From Empire to Humanity

From Empire to Humanity

The American Revolution and the Origins of Humanitarianism

To karl with admiration

AMANDA B. MONIZ

OXFORD
UNIVERSITY PRESS

OXFORD
UNIVERSITY PRESS

Oxford University Press is a department of the University of Oxford. It furthers
the University's objective of excellence in research, scholarship, and education
by publishing worldwide. Oxford is a registered trade mark of Oxford University
Press in the UK and certain other countries.

Published in the United States of America by Oxford University Press
198 Madison Avenue, New York, NY 10016, United States of America.

© Oxford University Press 2016

Library of Congress Cataloging-in-Publication Data
Names: Moniz, Amanda B.
Title: From empire to humanity: the American Revolution and the origins of
humanitarianism / Amanda B. Moniz.
Description: New York, NY: Oxford University Press, 2016. |
Includes bibliographical references and index.
Identifiers: LCCN 2015045811 (print) | LCCN 2016016061 (ebook) |
ISBN 978-0-19-024035-6 (hardcover: acid-free paper) | ISBN 978-0-19-024036-3 (Updf) |
ISBN 978-0-19-024037-0 (Epub)
Subjects: LCSH: United States—History—Revolution, 1775–1783—Social aspects. |
United States—History—Revolution, 1775–1783—Influence. |
Humanitarianism—United States—History—18th century. |
Humanitarianism—Great Britain—History—18th century. |
Humanitarianism—West Indies, British—History—18th century. |
Social reformers—History—18th century. | Political activists—History—18th century. |
Physicians—Political activity—History—18th century. |
Imperialism—Social aspects—History—18th century. |
Cosmopolitanism—History—18th century. |
BISAC: HISTORY / United States / Revolutionary Period (1775–1800).
Classification: LCC E209.M65 2016 (print) | LCC E209 (ebook) |
DDC 361.70941/09033—dc23
LC record available at https://lccn.loc.gov/2015045811

For David and Raia

Contents

Acknowledgments

EIGHTEENTH-CENTURY PHILANTHROPISTS KNEW their achievements rested on the contributions of many. I know keenly that mine do too.

I appreciate profoundly the people who have done the most to train me in the historian's craft. David Hancock inspired me to study the eighteenth century and to approach it from an Atlantic perspective. He has also taught me how to turn a mass of details into a meaningful narrative and has offered me much wise counsel over the years. Susan Juster and Michael MacDonald helped me grapple with the history of humanitarianism and helped me think about the feel I wanted to bring to my writing. At Yale University, Joanne Freeman, David Blight, Jon Butler, Steve Pincus, and Harry (Skip) Stout helped me sharpen my thinking about eighteenth- and nineteenth-century America, Britain and the British Atlantic, and beyond. Gordon Wood and the late Abbott (Tom) Gleason first spurred me to consider becoming a historian. Special thanks to go to Anne Boylan, Robert Gross, and Conrad Edick Wright for serving as my mentors in the exploration of the history of charity and philanthropy, and to Cathy Matson for supporting and guiding me through various stages of intellectual and professional development. Working at the National History Center and the American Historical Association has broadened both my intellectual horizons and my understanding of what it is to be a historian. It is a privilege to work with Dane Kennedy, James Grossman, Dana Schaffer, Eric Arnesen, and a fantastic group of colleagues. Kathleen Franz has also helped me grow as a historian, and I am grateful to her for that.

I am most appreciative for the support from the following institutions: the American Historical Association for its Albert A. Beveridge Grant; the Gilder Lehrman Institute of American History; the Massachusetts Historical Society for an Andrew W. Mellon Fellowship; the New England Regional Fellowship Consortium for a Colonial Society of Massachusetts Fellowship; the Program in Early American Economy and Society Fellowship of the Library Company of Philadelphia; the Social Science Research Council Program on Philanthropy and the Nonprofit Sector; the University of Michigan, including the History Department, the Rackham Graduate School, and the Joan B. Kessler Award fund; and Yale University, where I held a Cassius Marcellus Clay Postdoctoral Fellowship.

My research has been made possible because of the staffs at many libraries and archives. I am indebted to the those at the following institutions: the Beinecke Library; the Boston Athenaeum; the British Library; the Francis A. Countway Medical Library; the Historical Society of Pennsylvania; the Library Company of Philadelphia; the Library of Congress; the Maryland Historical Society; the Massachusetts Historical Society; the New Hampshire Historical Society; the New York Academy of Medicine; the New-York Historical Society; the New York-Presbyterian Hospital/Weill-Cornell Medical Center Archives; the New York Public Library; the Pennsylvania Hospital Archives; the Royal Humane Society; the University of Michigan Libraries; the Wellcome Library for the History and Understanding of Medicine; and Yale University Libraries.

Over the years, this book has been shaped by conversations with many colleagues including Richard Bell, John Brooke, Christopher Brown, Bruce Dorsey, Katherine Carté Engel, Charles Foy, Travis Glasson, Reeve Huston, Julie Kim, Sarah Knott, Albrecht Koschnik, Daniel Livesay, Jen Manion, Will Mackintosh, W. Caleb McDaniel, Michelle Craig McDonald, Roderick McDonald, Matthew Mulcahy, Johann Neem, Richard Newman, Matthew Warner Osborn, Daniel Richter, Jessica Choppin Roney, Anelise Shrout, Karen Sonnelitter, Peter Stamatov, Kyle Volk, the late Renate Wilson, Bradford Wood, and Serena Zabin. I am also indebted to my fellow students of humanitarianism and philanthropy for helping me situate the era I study within longer term developments. I have especially benefited from conversations with Thomas Adam, Michael Barnett, Richard Huzzey, Julia Irwin, Kathleen McCarthy, Sonya Michel, Sarah Snyder, Benjamin Soskis, and Olivier Zunz. At a critical point in the writing of this book, Rick Bell and Holly Brewer pushed me to be bolder and I am particularly grateful for their encouragement. I am also obliged to the many people who have offered ideas when I have presented my work. A big thanks to Marilyn Young for suggesting *From Empire to Humanity* as the book's title.

At Oxford University Press, Susan Ferber believed in this project and shepherded me through an unfamiliar process. Her insightful feedback and spot-on editing have strengthened this book. The manuscript is also stronger thanks to several people who gave generously of their time to read and comment on parts or all of it. My deep thanks to John Brooke, Kate Carté Engel, Bob Gross, Caleb McDaniel, Johann Neem, Sarah Snyder, Gordon Wood, and an anonymous reader. I appreciate also Maya Bringe's and Patterson Lamb's contributions to turning words on paper into a finished book.

My greatest debts are to friends and family. In graduate school, during fellowships, and beyond, Rebecca Brannon, Tamar Carroll, Brad Jones, Vasiliki Karali, Kate Luongo, Jen Manion, Michelle and Roderick McDonald, the late Mary O'Reilly, Matthew Osborn, Jess Roney, Honor Sachs, Dana Schaffer, and Sarah Snyder have offered practical assistance, moral support, and very welcome camaraderie. So have Shatha Almutawa, Alona Bachi, Keren Bachi, David and Louise Betts, Mira Edmonds and Doug Guthrie, Jenny Couzin-Frankel and Rich Frankel, Nils Henning, Jean Kohanek, Elisabeth Kvernen, Robin Leon, Heather Nickerson and Greg Holeyman, Ben Soskis and Rebecca Deutsch, Aviva Zierler and, last but not least, the best of friends Nuna Kim, who is always ready to listen to anything and everything on my mind, typically while we share a good meal. I treasure also the warmth and encouragement of Kathryn and Richard Lenter, Ellen and Tom Swengel, and Adam and Jamie Lenter, and the sweet spirits of Jacob and Noah Lenter. Not only have Debby and Marc Fuller and Jeanne Paul and Tom Nicely buoyed me throughout my life, but also Debby and Marc put me up during a research trip and Jeanne long ago nurtured me as a writer. Lisa Fuller's humanitarian globetrotting reminds me of my questions' currency. A crucial source of strength in this and every undertaking has been the love and steady confidence in me of my parents Judy and J. Webb Moniz and my sister Suzanne Moniz, and the summer Suzanne and I lived together while I did research in Boston was a special time in this project. For her part, Charlotte Moniz is a constant source of delight.

David Lenter has been a partner in this endeavor from before it began. Over many years, he has bandied about ideas, supported me in countless ways, and believed in me. I appreciate all his help, but, most of all, I cherish his love and our life together. Raia Moniz-Lenter has contributed too. She brings me immense joy. Moreover, she spurred me on during the final days of this long project by suggesting we have a pizza-and-ice-cream celebration when I finished. I dedicate this book to David and Raia with much love.

From Empire to Humanity

Introduction

THE NAME OF the charity, its president, Dr. John Murray, had to confess, was unpopular. The group had been formed in Norwich, England, in 1775 as an ethnic aid society for Scots in the region. By 1782, at the annual meeting, held on St. Andrew's Day—November 30—Murray acknowledged that the name "The Scots Society" no longer quite fit. The group had decided a couple of years earlier that it would help not just fellow Caledonians but distressed migrants anywhere in the world who lacked other sources of aid. Some questioned the new mission, he noted, while many others disliked the old name.[1]

Murray had much else to say. Reporting on the Society's efforts to establish branches of the charity in "revolted America," where several of his relatives lived, he noted that "reconciliation" was said to be "near at hand between Great Britain and her colonies," and he hoped that "whenever peace return[ed]," it would "come with healing in its wings."[2] Later that very day, American and British commissioners meeting in Paris signed preliminary articles of peace.

Over the following year, members of the Scots Society considered various names. The Universal was one possibility. The Philanthropic—the word then invoked "love of mankind"—was another. Not all members were sure about those expansive terms. As a compromise the group agreed to call itself the Scots Society, or Society of Universal Good-will. A year later doubts had waned and the group jettisoned the original name, calling itself simply the Society of Universal Good-will.[3] The group had struggled with its identity and purpose over the decade in which the transatlantic community had fractured. Once it was time to forge a healing peace, the society finally, fully, shed its character as an ethnic aid charity and embraced a global philanthropic mission. Its remaking heralded the transformation in humanitarianism that American independence would bring in its wake.

The American Revolution unsettled boundaries of moral responsibility in the Anglo-American world. For decades, as members of the same polity,
Americans and Britons had shared the view that charitable activity should and
did serve the empire. Efforts to evangelize native peoples in North America and
bring them into the British fold aimed at strengthening British military might.
Projects to build hospitals and preserve lives in London did also. Holding common understandings, philanthropists on both sides of the Atlantic increasingly
cooperated in benevolent ventures, and ordinary men and women donated to
help faraway members of the British community. The transatlantic struggle over
control of governance, the resulting war, and American independence dissolved
Americans' and Britons' imperial union and, with it, their common imperial
humanitarianism.

Political estrangement did not end transatlantic relationships, perspectives,
or practices developed in the colonial era. Often resentful toward one another
before and during the war, Americans' and Britons' ill will subsided with the
war's end and they readily renewed acquaintances.[4] The nature of their enduring ties, however, demanded a reckoning. How could a community cohere when
compatriots became strangers? How would peoples who had become foreigners relate? And what were the boundaries of moral responsibility when political boundaries changed?[5] No mere abstractions, these were compellingly real
questions for transatlantically oriented activists, such as Philadelphia's Benjamin
Rush and London's John Coakley Lettsom.

The erstwhile compatriots faced other challenges. Newly independent
Americans strove to define institutions, social relations, and modes of self suit-
able for a republic, and they sought to win recognition of the new nation abroad.
Meanwhile, Britons reconsidered the empire's character after the loss of the
Thirteen Colonies and, in time, turned their imperial energies toward the east.
Alongside these national projects of forging new institutions and new directions
was another, transatlantic project of reimagining bonds with now-foreigners.[6]
Ambitious American and British activists who had come of age before the
American Revolution addressed these intertwined concerns by crafting a new
universal approach in beneficence.

This book explores the revolution in humanitarian sensibilities and practices in the eighteenth-century Anglo-American world through the experiences of a generation of activists from the British Isles, North America, and
the West Indies. It follows a group of leading philanthropists as they came of
age in the pre-Revolutionary Atlantic world, faced a civil war, and then remade
their ties as they collaborated in a range of causes after American independence. Over the postwar decades, as they grappled with their political sepa-
ration, these activists and their contemporaries fashioned new philanthropic

institutions, projects, and norms. Their legacy was to make the care of suffering strangers routine.[7]

This story has not been told before. The history of the era's charitable and voluntary activity has typically been studied within the parameters of distinct nations or particular movements, such as antislavery or prison reform, although the parameters of neither nations nor movements contained the lives or activities of the era's humanitarians.[8] Many sojourned or traveled far from home at some point and more had connections to faraway places, and those experiences shaped their approach to philanthropy. Studying humanitarianism through their lives reveals the personal, professional, religious, and political reasons activists extended charitable movements and expanded their aspirations without heed to the borders created by American independence. Bringing to light their role in renewal of an Atlantic community, an activist-centered approach also paradoxically illuminates the strength of national loyalties among these citizens of the world. Far-flung activists readily corresponded about their projects, but Americans and Britons brought different priorities, attitudes, and expectations to their exchanges, while their shared commitment to universal philanthropy sometimes rested on national feelings. By bringing out the commonalities and the conflicts among American and British philanthropists, an Atlantic vantage point reveals how contemporaries were imagining their belonging in various communities at this moment of reconfiguration of the state system.

Focusing on activists instead of on particular causes or institutions also brings new insights to the relationships among various movements and, most important, between the antislavery movement and humanitarianism more generally. Scholars often use the emergence of the antislavery movement as the starting point or a stand-in for understanding changing moral sensibilities more generally. As crucial as the emergence of the movement to abolish the slave trade and to end human bondage was, the antislavery cause was part and parcel of a broader cultural development that it alone cannot explain. Indeed, as one historian has noted, making antislavery a case-in-point for humanitarianism writ large lets the winners of a historical debate over what constituted humanity define the contested concept.[9] Studying people, who were typically involved in various benevolent campaigns, highlights the fruitful borrowings and sometimes the jockeying among institutions or causes. In the case of antislavery, this approach uncovers activists' use of seemingly unrelated movements, such as the movement to save drowning victims, to express opposition to the slave trade or support for black citizenship. Following activists, then, brings out unappreciated dimensions of particular causes.

Similarly, a generational perspective offers new insights into what the American Revolution did and did not transform in philanthropy. In the decades after independence, Americans reformed penal practices, founded a host of new charitable and voluntary associations, embraced Freemasonry, and more, and historians often take the founding of the United States as the point of departure for studying these developments. The crafting of the new nation indeed unleashed creative energies. Activists, however, brought earlier experience with and expectations about beneficence to their postwar undertakings. Their stories point up that the Revolution was not a starting point for expansive benevolence, but a turning point as activists' recast the familiar imperial charitable tradition for a world in which fellow nationals had become legal aliens to one another.[10]

The beneficent practices inherited and, in time, remade by eighteenth-century activists had roots that were laid centuries earlier. For medieval men and women, charity was a reciprocal act: In exchange for a donor's gift, the recipient was expected to pray for the benefactor's soul. In early-modern Europe, charity began giving way—though it has never done so fully—to philanthropy, with Christian humanist thinkers and religious reformers remaking poor relief by rationalizing the provision of welfare and bringing it under lay control. The focus of sixteenth- and seventeenth-century donors' efforts remained by and large local. Early moderns were, however, grappling with the question of what their moral obligations were to strangers—people different from themselves. Religious turmoil led to impressive international undertakings to aid foreign co-religionists, and some were also raising their voices against the injustices suffered by very different peoples.[11] The sixteenth century saw people in the Spanish empire extending their moral concern to faraway fellow subjects. In the seventeenth and, even more so, the early eighteenth centuries, people in the English and then British empire followed suit. The American Revolution would unsettle and begin to universalize the charitable practices that came out of European imperial trajectories.[12]

A word—philanthropy—that came into vogue on both sides of the Atlantic over these years captured the universalizing thrust in charitable activity.[13] Using long-familiar language, eighteenth-century Britons and Americans spoke and wrote of living in an "Age of Benevolence." The era, they believed, was defined by kind feelings toward others—"benevolence"—that might prompt good actions on behalf of others—"beneficence." In the postwar years, contemporaries also increasingly used the word "philanthropy." As they understood it from the original Greek, "philanthropy" meant "love of mankind" and indicated a sentiment.[14] It was a sentiment they invoked more and more often in the postwar years as they found ways to aid sufferers who were distant and different from them through new types of medical charity, prison reform, abolition and antislavery, poor relief, and more.

Today similar endeavors are dubbed "humanitarian." In the earlier era, that word referred to a theological concept, that is, the view that Jesus's nature is only human, not divine. Increasingly, nineteenth-century commentators gave "humanitarian" a meaning closer to that of the present day, but they used the word negatively to criticize what they saw as misplaced or disproportionate do-gooding. Only in recent decades has the word come to be a generally positive term referring to far-reaching efforts to improve the lot of humanity. The subjects of this study were likewise ambitious. The eighteenth-century missionary charities that gave some of them their starts in benevolent activism might not strike today's observers as "humanitarian." Missions aimed to save souls, not to lessen earthly distress. Yet the difference between missions and antislavery—the cause now seen as radically new in its concern for the corporeal suffering of often distant others—is less stark than it first seems. For many contemporaries, antislavery had spiritual aims.[15] Both the missionary and the abolition movements asked people to extend their moral responsibility to others who were previously outside its ambit. Other causes did too. Whether called humanitarianism or philanthropy, the boundaries of moral responsibility grew over the Revolutionary and postwar years as Americans and Britons became strangers.

Historians examining later eras debate the impact of various wars on humanitarian and, relatedly, human rights developments.[16] Late eighteenth-century humanitarianism, by contrast, has more often been explained in terms of shifts in the economy. Indeed, economic change did play a role. The expansion of the market economy gave more middling people discretionary income to devote to charitable undertakings. It also gave rise to new class relations: philanthropic endeavors, historians have explained, offered the well-to-do opportunities to experiment with new forms of labor discipline and social control as artisanal skills and paternalistic apprenticeships were being replaced with industrial degradation and growing distance between employer and employee. Moreover, the burgeoning commercial economy nurtured cultural developments. Novel reading became ever more common, and scholars have attributed sympathy for the sufferings of others to the imaginative connections fostered by narratives, whether fictional or real. Scholar Thomas Haskell has also famously argued that an increasingly global economy taught new lessons about cause and effect. Individuals' new perceptions of their ability to have an impact on faraway events and in the future made it possible, this argument goes, to imagine that they had the capacity to improve the lots of suffering strangers.[17]

There is truth to these perspectives, but they miss important facets of eighteenth-century developments. Observing that the period from 1750 to 1850 saw a change in the conventions of moral responsibility, Haskell submits that this development owed to the "explosive growth of contract law in the century following 1770."[18] This is a neat formulation: The rise of capitalism—here understood as a contractually bound economy of exchange—led to the rise of humanitarianism.

But it rests on two misunderstandings. First, it misses the extent of long-distance charitable activity before 1750 and therefore cannot fully appreciate the changes later in the century. Second, it overlooks entirely the profession—medicine—at the forefront of philanthropy's expanding reach in the latter eighteenth century. Were contract law as critically important as Haskell has suggested, merchants, not doctors, should predominate.

From Empire to Humanity: The American Revolution and the Origins of Humanitarianism considers changes in humanitarianism through the experiences of a couple of dozen men who led in philanthropic circles. For much of the eighteenth century, women donated to benevolent associations and were acknowledged as supporters. They also staffed charities such as hospitals. They did not actively lead charitable organizations or publicly set their agendas, however, until the end of the century. Women, along with men and children, also used welfare institutions, although charities' recipients feature little in this book. Their voices and an understanding of the impact of these institutions on beneficiaries require a different approach, more rooted in particular urban environments and the charitable systems that they tapped as part of their survival strategies. The subjects of this study, then, are, almost entirely well-off men. They include merchants, such as Thomas Russell, a leader of many of Boston's charities in the 1780s and '90s; cultural entrepreneurs, such as "the blind Scotsman," itinerant scientific lecturer Henry Moyes; clergymen, including New York's Reverend John Rodgers; and one lucky soul whose landed wealth meant he did not have to work for his keep, English prison reformer John Howard. Most important are doctors, including West Indian-born John Coakley Lettsom; Scotsman John Murray; Philadelphia's Benjamin Rush; Samuel Bard of New York; and John Crawford, whose life stretched from Northern Ireland to India, Barbados, Demerara, and finally Baltimore.

Medical men played an outsized role in the late eighteenth-century's humanitarian revolution. Some are familiar to historians, who often consider them and other philanthropic leaders in terms of their religious affiliations.[19] Activists' religious beliefs, identities, and ties were, indeed, of great importance to these men, and their charitable activity showed it. They bestowed charity on needy co-religionists and they burnished their communities' images by working with members of their tribes for the good of outsiders. Others did much the same with ethnic aid groups. But it was doctors' membership in a professional community that was of such importance to their expansive approach to philanthropy. With their university medical educations, they had joined the "republic of medicine" and had taken up the mantle of "benefactors of mankind."[20] They had ties to fellow doctors far and wide, a professional imperative to correspond with their colleagues, and a professional identity that inclined them to pursue the welfare of humanity. Influenced, certainly, by the burgeoning commercial economy of their day, they corresponded with one another and with other friends in the broader republic of letters about medicine and philanthropy, current events, and politics. Their lives and letters reveal former compatriots grappling through humanitarianism with the reordering of the transatlantic community after the American Revolution.

Unfolding as a loosely chronological story, the book opens with a look at the world of imperially oriented beneficence in which postwar activists grew up. Several decades before they were born, tighter British oversight of the American colonies at the end of the seventeenth century and, a few years later, the Act of Union joining England and Scotland had brought a new British Atlantic world, and new charities, into being. Prompted by the empire's growth, philanthropic innovators such as the Reverend Thomas Bray and Captain Thomas Coram established or envisioned missionary, educational, and other charities, such as the Society for the Propagation of the Gospel in Foreign Parts (SPG) and London's Foundling Hospital, on both sides of the Atlantic to safeguard the heterogeneous polity's strength and character from outside and within. As donations showed, many shared their belief that charity served strategic ends. Growing up in this far-flung, increasingly tightly knit community taught activists that their charitable obligation went beyond the local to encompass faraway fellow subjects of Britain's empire.[21]

The men who led the late century's expansive humanitarian endeavors had typically been born in the 1730s, '40s, and '50s into comfortable families—as Benjamin Rush and John Coakley Lettsom had been—and they had grown up in the dynamic, interconnected British Atlantic world before the Revolution. From the newspapers, books, and periodicals they read, to the clothes and home furnishings they used, and the foodstuffs they consumed, from their encounters with celebrities like George Whitefield and Benjamin Franklin to the educations, occupations, and activities they pursued, the lives of these future philanthropists stretched around the British world. Indeed, a surprising number had traveled or moved around the Anglophone Atlantic and, through those experiences, forged ties with future colleagues, gained new perspectives, and trafficked in models of benevolent institutions. For budding medical men, whose schooling and training often required sojourns abroad, this was especially true.[22]

The imperial crisis that began soon after the Seven Years' War ended shook this world. On both sides of the Atlantic, British victory had swelled pride. Victory, however, had brought Britain a larger, more polyglot empire. Seeking to govern its extensive territories more uniformly and effectively, the British government pursued measures that threatened many white Americans' understanding of their liberties. As tensions mounted, they began to take their toll on charitable cooperation. Beneficence, many knew from the missionary and other charities of their youth, had a political salience.[23] Philanthropic practices and, more so, conceptions of moral obligations, then, were at stake with the American Revolutionary war.

The turn toward a new approach began while the longtime compatriots were fighting. The war caused dislocations on both sides of the Atlantic, but American civilians faced greater disruptions and often felt great anger toward their British counterparts. More conflicted about the transatlantic relationship than their American brethren were during the war, Britons wrestled with the question of moral obligation in a fracturing community first, with John Murray guiding the reinvention of the Scots Society of Norwich, England, as it became the Society of Universal Good-will.

John Murray's aspirations were ambitious but not unique. Other American and British activists likewise rethought and transformed the conventions of moral responsibility in the postwar years. With doctors' professional networks structuring broader conversations, far-flung philanthropists corresponded about medical charity, antislavery, prison reform, poor relief, education, and more for the well-being of humanity at large. These activists and their contemporaries shifted to a universal approach not because of the lessons taught by the market economy but because the restructuring of the Anglophone Atlantic polity left them with the challenges of redefining their relationships to each other and to the broader humanity they sought to serve. American independence had shattered their political bands and extinguished the old conventions. No longer members of the same empire, Americans and Britons no longer shared concerns about imperial security, strength, or identity. No more could imperial moral responsibility ground their philanthropic cooperation. Indeed, the passing of the old conventions affected more than transatlantic collaboration: London charities, one historian has noted, lacked focus in the 1770s and '80s.[24]

The basis of activists' cooperation had changed. They kept, however, to a central tenet of the earlier imperial approach. They continued to assume that philanthropy carried a political cast. Their charitable activity was not motivated by politics, but they believed that it had a political valence and brought this view to their postwar cooperation. Politics, and especially the politics of empires and nations, absorbed their attention.[25] Americans and Britons alike filled their letters with news of wars and revolutions, opinions about governments and policies, and thoughts on the remaking of states and societies. Preoccupied with politics and certain that philanthropy had a political tenor, they often saw their joint endeavors in the cause of humanity as a peaceable force in a world where states were in flux rather than, as with colonial-era charitable cooperation, a buttress of the British empire.

Philanthropy held an irenic power, except, alas, when it was a source of conflict. In the wake of their legal alienation, Americans and Britons looked to universal philanthropy as a new basis of transatlantic cooperation, a new grounding for an enduring community that was no longer a polity. And yet they also sparred over this shining ideal. After their loss of the Thirteen Colonies, British leaders redefined their imperial rule as a liberal humanitarian project. As this thinking developed, however, it brought out old divisions within Britain. In the late 1780s, English and Scottish admirers of the acclaimed English prison reformer John Howard, whose prison tours took him around Europe and beyond, clashed over whether he represented English or British benevolence. For their part, Americans used their celebrations of Howard to insist that the pursuit of universal philanthropy was a joint undertaking, not the province of Britons alone.

Despite these tensions, the transatlantic philanthropic community persisted as activists moved within the Anglophone Atlantic world. Men like repeated-migrant John Crawford helped to spread unfamiliar causes around the British Isles, North America, and the West Indies. Born in Northern Ireland, Crawford served as a surgeon on East India Company ships before heading to Barbados in 1779, where in time he led the founding of a dispensary providing free medical care to the poor and a charity to save drowning victims. The next decade found him sojourning in the Low Countries and then living for several years in Demerara (part of today's Guyana). Quitting South America, Crawford decamped to Baltimore, where he also worked to introduce the dispensary and lifesaving movements. When he died, contemporaries hailed him for embodying the ideals of universal benevolence that others engaged in through letters and print. He was among the humanitarians who helped to sustain bonds in the years after American independence.

Old and new friendships eased cooperation among individual activists in the postwar years. For organizations, the shift was harder, particularly for American groups. Britons had contended during the war with losing the Thirteen Colonies, but they soon began rethinking their imperial identity. Americans, by contrast, grappled with their new status as citizens of an independent nation and their new relationship as foreigners to Britons after the war and into the 1790s. Founding and running charitable institutions raised questions about what had changed with American independence, as men in a lifesaving charity, the Massachusetts Humane Society, particularly found.

The lifesaving movement had begun in Amsterdam in 1767 and, building on medical networks, spread around Europe and across the Atlantic. Known typically as "humane societies," lifesaving charities in the Anglophone world disseminated information, promoted new research and new technologies, and encouraged intervention in cases of drowning, suffocation, and certain other

life-threatening situations. Because these medical emergencies might befall anyone, humane society advocates touted that they made it possible to save the life of
any person regardless of background. As the abolition and antislavery movements
developed in the 1780s and '90s, activists used humane societies' insistence on the
value of all lives to challenge slavery. Britons and Americans drew on humane
societies' universalism, however, in distinct ways. While Britons attacked the
slave trade for causing deaths by drowning, Americans showcased African
Americans' fitness for republican citizenship by highlighting their benevolence
in rescuing people from drowning.

Americans and Britons may not have noticed differences in their intertwin-
ing of resuscitation and abolition. Men in the Massachusetts Humane Society
did discover, however, that involvement in a common cause could obscure the
effects of the transatlantic estrangement. Eager to prevent the loss of lives among
mariners in the North Atlantic, the Massachusetts Humane Society sought
to address the problem of shipwrecks with its London counterpart, the Royal
Humane Society, on the basis of shared moral responsibility for all humanity.
The Massachusetts men found themselves struggling to collaborate with their
erstwhile compatriots because they initially did not appreciate what had changed
with American independence. They asked for the wrong things and, moreover,
they mistakenly expected their British colleagues to lead in a shared endeavor. In
time, the Massachusetts Humane Society and especially its president, Thomas
Russell, recognized that they would have to approach now-foreigners differently
than imperial brethren. Instead, Americans insisted and their British colleagues
eventually conceded that the former fellow nationals could work together on
behalf of the good of all humanity.

With their shared belief in the political valence of philanthropy, the former
compatriots considered their cooperation to be a force for transatlantic reconciliation. Their common view also left their joint efforts in the cause of humanity in
danger from the new revolutionary forces erupting at the end of the eighteenth
century. In the face of the French Revolutionary and Napoleonic Wars, activists and organizations lost their cosmopolitan voices and stressed more strongly
patriotic themes. Long-standing practices continued, however, as activists kept
working with far-flung colleagues. Notably, in the field of medical philanthropy,
proponents of the newly discovered smallpox vaccination built on the humane
society movement to achieve a worldwide humanitarian reach in the early nineteenth century. Activists fashioned worldwide networks of philanthropy—laying
the groundwork for later generations' global institutions—even as nationalist
moods trumped expressions of catholicity.

By then, the American and British activists who had grown up in a shared
British Atlantic world were dying off. They left their successors norms and

practices forged as they came of age in the pre-Revolutionary British empire, confronted the strains of a civil war, and then repaired their ties after American independence. The culture of aid to strangers in the Anglo-American world developed as former fellow nationals wrestled with how to be a community without being compatriots.

I

Protestantism, Empire, and Transatlantic Philanthropy, 1700–1760s

AFTER AMERICAN INDEPENDENCE, the outburst of charitable activity in the United States from the 1780s to the 1810s would look like the start of something new. And in important ways, it did express Americans' Revolutionary exhilaration, republican hopes, and patriotic determination. But as citizens of the new republic built the structures of global humanitarianism with their British colleagues in the post-Revolutionary decades, they remained faithful in many ways to the world they had grown up in. To understand what American independence did and did not change requires understanding that the Revolutionary generation grew up in a world in which benevolent activity was burgeoning, transatlantic charitable cooperation was familiar, and philanthropy, especially religious and educational philanthropy, was a tool for strengthening the British empire.

Revolution, Union, and Religious Philanthropy

The Reverend Thomas Bray was vexed. He had been appointed as a Church of England official for Maryland in 1695 and held the office until 1700, though he spent a mere few months, in 1700, in the colony.[1] What he learned before and during his time there proved worrisome. Dissenting Protestants predominated in the North American colonies with Anglicans barely tolerated in New England outside of Boston. The Papists too seemed vigorous, although Catholics' numbers were actually dwindling. Meanwhile, Anglican clergy were few on the ground and Anglican churches few on the landscape. Worst of all, in Bray's mind, the Quakers—"'a Heathen Nation'"—seemed to be thriving in the colonies and they persisted in England, despite decades of persecution and out-migration.[2]

Bray was not alone in his dislike for religious heterodoxy. Not many years after he deplored the state of the Anglican Church in America, a group of Presbyterian Lowland Scots fretted about a similar situation. It was not the colonies but the peripheries of Scotland that concerned them, as Caledonia and Albion united into Britain. Rather than the Quakers, Deists, and assorted other deniers of orthodox Christian beliefs, it was Highland Catholics who so bothered the Presbyterian Lowland Scots, never mind that more Highlanders were Episcopal than Catholic.[3] Disturbed by the religious troublemakers in their midst, Bray and fellow Anglicans and their Scottish counterparts responded by founding religious charities to bring marginal peoples into their folds—groups that presaged the political salience of transatlantic philanthropy for decades to come.

The motley state of religion in the American colonies and Britain was not new, but recent revolution and reform that together created the British Atlantic world had made the heterogeneity unsettling to members of England's and Scotland's established churches. The first of these developments were England's Glorious Revolution and the loss of the American colonies' autonomy. From the beginning of English settlement in America, economic, legal, political, cultural, religious, and familial bonds had linked settlers in America to their compatriots in England and in other colonies. Yet, in important ways, England's North American colonies, especially those in New England, had been independent for much of the seventeenth century. Colonial assemblies, not the Crown or its officials, controlled taxes, and in most colonies, governors were elected or appointed by proprietors. Moreover, before the end of the seventeenth century the Church of England was the established church in only one mainland colony—Virginia—and had scant presence anywhere in North America.[4]

The degree of autonomy the colonies had enjoyed varied, but from the late seventeenth century, all the English plantations faced greater Crown oversight, beginning with the policies of King James II. The Catholic James, who came to the throne in 1685, was a believer in absolutist rule. To free himself from checks on his power that came with relying on Parliament's taxing authority within England, he sought to wring as much money out of the colonies as he could since levies on the goods they produced, such as sugar or tobacco, went into Crown coffers. The upshot was a series of reforms that drastically expanded Crown power over the colonies, to the great resentment of many colonists. James's style of rule likewise offended many English people. In 1688, with the connivance of a number of peers and Anglican bishops, the Dutch Protestant prince William of Orange, nephew and son-in-law of James, invaded England and claimed the throne with his wife Mary. Dubbed by supporters the Glorious Revolution, William's coup was endorsed by Parliament, which regained its role in governing with the monarch.[5]

In the spring of 1689, when colonists learned of the Glorious Revolution, they effected their own revolutions against James's governors in New England and New York and against the Catholic proprietary governor of Maryland. The American governments would not, however, recover the autonomy they had had before James's reign. To help strengthen his authority in England and his capacity to wage war against France, William maintained and furthered James's reforms. Governors appointed by the Crown (or, in a few cases, proprietors) became the norm from New England to the West Indies. In addition, the Crown had to approve laws passed by colonial assemblies. Moreover, the Board of Trade was created in 1696 to oversee colonial policy. Those developments, plus economic, military, and cultural ties, bound British America more tightly to the mother country, and many colonists in the eighteenth century cherished being Britons, the freest people, to their minds, in the world. Nevertheless, the colonies' self-government had waned.[6]

Scotland's experience was similar. Since 1603, England and Scotland had shared the same monarch but remained formally separate. In 1707, impelled by economic struggles on Scotland's part and strategic considerations—fear that a French army could invade through its northern neighbor—on England's, the two countries (plus the Principality of Wales, long subordinate to England) united through an Act of Union. Scotland kept its established church plus its own legal and poor relief systems. Many Scots would benefit greatly from their new economic opportunities, while learning and culture flourished in Caledonia's cities in the eighteenth century. Nonetheless, Scotland had lost its independence when it abolished its parliament and took seats in the Westminster Parliament, thereby creating Great Britain.[7]

These developments led Bray and other Anglicans and like-minded Scots to found three new charities to further integration across the Atlantic and within the British Isles. The Society for Promoting Christian Knowledge (SPCK), founded in 1699, and the Society for the Propagation of the Gospel in Foreign Parts (SPG), chartered in 1701, were Bray's brainchildren. He and colleagues set up the SPCK to help build the Church of England in the colonies, but the group soon changed course and instead focused on countering the influence of Dissenters domestically by revitalizing the Anglican Church, most notably by encouraging the founding of charity schools for the poor throughout England.[8] Meanwhile, the work of building the Church of England in the colonies was spun off to the SPG. Like the SPCK, the SPG sought to buttress the Church of England and bring more people—Dissenters, Africans, and native peoples alike—into its fold.[9] Their northern counterpart, the Society in Scotland for Propagating Christian Knowledge (SSPCK), was set up in 1701 based on several Edinburgh gentlemen's earlier experiences in a moral reform society. The group received a royal patent in 1709. Combating the Catholic menace within Scotland by spreading the Presbyterian Church of Scotland (the Kirk) was its main goal. From its beginnings, however, the SSPCK also anticipated spreading Christianity in "'Popish and Infidel Parts of the World'"—work it would begin in the 1730s.[10]

The missionary charities worked in the realm of religion, but their aims were as much political as cultural. The SSPCK's effort to combat "the Ignorance, Atheism, Popery and Impiety, that did so much abound in the Highlands and Isles of *Scotland*" had broader ends than winning Highlanders to the Kirk. Besides generally holding religious beliefs abhorrent to Lowlanders, the often-impoverished Highlanders spoke Gaelic, were less literate, and were overall a people apart from the dominant—Lowland—society. To SSPCK supporters, the fraught political situation of the early eighteenth century made these divisions untenable. Scotland had just lost its independence through union with its larger, stronger neighbor. Moreover, it was only in 1701 that England's and then Britain's Protestant character had been assured when the Act of Settlement named the German Protestant house of Hanover successors to the English (then British) throne in place of the Scottish Catholic Stuarts. Many Highlanders, however, continued to view the Stuarts as the rightful monarchs and would support the '15 and the '45, the uprisings led by the Stuart Pretenders, who invaded from France in 1715 and 1745. By teaching English to "extirpat[e]" Gaelic and by inculcating "the true Christian religion, good Morals, and an Industrious Way of Living," the SSPCK sought to undermine Highlanders' loyalty to the Stuarts. The group also aimed to foster a uniform Scottish culture. Finally, it promised supporters that, thanks to their endeavors, Highlanders "might be induced to take some honest Imployment for their Subsistence," thereby improving the region's under-developed economy.[11]

The origins and aims of the SPG likewise went beyond the religious. The founding of the group, a clergyman explained in 1718, came about after "the dependence of these [American] Colonies [had been], in some measure, secured to the Imperial Crown of these Realms." That is, the SPG was founded after the colonies had lost their autonomy and integrating them more closely with the mother country became a priority for British leaders. "At the same time," he went on, "GOD hath put into the Hearts of some few Good Men to regard also the state of Religion there"—in other words, to tend to the sorry state of the Church of England in the colonies in light of their newfound importance to Britain. The SPG activists were sincere in their concerns. By their lights, converts had everything to gain since the states of their souls for all eternity were at stake. Bringing people in America into the Anglican Church would have additional benefits. "Agreeing in the same Faith and Worship" would ensure "civil Unity"—that is, it would prevent the colonies' "revolting from Us," something many Britons feared might one day happen. Deepening transatlantic bonds of religion would also benefit the metropolitan economy: If the colonists fell prey to the Papists, who were *"laying always in wait,"* Britain would "be in great Danger of losing the Fruits of [colonists'] Industry." In addition, winning native converts would enhance Britain's military strength because "every single *Indian* we make a Christian, we make a Friend and Ally at the same time."[12] Charitable activity, these men made clear, was a tool for strengthening the British polity.

Religious Rivalry

Papists lying in wait were a major concern to the men and women involved in transatlantic benevolence before the American Revolution. Rivalry with Catholics loomed large in Britons' and British Americans' thinking about the world. British anti-popery drew on memories of old persecutions and threats dating back to the reformations of the sixteenth century, but, more vitally, it flourished in the face of the strategic danger that France posed to Britain and its colonies. The series of conflicts with different names on either side of the Atlantic—the Nine Years' or King William's War (1689–97), the War of Spanish Succession or Queen Anne's War (1702–13), the War of Austrian Succession or King George's War (1739–48), and the Seven Years' or French and Indian War (1756–63)—pitted the British and French empires against one another in struggles over dynastic and then territorial power. Persistent strife against a Catholic foe made Protestantism a force for common identity in the newly formed Great Britain and it fostered stronger bonds across the Atlantic. The wars paid dividends in charity too. For much of the eighteenth century, British transatlantic activism would rest on fear of Catholic power and concern to bolster the "Protestant interest."[13]

Hostile to Rome, Protestants in the British world nonetheless worried that their charitable endeavors lagged behind those of Catholics. One source of anxiety was that, compared to welfare infrastructures in Catholic communities, Protestants' beneficence toward their local poor seemed inadequate. English writers on charity sought to counter the view that "Charity is a Mark of the Catholick church exclusive to all other Churches." The Catholic publisher of *Pietas Romana et Parisiensis*, a 1687 English edition of European charitable pattern-books, had implied as much and, worse, *"thence invited [Protestants] to Reunite themselves to"* Rome. A Protestant responded with *Pietas Hallensis*, a laudatory account of the influential foundations in Lutheran Halle. Nonetheless, the author of a preface to the English edition of *Pietas Hallensis* betrayed an ongoing concern that Catholic charity *"surpass[ed] all that is generally to be found among Protestants."* A few decades later, another English writer fulminated against "Papists'" accusations that Protestantism was "unfruitful of good Works." Such views were baseless. England had "numberless Charities." Indeed, they were superior, the author argued with creative logic, since they did not "raise Envy" or spur fraudulent claims of poverty as did the more numerous, wealthier, and more splendid Catholic foundations.[14]

Advocates of charity did not confine their use of religious rivalry to comparisons with Catholic communities. The Boston minister Cotton Mather pointed to fellow Protestants—Dutch and Danish missionaries in the East Indies—as worthy of imitation by New Englanders. He even invoked Islam, noting that it says "Three Times in the *Alcoran; God Loves those that are inclined to do Good*," to prod his readers to action. Members of other religions, these writers suggested, were not merely reprobate menaces to God's truth, but generous to those in need. To their way of thinking, charity was a mark of faith and a measure of different faiths. What troubled them was that British and British American Protestants' beneficence seemed to fall short in their own local communities.[15]

The preeminent arena in which they measured themselves against religious rivals, however, was in spreading the gospel. *"Popish Idolaters,"* observers noted, outstripped Protestants in missionary activity. The missionaries organized by the French priest Vincent de Paul, a seventeenth-century trendsetter in charity, not only traveled around France and ministered to Christian slaves in North Africa but also labored in Madagascar, the Hebrides, and Ireland, as the 1687 Catholic charitable manual told English readers. The Jesuits, whose diligence shamed Cotton Mather, ranged over an even greater portion of the earth. Catholics' commitment to the hard work of spreading the gospel cast Protestants in a bad light. English colonists "have been more careful to make a booty of them [Indians]," charged a prominent minister, rather "than to gain them to the practice of Religion."[16]

Most important, Catholic missionary activity magnified strategic dangers, especially in North America, by bringing more people—potential military might—into the Roman fold. Britons on both sides of the Atlantic harped on this theme time and again. Catholic missionaries "[took] Care to instruct both [Indians] and their Negroes, in the *Popish* Religion." Moreover, "both *French* and *Spaniards* have intermarried with *Indians*, to the great Strength, Security and Increase of their Colonies" and to the detriment of British settlements in America. Britons and British Americans knew all too well what Indians' alliances with the French empire meant: insecure borders, dead or captured soldiers and colonists, and ruined towns. (For their part, native peoples knew what the European presence in America meant: dispossession from their lands and death.)[17]

All those considerations were of deep concern, but the prospect of captivity mattered in a distinct way because it raised questions of cultural and religious loyalty. Bondage was no new threat in the eighteenth century. As England, then Britain, built an empire, thousand upon thousands of its people were taken in conflicts in North Africa, North America, and the East Indies. Many were redeemed. But when they were, they found themselves facing concerns about their cultural integrity and, most of all, their fidelity to Protestant Christianity. And no wonder, since, from the beginnings of English and Scottish expansion overseas, "going native" was part and parcel of British experience. For many people, a degree of acculturation was no more than sound practice. Adopting exotic customs or clothes aided commercial interactions and promoted safety. Others, however, willingly embraced foreign cultures or religions. Even captives, as New Englanders knew too well, "are become either Pagans or Papists, and continue still in a Foreign Land," refusing to be redeemed. Whether done under duress or voluntarily, sincerely or expediently, thousands of Britons crossed cultural borders, and through captivity narratives, ballads, and firsthand experience, many of their fellow subjects knew it.[18]

This malleability could be worrisome. The influential Massachusetts minister Solomon Stoddard hoped the "conjecture . . . that the Christians in *America* will *Indianize* . . . [would] prove a Mistake." But if Christians could become Indians, Indians could become Christians—Protestant Christians (and, hoping for a virtuous circle of adoption and emulation, Stoddard thought Indians' conversion might stoke colonists' faith). Highlander Scots could become Presbyterians and English-speakers like Lowland Scots, Germans in British America could be assimilated, Dissenters and Catholics could be brought into the Church of England's fold, and Africans in the West Indies and North America could be Christianized. The perceived threats varied by time and place, but the fluidity familiar to people in the heterogeneous Atlantic world both disturbed members of dominant groups and suggested that through missionary and educational charities, they could strengthen the British empire.[19]

A World of Connections

If ever someone saw the chance to use philanthropy to buttress the British empire, it was Thomas Coram. Born to a middling family around 1668 in Lyme Regis, Dorset, on the southern coast of England, Coram is mainly remembered for instigating London's Foundling Hospital. Most of his charitable endeavors, however, focused on North America, where he had lived from 1693 to 1703 in Boston and Taunton, Massachusetts. Coram, a mariner and shipwright, had begun what promised to be a successful shipbuilding venture in Taunton. Although he would have a happy marriage to a Boston Puritan woman who continued to worship at a Congregational meeting once the couple moved to London, the staunch—and combative—Anglican clashed with his Puritan neighbors in Taunton. The conflict led to the attempted assassination of Coram, much litigation, and the ruin of his business. In 1703, he returned to England deeply in debt to the London merchants who had backed his shipyard. Nevertheless, until the 1730s, Captain Coram, as he was known, imagined he would move back to America. Not until 1743 did he sell his house in Taunton. He repeatedly sought offices in America, to no avail. Instead, he made a living, although never a fortune, trading in naval stores, and he also made a name for himself in the world of benevolence.[20] The period of his most intense activity coincided with an acceleration in the integration of the British world that spurred a surge in transatlantic charitable ventures that further tightened bonds.

Not suddenly, but strikingly, the transatlantic community drew closer from the fourth decade of the eighteenth century. People—men far more often than women—in England and Scotland had crossed oceans and seas in the early modern period while colonists had returned home, migrated onward, or voyaged abroad for trade. The extent and depth of connections, however, grew dramatically in the Georgian era. English movement to the colonies dropped from 350,000 migrants in the seventeenth century (most of whom went to the West Indies) to 80,000 from 1700 to 1775. In their place came 145,000 Scots between 1707 and 1775, and 100,000 Germans before 1780. One hundred and sixty thousand Huguenots, who had left France after the Revocation of the Edict of Nantes in 1685 for various parts of northern Europe, moved to England, with some going on to America. European arrivals to the colonies were dwarfed by the million and a half African captives transported to British America, mainly to the West Indies.[21] The new streams of migrants propelled a web of ties around the Atlantic that built on ethnic and religious groups' distinct networks. Travel went west to east too, with well-off colonists sending sons to England and Scotland for education and, after 1760, increasing numbers of colonists living in London.[22]

Commerce was another, principal reason for people on the move. By the late 1730s, 1,500 transatlantic crossings each year bridged the ocean. Over the middle of the century, the British Atlantic economy became both more integrated and more globalized as merchants traded in more multifaceted directions. Manufacturers dangled new wares before the buying public. As consumers took advantage of the swelling variety of goods on offer, the material lives of those who lived comfortably and even modestly around the Atlantic became more

FIGURE 1.1   Portrait of Thomas Coram, after Hogarth. W. Nutter and R. Cribb, 1796. Wellcome Library, London.

similar. Most notably, from the 1740s colonial society became more like metropolitan Britain's as colonists increasingly appointed their homes with carpets, linens, china, and silver; wore imported fabrics, hairpins, buttons, and buckles; and entertained friends with tea and sugar served in the proper vessels—trends well appreciated by British merchants and manufacturers. For their parts, more Britons enjoyed pleasures of life, such as sugar, coffee, and tobacco, produced by Caribbean and North American slaves.[23]

A booming array of print media also put transatlantic communities in closer touch. Starting in the late seventeenth century, as the British empire expanded, means of communicating across the Anglophone world expanded too. Pamphlets and books were joined around the beginning of the eighteenth century by regular newspapers and journals. London's nine weekly newspapers including one daily in 1704 rose to five dailies, eight tri-weeklies, and four weeklies in 1770. The one provincial newspaper, founded in Norwich in 1701, had mushroomed to thirty-five by 1760. Likewise, the American colonies began with the *Boston News-letter*, first published in 1704, and had thirteen newspapers from Boston to Bridgetown in 1739. Beginning at the start of the century, journal production also grew in England. The 1730s saw the establishment of the popular periodicals, the *Gentleman's Magazine* and the *London Magazine*. From the 1740s, American printers tried—and failed—to found similar magazines, but American readers stayed current with their counterparts across the water by reading English journals.[24] With their coverage of wars, politics, diplomacy, learned affairs, human and natural history, natural disasters, ship traffic, and the activities of clubs and societies plus advertisements for all manner of goods, periodicals made it possible for members of the far-flung British community to know more about one another—although they knew less than they perhaps realized.

With the growth of print media came interconnected religious revivals, which were critical in binding British Protestants together. These outbursts of faith burgeoned in the 1730s as the expanding world of print and epistolary networks spread news about revivals. Reports about the progress of religion elsewhere not only stirred excitement and spurred further revivals but also fostered a sense of community among believers. No one did more than George Whitefield, the "Grand Itinerant," to forge bonds among evangelicals in the British world. Starting with his outdoor preaching in London in 1737, Whitefield incessantly traveled throughout the British Isles and the British North American colonies, which he first visited in 1739. The first transatlantic celebrity, Whitefield propelled stronger ties, but his incredible success in the 1740s also owed to the new density of connections coalescing around the time he became a phenomenon.[25]

As the American colonies drew closer to the mother country, they fired the imagination of metropolitan activists, perhaps Captain Coram above all. New colonies could be planted in border areas as bulwarks against the French. Foreign Protestants might be settled in the colonies. Former prisoners and other dregs of society could be sent to populate British America too. Indians and others should be converted or ministered to. Coram and other men mulled ideas for such projects for years.[26] Starting in the 1730s, he and his colleagues launched ventures, which often cascaded into others, in hopes of making their ideas reality. The SSPCK began its long-contemplated program in America with missions to both Highlanders to America and Indians in border areas of several North American colonies. Also in the 1730s, the Associates of Dr. Bray began their work in earnest. The group had been set up by the indefatigable Thomas Bray in 1723 when he received a bequest from a Huguenot friend to fund efforts to convert Africans in America. Reorganized several years later, after Bray's death, the charity aimed to Christianize negroes and to found a new colony in America thanks to another legacy. Soon the task of planting a colony to "save wretched People" was spun off to a separate, but overlapping group, the Georgia Trust, formed in 1731/32, that drew in men who had been pushing schemes for settlements in America for years.[27]

The common link among Coram's North American projects was their focus on advancing the British interest there. Indeed, London's Foundling Hospital, the charitable institution that made him famous, belonged to the same agenda. Disturbed at the sight of deserted young children dying in London's streets, Coram began campaigning for a secular incorporated charitable association to care for foundlings—children born out of wedlock—in 1722. Novel in both organization and mission, the idea met much moral opposition from the many who thought such a charity would foster sex outside marriage, although the ubiquitous Reverend Dr. Thomas Bray early approved the hospital and urged English people to follow the example of a Parisian female Catholic charity that tended foundlings. Eventually, after a clever appeal to aristocratic ladies and with a rise in infanticide causing public concern, Coram won support. In 1739, the hospital was established with input from several similar institutions in Catholic Europe.[28]

His American projects were of a piece with the Foundling. Undeniably, Coram had been moved by moral outrage and by compassion for children—stories tell of him giving gingerbread to youngsters in his penurious old age. In addition, it was an eighteenth-century commonplace that a nation's strength lay in the size of its population, and the hospital served the aim of buoying British might by saving lives. (Lest the point be missed, some Foundling infants were named after noted British admirals.)[29] Likewise, the transatlantic ventures that Coram had a hand in—colony schemes, the SPCK, the SSPCK, the Bray Associates, the Georgia Trust, an Indian girls' boarding school plan, and a proposed Anglican college—all sought to build British strength in an era when Britain and France were locked in a struggle for control of the North American continent.

Coram's fellow activists on both sides of the Atlantic likewise sought to bolster Britain through their benevolence. The venture that first took George Whitefield to America was one example. After the Georgia colony's establishment, two of its leaders "concerted a scheme" to set up an orphanage in the colony. The idea captivated Whitefield, who went to America to launch the charity he would call Bethesda or House of Mercy. Whitefield was an evangelist and naturally invoked religious motives and goals for the orphanage, but he also plugged Bethesda as a contribution to the national undertaking of planting a new colony: An orphanage would help lure poor settlers, who might otherwise have fretted that if they died in their new home no one would care for their children.[30]

Among the ideas that came out of the widely shared concerns about the British interest in the 1730s and '40s were sundry educational schemes to better integrate various peoples in America into British culture. Some focused on Africans. Whitefield launched plans in 1740 to set up a "'Negroe school'" in Pennsylvania, where presumably reading and Christianity would have been pillars of the curriculum. The death of a key associate sank the venture, but with the support of a wealthy South Carolinian, Whitefield set up a reading school for Africans in Charleston, with conversion to Christianity the end goal, and he inspired, both positively and negatively, a handful of other endeavors to teach Africans.[31]

Indians were also targets, and while metropolitan Britons were more supportive of converting or educating Indians than British Americans were, some British Americans advocated charity schools to Christianize and "civilize" native peoples. Comparable endeavors aimed at Africans mostly originated with metropolitan Britons, Europeans, or Americans born and bred in Europe, such as the saintly Huguenot-refugee-turned-Quaker-Philadelphian Anthony Benezet.[32] But British Americans and metropolitan Britons shared strategic concerns and cultural attitudes about Indians. So in 1743 when the New Jersey–born missionary John Sergeant, frustrated with his floundering outreach to the Housatonic Indians in western Massachusetts, sketched plans for an Indian boarding school, he expected to win help from British counterparts. A friend sent his plan to Thomas Coram who "was so charm'd (to use his own Expression) with Mr. SERGEANT'S undertaking, that he exerted himself abundantly to promote it." Evidently inspired by Sergeant's proposal, Coram also championed the idea of a school for Indian girls—a "very political Contrivance" in the words of his approving eulogist. By educating girls in Christianity, "the *Indian* Children of both Sexes of the next Generation, [would] be brought up Christians," and the end result would be to "unit[e] the *Indians* in *North-America*, more closely to the *British* Interest."[33]

Coram's proposed Anglican college in Massachusetts was another part of this agenda. Back in 1703, he had donated property for an Anglican Church in steadfastly Congregationalist Taunton motivated by his devotion to the Church of England; perhaps less noble reasons for his gift were his limited options for disposing of land he had won in a lawsuit and the spite he felt because of his poor treatment in the town. In the late 1740s, he had another idea for how to buttress the Church of England in America and tighten transatlantic bonds— goals that he and many metropolitan Britons believed were complementary but that many British Americans felt were contradictory. Disturbed by the thriving

Dissenting college Harvard, Coram urged the Archbishop of Canterbury to build an Anglican college in Cambridge, Massachusetts. The school would be called King's College and would educate Euro-American and Indian students alike. Had it been so much as mooted in Massachusetts, many New Englanders would have been furious.[34] The precise goals revealed critical differences among members of the British world, but the thinking was the same: Benevolence should strengthen the nation.

And it did. Thousands of people on both sides of the Atlantic donated to Whitefield's Bethesda project, thereby banding together with their fellow subjects to help needy folks on the fringes of the British community.[35] Similarly, the SPG's program connected many in England to the colonies. Each February the Society broadcast its mission with a sermon given at the church of St. Mary-le-Bow in London by a prominent cleric. Printed (with appendices detailing the SPG's work colony by colony) and disseminated to all parishes, the sermons reached people throughout England and Wales. Time and again they were told that their charitable obligations extended across the Atlantic. That obligation rested in part on a general reciprocity. The colonies were "Mines of Wealth" and the key to British commerce and naval strength. Colonists' backgrounds lay (although this was decreasingly true) in "our own mother country," potential donors were told. Enslaved Africans were "creatures of God" and labored for the benefit of British commerce. To native peoples a special duty owed thanks to "having gotten possessions in their country." These appeals were effective. Over the decades, thousands gave to the charity, with occasional gifts coming also from Protestant churches in Europe.[36]

As donations to the SPG from foreign Protestants suggest, Britons and British Americans were part of a broader charitable world. The defining trait of that world was the exchange of ideas across national and confessional borders. Activists borrowed freely from foreign and even hated peoples in organizing the new charities. Thomas Bray, in particular, had looked to the enemy. The Roman Catholic Congregation for the Propagation of the Faith was his model for the SPCK. Similarly, when he and his colleagues set up the SPG, they initially emulated a successful technique innovated by Bray's bête noire, the Quakers. Founded in mid-seventeenth-century England, the Society of Friends had become a transatlantic body with the migration of tens of thousands of Quakers to the West Indies and North America, especially Pennsylvania, in the late seventeenth century. By effectively deploying a traveling ministry, Friends had built a forceful organizational structure and had knitted together the dispersed Quaker community into "one people" by the end of the seventeenth century. So, it was to an itinerant missionary that Bray first turned to pursue the goal of "the reduction of Quakers," with only modest success.[37]

The SPG had looked not only to Quaker institutions to define its mission and methods but also to the Puritan New England Company. The first Protestant missionary group operating in North America, the New England Company had been founded in 1649 to bring Indians to Christianity. Like its counterparts formed in the next century, the Puritan organization was a transatlantic undertaking with tasks divided between men on either side of the ocean. Members in England raised and managed funds, while the New England–based commissioners paid out money to the missionaries in the field—or rather, for much of the seventeenth century, to the Company's one, dedicated evangelist. Organizationally, the SPG and the SSPCK with its American work, and later other transatlantic projects in the colonial era, would more or less mirror the New England Company: Financial power and final control lay in Britain, while operational capability and initiative lay with men in America.[38]

Activists also turned to foreign friends for institutional examples. At the beginning of the eighteenth century, Bostonians founded three, short-lived charity schools based in part on the example of the SPCK.[39] A few decades later when planning his Georgia charity, George Whitefield was deeply impressed by a famous orphanage founded by German Pietist A. H. Francke in Halle, Saxony, a university city that had an outsized influence on international Protestantism and on charitable agendas in the eighteenth century. Whitefield was influenced by Francke to such an extent that he not only hewed to Francke's practices but also modeled his account of Bethesda's rise and progress on the Pietist leader's account of his foundations, particularly by recounting how God's favor saved Bethesda time and again from financial troubles in the nick of time. (God had His work cut out for Him since the charity was on shaky financial footing for decades.)[40]

Many thousands of people's donations and actions brought forth the charitable projects that led contemporaries to deem the eighteenth century an "Age of Benevolence." Nevertheless, a far smaller number of individuals repeatedly turn up as leading organizers and conduits among their fellow philanthropists, and not just in London where an activist could rub shoulders with colleagues at meetings of the Georgia Trustees, the Bray Associates, the SPCK, and St. George's Hospital as one busy man did. Boston minister Benjamin Colman, a mover and shaker in New England charity, talked parochial libraries with Thomas Bray in London and orphanages with George Whitefield in Boston. Through letters, he sought resources from British groups and swapped ideas with Thomas Coram, the New England Company–funded missionary John Sergeant, and even a Jesuit missionary, and he served as a local commissioner for the SSPCK's missionary work in New England and for the New England Company. Less well-connected activists appreciated the position of someone like Colman.

Benjamin Colman, the evangelist John Sergeant hoped, would introduce him to Colman's "Correspondents Abroad" to help his projected Indian boarding school, which had much in common with Whitefield's Bethesda—no coincidence since Colman had urged Sergeant to be guided by the spirit of the renowned A. H. Francke in drawing up his plans.[41]

Perhaps a source of understanding among these disparate movers and shakers was that many of them hailed from middling backgrounds. The zealous Thomas Bray, the bluff Thomas Coram, the media-savvy George Whitefield, and his clever American friend Benjamin Franklin were all born into families of modest means. An enterprising character moved these men, who were nurtured into charitable entrepreneurs in the British Atlantic world. Exposure to new and different institutions, the ability to tap growing middling wealth, the increasing acceptance of ambition and the loosing of its energies made it possible for ordinary men to bring forth benevolent plans. As they moved around the variegated but evermore connected community, they found new problems and new possibilities.[42] To address them, they turned to voluntary associations, the quintessential middling organizational form of the eighteenth century.

The associated-philanthropy form was one of the defining traits of eighteenth-century beneficence. Such charity, based on the joint-stock company structure of a group of subscribers supporting a venture, emerged in England at the end of the seventeenth century and was preferred to the previously common endowed form by which individual testators funded charitable foundations. Associated beneficence gave donors greater control than trusts set up by testators; at the same time it addressed the contemporary concern that trusts robbed heirs of their inheritances. Moreover, it both took advantage of rising middling wealth and gave middling men voices in community governance. Such men made voluntary associations a force for shaping not only their communities but also the British transatlantic community.[43]

The associated-philanthropy structure and the multiple and overlapping networks among key activists, along with a developing sense of a common British Protestant identity and shared concerns about the British community's interests, made possible many-sided cooperation among organizations. Importantly, this collaboration often crossed denominational lines. The SSPCK, close to though formally separate from the (Presbyterian) Church of Scotland, depended on the contributions of Protestants from an array of backgrounds to undertake its American missions—really joint ventures with other bodies. Besides a conditional legacy that catalyzed the SSPCK's overseas activities, monies came from the fisc of Congregational Massachusetts and the primarily Congregational New England Company, plus individual donors. The SSPCK's endeavors also drew on Anglican support. The Bray Associates sent books to the Society's missionaries through the hands of ardent Churchman Thomas Coram, who also offered his friend Benjamin Colman pertinent advice on money matters. The participation of "all Denominations of Protestants" was a selling point for charities; the SSPCK touted it as one reason would-be supporters need not fear financial mismanagement. Similarly, the hospital movement then burgeoning in Britain entailed cooperation across political and religious lines, and advocates of those charities lauded their impartiality—though sometimes disingenuously. More was at play than leaders' heartfelt catholicity. For transatlantic ventures, financial as well as logistical considerations demanded interdenominational cooperation.[44] As organizations bowed to necessity and then puffed their Protestant cosmopolitanism, the public legitimacy of many charitable ventures increasingly depended on cross-denominational cooperation.

Close ties and common aims did not mean harmony. The busy activist Viscount John Percival vented in his diary about the "very cold and evasive letter" the SPG had sent in reply to a request by the Bray Associates to help lobby the Crown to press the South Carolina governor to "procure" the province's Assembly in passing a law "settling one or more negro Catechists" there. The SPG annoyed many American Dissenters, who resented its efforts to convert their numbers. Yet while Benjamin Colman could protest the activities of one Anglican missionary charity (the SPG), he worked with another (the Bray Associates), and even that bastion of Congregational orthodoxy, Yale University, accepted gifts of books from the SPG. Percival thought another Anglican gift to Yale, money from a noted divine to fund three divinity students of any religious background, "had greatly softened the Dissenters to the Church of England." Perhaps. But he and his fellow Bray Associates had been mistaken in believing that the South Carolina governor could pressure the Assembly to pass a law supporting catechists to slaves. Not only did slaveholders oppose missions to the slaves, but colonial governors did not have the sway over colonial assemblies that the British Ministry had over Members of Parliament. Benjamin Colman likewise saw what he wanted. In an account published in the *New-England Weekly Journal* in March 1735, Colman reported on three charitable ventures fathered by Thomas Bray—the SPG, the establishment of parochial libraries, and the Georgia colony—and explained that they were all "in special Favour of the *Protestant America.*" True enough, but the *"Venerable Man* of GOD, Dr. *Bray"* had aimed first and foremost to strengthen the Church of England in the colonies, a goal inimical to most American Protestants. For the time being, however, wishful thinking and misperceptions did not deter growing closeness. Instead, over the 1730s and '40s, they sparked plans for transatlantic projects. Ideas flourished more readily than institutions, but even the plans that went nowhere helped build the British Atlantic world. Some laid the groundwork for later endeavors while the others deepened ties that were making a diverse polity into a community.[45]

A British Atlantic Community

By mid-century, not only had the bonds between the North American colonies and Britain grown closer, but the colonies, although always less valuable to the British fisc than the West Indies, also mattered more than ever to the metropole's economy, as British Americans' spending helped spur British manufacturing. Colonists, none more so than Benjamin Franklin, knew it. As he saw it, "the Foundations of the future Grandeur and Stability of the British Empire, [lay] in America.'" Thus, well-connected people in the colonies increasingly imagined notable roles for themselves in the British polity. For their parts, ordinary colonists saw themselves as full-fledged members in the British community, especially by the end of the Seven Years' War, a conflict that, in another sign of the colonies' enhanced importance, had begun in America. Also by mid-century, colonial society had matured, not always in healthy ways. With the growing wealth that allowed many to buy "the baubles of Britain" came new depths of poverty: A more developed society meant a more unequal one.[46]

During the middle decades of the century, British Americans expanded their civic and welfare infrastructures in ways that reflected these changes. Among the earliest institutions founded in the mid-century wave were the College of New Jersey, established in 1746, and the Philadelphia Academy, established in 1749, on colonists' initiative. Religious rivalries among Presbyterians drove the founding of the College of New Jersey (now Princeton University), but the undertakings also signaled colonists' self-assurance and commitment to the improvement of their societies, a concept that to elite Americans entailed heightening distinctions of rank. New undertakings to relieve and supervise the growing underclass responded to the downside of economic development. Public poor relief in northern cities expanded, and a hospital and orphanage opened in Halifax, Nova Scotia, in 1752 joined almshouses and workhouses— public institutions that also might receive private donations—from Boston to Charleston. Colonists also increasingly elaborated the voluntary charitable landscape, laying the groundwork for much greater expansion in later decades. In 1748, the Boston Society for Encouraging Industry and Employing the Poor set up a linen manufactory in a failed experiment to cope with the rising problem of destitution, and residents in Newport followed suit. More successful was Pennsylvania Hospital, established with public and voluntary funding in 1751 and still in existence. Typical for its time, the hospital cared primarily for poor patients.[47]

These mid-century developments put the colonies—though less so the southern and Caribbean slave societies where extremely stratified economies hindered voluntary activity—squarely in the British charitable mainstream. The increasing number of mutual aid groups organized generally along occupational or ethnic lines, along with a panoply of other clubs and societies, belonged to a larger trend throughout the British world. The manufactory in Boston, for instance, drew on a model from England, where workhouses were in vogue. When Pennsylvania Hospital was founded, the voluntary hospital movement in the British Isles was in full swing.[48] Moreover, the hospital managers, in a practice typical in Britain, recycled copy from an English institution's publicity materials in their pamphlets.[49]

In ways large and small, benevolence was furthering transatlantic integration, a trend that accelerated with the Seven Years' War. The particular problems and solutions differed, but Britons on either side of the water created new charities to strengthen Britain against its foes. London saw most notably the founding of the Marine Society in 1756, the same year that the conflict already under way in America began in Europe. The Marine addressed two problems—insufficient naval manpower and disorder caused, in supporters' minds, by young rowdies roaming the streets—by outfitting poor boys for the navy. That charity, quite ingenious if one were well off, had been instigated by retired merchant Jonas Hanway. Inspired by what his biographer terms "Christian mercantilism," Hanway was a prime mover on London's charitable scene. Many of the undertakings he had a hand in drew on institutions he had encountered during the many years he spent living in Portugal as well as on other European models. Among them was the Magdalen charity for penitent prostitutes. By reforming prostitutes, the Magdalen promised to boost British population and thus military strength by restoring women to their proper reproductive roles. Or, if the redeemed women settled in the colonies, it would answer a similar end, and thus one enterprising Magdalen governor sent a number of penitents to the swamps of Florida in an effort to marry solving social problems to colony building.[50]

Men active in American philanthropy did not advocate population-boosting charities for the colonies. Because British America had less extensive—albeit rising—poverty and a growing population, its conditions did not foster identical needs. Rather, the prospect of a new conflict provoked the same unease among Anglo-Protestants that the creation of the British Atlantic community had. During the French and Indian War, activists took new steps to strengthen the British interest in America.

Even before the renewal of war, Anglophone Pennsylvanian activists and their coadjutors in London worried that a marginal group, in this case Germans, threatened cultural unity. Just as strategic concerns had played a key role in the establishment of missionary charities early in the century, so too did they here. Many German immigrants belonged to pacifist churches and therefore would not bear arms for Pennsylvania or Britain, and some Anglophones worried that those peculiar Moravians might secretly be Catholic. Moreover, in French North America there was "a considerable body" of German Catholics, "who, as they are countrymen, and speak the same language, may more easily seduce and corrupt" Germans in British North America. Again activists' response was to establish charity schools to integrate the outsiders. The supporters of the Society for Promoting Religious Knowledge and English Language among the German Immigrants in Pennsylvania, established in 1753, sought to teach English to German children plus "the plain and uncontested principles of Christianity" and "no farther degrees of knowledge, than are suited to their circumstances and occupations." These measures, proponents hoped, would keep the Germans from joining with the enemy. (Initially, German families supported the educational plan and by 1759, eight schools, teaching more than four hundred children, were in operation. Surmising correctly that the real goal was to assimilate Germans—who had resolutely remained separate—to the dominant culture, a German-language printer stoked opposition to the schools, and by 1764, they had folded.)[51]

Germans, who were arriving in force in the 1740s and '50s, were new objects of transatlantic charitable action in America. In addition, native peoples and people of African descent also were the targets of undertakings pursued during the war. Moor's Indian Charity, launched by the overbearing and underhanded Eleazar Wheelock in Lebanon, Connecticut, realized the goal of an Indian boarding school that had so animated John Sergeant and Thomas Coram. Wheelock, who cited Sergeant's model, had had plans for a school for a while. To his mind, the outbreak of war threatened to disrupt his efforts, although he also touted the familiar strategic justifications for such a venture. But besides funds raised in America, money flowed across the Atlantic during the conflict. Similarly, the Bray Associates set up negro schools in several cities starting with Philadelphia in 1758. Again, the idea rested on earlier efforts. The Associates had been funding catechists for years, to little effect. Then in 1751, the Associates and SPG jointly hired Joseph Solomon Ottolenghe—an Italian Jewish convert to the Anglican Church and former imprisoned debtor who had fallen out with his relatives in London—as a catechist in Georgia at the behest of the Georgia Trustees, whose interest lay in Ottolenghe's expertise in silk cultivation. Ottolenghe had no better luck with his mission than anyone else. His letters to the Bray Associates, however, seem to have focused more of the Associates' attention on the task of converting people of African descent, and in 1757, one of the Associates asked Benjamin Franklin for his thoughts on how to structure an educational mission "for the Service of the blacks" in Pennsylvania. The upshot was the founding of the first of five schools. The Bray Associates' record does not invoke the war as a reason for their new undertaking, but the Associates moved in circles that deemed it "a national Duty at this Time"—1756 was when an SPG preacher spoke these words—"to endeavour to preserve the Communion of our Colonies."[52] Toward that end, activists brought ventures to fruition during the war—the Associates' negro schools, the German schools, and Moor's Indian Charity school—that attempted to bind marginal groups to the British empire through religious culture.

Even without those efforts, bonds across the ocean had grown stronger throughout the 1750s and charity showed it. When, in 1751, the Foundling governors named a baby after the American missionary John Sergeant, they signaled not only that disparate charitable endeavors shared common goals but also that Britons around the Atlantic belonged to one community. Moreover, London periodicals paid increased attention to the colonies, especially those in North America, and showed new interest in charities there. Money tells the same story. Within diasporic groups—such as Quakers and Pietists—that structured the British world or linked it with Europe, aid to faraway members became familiar. Britons raised funds for welfare ventures throughout the community, often through religious and mercantile networks. In terms of transoceanic giving, the capital-poor colonies were more often on the receiving end of benefactions from Britain and the West Indies, while charities in Britain took in gifts from compatriots in the East Indies. But some people in America sent donations to London charities—American support for the Marine Society mirrored British support for Christianizing Indians—and the London ladies' charity that asked New Yorkers in 1761 to help impoverished genteel women by buying fashionable goods signaled that Britons expected the colonies to be a source of charitable funds. Most telling, however, is disaster relief: After 1740 when hurricanes, earthquakes, and other natural catastrophes struck, it became routine for people around the British Atlantic to contribute to campaigns to aid the sufferers.[53]

The Dilemma of Moral Responsibility

Even as men and women donated to help far-flung fellow Britons and even as activists undertook ventures that tightened the bonds of their polity almost up to its dissolution, they debated the nature of charitable obligation. It was only "narrow Opinions, and mistaken Politics" that led some people to think "their Charity should begin, continue, and end at home," wrote a publicist for the new colony of Georgia in 1733.[54] Bashing people who believed that moral responsibility to local folks should be paramount may not have been the best way to win supporters, but fundraisers knew they had to contend with that perspective. Ambivalence about the boundaries of moral responsibility would nag at members of the British Atlantic world as wars, migration, and political reforms continually remade their community—and communities. The uncertainty about the nature of charitable obligation, however, also belonged to a larger debate about human nature that intensified with the growth of a market economy in the eighteenth century.

To heal divisions after the Civil Wars in the British Isles, moral philosophers in the late seventeenth century had begun to argue for the natural compassion and sociability of human beings. The growth of commerce, and consumerism with it, added new urgency to efforts to understand human behavior. Gathering pace from the late seventeenth century, manufacturing and trade were making new goods available and with them new routes to wealth and status. These developments could be threatening. "Common is the Complaint we hear, that Publick Spirit is lost among us, and that no one pursues any Dictates of his Interest," observed Benjamin Martyn, the Georgia publicist. Not surprisingly, Martyn's solution to rampant self-interest was to urge a show of public spiritedness through support for the new colony. Moral philosophers approached the problem differently—although their conclusions would be a great boon to charities' fundraisers. They reacted to worries about the changing social order and about how to keep people's grasping ways in check by dissecting human nature. Ultimately, they found that nature to be benevolent.[55]

Not everyone joined the ranks of optimists. In what became an infamous pamphlet, Bernard Mandeville, a Dutch-born physician and writer living in London, attacked the developing view and instead rooted people's behavior in innate selfishness. Even worse, as he explained in a pamphlet published in 1723, "private vices" had "publick benefits." Greed and vanity, for example, fostered economic growth. Mandeville did not champion immoral behavior. Rather, he charged contemporaries with hypocrisy for denouncing and denying self-interest while enjoying its effects.[56]

Mandeville's many critics rejected the private vices, public benefits formula. But as they reacted both to his harsh analysis of human nature and to the pressing need to make sense of a social structure in flux, they tamed self-interest, the base of a market economy. Self-interest would not run amok because people recognized their reliance on others and would control their worst instincts. Commerce would even foster new social bonds with old enemies. The increasingly mercantile, consumerist character of Britain and America need not be disturbing, many concluded.[57]

This line of thinking helped further changes in the intellectual underpinnings of beneficence that had begun in the late Renaissance and Reformation eras. In medieval and early modern thought, the rich were stewards of wealth to which the poor had a rightful claim. Charity, which encompassed righteous treatment of others as well as alms-giving, bound communities together. The rise of commercial economies and the growing acceptance of self-interest sapped justice from conceptions of charity. Clergymen came to highlight not the rights of the poor but the gratification of the well-off. Indeed, Mandeville had been reacting to this shift when he asserted that "'Pride and Vanity have built more Hospitals than all other [Christian] Virtues together.'" Few would have put it that way, but contemporaries increasingly couched appeals for donations in terms of the benefits to the donors. Because eighteenth-century charitable ventures typically were organized as associations seeking funds from many subscribers, this was a savvy tactic to tap the rising wealth of the middling sorts. Boosters thus promised material and even spiritual rewards to individuals. They explained that beneficence would assure a stable social order, no small concern to people doing well in the new economy, and would enhance the British community's wealth, strength, and security. Most of all, clerical fundraisers stressed time and again that doing good "'[was] the most pleasant enjoyment in the world.'" This view—that charitable activity was "'the Greatest Pleasure of Life'"—rested on the felicitous finding that people were innately sympathetic and pained by the suffering of others. Relieving others' distress, therefore, brought donors happiness. Their delight became central to understandings of benevolence.[58]

By the mid-eighteenth century, then, there was widespread agreement that human beings were sociable and sensitive to their fellow creatures' feelings. Yet the possibility of *universal* benevolence remained in dispute. Moral philosophers David Hume and Jonathan Edwards took extreme positions: Hume, a Scot, denied the existence of universal benevolence, believing that to feel for another, one needed a relationship with that person. The New Englander Edwards, on the other hand, believed that "'general benevolence'" followed from love of God; anything less fell short of true virtue. Many moral philosophers steered away from those poles and instead endorsed the idea that people felt concern for all humanity. Due to "the weakness of [man's] powers," however, charitable actions should be confined to a man's "family, his friends, his country," in Adam Smith's words, and many thinkers agreed that pragmatic considerations and the primacy of responsibility for family, friends, and neighbors demanded those limits.[59]

As the world shrank in the eighteenth century, questions about aiding strangers were becoming more pressing—and they would become even more so after the American Revolution—but the issue was hardly new. Indeed, contemporaries looked back millennia as they considered the nature of charitable obligation. The parable of the Good Samaritan, the story from Luke 10:33 about a passerby who tended to a unknown man injured and lying in the road, was a perennial favorite among clergymen and other advocates of charity throughout the century. Other sections of the New Testament, as well as the Old, likewise counseled compassion for those outside one's community. Non-scriptural sources, and even the modern example from Muslim regions, were called on to teach the same lesson. As the May 1733 issue of *The London Magazine* reminded readers, Homer's verses celebrated those who cared for strangers. "These principles of *Humanity* were so strongly established among the *Eastern* Nations," the contributor of the lines from *The Odyssey* commented, "that the *Turks*, to this Day, retain them in some Degree" and provide free lodging to "*Travellers* of whatever Country or Persuasion."[60]

Like the biblical figures and foreign peoples they cited, Britons and British Americans also helped people outside their community, but not without controversy. King George II sent funds—taxpayers' funds—to "the distressed people of *Portugal*" after the 1755 Lisbon earthquake that killed 30,000 in that city. The same year, at the behest of Quaker philanthropist Anthony Benezet, the Pennsylvania Assembly voted money to care for a group of Acadians—French-descended Catholics—who were languishing in Philadelphia after they had been expelled from their homeland in Nova Scotia in a land grab justified as a wartime necessity. The next year, Pennsylvania Quakers founded the Friendly Association for Regaining and Preserving Peace with the Indians by Pacific Measures to do just what its name said. Englishmen at the same time responded to the plight of French prisoners of war by raising funds to clothe them. Because the Friendly Association seemed to many non-Quaker Pennsylvanians to put the welfare of Indians before that of their fellow Euro-Americans in the midst of Anglo-Indian warfare, it faced immense hostility. Likewise, the Committee to aid French Prisoners came under criticism for "lavish[ing] pity on our enemies" while "there remain many Englishmen unrelieved." Magnanimity to captive, fellow European foes was more palatable than sympathy for savages. Where the Friendly Association reaped opprobrium, the argument of the prisoners' relief committee that succoring the French "would soften the acrimony of adverse nations" brought great sums into its coffers. Even an Antigallican club donated a sizable £50. Nonetheless, charity within the British community, including to those marginal figures who Anglo-Protestants wanted to assimilate, was much more common than aid to those outside it.[61]

Yet even within the British world, charity to distant fellow nationals was not always popular. Transatlantic benevolence swelled over the first several decades of the eighteenth century, but most charity went to local folks. Moreover, there was a persistent assumption that responsibility for routine aid in the diverse community lay with one's own. Thomas Coram thought so. Public poor relief structures and charities alike generally did not provide for penurious outsiders, and,

after encountering some needy New Englanders in London who had been succored individually by people they knew, Coram thought about a more systematic
approach to the problem. Well-off New Englanders, he concluded, should fund an
institution to aid their down-and-out compatriots abroad. The Scots in Boston,
he told Benjamin Colman in asking for help with this idea, had such a "Bank . . .
for the reliefe of such of their Country as fell into Distress in New England,"
not to mention similar institutions in London and Europe. When people were
away from home and landed in need, it was the duty of their countrymen—here
Scots were Scots, New Englanders New Englanders, not Britons—to help them
out, thought Coram and his contemporaries. Hence, migrants, who were eager
to maintain their cultures, set up organizations based on ethnic and religious
ties, with the influx of newcomers in eighteenth-century British America leading
to a boom in such groups.[62]

Two decades after Coram shared his idea with Colman, one of the founders
of the new Pennsylvania Hospital worried that the institution would attract people from other provinces.[63] Moral responsibility to neighbors trumped the lesson
of the Good Samaritan. The managers of charities on both sides of the Atlantic
shared that view. Moreover, finite resources and the need to manage funds carefully to keep attracting more, along with ambivalent views of the poor, made managers fear fraud by applicants for aid. Crafty outsiders, the thinking went, could
hoodwink benevolent souls. Moreover, aid to faraway strangers took money away
from local needs. In Britain in 1762 to fundraise for the College of Philadelphia,
the school's provost encountered that view when a nobleman opined to him that
"many Things at Home . . . were much more Objects of Charity" than the faraway colleges. The provost also found that Londoners resented his appeal. They
were constantly being asked for donations, the Philadelphian was told, and, in
addition, there was a "Scarcity of Money owing to its being all locked up in the
Funds & Stocks" that had financed Britain's effort to expel France and its menac-
ing Catholic presence from the colonists' vicinity.[64]

In 1763, the Treaty of Paris ended the Seven Years' War. Britain had succeeded in eliminating France from North America and had become a worldwide
power. Yet the phenomenal victory had exposed rifts. Not only did some Britons
resent American appeals for money—even while many donated generously to the
several colonial college fundraisers who arrived as soon as it was safe to cross
the Atlantic—but Americans had hard feelings of their own. Dissenters in New
England had always been irritated that the SPG sent missionaries to that region
where, as Boston minister Benjamin Colman protested to an English bishop,
"the Gospel is received and preached, and Churches gathered in very good Order
and Manner."[65] Tiring of the SPG's meddling in Dissenting New England, a
group of Bostonians tried to found their own Society for Propagating Christian

Knowledge among the Indians in North America in 1762, which the Crown vetoed.[66]

Three years after the war's end, readers of the fashionable *Gentleman's Magazine*, published in London, could be forgiven if they were confused about their charitable obligations to strangers and, indeed, about who was and who was not a stranger. A commentator in April 1766 frowned on an English clergyman for spending too much effort fundraising for "for an *American* charity" rather than for his fellow clerics' orphans. A letter that September, by contrast, seemed to bring a ringing endorsement of a broad approach when it reminded readers that Britain had won praise for aiding prisoners of war in the last war, not to mention "strangers, thrown on our coast by accident, on the return of peace." But, as it turned out, the writer recalled those efforts as part of a favorite fund-raising tactic—a time-honored technique known today as the guilt trip—to spur donations for Britons' "Brethren and Friends" in Bridgetown, Barbados, where a fire had recently devastated the town.[67] The message was mixed. Transatlantic charity was by now commonplace, but contemporaries were torn about their responsibility to help faraway members of the British Atlantic community. The philanthropists active after the American Revolution grew up in a world where benevolence might serve political ends, where far-flung activists exchanged ideas, and where imperial growth raised questions about the nature of charitable obligation.

2

Coming of Age in the Atlantic Community, 1740s–1770s

WITHIN A FEW years of hailing the success of "our forces" in Havana after Britain took the port, Benjamin Rush would be railing against Parliament's "infernal scheme for enslaving America." He and his generation came to adulthood during a struggle over the nature of their polity and authority within it that began soon after members of the British polity on both sides of the Atlantic thrilled at victory in the Seven Years War. When the political conflict ended, this generation would turn to philanthropy to repair transatlantic bonds. Those born during the reigns of Anne and George I, men such as Jonas Hanway and Benjamin Franklin, were still active in beneficence in the postwar years, but they were passing from the scene. The movers and shakers in the late eighteenth-century "empire of humanity" had been born during the 1730s, '40s, and '50s and grew up before the British Atlantic community fractured. They would later work as "benefactors of mankind" based on their experiences coming of age in a world of mobility and interconnectedness.[1]

The people who stand out as leaders in philanthropy in the late eighteenth century, though quite accomplished, are not household names today.[2] Englishman Thomas Percival (1740–1804) pioneered in demography. West Indian–born John Coakley Lettsom (1744–1815) was the force behind the founding of the Medical Society of London, while New Englander Jeremy Belknap (1744–1798) was the prime mover in the establishment of the Massachusetts Historical Society. Philadelphian Benjamin Rush (1746–1813) signed the Declaration of Independence. John Crawford (1746–1813), whose life began in Northern Ireland and ended in Baltimore with a sojourn in the West Indies in between, is noted for early work on germ theory. Benjamin Thompson (1753–1814), the Massachusetts boy who became a nobleman in the Holy Roman Empire, made

important findings in the science of heat and light. Their fellow charitable leaders are remembered for their contributions to medicine, history, and ethics as
well as to philanthropy.[3]

Most of these future activists were born in the British Isles, North America,
the West Indies, and Europe. Born in one place, some settled in other parts of
the British world while most of them visited distant parts of it at some points
during their lives. A few had experience in the East Indies. They were Anglicans,
Congregationalists, Friends, and Presbyterians, with some maintaining ties to
more than one community. A few had Huguenot ancestry.[4]

Like their predecessors, these men generally hailed from middling backgrounds. They eventually might rub shoulders with aristocrats, but by and large,
they would work for their bread. The true elite, by contrast, lived off landed
wealth, not sullying themselves by labor, although some were actively involved in
the seamy world of trade. Many of the future humanitarian activists would gain
prominence and sometimes fortunes, though some died in debt.[5] Their fathers'
occupations were a reminder, however, that often they had moved up in life. The
sons of farmers, merchants, artisans, and craftsmen, and even a doctor, a West
Indian planter, or a lawyer-turned-royal governor would not have forgotten that
they had to cultivate their gentility. As they well understood, genteel status costs
money. Happy must have been the young man whose father told him, "You Judg
very right when you suppose I would not have you neglect any Expence relating
to your Education or the appearing like a Gentleman."[6]

Hierarchical relations structured the world they were born into. In the
ideal, bonds of obligation and reciprocity up and down the social ladder held
society together. From the monarch down to the lowliest slaves, all members of
society had—and knew—their places. People's positions vis-à-vis one another
determined the nature of social interactions—dictating modes of address, for
instance, but also allowing high- and lowborn men to mingle at, say, sporting
events. In this system, people at the top maintained and enhanced their authority by patronizing those below them who were then expected to defer to elite
leadership, while those lower down gained access to opportunities or merely
survived by cultivating the patronage of their superiors. The distance from top
to bottom was greater in Britain than in America, which lacked nobles or great
depths of poverty among Euro-Americans, but with inequality rising in America
so too was social stratification.[7]

This hierarchy was under stress, however. Even as the burgeoning market
economy heightened disparities in wealth, the traffic in goods then integrating the Atlantic world also blurred lines between the genteel few and the vulgar
masses. Manufacturers pioneered new products and new ways of selling them.
Merchants advertised their wares with growing care. Culture—from the arts to

religion—became a commodity, as did science and beneficence. The upshot of a thriving consumer culture was a world in which people could fashion themselves for public consumption. Through their clothes, homes, and leisure activities, individuals crafted their images, and through print those more eager for notice told stories about themselves. From enormous transatlantic successes such as George Whitefield and Benjamin Franklin to minor and fragile successes like Margaret Rudd, a social climber put on trial in London in 1776 for forgery, the eighteenth century was an era of self-invention and self-promotion. For more typical middling people, that could mean the chance to reach not the heights of a Franklin but respectability.[8]

In later life, members of the "empire of humanity" rarely commented on their early years, although the effects of growing up as a consumer economy boomed would show in their approach to charitable activity and their assumptions about the poor. The few who did record memories of their early years, however, recalled things that located them in a dynamic Atlantic community even as youngsters. Benjamin Rush, who attended a school in Maryland run by his uncle, an Irish-born Presbyterian cleric, had "met Mr. [George] Whitefield when a boy in America." (And as a young man, Rush heard Whitefield preach in Philadelphia, Edinburgh, and London and visited with the "great man" in London.) *Robinson Crusoe*, the tale of a castaway's adventures in the Americas, that "might probably inflame some of the boys with a spirit of enterprise," was one of the favorite books of John Coakley Lettsom and his classmates at a school near Lancaster, England.[9] With Whitefield and Robinson Crusoe as childhood influences, no wonder they would think across oceans as adults.

Education and Training

Parades of goods from distant places, celebrity preachers, and a world of print introduced future philanthropists to a transatlantic community. What made them members of it, however, were their own experiences of moving around and beyond the British world. Not every leader in the empire of humanity traveled far or wide. But many of them—and especially those who instigated new charitable undertakings—moved around the Atlantic with remarkable fluidity. These men's voyages generally did not rival the experiences of many people of African descent whose extensive migrations were coerced or constrained by narrow options. But compared to one group of peers, the fifty-five men who would be delegates to the United States Constitutional Convention, they were a mobile lot.[10]

Some traveled for their educations. John Coakley Lettsom left Little Jost Van Dyke in the British Virgin Islands at around age six to be schooled in England, where he would spend the majority of his life. More typically, however, colonists ventured across the ocean for medical schooling and perhaps some hands-on training with older doctors after their college years. No degree was necessary to practice medicine on either side of the Atlantic—university-trained physicians provided only a fraction of health care and not necessarily the best treatment— but for young men whose families could afford it, a "Doctors Degree" promised places in society's upper strata. Medical schools did not open in the colonies until the second half of the 1760s, so young Americans of means headed to Europe, usually to the University of Edinburgh, the preeminent medical school of the day. Unlike Oxford or Cambridge, Edinburgh was open to Dissenters, and its pupils "were collected from several parts of the continent of Europe, as well as from every part of the British empire." Not all Anglophone medical students went to Edinburgh. Some—Anglicans only—studied at Oxford or Cambridge and thus became eligible for the highest status in the English medical profession. In addition, a decent number went to Leiden, often after some time at Edinburgh, and some took their degrees there.[11]

To round out their educations, budding doctors "attended the lectures and dissections" of eminent doctors at hospitals in other European cities. Leaving Edinburgh after "the happiest period of [his] life," Benjamin Rush headed to London. Although he did not expect to learn much in the hospitals of the metropolis, he thought his "reputation may be influenced by" his time there. Not everyone was motivated by such tawdry concerns as image. "I did not so much look at the little reputation which the vulgar generally attribute to a Physician who is travelled, be it ever so little," insisted a newly minted English doctor in 1740 after traipsing through Belgium, Germany, and Holland, "as the use that I hoped would accrue from establishing an acquaintance with some ingenious people abroad."[12]

And make connections they did at university and on the medical tour. A good reason for his son to stay at Edinburgh "a further season," thought one New York father, was that it gave the young man more time to develop "a foundation of a Lasting and uninterrupted Friendship" with a couple of promising young men. Often ties forged by fathers and their friends, co-religionists, or hometown acquaintances opened doors for medical students. The "friends"—patrons— they came to know thanks to these recommendations might advise their courses of studies. They also introduced the young men to notables and to their peers, with famed London Quaker physician John Fothergill alone introducing several future philanthropists to one another.[13]

In addition to connections, young men took a sustained exposure to benevo- lent institutions from these years. Still vivid to John Coakley Lettsom decades after his days as a surgeon's dresser at St. Thomas's Hospital was the harsh way in which one doctor treated patients. "Sometimes he would order some of the patients on his visiting days to precede him with brooms to clear the way, and prevent the patients from too nearly approaching him," recalled Lettsom. "On one of these occasions, [one] of the governors upbraided him for his cruel behaviour. 'Know' said he 'thou art a servant of this charity.' "[14] Besides absorbing lessons at the hospitals where they trained, medical students visited hospitals and other charitable institutions on their trips to Europe. The layout and furnishings, management, staffing, and patient populations drew their attention for better or worse. Benjamin Rush found the Hotel Dieu, a large Paris charity caring for the poor, to be "crowded and offensive. [He] saw four persons in one bed." Also noteworthy was that "it was open to the sick of all religions and countries."[15]

Medical students were not the only young men traveling for training. Aspiring clergymen also left home to attend universities or academies. By the 1760s, the British Isles and British American colonies were well stocked with institutions to school men for the ministry. (The Society of Friends did not have ordained clergy. Its Public Friends—akin to clergy—honed skills in their local meetings before undertaking their travels.) Unlike their peers destined for medicine, therefore, clerical students did not cross oceans for their educations though they might go far from home. The only fledgling ministers who did have to travel across the Atlantic were American Anglican clergy, who had to be ordained in England until the establishment of the Protestant Episcopal Church in the 1780s.[16]

Merchants-in-training, by contrast, were inducted into an almost borderless world. Youths who "caught the spirit of enterprise" rarely attended university.[17] Rather, in their mid-teens they went to work for established merchants, sometimes in formal apprenticeships. Often, their families sent them to live overseas so they could learn skills and make connections. In addition, young merchants were dispatched abroad early in their careers to manage cargoes and transact business for their masters or more senior partners, as was twenty-two-year-old Bostonian Thomas Russell (1740–1796) when he "embarked with a cargo for the West-Indies" in 1762. Merchants' travels and foreign sojourns made them quite cosmopolitan as they traded across religious, cultural, and imperial lines—to the dismay of more chauvinistic types and the consternation of state authorities struggling to enforce regulations that confined much commerce within imperial boundaries.[18] The ties they formed, however, would not be as important to developments in philanthropy as the medical students' connections would be.

Surviving: The Charitable Landscape in the 1760s

In 1765, Thomas Russell was long back from the West Indies and perhaps also from London, where he had traveled soon after his return from the West Indies to sort out a business crisis. Benjamin Rush began taking medical courses in

Philadelphia while John Coakley Lettsom was apprenticing to an apothecary in Yorkshire. Thomas Bernard (1750–1818), born in Lincoln, England and son of the last royal governor of Massachusetts, had begun Harvard the previous year. By the mid-1760s, Englishman Thomas Cogan (1736–1818) was practicing medicine in the United Provinces (the Netherlands), where he had moved intending to settle for good.[19] Their work augmenting the charitable landscape would generally begin over the next decade, but for now these young men of means were mainly anticipating "lives of usefulness and benevolence."[20]

For the men, women, and children who used institutions their social superiors built, life was much tougher. In England, maybe a third of people received relief through the poor law at some points in their lives, with roughly 10 percent of the population "on the parish"—that is, receiving weekly doles from the poor laws—at a given time. Likewise in Scotland, poverty was widespread, so much so that one commentator in the 1780s noted that "'the poor in Scotland are supported by the poor.'" Indigence was a fact of life in North America too. Almost all migrants—a group including bound servants and captive Africans—arrived in poverty and many never escaped its grip as economic insecurity rose in both urban and rural areas over the eighteenth century. In Philadelphia, British America's preeminent city, one-quarter to one-third of free residents in the eighteenth century, estimates one historian, lived in danger of falling into penury. Perhaps the greatest stratification in the British Atlantic world was in the British West Indies, where the vast majority of the people were enslaved and destitute. Need stalked the white population too. In Bridgetown, Barbados, from the 1750s to the 1820s, half of whites were poor.[21]

Privation was a constant in these societies, but in individuals' lives it could ebb and flow. Economic growth and contraction—forces that the shifts between war and peace heightened—were one reason for people's changing fortunes. Seasonal fluctuations in the availability of work also played a role, with hard winters idling workers in shipping and building industries. A fire or hurricane could leave people homeless, while bitter cold could upend fragile budgets by both creating the need for extra fuel—usually wood—and raising prices. Likewise, "should any Distemper seize and afflict" a poor man, "should any sudden Hurt happen to him, which should render him incapable to follow the Business of his Calling, unfit him for work, disable him to labour but for a little Time. . . . How great must be the Calamity of such a Family!" Even worse, if he died, his wife and children could be left "perishing" with "no covering for [their] head[s] but the clouds." Besides the disasters that might suddenly beggar someone, want waxed and waned over a lifetime. Those whose parents could not fund education or training to set them up in life might enter adulthood on the economic margins, achieve a modicum of stability in their middle years, and then return to insecurity in old age. Many people, then, knew what it was to lack "the common necessaries of life."[22]

To cope, the impecunious used various, complementary means. They relied on one another. As everyone "[knew], many Mouths are fed, many Bodies cloathed, by one poor Man's Industry and Diligence." Women contributed to the family fisc also, although their wages were lower. The same was true for children, whose tasks could include collecting, fetching, carrying, tending, and cleaning. In addition, "the Help of Some friends" (most likely meaning kin) could make someone "Capable of getting [her] Bread," while a man might have a place to sleep thanks, say, to permission to bunk in another's stable.[23]

Mutual support among the poor was part of the fabric of their lives. On occasion, their aid to one another was noteworthy to the minds of the well-to-do. "At the admission of poor women to the Lying-in hospital in *Brownlow-street* [London], a *Scotch-woman* drew a white ball, which entitled her to be received into the house; an *English-woman* drew a black ball, which excluded her." What happened next so moved observers that someone ensured the incident saw print. "The *Scotch-woman* seeing [the Englishwoman] ready to sink at the disappointment, ran up to her at once, and *Do not lose heart, Mistress*, said she, *I will change*

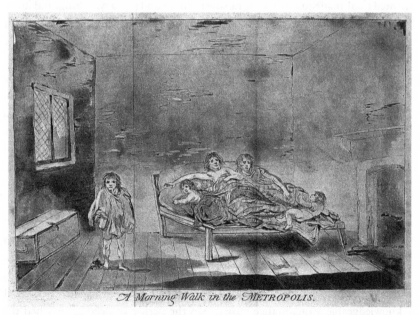

A Morning Walk in the METROPOLIS.

FIGURE 2.1 This depiction of a destitute family in late eighteenth-century London was sketched by John Coakley Lettsom in 1779 after a visit to the family's lodgings. He published it in the *Gentleman's Magazine* in 1780 to educate the comfortably off about needy people's suffering. Wellcome Library, London.

balls with you, and accordingly did so. The governors, struck with the poor *Scotch-woman's* generosity, gave orders that she should be admitted whenever she should apply."[24] The lower sorts could give their social superiors lessons in charity, they acknowledged.

The survival strategies of the poor were not typically so heartwarming. People might take in lodgers to help pay the rent. To cut their budgets, they ate less or cheaper foods. For laborers, less meat and more grains was not a healthy choice but one that courted sickness and made their physically demanding work harder. Sometimes parents found they "must part from" children if they could not support them. By binding youngsters out as apprentices, families reduced their expenses. By contrast, begging in the streets, a strategy best employed by the disabled and women with children, brought in some income. So did casual labor in exchange, essentially, for alms that could take the form of money or of "some cold victuals, and an old petticoat, and an old curtain to make a gown." Supplicants often approached the well-off deferentially, but not always. "God bless your honour, remember the poor mob," was how one boy announced that giving him a little money was not an option. It took the mob's arrival, however, before the terrified householder got the point. Stealing and prostitution also formed part of survival strategies. Slaves, especially in the West Indies, supplemented their inadequate diets by raising produce and poultry, fishing, and hunting. Like other poor people in Europe and America, they lived "by hawking or begging or stealing, by endurance or industry or guile" and by relying on one another.[25]

Poor people also turned to the poor law to help them survive. Distinct among European countries, England had a national, parish-based poor relief system. Drawing on existing local practices, Parliament established the poor law in a series of acts over the late sixteenth and early seventeenth centuries. By the late seventeenth century, the system operated nationally, but it was administered locally, and colonists imported the same basic infrastructure to British America. Parish overseers of the poor assessed and collected taxes from ratable residents, with people whose incomes were precarious exempted. The overseers were also responsible for providing relief to residents who were both legally eligible—based on having settlements in particular parishes—and deemed worthy—judgments made based on age, disability, sickness, widowhood, and other similar factors. When she petitioned for relief, therefore, a widow might stress that she "'ha[d] been very Ill a Long time and Oblidged to have a Doctor to attend'" her. Or, if a knowledgeable acquaintance rather than the person in need approached the authorities, she might explain that "'a poor man who lodges at her house [was] very destitute of every thing necessary to support life and must perish if not speedily relieved.'"[26]

Officials responded variously. They refused to succor some people (decisions that could be appealed). When officials found paupers' supplications meritorious, they could provide aid in several ways. They made occasional payments to people coping with sudden or short-term crises and disbursed weekly pensions to others, such as the aged or disabled. They also spent parish funds on medical care, burials, clothing, fuel, and other necessaries for the penurious, including sometimes for people who were not entitled to relief based on their settlements. In addition, overseers housed paupers in almshouses or workhouses, an option poor folks generally disliked although their inmates could—for better or worse—become family.[27]

People in need also sought aid from voluntary charitable institutions, which typically gave aid based on religious, national, occupational, or personal ties. In the eighteenth century, there was no sharp line between the poor law and what today would be understood as private philanthropy. Separate from their tax payments, individuals donated to public relief measures, while voluntary institutions received funds from the public fisc as well as from the ruling members of society. Moreover, in bigger cities, public and voluntary poor-relief organizations worked as a system, with an indigent person moving among different institutions over, say, the course of an illness. In recognition of the complementary, interconnected relationships among public, private, and religious institutions (not distinct spheres to eighteenth-century men and women), scholars now speak of the "mixed economy of welfare."[28] The various parts, they stress, functioned as one infrastructure—something poor people, who survived thanks to an "economy of makeshifts," already knew.

When paupers looked to voluntary charities in the mid-1760s, their prospects varied by city. "The mad extravagance of the present age [was] *charity*," and the crowded welfare landscape of London, a city familiar to many British and American philanthropic leaders, showed it. Anchoring it were five hospitals—a word then evolving toward the modern meaning but that still could encompass non-medical refuges—founded centuries earlier and jointly run, each specializing in a particular type of patient: two cared for the sick and wounded, one took in orphans, Bethlehem (enunciated as Bedlam) treated lunatics, while the fifth served as a house of correction for "strumpets, night-walkers, pick-pockets, vagrant and idle persons . . . also incorrigible and disobedient servants." In 1765, over 15,000 people kept body and soul together in the hospitals.[29]

Dozens of other institutions also provided relief. Not far from Westminster Abbey stood a hospital founded in 1720 by SPCK men, the first in the English voluntary hospital movement. Nearby, three charity schools variously taught, clothed, and "put out apprentice" children. At one, the children "[wore] blue coats, to distinguish them"—not a bad idea since nearby were the

Grey-coat-hospital, with 110 youngsters in the charity's eponymous garb, and the Green-coat-hospital for parish boys. A "house of correction, adjoin[ed] to the east end of the *Green-coat-hospital*." Not far away was one of the countless small almshouses—this one for "six poor people, who have each 5l. [pounds] per ann. and a gown"—that could be found throughout London. Often endowed by testators in the seventeenth or even sixteenth century, these small charities supported men, women, and occasionally children based on whatever criteria the donors had named.[30]

Walking through St. James's Park and north across Piccadilly and Oxford Street led to the financially unstable Middlesex Hospital, where Benjamin Rush studied in 1768. To the east in Lamb's-conduit lay the Foundling Hospital. There mothers seeking care for their infants left them with trinkets to later identify them, although most of the little ones would die. The well-heeled visited the Hospital to view its famous paintings and listen to Handel perform the Messiah. Heading away from the Foundling down Gray's Inn Lane led to the smallpox or inoculating hospital, where young Rush learned about inoculation. To the east, past the neighborhoods of Clerkenwell and Smithfield, was the French Hospital, established in 1718 for poor Huguenots. Elsewhere there was another French hospital; London also had a Scots Hospital.[31]

Heading south toward the Tower of London, "we find a modern institution, ([founded] in the year 1758, for the reception of penitent prostitutes." "To prevent the prying curiosity of the public . . . the windows next the street [were] concealed by wooden blinds" that "admit[ted] the light only at the top." Farther west, in the Royal Exchange—partway between the Tower of London and St. Paul's Cathedral—was the office of the Marine Society, the charity that kitted out men and boys who "would probably have been a nuisance to society" for the navy. North of St. Paul's, on Aldersgate-street—"more noted for the remains of its ancient grandeur than for the modern taste of the buildings"—stood a lying-in hospital established in 1750 in a decayed former palace renovated for the purposes of caring for "married women in the last stage of pregnancy, time of labor, and month of lying-in." Poor, respectable women could also seek admission—and did in great numbers—at one of the other four lying-in institutions set up in London between 1747 and 1765.[32]

Smaller cities also had a variety of institutions, although they lacked the degree of specialization that characterized London's charitable infrastructure. In the mid-1760s, the poor in the small manufacturing city of Norwich, England, might live in the boys' or the girls' hospital, each more than a century old; a hospital for poor lunatics, endowed by a woman in 1713; the ancient St. Giles's Hospital, where one wore blue, or Doughty's Hospital, whose residents donned purple outfits and had to obey the rules against "cursing, swearing, and drunkenness." Other almshouses, workhouses, and charity schools rounded out the landscape of relief.

By mid-century, the welfare systems in British North American cities were growing too. British American cities had few of the large institutions found in British cities, especially London, but their residents had set up a range of benevolent outfits by the mid-1760s. Philadelphia, the biggest and most heterogeneous city, had the greatest mix. Various charity schools, the Quaker almshouse, and Pennsylvania Hospital—which cared for lunatics as well as the sick and injured—were joined in 1767 by the Bettering House. The workhouse-cum-almshouse was funded by public and private money and, in spite of the managers' promises that it would reduce poor relief costs, it immediately ran debts. A few years later, a bequest added to the landscape an almshouse for twelve poor Anglican widows. If they met the right criteria, poor folks might seek succor from the long-established Carpenters' Company, the Society of Ancient Britons' (for Welsh people), the St. Andrew's Society (for Scots), or the newly founded German Society and the Society for the Relief of Poor and Distressed Masters of Ships, their Widows and Children.[33]

Settling Down

That, then, was the landscape that philanthropic leaders would build on in the late eighteenth century. They could play active roles in that endeavor for two key reasons. For one, they were men. Women had a place in the world of beneficence. Like men, they dispensed alms on a personal basis, gave donations, subscribed to charitable associations, and left bequests. Indeed, the canny managers of Pennsylvania Hospital targeted "the charitable Widows, and other good Women of the City" to pay for the Hospital's initial supply of drugs. Women, and men, of modest means also gave their mites when they dropped money in charity boxes. Society, however, frowned on female forwardness in public life and not until the very end of the eighteenth century did women initiate and run organizations in their own right.[34]

The other reason that future movers and shakers in beneficence could play active roles was that they generally settled in urban areas after their education and training. "A great city is . . . the school for studying life," observed Samuel Johnson. Not all cities in the British world rose to the level of great. But the urban growth of the eighteenth century meant that even Boston, a town of fewer than fifteen thousand people at mid-century, had an "'abundance of men of learning and parts, so that one is at no loss for agreeable conversation.'" Along with many people, cities had more spaces for conversation and more options for intellectual stimulation. Coffeehouses offered beverages, newspapers, and meeting places for "talkers," though not female talkers. Taverns, displacing coffeehouses in popularity, were places for men and sometimes women to socialize. (They were also places for attendees at the male-only benefits, such as the feasts to raise funds for new medical charities, to "eat and drink themselves into disease, to prevent it in their fellow-creatures.") Newspapers provided the "freshest advices" from around the Atlantic and beyond. Booksellers sold "a Very extensive Assortment of Books, in History, Divinity, Law, Physic, Poetry &c." plus "the Reviews"—for instance, the *Monthly Review*, published in London—and "the different Magazines." Libraries, both the membership variety and the fee-to-borrow circulating libraries that were part of booksellers' ventures, gave readers access to more of the pricey goods.[35] Taking advantage of and supporting all those institutions were the many clubs and societies that made city life so pleasurable for the middling and wealthy white men who could join them. For men who envisioned "lives of usefulness and benevolence" and embraced "rational entertainment," groups dedicated to learning, improvement, sociability, and charity were a draw.[36]

The chance to earn a living was another draw. Cities offered employment opportunities for the ambitious, if they could find positions or patronage.[37] Compared to their peers in other occupations, new clergymen had perhaps the least control over where they landed. A Dissenting cleric needed a call—a job offer—from a congregation, who would have the candidate audition before issuing the call. For some, this could mean a long time far from any urban center. Not until he had spent two decades as a minister in rural Dover, New Hampshire, did the ambitious Boston-born Jeremy Belknap (1744–1798) get back to his hometown. The English-born Thomas Cogan (1736–1818) had a different problem. Educated to be a Dissenting minister but unable to find a pulpit in England due to his unacceptable theological views, he decamped for Amsterdam, where he found a position in a Presbyterian church in 1759. The process was different for Anglicans such as William White (1748–1836), born and bred in Philadelphia. Rather than being called by congregations, Anglican clergy were appointed by the relevant authorities for particular churches, with White made a minister at Philadelphia's Christ Church.[38]

In contrast, elite medical men had more choice about where to live once their schooling was completed. After their sojourns abroad, young Americans often returned to their hometowns—Benjamin Rush to Philadelphia, the Anglican Samuel Bard (1742–1821) to New York, and the Quaker Benjamin Waterhouse (1754–1846) to Rhode Island (before moving to Boston in the 1780s). Their British contemporaries—often their friends—commonly redistributed themselves to cities around England after finishing their educations and medical tours. John Haygarth (1740–1827), an Anglican from the West Riding of Yorkshire, and his friend Thomas Percival (1740–1804), a Dissenter from Warrington,

England, moved to Chester and Manchester, England, respectively. For his part, the Scottish James Currie (1756–1805) sought a position in Jamaica until relatives urged him to reconsider. Instead, Currie wound up in Liverpool after a kinsman introduced him to friends there.[39]

For Currie and his fellow doctors, connections were essential to setting up their practices. A father who was a doctor (in Samuel Bard's case), a co-religionist patron (in John Coakley Lettsom's), or a friend's ties (in Haygarth's) brought them patients or hospital positions. Benjamin Rush, however, was bereft of a local patron or powerful family connections and wary of exploiting his Presbyterian ties when Quakers and Anglicans hated his co-religionists. Thus he pursued "the only mode of succeeding in business which was left for [him] and that was by attending the poor," as two British physicians he revered had done. Thanks to the patronage of the famed London physician who was also Lettsom's mentor, Rush was named professor of chemistry at the College of Philadelphia.[40]

Not all philanthropists followed these paths. Some were lifelong residents of their natal cities, such as William Hawes (1736–1808), who was born, schooled, and apprenticed in London and took over his first employer's practice as an apothecary and surgeon. Others, such as the Philadelphia-born Quaker merchant Thomas Eddy (1758–1827), moved around before settling—in Eddy's case in New York. Crucially, however, they made their marks in philanthropy once they made their lives in cities.[41]

Settling down meant more than getting established in one or another line of work. Most of these men married, usually by the age of thirty. A few gained fortunes through their wives. Settling down also meant enrolling in voluntary associations. Growing and mobile populations, growing disposable incomes, and growing demand for commercial leisure activity plus "social confusion" about status, among other factors, fueled a boom in clubs and societies. Wherever a man's interests lay, there were—or would be—groups for him to join. Some, especially the medical men, gravitated to learned conversation clubs and more formal learned societies. A few became Freemasons or members of other fraternal bodies. As urban dwellers who often had experience in other organizations, they were well placed to be leaders of the philanthropic groups they joined.[42]

Transatlantic Communities

These men looking for missions had grown up in a world of connections and mobility, and they expected that as adults they too would lead lives that went beyond the places where they settled. As they built their lives locally then, they also participated in far-flung communities as a matter of course. Even as ministers in Whitehall stoked political tensions in their attempt to deal with the challenges to public finance and imperial administration that grew out of the Seven Years' War, Americans and Britons strengthened the empire's sinews by pursuing transatlantic ties.

Kin stretched some men's lives across space. For no one was this more true than John Murray (1721–1792), the would-be founder of a worldwide chain of poor-relief societies. Murray, an Anglican Scot, had been born in 1721 in Unthank, Scotland, to John Murray and Anne Bennet. In 1728, John's father died and left the boy a legacy of £100. His elder brother James, ten years John's senior, planned a career for John in medicine, and in 1739, after completing his training in pharmacy and surgery, John embarked on a twenty-year career as a British navy surgeon. During that time, he was often in America and at least once visited with a sibling in Jamaica. In 1751, he moved to Wells, Norfolk, England, and two years later married Mary Boyles. By 1757, when Murray received a medical degree from the University of St. Andrews, the couple had had the first three of their eleven surviving children. In 1768, the Murrays moved to Norwich because the city offered a larger practice for Murray and better educational opportunities for the Murray children. Nonetheless, Murray struggled to maintain his brood and over the years received help from his sister Elizabeth, a wealthy businesswoman in Boston.[43]

After settling in Norwich, Murray did not move again, but his family fanned out across the Atlantic. Two of his siblings made their homes in North America. The youngest Murray brother, Will, joined the army; 1761 saw him in Senegal. A cousin was British consul in Madeira. Despite being separated by distance, the family stayed involved in each other's lives. Distant relatives wrote, helped each other with business matters and with finances, raised each other's children, and periodically visited one another. From the 1750s, nephews and sons of friends from America lived with John Murray's family. In the early 1770s, Murray sent his three eldest children to Boston to live with their aunt.[44]

Religion too tied many people to faraway places. Confessional bonds made the Atlantic world a community, indeed, many communities. These bonds laid the basis for long-distance business relationships, although less so than in the past, and spurred business developments, for instance in publishing, in response to spiritual and denominational aspirations. They also shaped political loyalties and hostilities. Religion created long-distance fellowships for just about all white members of the British world, small but increasing numbers of people of African descent, and very small but celebrated numbers of Indians who shared expansive outlooks and reaches.

Striving, philanthropically minded men found different entry points into these communities. After graduating from the College of New Jersey in 1763, John Lathrop (1740–1816), a Connecticut native, plunged into the world of transatlantic, mainly Congregational and Presbyterian, missions when he worked for several months at Moor's Indian School in Lebanon, Connecticut. For Lathrop's future correspondent John Coakley Lettsom, ties to the Quaker Diaspora were almost a birthright. Moreover, his patron John Fothergill served both as the correspondent between the Philadelphia and London Friends' Yearly Meetings and as a manager of the Quaker-dominated Pennsylvania Hospital, with responsibility for the charity's finances in London. As Fothergill's frequent amanuensis, Lettsom would have become even more familiar with co-religionists in North America. Meanwhile, Philadelphian William White, who would share prison reform circles with Lettsom, spent a year and a half in the early 1770s in London preparing for Anglican ordination. As they went about their lives, then, these three and men like them forged ties to their faraway brethren.[45]

Like family and religion, medicine made men part of a larger world. Their common experiences as students in Edinburgh or London initiated them into "the republic of medicine." Besides mixing with peers from far and wide, they had relished the stimulation of student societies and "medical conversation part[ies]" with established doctors. After finishing their schooling, they redirected their conversations into writing. Medical men prized this "literary [i.e., learned] correspondence" with their distant colleagues. They thrived intellectually on discussions about the latest empirical knowledge, new treatments, new ideas about diseases, and better management of patients. Doctors understood themselves to be "benefactors of mankind," a phrase they used time and again. Being citizens of the world was fundamental to their professional self-images, and their actions bore out the ideal. They conversed through letters, pamphlets, and books across borders of nation, empire, and religion to help advance "the common stock of medical knowledge" for the benefit of all humankind. When "soon after his return to Philadelphia" Benjamin Rush began what would be a lifelong correspondence with John Coakley Lettsom, a friend from his days in London, and when not long after starting his practice Thomas Percival published *Essays Medical and Experimental*, they were staking out places in a cosmopolitan professional fellowship that would sustain them throughout their careers.[46]

As Percival's eagerness to get into print suggests, print culture enlarged their lives. Books, pamphlets, periodicals, and newspapers were critical to the making—and ultimately undoing—of the British Atlantic community. Throughout their lives, Percival and his peers filled their letters with discussions of what they were reading and writing, and their eulogies and biographies often include lists of their publications.[47] These men recognized, as the generation of Whitefield and Franklin had, that by committing their words to print and by reading the works of others, they joined and shaped transatlantic conversations. At times, they professed to be worried about the response to their writings, but it was the cut and thrust with words before a far-flung audience that made their experiences as readers and writers so exhilarating.[48]

In addition to family, religion, medicine, and print culture, another institution united philanthropists in a transoceanic community: slavery. Besides the indirect ties they all had to the central institution of the Atlantic world, many philanthropists had firsthand experience with slaves and slave ownership. Americans lived in societies where slaves could range from a few percentage of the population in New England—higher in cities—to 40 percent in Virginia and 90 percent in the West Indies. Encounters with bondspeople were, therefore, an ordinary part of all European Americans' lives.[49] Slaveholding was also, and not only among Southern and West Indian whites. Boston clergyman John Lathrop married into the family that owned Phillis Wheatley, the celebrated African American poet. Likewise, Benjamin Rush, whose childhood household had included an enslaved girl, owned a man named William Grubber for at least fourteen years, while slaves toiled in the home of New Yorker Samuel Bard.[50]

In Britain, people of African descent—whose status lay between that of slaves and servants until court cases in 1772 and 1778 effectively prohibited slavery in England and Scotland—were a much smaller proportion of the population but not unfamiliar. A surprising number of British-born philanthropists, however, had spent time in America where they were exposed to slavery. During their youth, the Scotsmen Andrew Bell, James Currie, and Patrick Colquhoun each lived for a few years in a slave society, Virginia. John Murray, the naval surgeon who had spent "much time in the West Indies and other parts of America," not only managed a naval hospital in Jamaica in 1744 where he was in command of enslaved nurses, but he also helped his brother James purchase bondspeople. In Massachusetts, Thomas Bernard's family owned an enslaved man, Cato, who served as the household's cook; he was eventually manumitted and baptized in England. John Coakely Lettsom held slaves himself, after inheriting them along with other property in Tortola from his father. During a brief sojourn there in 1767–68, the emotionally intense Lettsom freed those bondspeople. His "heart [had] melted," he later explained, at the sight of them and he "could not for [his] life make them labour by compulsion." He continued to own other slaves, however, for decades, manumitting Teresa, a favorite, in 1782 and others in 1792.[51] Personal experiences with slavery would not necessarily turn men inclined toward philanthropy into abolitionists, yet their familiarity with the institution underscores their coming to adulthood in an interconnected transatlantic world.

Equal Partners?

Building the Atlantic community and especially Americans' place in it was not simply the outgrowth of people going about their lives but was the result also of conscious efforts to build ties across the ocean. Through missionary charities, people in Britain had long been working to bind colonists to the mother country. Leading American activists too aimed to strengthen the British interest with schools for Indians and Germans, and they drew closer to Britain, increasingly so from the mid-century, by participating in its charitable trends. The goals in both America and Britain were largely complementary, yet with ultimate financial control of joint undertakings in London, Americans had not been full partners. When a new religious charity, the Society for Promoting Religious Knowledge among the Poor (SPRK), offered equal membership, American activists responded enthusiastically, with many joining before imperial tensions reached a crisis point at the end of the 1760s.

A group of Dissenters had set up the SPRK in London in 1750 to distribute the Bible and other religious works to the poor. Like the Society in Scotland for Propagating Christian Knowledge, among others, the SPRK drew support from Dissenters of various persuasions and Anglicans, primarily those of an evangelical bent.[52] Like the (English) Society for Promoting Christian Knowledge, the SPRK had a network of supporters throughout England, and it also operated in North America. What made the SPRK distinct was that neither members nor objects of the charity in America were treated differently from their counterparts in England.

People in North America had begun joining the SPRK in the mid-1750s. One minister in Virginia subscribed in 1755. The next year several men in South Carolina followed suit. By 1769, forty-six people—including three women—in America had subscribed, making up about 6.5 percent of the nearly seven hundred subscribers that year. Laypeople far outnumbered clerics, and more Southerners joined than Northerners. In return for their minimum one guinea annual subscription—plus payment of "(at least) one guinea" at joining—members received "parcel[s] of books" to give to the "poorer sort" who, the founders and members thought, were generally in need of "aids to Christian piety and benevolence." When it was their turn, London-based members could pick up their books at monthly meetings. Different arrangements were made for subscribers outside the metropolis to receive their allotments. Other than that provision, all members participated on the same terms. And all—men and women, clerics and laypeople, Britons, Americans, and the lone subscriber in the East Indies—furthered the Society's mission by distributing books in their own neighborhoods to recipients of their choosing. Some Virginians used the society's materials to teach slaves to read and to bring them to Christianity. Others met local people's yearning for spiritual nourishment: a Mrs. Elizabeth Smith in New York and the Reverend Devereux Jarrat of Dinwiddie County, Virginia, both explained they could not keep up with the demand for books.[53]

Americans, however, appreciated the Society for reasons beyond religion. Through it, they had found a way to be full partners in a metropolitan venture. The colonies had grown closer to the mother country during the mid-eighteenth century, but in the process, colonists increasingly recognized and resented their inferior position to metropolitan Britons. During the French and Indian War, Americans—from leading men such as George Washington to ordinary soldiers—chafed at regulations that made British regular officers superior to colonials and bristled at British officers' disdain toward them.[54]

Worse yet were the policies pursued by the British government since the end of the Seven Years' War. In Americans' own eyes—though not in the eyes of British commanders and ministers—Americans had made critical contributions to the war effort and expected now to be treated as equal partners in the empire. British ministers had a similar expectation. Britons in the metropole were staggering under the tax burden from the war that expelled the French from eastern North America. To share the financial burden with colonists—great beneficiaries of the changed strategic situation—the government imposed a series of new taxes on colonists, an equality Americans failed to appreciate. The government also pursued other measures to defend and better control the colonies, such as stationing troops on the American frontier and improving customs regulations to hold down rampant smuggling. Most obnoxious of the new policies was the Stamp Act, passed in 1765, which mandated tax on any and all paper—from newspapers to court documents to almanacs and much more—that Americans used. Because it was so intrusive, the act raised fundamental issues of liberty and slavery. Britons on both sides of the Atlantic understood power and liberty as perpetually embattled. To remain free required constant vigilance against rulers' attempts to encroach on individuals' rights and property, the basis of a person's independence. The alternative if they failed to maintain their independence was slavery, that is, being under the arbitrary control of others.[55] In colonists' minds, then, acquiescing to be taxed without representation by allowing the Stamp Act to go into effect would be consenting to "an infernal scheme for enslaving America." In their furious response to this evidence of "venality, bribery, and corruption," colonists rioted, tore down houses, and burned stamp collectors in effigy—a tactic Benjamin Rush not only applauded but also wished to see employed in Philadelphia.[56] They spoke and wrote against the Stamp Act, initiated non-importation agreements, and organized a congress to discuss the crisis. When Parliament revoked the Stamp Act in 1766, Americans rejoiced, and transatlantic relations seemed to return to normal.[57]

The period of tranquility was brief. In 1767, the crisis deepened when Parliament passed the Townshend Duties, which taxed various goods, including lead, glass, and paint, that Americans were prohibited by law from manufacturing for themselves. Even worse, taxes raised from the Townshend Duties would pay royal governors' salaries. Until this point, colonial legislatures had paid governors, thereby holding them in check. The new arrangement threatened colonists' liberty by removing the power of the purse. Colonists rejected these new duties as unconstitutional, a position articulated in a Circular Letter issued by the Massachusetts House of Representatives and sent to the other colonial assemblies. When the Massachusetts House refused orders to revoke the letter, Governor Francis Bernard dissolved the legislature, and colonists responded with mob violence. In October 1768, British troops began arriving in Boston to take back control of the province—proof to Americans of the plot to enslave them.[58]

These developments strained the British community. To many metropolitan Britons, Americans had a responsibility to help support the government that protected them and the empire in which they were thriving. American opposition to the taxes was a betrayal of their obligation to their fellow subjects.[59] The imperial crisis did not simply alienate fellow national from fellow national. Indeed, it strengthened bonds among some members of the British world. Some Britons, especially Dissenters, shared American fears of an overweening government, and Americans celebrated and corresponded with their right-thinking brethren. John Wilkes was "an enthusiast for AMERICAN Liberty," reported Benjamin Rush, after meeting the famous politician in London. Many West Indian whites also shared American hatred of the Stamp Act, and some of those in London worked with their North American counterparts toward its repeal.[60] Meanwhile, as reminders that there were deep tensions among Britons, some Englishmen such as Wilkes assailed Scottish Members of Parliament as collaborators in tyranny.[61] The most important reaction to the new imperial policies for the future of Britain's hold over the Thirteen Colonies was Americans' disaffection. They had expected to be partners, but Euro-Americans felt they were being treated, in their English champion William Pitt's words, as "the bastards of Englishmen."[62]

Well-off Americans had begun joining the SPRK in the heady days of the French and Indian War. Partnership in the empire was possible, the charity had suggested. Hence, after 1769, when the British government's policies increasingly dashed colonists' expectations of equal membership, no more Americans joined the SPRK, with two exceptions—a Swiss-born clergyman in Georgia in 1774 and a New Hampshire man in 1784.[63]

By shunning the SPRK, Americans displayed their alienation from Britain. Some were beginning to go further. In 1762, a number of Bostonians had tried to set up their own society for promoting Christian knowledge. A decade later, in 1771 two American Presbyterians who had earlier supported the SPRK, the New York–based Reverend John D. Rodgers and his correspondent Benjamin Rush, were likewise mulling plans for an American missionary organization. The two men should talk about the idea of "creating a Society for the Distribution of pious Books among the poor especially on our frontiers," Rodgers suggested, when they next met in person.[64]

Thanks to the importance of a shared Protestant identity, religious philanthropy was an especially sensitive gauge of the state of the transatlantic community. By 1770, Americans signaled disaffection by their loss of interest in the SPRK. Colonists, however, were not ready to break all ties. Indeed, through medical charity, they were drawing closer to their British counterparts. Most tangibly, in the early 1770s New Yorkers established a hospital with help of colleagues in Britain. Doctors in New York had worried for some time that their city lagged behind Philadelphia in terms of medical education. They thus advocated founding a public hospital to care for the sick "labouring Poor," with Samuel Bard and his father John, also a doctor, playing leading roles in the effort. The institution, Samuel Bard explained in a commencement address at King's College in 1769, would also give physicians the chance to study the "particular Diseases" of the region and provide "the best and only means of properly instructing Pupils in the Practice of Medicine." In 1770, men began fundraising for the hospital in New York, and the following year the colony's governor granted a charter for the charity.[65]

With the local preliminaries behind them, the hospital governors soon reached out to British associates for help with the next steps. In November 1771, the governors—many of them merchants—appealed to English and Irish merchants trading with New York for subscriptions. They also requested "Aid and Assistance" from John Fothergill and from "one of the Queens Physicians, who is soon expected in America." Some months later, the governors authorized two men—including John Jones, a doctor who had trained in London in the 1750s—to solicit donations during their upcoming trips to England, and in 1774, they empowered a well-wisher in Jamaica (possibly from a New York family) to raise funds there. Besides funds from abroad, the New York Hospital governors, like their fellow activists around the British world, drew on existing institutions in Britain for plans for the building.[66] In setting up the charity, then, the New Yorkers were not just responding to local needs, nor just keeping up with their rivals in Philadelphia. Rather, they were consciously joining the movement that had led to the establishment of hospitals in England, Scotland, and Pennsylvania.

By the time New York Hospital was founded, many Americans had grown increasingly angry with the British government. Men like Samuel Bard, however, had been raised in an Atlantic world, as had their British counterparts, and even with transatlantic tensions mounting, they understood their community—the core of charitable endeavor—to extend across the ocean. How better could the New York Hospital men recognize that understanding—and garner benefits for the charity—than by electing Dr. Fothergill to the board of governors?

3

The Unnatural War

JOHN FOTHERGILL DID not keep his place on the New York Hospital board for long. The friend to so many young American doctors, manager of the New York and Pennsylvania Hospitals, and donor to the colleges in New York, Philadelphia, and Williamsburg was ousted in May 1774, on the day that New Yorkers heard about the impending closure of the port of Boston in punishment for colonists' defiance of Parliament with the Boston Tea Party.[1] Eleven months later, compatriot began to fight compatriot.

While the civil war is often seen within national frameworks as a beginning or ending point, to men and women who had grown up in the British Atlantic world, the "unnatural war" was not a neat break.[2] The conflict unsettled lives on both sides of the Atlantic and relationships across it. Moreover, it was a crisis of community that led Britons during the war (and Americans after it) to reckon anew with conceptions of moral obligation as they tried to make sense of their disordered world. Out of the confusion came one of the era's most astonishing endeavors to extend charity on a universal basis.

Dislocations

Ironically, during the leadup to and early stages of the war, the government did much to foster unity in the Anglo-American community: Few approved of how the ministry handled the imperial conflict. Imperial "administration ha[d] been and [was] undoubtedly much to blame" for the "present unhappy disputes," thought the youthful Scotsman James Currie, then living in Virginia, although he also believed "the colonies ha[d] certainly carried things to a very extravagant height in consequence of it." John Murray, the Scottish doctor living in Norwich, England, also faulted the ministry. With war in the offing, he counseled his son in Providence, Rhode Island, that "Loyalty to the lawful Sovereign is the Character of your family." Although he supported efforts "to subdue our rebellious children should they continue to resist parental authority and lawful power," he regretted that Britain had not earlier "acted with common sense in the conduct and management of American affairs." Englishman Granville Sharp went further. To his mind, "the impending Evils which threaten[ed] the Colonies abroad" were coupled with a dangerous "misunderstanding of the British Constitution" at home"—a view that surely gratified his correspondent Benjamin Rush, who regularly denounced the iniquitous policies of Parliament yet assured Sharp in 1774 that "not a *man* in America . . . wishe[d] for the independence of the colonies." American Loyalists too shared the general view. Samuel Bard predicted that the "British ministry . . . [would] never get a revenue out of us which will pay the expense of collecting" it by force.[3]

The government's mishandling of the colonies dismayed many. The likely results of the ministry's bungling, they accurately predicted, were "the horrors of a civil war." The American Revolution was a civil war several times over. Not only was the American population divided overall, but people of European, African, and native descent also fought on both sides. But most salient to transatlantically minded contemporaries was that the conflict divided "people of one Religion, family and tongue, and . . . of one principle" on either side of the Atlantic.[4]

Men who were or would be in philanthropic circles found their lives upended by the strife in many ways. Some found themselves separated from correspondents and publications across the ocean. For Americans especially, the inability to swap letters and writings with colleagues abroad or read the newest works meant being isolated from the latest "discoveries" in Europe. A greater worry was the disruption in trade. The war, joined in 1778 by France and Spain, halted much commerce in the Atlantic world and impeded internal American trade. The personal impact of the standstill varied, but affected many. John Murray, the doctor in Norwich, England, fretted about his eldest daughter's unsettled mercantile affairs. Thomas Russell, the Boston merchant, lost part of his fortune when the British attacked the city in 1775. For his part, James Currie, still then learning trade in Virginia, found himself anticipating that "the last year of [his] apprenticeship [was] likely to be a very idle one," a state of affairs that "must be destructive to a young fellow in [his] situation."[5]

Faced with declining prospects in Virginia, Currie (after various misadventures from conscription in Virginia to a run-in with an American privateer) returned to Scotland and trained to be a doctor. He was not alone in quitting his current home because of the war. Several would-be leaders in the empire of humanity also found themselves impelled to move and resettle because of it. Among the first to have his life disrupted by the conflict, well before fighting started, was Thomas Bernard. Bernard was a student at Harvard when the imperial crisis began. In 1766, this son of the royal governor of Massachusetts had joined his classmates in a protest of the college authorities inspired by the defiant mood of the day. Over the next few years, however, his father, struggling to maintain royal authority in the colony, became a figure of abuse, and in 1769 Thomas Bernard withdrew from college to serve as his father's secretary. Within months, he returned to England when his father was relieved of his office.[6]

Benjamin Thompson (1753–1814), who would become a friend of Bernard's in London, was also forced to move by the American Revolution and turned those circumstances to spectacular, if lonely, success. The future Count Rumford was born into a middling family in Woburn, Massachusetts. His education consisted of schooling to the age of thirteen, apprenticeships to a storekeeper in Salem and then a physician in Woburn, and attendance at some lectures at Harvard. In 1772, he moved to Rumford (now Concord), New Hampshire, to teach school, and there met and married the well-off widowed daughter of a clergyman. In New Hampshire, Thompson gained the patronage of Governor John Wentworth, who made Thompson a major in the New Hampshire militia. As the imperial conflict deepened, Thompson remained loyal to Britain. His efforts to return deserters to the British army in 1774 aroused the ire of "the people of Concord," and Thompson was tried "at the bar of the Populace" as "an enemy to the cause of America." The charges were not proven, but fearing the "Rage of this Popular Whirl-wind," Thompson fled the town.[7]

Leaving his wife and young daughter behind, he sailed for England in 1776. There the man with a talent for ingratiating himself with superiors became private secretary to Lord George Germain and later secretary to Georgia, and then, in 1780, Undersecretary of State for the American Department. During this time, Thompson faced accusations of embezzlement—for the first, but not the last, time—and treason. To further his career, Thompson raised a regiment of the King's American dragoons. With it, he went, in 1781, to America, where he distinguished himself by desecrating a Long Island graveyard which he used for military purposes. In 1783, he returned to England. After retiring from the army on half-pay, he traveled in Europe. Through military ties, he met the modernizing Elector of Bavaria, Karl Theodor. With the permission of George III and a knighthood to boot, Thompson accepted a position as a colonel and aide-de-camp to Karl Theodor. Within a few years, he had reformed the Bavarian army, a feat that led to his later work in social policy and philanthropy.

Other Loyalists also decamped to communities that would be more welcoming to their politics. Thomas Eddy, a Quaker and an opponent of "the shedding of blood," left his native Philadelphia for the British-occupied New York where he worked to establish himself in business. The war years did not pass placidly for him, however. A romantic errand to New Jersey one night landed him in custody of the Jersey militia for several weeks, with a spell in a "miserable dungeon," before he was exchanged and sent back to New York. (In the end, though, he got the girl.) [8]

Americans on the other side of the political divide likewise fled their homes due to the hostilities. The Reverend John D. Rodgers of New York moved several times during the course of the conflict, dislocations that separated him from his flock. John Lathrop, minister at the Second (Old North) Church in Boston, and his parishioners similarly dispersed after the British took Boston in 1775, with the clergyman filling a vacant pulpit in Providence for a few months before moving to his hometown of Norwich, Connecticut. Farther south, in December 1776, with a pending invasion by the British, Benjamin Rush joined his fellow Philadelphians and fellow members of the Continental Congress in an exodus from the city.[9]

Rush returned to Philadelphia in the spring and spent the next few years in and out of the city. He was busy with his work as a congressman until his opposition to the new Pennsylvania Constitution led to him to lose his political position. He kept up with army medical duties until clashes with colleagues led to his resignation as physician general of the Continental Army's Middle Department. Public and professional conflicts tried him, as did the "banishment" from family and home. Rush missed the company of "a most affectionate wife," instead having to settle for "the society of strangers." He rued having had "to exchange a *whole* house for a *single* room" and he disliked having "to *request*," as a boarder did, "instead of *commanding*" as a head of a household. Many, many others, he knew, faced these hardships too. "The country families," he noted, had been so "crowded with refugees" from Philadelphia and nearby cities that it was difficult for the displaced to find "tolerable accommodations."[10]

Being forced from their homes was bad enough, for Loyalists and Patriots alike. Many Loyalists would not be able to return to their homes, and their wartime flight was often just the beginning of a series of moves that would scatter them around the world. Unlike their Loyalist relatives, friends, and neighbors, Patriots could return home, but when they did, thousands found that their communities had "been pillaged and burned." In Lathrop's Boston, "between 4[00] and 500 houses were pulled down and burnt, while the town was held by British troops," and even his church, the Old North, had been "torn to pieces" by the enemy. Towns from Falmouth, Massachusetts, to Norfolk, Virginia, had also been razed, the clergyman railed in a chronicle of ruin that presented citizens of the nascent country united in woe.[11]

Besides experiencing the "wanton destruction" of their towns and cities, American civilians, unlike their British counterparts, also saw friends, family, and compatriots maimed in battle and sickened from infectious diseases that spread so easily in wartime, and they lamented the poor souls who succumbed to combat or contagion. Their ordeals were awful, but if a soldier met death honorably, as Benjamin Rush felt General Hugh Mercer had, after being wounded at the battle of Princeton in 1777, then his friends might channel their sorrow into suggesting "funeral honors." When Patriots came in for mistreatment at the hands of the British, however, Americans reacted with fury. John Lathrop fulminated about the "many [American prisoners of war] who have suffered in the most shocking manner and died in [British] prisons and guard-ships." After Rush's own father-in-law, Richard Stockton, also a member of Congress, was abused by the British who held him prisoner, "every particle of [Rush's] blood [was] electrified with revenge." Some weeks later, Rush raged at the news of an American militia chaplain "murdered" in "cold blood" by "savages." Like the native people more often tarred with that term, the British were now emotionally alien to him.[12]

Except when they weren't. Over the course of the war, Americans, Rush included, faced affliction and felt patriotic anger. Nonetheless even a few years into the fighting, even as an ardent patriot, Rush could experience the conflict as a civil war. A young man Rush "knew . . . intimately in Scotland" was killed in the battle of Princeton. The American "wept, for the first time, for a victory gained over British troops." Most poignant to Rush was that the two old friends' "attachment to each other was reciprocal." The Scot had mentioned Rush, reported a fellow soldier, "a thousand times" as a "personal friend," not a "political enemy." Rush later told his friend's family that he had had the body properly buried and the gravesite marked.[13]

Civil War and the Crisis of Moral Responsibility

American Patriots might grieve for British friends but seethe at the friends' army for the miseries it was inflicting on their soil and among their fellow citizens. After the fighting ended, they would be perplexed about their relationship to the former compatriots turned foreigners. This reckoning came first for Britons. With the war's battles at a distance, British civilians could feel torn about the people their soldiers were fighting. Were the Americans "rebellious children" of Britain, "trans-atlantic brethren," compatriots, or foreigners?[14] In the face of this confusion about who belonged to their community, some Britons embraced a universal approach to moral responsibility.

People's senses of the community or communities they belong to shape the boundaries of their moral responsibility. With the transatlantic family in crisis but with the most immediate disruptions of war thousands of miles away, Britons wrestled with the nature of moral obligation. Writer Samuel Jackson

Pratt addressed the issue in his epistolary novel, *Emma Corbett*, published first in 1780 and subtitled in some editions *The Miseries of Civil War*. *Emma Corbett* is the story of two English families whose close friendship is threatened by the war. In the Corbett family, the father, Charles, and son, Edward, side with the American rebels while Henry Hammond, dear friend to Edward and beloved of his sister Emma, takes up arms for Britain. Henry Hammond is ardent in his beliefs, but Charles Corbett is almost violent in his.[15]

The moral hero of the story is Charles's friend, Sir Robert Raymond. In shocked response to Corbett's tirade against Henry, Sir Robert champions a cosmopolitan outlook toward this war and war in general. "I imagined *you* were, like *myself*, a citizen of the earth, and of no particular party," he tells Charles. He had traveled widely, Sir Robert continues, and "beheld amongst every people, whether savage or civilized, many things to like, and many to dislike, but not *one* to cut them wholly from [his] tenderness." Moreover, he "deplore[d]" war. Although he had discovered war is universal, Sir Robert believed there were people in all armies worthy of love. Furthermore, often both sides were wrong and even if one were right, many innocents died.[16]

Eventually swayed by Sir Robert's ethical leadership, Charles repents for his extreme attitude and wishes he had "prayed fervently for the returning embrace of a divided people. *That* would have been true patriotism and true philanthropy." The war raised the question of to whom Britons owed moral obligations—whose welfare they should care about—and Pratt, through his characters, answers that they should love country *and* love mankind. (Pratt's character, typical for people in the eighteenth century, used philanthropy in the sense of its literal Greek translation, "love of mankind.")[17]

The author closes by driving home the idea that the boundaries of moral responsibility are at stake in the civil war. By the end of the story, the four young people—Henry Hammond, Emma Corbett (who had married Henry after she intrepidly tracked him down in the midst of the fighting in America), Edward Corbett, and Henry's sister Louisa (who had secretly married Edward before the war)—are dead, and Charles Corbett is a broken man. The person left to raise the orphaned children is Sir Robert. His stance had been ethically correct and therefore he is the only one fit to nurture the next generation of the transatlantic community, symbolized by a boy conceived in England and a girl conceived in America.[18]

Samuel Jackson Pratt was not alone in reflecting on the nature of moral bonds in reaction to the civil war. The transatlantic crisis raised the same issue for John Coakley Lettsom. In 1778, he had hoped for the "permanent reconciliation" of a divided people, and he ruminated on the topic in a memoir of John Fothergill. In 1782, Lettsom read a eulogy of his late patron to the Medical Society of London;

the memoir was first printed in 1783 and later expanded. After a long discussion of how Fothergill had tried to prevent the war and then tried to make British leaders realize how harmful the conflict was to the country, Lettsom turned to the issue of national loyalties. He admired Fothergill because he had "a natural attachment to his native country, . . . yet, in the philanthropy of his breast, his affections expanded beyond the confines of empire." Invoking his patron's beliefs to bolster his case, Lettsom rejected the idea of "*natural* enmity of nations" as "impolitic and irrational." Instead, drawing on the hotly debated view that commerce softened interactions among peoples, he advocated mutually beneficial relations among nations. He used Britain's relationship with France as an example. By then, the fight against France mattered more to Britons than the colonial rebellion and France was Britain's traditional foe so it was a natural choice for Lettsom's lesson. But it was the question of Britain's relationship with America that had gotten him started on the topic. The breach in the transatlantic community had stoked concerns about the boundaries of moral responsibility.[19]

Those concerns had broad resonance. Before the war, members of the British Atlantic community had extended their beneficence to one another across the empire's subdivisions mainly on an ad hoc basis, though some carped about the growing practice. During the war, Britons' charitable funds continued to flow to America or Americans. With money, rather than words, they announced that the boundaries of community and therefore of charitable obligation were at issue, although how people defined those boundaries varied. Some aided co-religionists. The Society for the Propagation of the Gospel raised funds for Anglican missionaries, generally English-born, in America. Likewise, the "*Quakers of Europe*" took up a subscription "for the service of their fellow-subjects beyond the Atlantic."[20]

The suffering of American prisoners of war in England drew attention also. Two years into the war several hundred people donated to a charity drive to provide clothing and other necessities to men whose government was ordinarily expected to care for them—an obligation the nascent United States could not fulfill. Several hundred people contributed, from aristocratic parliamentary leaders sympathetic to America, London aldermen, merchants trading to America, and comfortably off friends to America such as John Coakley Lettsom, to a "journeyman baker, [who], if his circumstances kept pace with his good wishes, would have given more." A few donors identified themselves as Americans. Others used their anonymous gifts to make political points. "Altho' a Briton born, a well-wisher to America" was on one side and "A Friend to Government" was on the other. As one historian has persuasively explained, this fundraising effort for the American prisoners shows that "many Britons continued to harbor lingering familial obligations toward the colonists." Yet a few donors stressed not familial obligations but broader conceptions of moral responsibility. "A Friend to Humanity" and "Amicus Omnibus"—Friend to All—chose to express their motivations in universal terms.[21]

The Scots Society of Norwich

If the disorder in the transatlantic community led some Britons to conceive of the boundaries of moral responsibility on a universal basis, no one attempted to put a new vision into practice quite the way John Murray, the Norwich, England, doctor, did.

Since the early eighteenth century, Murray's kith and kin had made the expansive British world its home. The "unnatural bustle" interfered with the far-flung yet close-knit family's routine of exchanging letters, helping each other with business, visiting one another, and raising each other's children. Worse yet, the eldest son of the longtime British naval surgeon sided with the rebels. Jack Murray had moved to America in 1770 as a fourteen-year-old at his aunt's urging to train as a merchant with his cousin in Providence. Although his father had warned him in 1774 that the family expected loyalty to the government, by 1776 Jack sympathized with those "resist[ing] . . . lawful power." With the fighting under way, his sister "wish[ed] [her] Brother . . . was at home; his absence hurts both his Parents and they (particularly my Father) are more anxious for his principles than his personal safety, which cannot be feared." "Surely," she hoped, "he will remain inactive on the side he is, and if he does not he crushes [their] Fathers peace forever." Seven months later, the family was still anxious about Jack. "The boys all at home," reported another sister to a relative, "(except one who gives us more anxiety than all the rest)." The young man remained set in his beliefs. In 1778, John Murray's sister Elizabeth, in Boston, got wind that her nephew was thinking of joining the American army. Knowing if he did, it would be "farewell to his Fathers and Mothers happiness," she tried to dissuade him. The same year, John Murray was making plans to send another son, George, into the British navy. Also that year, Murray took "pains . . . to make [Jack] a visit, but Providence decreed otherwise." Murray's finances were straitened at the time and a trip to see Jack would have meant a costly voyage across a war zone, particularly irresponsible for a husband and father with eight children still to raise. Perhaps, then, Murray wanted more than "the pleasure of viewing and conversing with [Jack]" and thought that in person he could sway his son away from the Patriot cause.[22]

In the event, Jack seems not to have joined the American army. In a nineteenth-century family history, his son detailed an impressive record of Jack Murray's participation. Letters from the Revolutionary years, however, tell a different story. These sources place Jack in England and Europe, at least in part

FIGURE 3.1 Dr. John Murray, Murray Family Papers, New-York Historical Society.
This image has been cropped.
Photography © New-York Historical Society.

for business, at some points when he was supposedly serving the Patriot cause.
Likewise, Rhode Island military records make no mention of him. John Murray's
worst fears were not realized, but several relatives did fight on the rebels' side as
his eldest son had aspired to. The breach in the British family had created tensions in his own and was, therefore, deeply personal for Murray. Indeed, he could
not separate thinking about his own family from thinking about the state of the
transatlantic relationship as he inadvertently revealed when recounting a domestic incident from 1778. One of his sons had misbehaved and been punished. The
boy accused Murray of being "ill natured" so the canny father held a family trial

to judge the child's charge. He "was honorably acquitted" and the boy deeply chastened. "Had Great Britain thus treated the Colonies," Murray asked in conclusion to the story of this family drama, "what would have been the effect?"[23]

Alas, Britain had not acted so sagely. Unable to control the government's—or even, fully, his son's—decision making, John Murray responded through philanthropy. He would heal the divisions in the transatlantic family—and in his own—and renew his—and Britain's—fatherly role by crafting an institution to exercise his charitable powers for the good of the world.

The organization John Murray led began modestly. In 1774, Scots natives in the Norwich area at the annual dinner in honor of St. Andrew, patron saint of Scotland, had found an "overplus" after paying the dinner bill. Someone suggested using the money to aid needy Scots in the area. As the assembled party well knew, natives of Scotland living in England were generally ineligible for English public poor relief, and the party took up a collection to raise more money. At the 1775 St. Andrew's Day festivities, the group formally instituted itself as the Scots Society of Norwich, and at the 1776 gathering a constitution was approved. In 1777, the Earl of Roseberry, a Scot who had a home in Norfolk, pledged to help the Society in any way possible and was elected as the governor (patron) of the Society. That year or the next, the group made the signal decision to extend its aid to all foreigners in Norwich on the same terms as applied to Scots.[24]

Norwich Scotsmen had together formed the new charity, but John Murray was, his obituary reported, the force behind the Society, which faded after Murray's death. A few years before setting up the Scots Society, he had helped found the Norfolk and Norwich Hospital, a charity that first admitted patients in 1772. Murray served as its physician from its founding until close to his death.[25] He therefore brought to the Scots' Society some familiarity with charitable leadership.

With the expansive mission of aiding all needy foreigners in Norwich, the Society was responding to a real social problem. To qualify for public poor relief in England or Wales, an individual had to have a parish settlement. (Scotland had its own poor-relief system dating to before the Union of 1707; parish settlement was not a feature of the Scottish system.) Settlements were gained in several ways including by birth, for a woman by her marriage to a man with a settlement, by legal apprenticeship, by paying parish rates, and by property rental or ownership of certain amounts. People who fell on hard times away from their parishes of settlement could either be removed to their home parishes (an expensive process) or supported by their home parishes in their parishes of residence. Although critics at the time charged that the settlement laws limited labor mobility, it allowed the locally funded, national poor relief system to work by laying out administrable conditions for eligibility. Moreover, settlement laws conferred much-prized

guarantees of aid on the poor and fostered feelings of belonging to an intimate
community. The settlement laws made sense, but they excluded the foreign born
from parish relief. Similarly, access to aid from charities in the Anglo-American
world at the time generally depended on ethnic, religious, occupational, or personal ties.[26]

The Scots Society aimed to fill the gap between the English poor law and the
population of England and, in doing so, it followed the poor-law model in its
provision of aid. Thus recipients might receive weekly allowances as recipients of
parish relief generally would. Or they might be sent to the city's workhouses at
the charity's expense. Similar to—although less litigious than—parish officials'
removal of those people who were eligible for relief in another parish, the Society
gave errant applicants money to get home. Another type of aid the group provided was medical care. Like other charitable organizations in the Anglophone
world, the Scots' Society subscribed to a local medical charity, in this case the
Norfolk and Norwich Hospital, so that it had a right to send patients there.
Finally, it paid the funeral expenses of its beneficiaries who died, with any assets
of the dead used to reimburse its costs for the departed. If no heirs could be found
for anything they left, the rest went into the Society's coffers.[27]

Who were the recipients and what brought them to apply to the Society? To
qualify for aid, applicants' hardship had to be "occasioned by sickness or some
other unavoidable distress," namely, loss in trade, fire, or shipwreck. The Society's
records provide few details about recipients beyond aggregate numbers, though
some stories reveal the types of persons and problems that elicited the Society's
sympathy and succor. Typical of the people relieved by the Society was a middle-
aged man from Edinburgh who "had served in the navy, merchant service, and
on board private ships of war, with equal ill fortune in all, by suffering shipwreck,
imprisonment, and loss of health." "Naturally [he] became tired of so inauspicious a course of life, settled on shore, married and became a father. Adversity
still pursued him." His business failed to profit, and he wound up imprisoned
for debt. The man applied to the Society, which, with the aid of medical men
and a magistrate, helped the man and his family get on their feet. Besides men
with backgrounds similar to those of the Society's supporters, the Society aided
others, such as the eighty-four-year-old "deaf, blind and helpless" widow of an
Irishman whose family could no longer provide for her.[28]

Foreigners—about 20 percent of the total—helped by the Society were
in similar straits as the charity's beneficiaries from British or formerly British
dominions. The first non-Scotsman or non-Irishman aided by the Society,
Ismael, aka James, Bashar, a Constantinople native, had prospered in commerce
but had suffered reverses and a "variety of misfortunes [had] brought him" to
England. There, he scraped out an existence by peddling and "working in the

Table 3.1. National Origins of Recipients of Aid from the Scots Society of Norwich, or Society of Universal Good-will, 1778–1787

Natives of	Number
Scotland	263
Ireland	130
America	83
France	4
Germany	25
Italy	31
Turkey	6
Prussia	8
Sweden	6
Spain	5
Flanders	3
Portugal	2
Holland	4
Switzerland	1
Africa	2
Greece	1
East Indies	4
Jews	14
Uncertain countries	10
Wives and children of the above	474
Total men	602
Total	1076

Note: The order in which groups are listed follows the order in the Society's records.
Source: An Account of the Proceedings of the Society of Universal Good-will, from the Beginning of 1784. To the End of the Year 1787 (Norwich, n.d.)

tin and wire way." "Those failing him, he became at last an indigent vagrant in a strange land, in which he married, was converted to [C]hristianity, and had children." When he became sick, the Society relieved him and tried, without much success, to set him up in business. A foreign recipient in 1784, a German named Lewis LeFebure, was a demobilized soldier who had fought in America and was trying to get home. He was found perishing one freezing day outside Norwich and referred by a justice of the peace to the Society, which sent him back to Germany.[29]

The Scots Society innovated by not distinguishing between compatriots and strangers, though its policy of treating the stranger as a neighbor aroused anxiety. Some people worried, John Murray explained in his 1782 annual address, that the group's aid to penurious foreigners would harm natives of England: The Society's existence might induce migrants, who would compete for jobs, to come to the country. Murray thought that worry was unfounded. "Although it may afford great comfort to such as for various reasons emigrate from their native home, to know, that in cases of unavoidable distress, they and their families will not be left destitute," he argued, "yet no one, on that account only, would quit his parent soil, his dearest connections, and abandon the probable, if not certain means of subsistence, by his labour, skill and industry in his own country, merely that he may not be suffered to starve in a strange land." His view—and not the fear that a small Norwich charity would lead to an influx of foreigners eager to take advantage of British welfare institutions—prevailed. Indeed, a review in the London *Monthly Magazine* in April 1783 hailed the Society's "laudable design." "Too much cannot be said in praise of this humane institution (especially since the extension of their charitable plan [to all foreigners in England])," the reviewer added, "nor the zeal and genuine philanthropy of their President." Murray and his fellow Scotsmen had begun the Society to aid needy countrymen but had shifted to a catholic view of charitable obligation. While there had been challenges to the new practice of moral responsibility, the urge to embrace, in the words of the *Monthly Magazine*, "the purest principles of universal charity and benevolence"—was stronger.[30]

Rethinking the Atlantic Community

The Society had succeeded in expanding its mission in Norwich, but its next moves would prove too ambitious. First, in 1779, the Society decided that non-English and non-Welsh "dispersed through the kingdom of England" were now "objects of this society's attention." A few years later, the group had a yet grander vision. The Society, it announced in the early 1780s, "regard[ed] the whole of the human race as one family, and wishe[d] to extend the assistance thereof to every fellow-creature in distress, who is not provided for by law, any government or other charity." Murray and his colleagues realized that in an interconnected, mobile world, needy strangers far and wide must face difficulties accessing aid.[31] They would help their fellow creatures by "being stewards for the whole world."[32]

The group's records do not say who hatched the idea to work on a global scale, but the plan bears the hallmarks of John Murray's thinking. He was a man who contemplated the restructuring of the Anglophone Atlantic community during its moments of crisis or ferment. His first contribution to the problem of how to bind a community together came before the American Revolution. During the long period of imperial tension before the outbreak of the civil war, he had offered the government his ideas on the reform of the government of the colonies. In the early '70s, he penned a plan for better governing the American colonies based on his personal knowledge of America and presented it to the British government. In 1771, Murray told his sister that his "Plan [was] . . . much approved of in general except the Bishops." His obituary, however, remembered that it had been "without effect."[33]

In 1789, almost two decades after crafting his plan for the reform of colonial government, Murray put forth *"a Plan for the Gradual, Reasonable, & Secure Emancipation of Slaves"* in the West Indies. This proposal, published while he was still trying to expand the Society of Universal Good-will around the world, was his third and last scheme to remake the Atlantic community. Murray and his plan share many traits with other contemporary emancipation schemes and their writers. Other men weighing in on the subject had "active engagement with imperial questions," and, like them, Murray had lived and traveled in British colonies and had worked for a critical institution of the British empire, the navy. His attention to the management of African laborers dated to his days in Jamaica. Parliament's consideration of the slave trade prompted Murray to offer his thoughts to the public, and as with his colonial reform plan, he rested his authority to speak on the topic on personal experience with the issue at hand.[34]

For the time, the nature of his interaction with slaves was not unusual. As a young naval surgeon in 1744, Murray was in Jamaica and was named a surgeon's assistant of the new naval hospital in Port Royal. In the surgeon's absence, he was put in charge of running the hospital. On his first day, he found one of the wards in "very great disorder" because a delirious patient had "thrown his drinks" and the nurse—an enslaved black woman—"had refused to clean it." Murray "gently reprimanded," her to no effect. The next day the disorder had worsened and he learned that the nurse that "laughed at" and "abused" Murray. Later that day, after addressing the assembled staff and patients on the matter, he had the nurse whipped. He cited this incident in his 1789 pamphlet as part of his discussion on the proper way to treat slaves to prepare them for emancipation. His interest in the management of bondspeople had also prompted Murray to visit St. Domingue in 1749 with Admiral Knowles's squadron. The admiral had gone to visit the governor of the French island and Murray availed himself of the chance to "make himself acquainted with the police and customs of the French; in particular, how they treated their Negroes."[35]

Like other emancipation plans from the 1770s and 1780s, Murray's plan addressed the several concerns that bedeviled abolitionism, to wit, how to maintain colonies' and the empire's economic vitality, how to integrate Africans into the British community, and how to satisfy both slaveholders and enslaved Africans. Like other plans, Murray was confused and confusing. He began and ended his plan with both justifications for and condemnations of slavery. He justified slavery based on both "sacred and profane history," with special stress on the timelessness of Noah's curse on the children of Ham. Ultimately, Murray condemned the treatment of slaves as inhumane, unchristian, and impolitic. He wrestled with the topic, however, because as a believer in revealed religion, he had to square Noah's curse, understood by many to legitimate the enslavement of Africans, with his beliefs that the "Christian religion abhor[red]" inhumanity and that Africans "ought to be considered and treated as fellow creatures."[36]

Competing considerations marked Murray's plan—by turns, bigoted, feeling, comprehensive, and inconsistent. "The most immediate reform" that Murray thought needed to be made was in slaves' "language." Speaking a mixture of broken English and native languages "degraded" slaves as humans, and degraded the language of white children, while making it hard for masters to communicate with slaves. So he proposed first that white men be appointed to teach enslaved Africans proper English. Murray, whose views reflected widespread ideas about linguistic capacities, felt so strongly about the language issue that he thought eligibility for freedom should depend on enslaved Africans' mastery of proper English. He then proposed that a census should be taken of all slaves and tenures of enslavement, ranging from seven to twenty-one years depending on age and circumstance, specified for all slaves. At the ends of those periods, "the Negroes having served with fidelity" could choose to return to their native countries or the freed slaves could "hire themselves as they think proper or are qualified, in the same manners as the whites in a free country." Although in some ways he scorned Africans, Murray could also sympathize across racial lines with people separated from their families and friends. He therefore proposed "a three day Saturnalia" at the end of each seven-year period so "the Negroes of every plantation . . . all might have an equal privilege in enjoying their friends who are about to part, perhaps never to meet again." Plus, "some rites . . . a Jubilee, or Isthmian Games, or the like" should commemorate the end of the last seven-year period, when all slaves would finally be free. Murray's plan also covered work and training, slaves' formation of families, diet, health, recreation, and religious training, with the various parts working together to benefit Africans, slaveholders, and Britain. To oversee the whole program, commissioners were to be appointed in the various islands.[37]

Like other Britons, Murray struggled with the issue of emancipation because of common concerns about how ending the slave trade or slavery would affect British interests. But, in addition, his relatives held bondspeople, at least once he had helped buy humans, and his son worked with a leading Rhode Island slave trader. The issue was not abstract to him. Likewise, his views about aiding needy foreigners were shaped by his family's experiences. Many of his relatives had moved in attempts to improve their lots. Murray therefore appreciated the role that foreigners played in their new communities. "Agriculture, arts, manufactures and commerce, have severally contributed to the opulence and happiness of this still free nation: all of those have been promoted, some in a manner created by foreigners," he declared in his 1779 speech to the Scots Society. "Many families of high rank, many manufacturers of great wealth and eminence, have sprung from those, and are still in being." Migration resonated with him as a boon to countries that accepted immigrants, and he was also sensitive to the problems that migrants faced. Murray had long struggled financially, and he fretted about the futures of his children in America. "Oh my Children! Orphans in a Strange Land!" he lamented to his sister Elizabeth, then helping to raise three of his children, when she remarried unexpectedly in 1771, "what will become of you [his children], if Providence should remove your Aunt or any Cause alienate her affections?"[38]

The challenges he and his relatives faced as they moved around the Atlantic world made Murray sensitive to foreigners' needs. Most important to his efforts to extend the Scots Society to the whole world, however, was the civil war. It was in that crucible that he and fellow members of the Scots Society crafted a program—the second of his three efforts to remake the Atlantic community—based on universal understanding of moral responsibility. The men began adapting the Society's program to encompass non-Scots in 1778, the year Murray was mulling a trip to America to see his son Jack, and progressively expanded their aims over the next few years. At the annual meeting in 1780, Murray suggested trying "to extend our correspondence to Scotland, Ireland, America and other parts." He admitted that the hostilities created an unfavorable climate for the "principles and purpose" of the Society yet thought "the trial may be made" and urged his members to "unite in endeavouring to promote on earth, PEACE, and GOOD WILL, towards men." His feelings were not always so generous. His brother James and family friend Gilbert Deblois, a merchant, had both been exiled from their homes in New England as Loyalists. Their treatment angered Murray to the point that in 1782, he hoped the mooted independence for the "revolters" would "be a curse to them." Several months later, with peace in the offing, he worried about the fate of Loyalist refugees—but he also was eager to receive "all the information concerning the future establishment of the now independent America" he could. He had relatives who had stayed in the United States, including Jack, who was referred to in Society records for 1781 as a merchant in Providence, while other sons moved to the United States and a daughter and son-in-law went to Canada.[39] He had a stake, therefore, in the shape of the

Anglophone community at the end of the war. Rather than turn inward in the face of the Thirteen Colonies' rejection of Britain, he, like the novelist Samuel Jackson Pratt, sought to preserve transatlantic ties based on universal principles.

The Miscarriage of Universal Goodwill

With his new plans for his charity, Murray aimed to help rebuild the Anglophone community—and to ensure a leading role for Britons in it. First, however, he and his colleagues would have to build the Society outside Norwich and overseas. Things got off to a promising start. In 1779, the Scots Society of Norwich approved the formation of a London branch. Soon the Scots Society of Norwich, in London—as it was officially called—had some money coming in and could take pride in aiding its first few people. Plans were made for a regular correspondence between the Norwich headquarters and the First Branch—as it was more commonly known—and in 1782, John Murray "had the pleasure to meet the President and most of the members" of the London branch at its annual meeting.[40]

To spread knowledge of its mission, the Scots Society in Norwich took advantage of its members' travels to distant places. People in Birmingham, Bristol, Canada, the East Indies, Ireland, New England, and the West Indies knew of—and had contributed to—the charity by 1780. Within a few more years, news of the group had reached Devonshire, Rouen, and Scotland. The group also named agents, who had to donate one guinea per year, to conduct the Society's business outside Norwich, with agents named for parts of England, Ireland, Scotland, North America, and St. Christopher's. Their duties included collecting and disbursing funds and providing information to the Society in Norwich on faraway aid applicants.[41]

Agents' duties also included trying to found branches of the Society. Three or more members or agents in a place could, with permission from Norwich, found a branch. They could run their own operations under the aegis of the parent Society and would be expected "to send copies or abstracts, remit balances to, receive directions from, and hold correspondence with" headquarters. Once enough branches had been set up, a yearly meeting "of deputies from the original society, and all the branches" would be held to determine "the best and most proper methods of carrying on the various good designs, and humane purposes of the society, in different parts of the world."[42] With its global mission, the Scots Society in Norwich seemed too local a name. Moreover, by 1783, Scots no longer made up a majority of members. Hence, in 1784, the Society decided to be known as the Scots Society in Norwich, or the Society of Universal Goodwill. The following year, the Society changed its name to simply the Society of

Universal Good-will. The new name said it all. Murray was ready to care for the world.[43]

The Society was not expanding, however. At the 1782 annual meeting, Murray had related various agents' progress, or lack thereof. The Edinburgh agent had made no progress "owing to his not understanding the nature of the business intrusted to his care. Upon being again informed how to proceed, he promised to comply with our directions. We have however never heard from him since his return to Scotland." At the behest of the former Ireland agent, the Society had sent its materials to a bookseller in Dublin, "but we have heard nothing from that quarter since." "No intelligence has been received from our agent in St. Christopher's." "The present unfortunate situation of that and the neighbouring islands," Murray commented, "may possibly have obliterated from his memory, the very existence of this society." The Canada agent, to his credit, relayed news of his endeavors, albeit unpromising news. "'I have not been able to render your society any service, although I have mentioned it to several." "Those who emigrate from Europe to this country," he explained, "have purposes far different from those of charity." Finally, "our members who went to the hostile parts of America," Murray reported, "have sent us no official accounts." He admitted that "we have no great reason to boast of our success," but, he reassured his members, there was "no cause for despair."[44]

Murray may well have been disappointed in his agents, who were, after all, his family and friends. Three of John Murray's sons plus one of their business associates, Cyprian Sterry of Providence, had been named as agents in the United States. Murray's son-in-law, William Dummer Powell, the future chief justice of Upper Canada but at that point a young man with uncertain prospects who had married Murray's daughter without her parents' permission, was the Canada agent. At least one of the London branch founders was a Murray friend.[45] In the early 1780s, the Society named another Murray family friend as the Directress of the Society of Universal Good-will in North America. Mary Hayley, the "eccentric" sister of the London politician John Wilkes who championed liberty in the 1760s and '70s, was the widow of George Hayley. Her late husband, a wealthy London merchant, alderman, and Member of Parliament, had been one half of Hayley and Hopkins, a partnership trading to America. (Hayley, who had died in 1781, had supported the cause of the American colonies and been a leader of the charity for American prisoners of war.) John Murray had a tie to the couple through his daughter, Mary, who had bought goods from George Hayley for her short-lived mercantile venture in Boston in the early 1770s. About three years after her husband's death, Mary Hayley headed to the United States primarily to collect debts. The timing of her arrival, in May 1784, made her one of the earliest celebrity visitors to the United States. Newspapers followed her moves, and leading Americans feted her. If she made any efforts to promote the Society of Universal Good-will in America, however, no one seems to have noticed.[46]

Whatever his agents did or didn't do, John Murray was working hard to create his global charity. The compassionate, far-sighted doctor was trying to build a worldwide organization, but he was going about it the wrong way. Murray was trying to set up and supervise branches from the center. He did that with the London branch by participating in several of its meetings and by planning to make it the hub of the global Society.[47] And he did that more generally by appointing his family and friends as would-be leaders of overseas outposts. Top-down approaches to expanding worked well in some cases, such as with charities closely tied to hierarchical organizations—for instance, the Anglican Society for the Promoting of Christian Knowledge—with their natural pools of potential leaders and supporters.[48] Most movements in the eighteenth century, however, grew through a give-and-take between local activists interested in a particular cause and faraway advocates planting ideas and offering know-how. They did not grow through central direction.

Murray never recognized his mistake and he never lost hope. The one branch society failed to attract a patron early on or much prominent support, and in 1786 or '87 its treasurer went bankrupt with monies in his hands owed by the London branch to the Norwich body.[49] Still, Murray persevered with his plan for a worldwide body. In 1789, he drew up a constitution for the foundering, if not defunct, London branch; it could also be used as a model for branches elsewhere. Membership in his global charity would be open to women and men "of all ranks and degrees," and "of all nations, religions and sects, or of no religion or sect, of all descriptions or denominations already known, or which may hereafter become known." There would be envoys from every nation to serve as agents and interpreters to aid and vet non-English-speaking applicants. In addition, Murray wanted to promote the morals that, in his view, underlay universal goodwill. His model constitution therefore endorsed belief in a "CREATOR" as essential to advanced civilization and cited Jesus as the exemplar of the values on which the Society would be founded. Therefore, the Society should elect a chaplain, who could come from any monotheistic faith. Because Christ had taught moral duties, the Society should send out missionaries, if its funds allowed, to teach the morals necessary for peace and happiness. The moral missionaries might prepare the way for Christianity, but their purpose would be moral instruction, not evangelizing. In spite of all the setbacks with his plans, Murray's vision had not narrowed. He looked forward to finding that "an institution for the purpose of cultivating Universal Goodwill, [was] fully established throughout the world."[50]

In a way, John Murray was ahead of his time. Global organizations and annual meetings of activists from around the world were things of the future.

But in another way, he was behind the times. Murray tried to heal the rift in the Atlantic community with philanthropy—that is, with a universal approach to moral responsibility—by building a worldwide charitable organization that would be run from London. The particulars differed, but the same approach to reforming the transatlantic relationship had been tried before, and Americans were now independent. The transatlantic relationship could not be remade from the center before the Revolution, and it would not be now.

4

The Empire of Humanity

JOHN MURRAY WAS not alone in being puzzled by how the relationship between Britain and its former colonies had changed. With the war over, old friends across the Atlantic reached out to one another, but "the Interruption of our Epistolary correspondence by the unhappy disputes ... seems to have made it difficult to find a subject for a Letter," wrote an English Quaker to an American co-religionist. If members of perhaps the most tightly knit transatlantic community were unsure about where to pick up their relationship, others were positively inept. Before the ink was wet, never mind dry, on the final peace treaty recognizing American independence from Britain, Benjamin Rush asked British Dissenting cleric Richard Price to solicit donations for a new college in Carlisle, Pennsylvania. The request came too soon, his friend had to tell him. "Friendship [was] not yet sufficiently restored between the two countries" and Britons were "much overburden'd" with taxes. "America," Price hoped, "will learn to take care of itself." John Coakley Lettsom, also received a plea for books for the college, and he characteristically responded positively. The gift he sent, however—thirty volumes of *The Journals of the House of Commons*—showed that Lettsom was as misguided as Rush was. Since the Americans were busy writing new laws, Lettsom thought the journals would prove useful—an odd choice given that Americans had just finished declaring independence from the British government: Rush deemed the books not "worth to us their carriage to Carlisle."[1]

By not recognizing what had changed with political disunion, Rush and Lettsom bungled their first postwar efforts at charitable cooperation. Leaders of British missionary organizations, by contrast, quickly realized that they had to adapt, although legal strictures affected if and how they could revise their activities. The oldest transatlantic religious philanthropy, the New England Company, ended its work in the 1780s because its charter required the group to expend its efforts on behalf of Great Britain.[2] The Society for the Propagation of the Gospel in Foreign Parts initially wondered about its future in the United States. "With regard to our missionaries in North America, in what state they will remain after the great change which has so recently taken place on that continent is yet unknown," said the anniversary speaker in 1783. By 1784, however, the group had concluded that "foreign parts" meant "the British Plantations, Colonies and Factories beyond the Sea." By then, most of its missionaries in the United States had already left.[3]

For their parts, the Society in Scotland for Propagating Christian Knowledge and the Bray Associates continued their work after the war. They did not have much choice. Benefactors had given money for activities in North America and, facing the same constraints that later institutions receiving philanthropic funds know well, they could not "bestow this money upon any other object than that for which it was collected," as the SSPCK's Law Committee explained. Perhaps keeping faith with longtime colleagues in America and the people they were ministering to before the war was also a factor. If so, the SSPCK, for one, had first to overcome dismay about "the unhappy differences between Britain and America"—which had led to its "contemplation to establish missions among the Indians in the vicinity of the colonies [still] connected with the mother country." However the Bray Associates felt about continuing the schools for Africans in Philadelphia, the fact that they also opened a school in Nova Scotia after the war annoyed at least one of their trustees in the City of Brotherly Love.[4]

While many Americans celebrated independence and Britons quickly got over the loss of the Thirteen Colonies, the rupture also stoked initial uncertainty and inappropriate expectations about the transatlantic relationship. "The dissolution of [their] connection with each other as fellow citizens," as Benjamin Rush put it, did not, however, lead the erstwhile compatriots to turn away from one another.[5] Activists who had come of age before the imperial breakup shared an outlook shaped by growing up in the Atlantic world: Their common frame of mind helped them remake their ties as citizens of the world, that is, as foreigners. By, paradoxically, nurturing cosmopolitan practices, the wars they had lived through eased their adjustment, too. In the postwar years, they resumed and intensified the exchange of charitable knowledge familiar from their youth. The politics of transatlantic collaboration, they recognized, had changed. No longer working together to strengthen the British empire, Americans and Britons instead cooperated to aid suffering humanity at large. Through philanthropy, they would seek also to forge peaceable relations in the revamped Atlantic world.

Cosmopolitanism, Curiosity, and Improvement

Several elements of the war and its conclusion encouraged broad-mindedness among the recent enemies. On the American side, the Patriot cause rested on ideas about the universality of rights. The Revolution was no mere parochial affair but an event meant to "form a new era and give a new turn in human affairs." Independence further nurtured American elites' liberality. Loath to be or seem culturally insular, they bought European consumer goods and participated in transatlantic scientific networks to stake places in the world. For different reasons, English elites responded similarly. The effort to quash the Americans' quest for liberty had hurt Britain's enlightened image in Europe. Worried about their country's reputation and their own legitimacy, the British establishment in the 1780s turned to cosmopolitan ideals to bolster its authority at home and abroad.[6] Besides the factors particular to each side, philanthropic leaders shared a common liberality and they quickly adapted to collaborating as foreigners.

Many philanthropic agenda setters had seen and would see "much of the manners and customs of the world," or at least knew one or a few unfamiliar parts of it. A man with such a background "studied what he had seen. This gave him an easy variety of subject, which he could readily adapt to the capacities or wishes of his company."[7] More important than being adaptable in social settings were the efforts of these men to rise above partiality: Many surmounted some of their biases and endorsed liberality to get along in a heterogeneous world. Of course, most of them would have been steeped in intellectual traditions of toleration and the search for universal rules to explain human nature and structure human activities. But for many well-off Anglo-Americans, cosmopolitanism was more a practical way of managing experiences and less the psychological construct that it had been for the *philosophes*. Being a citizen of the world, as charitable leaders understood it, meant having the ability to participate in various and diverse communities (local, national, international, religious) and to rise above prejudices or narrow sympathies.[8]

Partiality toward one or another group, they had learned, was offensive while being above clannish loyalties was praiseworthy. "Illiberal prejudices," "A Citizen of the World" declared in an essay in the *New York Daily Advertiser*, "are the most contemptible principles of human nature." Bigotry was also injurious. "Britain "ha[d] suffered much," John Murray asserted in a 1782 speech, "but the cause of humanity a great deal more, from indulging, and, if I may be allowed the expression, the cultivating of religious and political prejudice." Of course people had biases, but worldly types "confessed" to them, as John Coakley Lettsom did when he admitted to a correspondent he had a "prejudice in favour of my White brethren, and consequently a bias against a near [i.e., procreative] alliance with our Black fellow-creatures." Impartiality, by contrast, drew plaudits. Late in life, as he recalled his experiences as a member of the Continental Congress, Benjamin Rush noted his impressions of his fellow congressmen and criticized or lauded several men on the basis of their chauvinism or lack thereof. Samuel Adams, Rush thought, had "more of the prejudices of a Massachusetts man than the liberal sentiments of a citizen of the United States," whereas Thomas Jefferson, in his view, extended his benevolence to "all nations and religions."[9]

The ability to overcome biases, contemporaries throughout the century attested, was fostered by traveling or living abroad. The London Quaker physician John Fothergill visited Flanders, Germany, and Holland in the 1740s in part because he "[thought] it one proper step to teach one to judge of other nations without prejudices." A few decades later, reflecting on his days as a medical student in Edinburgh in the 1760s, Benjamin Rush wrote, "My intercourse with other sects while I was abroad had led me to consider all denominations of Christians with a more equal eye than I had done in early life, and had divested me of an undue predilection for either [i.e., any] of them." John Murray, who had spent years traveling as a British naval surgeon, felt similarly. From his experiences at "different periods and in different countries," Murray believed in "the benignity of human nature," and he had come to distinguish between nations or religions at odds—or at war—with his own and their individual members. The Spaniards he met during the War of Jenkins's Ear, were "desirous of my private friendship, ambitious of my good opinions, and ready unasked to supply all my necessaries" in spite of the conflict between their countries.[10]

Being broad-minded, however, did not necessarily mean not having any biases or loyalties to one or more subsets of humankind. Distinct from universalism, cosmopolitan thought and behavior grew from a realistic recognition that people were divided into different groups: Philanthropic leaders were little animated by a philosophical ideal of identifying as nothing more and nothing less than a citizen of the world. There were good reasons to act above prejudice. Although religious or ethnic networks could and often did promote business or professional pursuits, elders counseled their children and pupils to engage in impartial behavior to further pecuniary interests. "I would not have you Indulge your self in the opinion of Parties [illegible] among us [e]specially religious Parties," New York doctor John Bard chastised his son Samuel, then a medical student in Edinburgh, in 1763: "It does not become one of your Profession, and it will always be [inconsistent?] with your Interest." Two decades later, Benjamin Rush drew a similar conclusion as part of the advice he gave to a medical pupil about to set out in the world. "Go regularly to some place of worship. A physician cannot be a bigot. Worship with Mohamitans rather than stay home on Sundays."[11] For doctors, at least, biases were bad for business.

Besides the financial benefits of cosmopolitan practices, knowing how to cope in diverse settings quite simply made life easier, as John Murray suggested in a long letter of advice to his son, Jack, in 1774. Among other things, Murray gave his son tips on dealing with discussions of religion with skeptics or with members of different sects. Jack was to explain his own faith to them in a calm and straightforward manner, "shun disputes concerning religion," and be aware that all sects had errors. Finally, "for the sake of improvement and occasionally to keep up conversation," he was to "become acquainted with the tenets of every religion that exists or has existed, there is something good in them all." In short, Jack should learn, as his father had during his years in the navy, to manage and even appreciate heterogeneity.[12] Rather than downplaying differences, Murray and his fellow activists heeded them and concluded that many were not threatening. As a result, interactions with peers from other religions or nations— experiences that often dated to before the transatlantic civil war—offered vital intellectual and emotional resources that were newly relevant as American and British philanthropists sought to reconcile a divided community.

In addition to the experiences of living in a mobile and heterogeneous world, activists credited their liberality to religious beliefs. Boston minister John Lathrop was "convinced it was the will of God there should be a great variety of religious opinions, and that there should be a variety of ways in which men offer worship to the One Supreme." Thus, while he remained content with his religious upbringing, Lathrop refused to judge others based on their religious beliefs, but rather "love[d] good men of all sects and denominations, as ardently as [he] love[d] good men of [his] own."[13]

Laymen Benjamin Rush and John Coakley Lettsom likewise rooted their cosmopolitanism in religious beliefs. From a historical vantage point, it is a chicken-and-egg question whether belief in universal salvation gave rise to cosmopolitanism in other realms or whether Enlightenment ideals of cosmopolitanism shaped religious beliefs. Rush, a Pennsylvania Presbyterian, and Lettsom, a West Indian–born Quaker who lived as an adult in London, were more tribally attached to their sects than perhaps either man would have cared to admit. Still, each also embraced universalist beliefs about God's relation to humankind and eschewed living primarily within the confines of their groups. As Rush wrote, his belief in "the doctrine of universal salvation and final restitution . . . [had] bound [him] to the whole human race." Similarly, Lettsom believed that all people were "equally children of one supreme beneficent creator" and that the global diversity of religions pleased God because it made divine mercy "accessible to every human traveller." Those views hewed to Quaker thinking on the universal accessibility of God's grace. Lettsom, however, saw his views as a forsaking of the "notions [he had been brought up with,] which encouraged ideas of a favourite people, of a little remnant, of a chosen few, and such like narrow principles." Through avid reading, Lettsom had learned to think for himself, realized that the Society of Friends "was in less proportion than a grain of sand to the great globe," and, therefore, "entertained more ample notions of the Universal Parent."[14]

Lettsom was a famously vain man with a robust regard for his own virtue. But as he lived his life, he put into practice (with much self-congratulation) his "more ample" religious beliefs. Lettsom reveled in his self-image as a citizen of the world and encouraged others to think of him that way. Thanking a friend for the gift of a "gigantic turkey," he noted that the bird had fed a "a group of different nations and sects"—an Englishman, a German, "a Scotchman, an Irishman, a Dane, an American, a West Indian, a Papist, a Presbyterian, a Quaker, a No Religion, a Sandemanian, and a Staunch Churchman"—at a dinner party he hosted in 1792. Besides socializing across national and religious lines, Lettsom routinely attended non-Quaker worship services as part of his involvement in various charitable ventures. He summed up the views guiding his activism when he volunteered to a friend: "He must be a niggard indeed, to set bounds to philanthropy"—that is, to set bounds to the love of mankind.[15] Rush, like Lettsom, socialized across boundaries and espoused catholic ideas of moral responsibility anchored in his Christian beliefs. His peers did much the same. Christian ideals of universal benevolence filled a well of inspiration that philanthropists drew from. But Christianity, in the parable of the Good Samaritan, had long enjoined care of suffering strangers. More than love of mankind or a newfound commitment to religious injunction impelled these men to work across boundaries.

A broad fascination with the world and its peoples defined the mindsets of philanthropic leaders and many of their middling-elite peers and made them open to borrowing ideas across borders. As they journeyed across space, unfamiliar customs from headgear to inter-communal cooperation captured their attention. Congregational minister Jeremy Belknap traveled from Dover, New Hampshire, to Philadelphia in 1785, and he learned something new. On his trip he attended Jewish worship three times, twice in Newport and once in Philadelphia. "[Jews] worship with their *hats on*," Belknap discovered on his first visit to a synagogue, in Newport. On his way back north, Belknap again attended the Newport synagogue and noted in his diary that the Rhode Island congregants behaved more decorously than their Philadelphia co-religionists. The Philadelphia Jews' whispering during a religious service disturbed Belknap's Protestant sensibilities, but another facet of Philadelphia's religious life impressed him. There Belknap found a religious diversity that he had not encountered at home. "The many Religious distinctions in [Philadelphia]," he mused, "have doubtless some *ill* effect on the Tempers of *Some* of the people," but, he concluded, for the most part Philadelphians lived tolerantly with others. They even "frequently assist[ed] each other, Persons of various denominations, to build churches & Schools." Philadelphia's water pumps, the meals served at the city's almshouse, and the use of umbrellas by Quaker women captured his attention too.[16]

Like Belknap, surgeon John Crawford gathered ideas about practices unknown to him as he moved about the world from his native Northern Ireland to the East Indies to Barbados and eventually to Baltimore. Crawford, also taken with umbrellas, would have liked to borrow that East Indian technology to guard against the sun. Alas, in the West Indies "the scarcity of hands renders this useful practice inconvenient," he lamented, "in the first [umbrellas] are carried by a Servant; in the last we are obliged to carry them ourselves, which in squally weather proves often very troublesome." To Crawford's way of thinking, the use of umbrellas could not be adopted easily. But other ideas could be transferred from one place to another: In the hospital under his control in Barbados, he implemented a rice-based diet suggested to him by a friend in Bengal.[17]

Even when activists did not go far, they were collectors of the world's knowledge. "Man ... can circum-navigate the globe, and please his taste with the produce of every clime," John Lathrop marveled in a sermon, "Or, by the use of letters, man may abide at home, and yet collect both knowledge and wealth from nations the most distant, and the least acquainted with each other." John Coakley Lettsom lived by that view, dispatching seeds and roots to his correspondents and asking to be repaid in kind. Likewise, from travelers he met in Philadelphia, Benjamin Rush learned about Hinduism and Laplanders and Persians' diets and the plague in Constantinople and dysentery in Peking, not to mention about the lack of suburbs in Madrid.[18]

These men weighed new knowledge and resources from faraway places critically. But, by and large, they believed migration and trade were beneficial. Not only were these activities boons to their societies in general, but new arrivals from distant places might also bring new tools for lessening suffering. John Murray had insisted that migrants bettered the communities that received them. The American-born Count Rumford went further. In his view, travel was a means to addressing social problems. "Those whose avocations" or "fortune" led them to visit foreign places, he observed, introduced "many improvements, and more *refinements*" into their home countries. So far he thought the well-to-do, not the poor, had gained from this exchange. Well-off travelers, therefore, had a responsibility to bring home information that "tend[ed] to facilitate the means of subsistence, and to increase the comforts and conveniences of the most necessitous and most numerous classes of society."[19]

Besides curiosity and an interest in knowledge from abroad, the idea of improvement, and the belief that things were improving or improvable, captivated and motivated well-off eighteenth-century men and women on both sides of the Atlantic. This "set of priorities" rather than a "philosophical doctrine or political program" came originally from the realm of agriculture and referred to turning land to more profitable use. Over the early modern period, and especially as the culture of scientific study burgeoned and widened, the concept broadened to apply to all manner of activities and comprehended a broad, optimistic outlook of progressive changes to use and make the world better. Improving their profits, their communities, their countries, the world, knowledge, and others and themselves fired the imaginations of landowners, farmers, planters, merchants, manufacturers, medical men, and other Enlightened gentlepeople. Their improving efforts ranged from using land more productively, running businesses better, founding new public institutions, and building faster transportation and communication systems to softening old enmities through commerce, learning more about most everything, updating and refining homes, adopting new comforts and new luxuries, and crafting projects to aid the poor and distressed to finally the very personal agendas of becoming genteel. Not everyone shared their faith in improvement, but among those who did, evidence of progress animated expectations of still more.[20]

Activists came from the ranks of improvers, whose outlook guided their beneficence, as the constant use of the words "improve" and "improvement" underscore. Although they never defined those words, when well-to-do philanthropists talked about improvement, they had a clear sense of what they meant. And what they meant was controlled, incremental change to make the world more orderly and to promote the security, productivity, and the happiness—something they stressed often—of the poor. Their conception of improvement lay between the older meaning of the word, as taking advantage of or turning to profitable use, and the newer, vaguer sense of the word, as making better. The last thing that the "friends of order and humanity," in Benjamin Rush's words, wanted was radical overhaul of the social order in which they had, in many cases, risen. Indeed, they were pragmatic people, not doctrinaire types working from a theory. They therefore opted for focused approaches that broke humanity down into ever-narrower groups whose troubles—generally poverty—they addressed with institutions dedicated to particular manifestations of indigence. Thus, for example, sick laborers were targeted with dispensaries providing medical care they could not easily afford. Or activists broke problems into component parts. They—free people—wanted to tackle abolition of the slave trade before emancipation, and fearful of the disorder that sudden freedom might cause, favored "gradually prepar[ing]" slaves to emerge from bondage. Raised in consumer societies, they also often used incentives to try to shape the behavior of the objects of their aid. Through appeals to beneficiaries' desires and ability to make choices rather than through overt pressure, they sought to encourage changes over time.

Furthermore, in their preference for measured improvement, activists bore in on the nitty-gritty details that would both better the condition of the distressed and make them more useful citizens. That is, they would improve the poor in both the new and old senses and, as a consequence, make the world a more disciplined and benign place.[21]

The Lessons of War

Of all the forces that undermined the humane order they sought, war stood out for its destructive power. Hostilities unsettled "happy days of peace and quiet" and brought "many Individuals to Poverty & Misery," as some activists knew firsthand.[22] Besides familiarizing them with suffering that many of them— comfortable souls—did not otherwise experience in the courses of their lives, bloody conflicts helped them define their philanthropy as an alternative form of political action. Yet, though they lamented war, they found positive lessons in it. Armed strife reinforced their faith in the idea of improvement. Moreover, it sometimes bred the goodwill to enemies that made philanthropic cooperation with foreigners meaningful.

To many leading men in philanthropic circles, war's ruinous power was no abstract thing. Thomas Bernard, James Currie, John Lathrop, Benjamin Rush, and others had been displaced by the Revolution, while Thomas Eddy had spent time in custody during that recent war. Like Eddy, the English prison reformer John Howard and the Boston philanthropist Thomas Russell had been held captive, although unlike the love-struck Eddy who had ventured across battle lines during the American Revolution, Howard and Russell had faced their ordeals during the Seven Years' War. Traveling in the midst of the conflict, each man had fallen into the hands of the French and each suffered at the hands of his captors. Howard, who, in 1756, had been heading to Portugal when a French privateer seized the vessel he was on, was at first deprived of food and water and then fed but little and given only the floor to sleep on. For his part, when Russell had been on his 1762 mercantile trip to the West Indies, a French cruiser captured the ship he was on and Russell endured "much personal severity." Most did not say whether their acquaintance with hardship quickened their inclination to relieve others. English prison reformer John Howard allowed that it did. The ill-treatment he faced in custody, he wrote years later, "perhaps . . . increased [his] sympathy" for the plight of prisoners.[23]

The inhumanity they encountered during times of conflict might spur on their beneficence. It also gave meaning to their endeavors. War, they knew, "desolates the world with fire and sword." With philanthropy, however, they were practicing "the milder virtues of making our neighbours and fellow men as happy as their frail condition and perishable natures will permit them to be." No less an authority than "General Washington, of America" had exalted charitable activity in a 1788 letter to a Massachusetts lifesaving group. Sent a copy of the missive by John Lathrop, John Coakley Lettsom read it to the Massachusetts group's London counterpart. Washington, Lettsom thought, "ma[de] a beautiful eulogy on the virtues of saving life, in contrast to that of taking it away."[24] Washington's comment was a commonplace, but the prevalence of war during their lifetimes made shedding blood versus saving life, or alleviating its miseries, a ready contradistinction.

War and beneficence, these men had learned in their youth, were not necessarily polar opposites. As the charities that operated or fundraised on both sides of the British Atlantic had insisted for decades, their activities could serve strategic ends. Men raised in the world of transatlantic missionary organizations, population-boosting hospitals, and other charities that aimed to bolster the British empire's military might continued to understand philanthropy as a pacific means of advancing aims also or otherwise pursued militarily. "I am exceedingly chagrined and distressed with the idea of a war with the Indian nations on the Western Frontiers," Jeremy Belknap wrote to Benjamin Rush in a 1791 letter that Rush had printed in the newspaper. Noting that, in his view, Moravian missionaries were succeeding in "reducing [native peoples] to a settled and peaceable mode of life," Belknap asked "whether it would not be better policy to encourage these *united brethren* in their attempts of this kind among the Miamis, Wabash, and other Western Indians, than to send armies into their country?"[25] War making and beneficence were not contrary to one another but could be alternative approaches to the same ends.

Activists looked to philanthropy to achieve strategic goals without combat's devastation. When their states were at war, they likewise understood charitable activity, most of all to prisoners of war, as a strategic and diplomatic tool. With many thousands of people taken captive during the strife-prone century's wars, contemporaries were well familiar with the problem of maintaining prisoners of war. The law of nations—what today would be called international law—expected countries to feed and shelter prisoners in their custody at the expense of the prisoners' own countries, with states settling accounts during prisoner exchanges or at the end of the war; sometimes nations appointed agents to provision their captives—who could include the womenfolk and children of combatants—directly. In some cases, states could not provide adequately for their imprisoned sailors and soldiers, and charities and people in host nations stepped in to help, as with the group aiding American captives in London during the War of Independence. While some Britons used donations to American captives to express support for the Patriots' cause or their enduring bonds to their departing compatriots, many understood their assistance to prisoners of war, particularly to their frequent French adversaries, in strategic terms. Such aid, one recent historian explains, showcased British morality and benevolence, curried divine support, and kept French soldiers and sailors out of combat against their British counterparts.[26]

Providing for foreign captives had strategic value during hostilities. Because, as philanthropists saw it, it also sowed peace for the long term, charity to prisoners of war bolstered their belief in the world's steady progress. "'The relief of enemies,'" John Coakley Lettsom quoted approvingly from Samuel Johnson as he ruminated in the 1780s on aid to French prisoners during the Seven Years' War, "'has a tendency to unite mankind in fraternal affection; to soften the acrimony of adverse nations, and dispose them to peace and amity.'" Not everyone shared this view, with critics charging that the charities strengthened the enemy by undermining the state's proper role or showcasing its incapacity. In the midst of war, others bristled more at the hardships their own prisoners suffered than they appreciated the aid those prisoners received. The passage of time allowed more positive assessments. Angry about the alleged mistreatment of American prisoners of war by the British during the Revolution, John Lathrop could say in 1790 that "wars are not carried on with as much savage cruelty as they were in former ages."[27] Warfare desolated, but charity during hostilities gave activists, on reflection, further proof that their world was improving.

While knowledge of organizational beneficence during wartime deepened activists' faith in betterment, memories of personal kindnesses during times of strife furthered their cosmopolitan leanings. John Murray long recalled numerous Spaniards' solicitousness of his well-being when he met them while their countries were at war in the 1740s and he knew others had had similar experiences.[28] Thomas Russell had likewise learned that people could rise above national animosities to succor strangers. In 1762, after he had been seized by the French, he had been taken to Martinique. There he was relieved of his goods—even his clothes—and mistreated. By a stroke of luck, however, Russell had with him a letter of introduction to a French gentleman in Martinique who not only tended to Russell's comfort and safety but also (evidently once the island had surrendered to the British and the war was winding down) gave him a loan that "laid the foundation of [Russell's] subsequent success." The Frenchman's kindness made such an impression on Russell that he shared the story with others, and decades later his eulogist related it again.[29] Less dramatically, John Howard, on a prison investigation trip in Spain in early 1783—when Spain and Britain were still at war—noted that a letter from the Spanish ambassador to Britain had opened many doors for him. Moreover, the ordinary Spaniards he met treated him well. "Never," he reflected, "were two Nations so often at Warr and Individuals have such esteem and Complacency one towards another."[30] By drawing attention to these incidents in speech and writing about philanthropy or philanthropists, these men publicly imparted the lesson they had learned personally: Humans were basically good and their moral capacities were a stronger force than war.

Trafficking in Benevolence

American and British activists' pragmatic cosmopolitanism, curiosity, and belief in improvement were born of growing up and living in the exhilaratingly interconnected and strife-prone Atlantic world. Rather than losing faith in those currents in the face of the communal rift, they appreciated them anew and trafficked keenly in charitable knowledge. This transatlantic exchange, however, took on new meaning after the Revolution. No longer fellow nationals joining together to strengthen the British empire, the postwar philanthropists were working with foreigners to lessen suffering among compatriots and strangers alike.

"Preserving the Health of the Poor" was one such effort. "A few copies of a tract" on the subject arrived in Philadelphia in 1790. Thomas Percival, a doctor and activist in Manchester, England, had sent the pamphlet, though Sir William Henry Clerke, a Jamaican-born High Church Tory, had written it. Clerke or Percival or both thought the ideas on maintaining poor people's health might prove useful in the United States, and so the well-connected doctor forwarded copies of the pamphlet to a friend in the City of Brotherly Love in hopes it would be published in the American press.[31] In this case, there is no evidence that the proffered plan was ever reprinted in the United States. The utter ordinariness of Percival and Clerke's effort to prevent illness in a now-foreign country, however, showcases how they and their former compatriots approached beneficence in the postwar years almost as if the Revolution had never taken place.

Percival and Clerke's effort to address a problem both locally and more broadly started with a concern—in this case, the health of the poor. Known to be compassionate to needy folks, Clerke wrote his pamphlet during an outbreak of epidemic fever—the eighteenth-century term for a host of infectious diseases—in Manchester. But he did not write, he stressed, simply in response to the immediate "local affliction." Rather, an earlier outbreak in Manchester and the resulting public health recommendations by Dr. Percival had shaped his views.[32]

Activists, however, turned their attention to particular social ills based not only on local situations but also on distant developments. The "astonishing success" of humane (lifesaving) societies and "the warmth and liberality of support" for them elsewhere swayed men in other cities to set up the charities in their own communities. Moreover, newspaper reports of drowning incidents far and wide made drowning loom larger as a local problem demanding action.[33] Similarly, when Thomas Percival thought about the problem of slave trade abolition, he did so by reference to affairs elsewhere. "Are you making any exertions at Chester [England] to suppress the Slave Trade?" he asked a friend. There was a bill in Parliament on the matter, he went on, and the "great" French minister Turgot opposed the trade. "Virginia, New-York, and Carolina," he added, "have now united in measures to put an end to it."[34] Preventing the spread of infectious disease was another topic of the day hashed out in periodicals and philanthropic circles, and its currency may have further inclined Clerke to publish a pamphlet on the topic.

More than inspiration came from faraway. Stay-at-home philanthropists, or those whose traveling days were behind them, also garnered useful ideas for their projects from practices elsewhere. Correspondents were one source of knowledge. Concerned about feeding the English poor, John Coakley Lettsom considered a foodstuff—squash—that he learned about from a British admiral who had first tried the vegetable in Turkey and from an American doctor, Benjamin Waterhouse, who ate it at home. Both men sent Lettsom specimens or seeds plus tips on cultivating and preparing squash. Besides friends, activists turned to books, pamphlets, and other publications for practical information. When he became focused on what he saw as a pressing problem—infanticide—Bostonian Jeremy Belknap turned to *London and Its Environs Described*, a guide to the city, to understand the workings of various relevant charities in the great metropolis before he drew up his own proposal for a dispensary and foundling institution in his city. For his part, to rebuff criticism that his plan was not workable, Clerke cited Chester, England, for its "experience of years" with regulations to check the spread of smallpox devised by Percival's friend Dr. John Haygarth. Unmentioned by, perhaps unbeknownst to, Clerke was that Haygarth had developed the Chester public health measures with help from Newport, Rhode Island, native Benjamin Waterhouse, who had shared Rhode Island's rules for preventing smallpox contagion with his English friend.[35] Often activists and, thanks to their writings, the funding public knew their endeavors drew on distant precedents, but at times they built charitable infrastructures as unwitting citizens of the world.

Philanthropists were as keen to disseminate ideas as to gather them. Their first priority was to implement them locally. For cosmopolitan, improvement-minded men, however, having an impact farther afield was almost as important, and activists sought to spawn favorite charitable institutions elsewhere through the complementary use of print media and letter writing. Like Clerke, many benevolent types wrote essays, pamphlets, and books to broadcast their ideas. The works were meant to persuade, but they also contained much practical

FIGURE 4.1 Plan of the General Dispensary at Aldersgate Street, established 1770. From "Of the Improvement of Medicine in London, on the basis of the public good" by J. C. Lettsom. This plan was typical of material philanthropists circulated to facilitate the adoption of charitable models. The letters in the floor plan correspond to information about what each room should be used for. Wellcome Library, London.

information about how to make undertakings work. Clerke's pamphlet included not only guidelines on hygiene, patient management, and disposal of dead bodies but also a method for organizing patient data and details on the costs of the program. With their publications, activists strove to sway or reassure local supporters, but they also aimed to make it possible to set up similar ventures elsewhere.[36]

Besides print media, philanthropists relied on letters to sow their ideas or keep colleagues up-to-date on their work on common causes. Activists wrote to friends and acquaintances in distant cities asking colleagues to "establish a Society for the recovery of the drowned" or to forward "such communications as may appear Interesting to the [abolition] cause." They also apprised colleagues of the recent goings-on in local charitable organizations, solicited advice, and ruminated on schemes they were developing. Often they sent pamphlets or charities' annual reports along with their missives. Indeed, so customary was the practice that Jeremy Belknap rued an occasion when it was not "in [his] power to send [his correspondent] any thing from hence in return" for an essay he had received. To participate in this commerce in benevolent ideas did not require that philanthropists constantly pen new works. They did dispatch their own writings, but more often they enclosed works authored by others, either friends or other people whose ideas they considered important.[37]

Activists hoped and anticipated that information they conveyed would be broadcast widely. Letters read aloud or shown to family or friends might carry philanthropists' words beyond their correspondents. In addition, letter writers expected their words or the materials they sent to be reprinted. Sometimes they asked recipients to insert works in the "periodical prints," as Thomas Percival did with his friend Clerke's plan, or to republish whole pamphlets. But even without explicit direction, recipients excerpted letters for publication—the marks showing what sections were blocked out for insertion into the press can still be seen on many letters—so that larger publics would learn about, say, the latest in prison reform or disease prevention. Because newspapers picked up pieces from periodicals in other cities, people far and wide might read philanthropists' news. Acceptable as the practice was, a well-understood etiquette governed printing material from friends' letters. Without permission, a recipient "did not mention [a writer's] name." Recipients were expected to exercise good judgment about what "concerned the public to know." When Jeremy Belknap proudly recounted praise he had received from several Boston African Americans he had worked to help after they had been kidnapped by a slave trader, he had thought it went without saying that the news was "an effusion to a private friend." His correspondent should have known better than to publish it in the press.[38]

Belknap's correspondent was Benjamin Rush and it was Rush to whom Thomas Percival sent Clerke's pamphlet. The Philadelphian, the United States' most prominent doctor, was also the country's best-connected philanthropist for a reason: Medical men were especially well organized and oriented for trafficking in charitable knowledge. Their profession, they liked to tell themselves, made them "benefactors of mankind." Their knowledge was "useful." Their "ruling principle" was "active benevolence." And they strived to understand "the unexplored regions of the *terra incognita Medicinalis*." Self-serving though it was, doctors' professional sensibility did incline them toward philanthropic cooperation. They sought both to counter their image as self-important money-grubbers and to win patients from quacks and empirics. Giving their time to medical charities furthered those ends and gave them information to share. Moreover, doctors deemed correspondence among gentlemen of the faculty (the contemporary term for the profession) essential to progress in medical knowledge, not to mention a boon to their reputations. As a result, they regularly traded letters with distant colleagues, covering all manner of medical matters, including the latest in charitable projects. More mundanely, but as important, many elite doctors had met during their student years or at least shared mutual acquaintances. They had, therefore, the strong bonds that gave body to a far-flung community.[39]

The "republic of medicine" was especially important to transatlantic philanthropic cooperation but many activists contributed to conversations about beneficence. Not everyone could participate. Women and people of African descent, including notables such as Hannah More, Richard Allen, and Olaudah Equiano, helped shape agendas through their writings or local activities. But in the eighteenth century, only men of European ancestry with claims or aspirations to gentility corresponded in the broad web of activists that Belknap, Percival, and Rush belonged to. Although narrower bonds, such as those among medical men or co-religionists, were critical, people swapped ideas across them. It was a point of pride with John Coakley Lettsom that his circle went far beyond his fellow Quakers, and, besides medical men from North America to Central Europe, his correspondents about matters philanthropic included two Congregational clergymen in Boston, an Episcopal minister in Virginia, an Anglican cleric, and a titled Norfolk, England, gentleman.[40]

The empire of humanity—Rush's term for the transatlantic community of philanthropists—was broad in other ways. Geographic isolation did not preclude participation and indeed could encourage it, as it did with a British enthusiast for the new rescue and resuscitation cause; living in Madeira, this man was eager to stay connected to London. Nor did social isolation. An activist from Bath, England, who one acquaintance described as an "odd man" and capricious to boot, perhaps unable to find men to join him in a local humane society, made his mark in the cause through the written word. The equally difficult New

FIGURE 4.2 Portrait of Benjamin Rush, engraved by James Barton Longacre from Thomas Sully painting done circa 1813–1815. Library of Congress.

Englander who maligned the Bath man likewise worked well with faraway fellow philanthropists but was shunned locally.[41]

For one of the busiest transatlantic channels, between Benjamin Rush and John Coakley Lettsom, distance helped, too. The men, who had met when Rush had been in London as a medical student, exchanged missives amicably for years and Rush routinely gave American pupils letters of introduction to the Londoner. Cooperation, however, did not mean esteem. Rush thought, in one of his student's words, that Lettsom "possess[ed] very moderate medical abilities." His own medical skills may not have been challenged (until the 1793 yellow fever epidemic) but better the thin-skinned Rush not know that a Newburyport,

FIGURE 4.3 Portrait of John Coakley Lettsom, by Thomas Holloway, 1787. Wellcome Library, London.

Massachusetts, activist thought the Philadelphian stood out for his "Pedantry." Some of his ideas were "*Stale*" too. But, remembering Rush was a friend of his correspondent Jeremy Belknap, the Newburyport man "for[bore]" further criticism.[42]

Carping may have been unkind, but it and forbearance rested on a sense of familiarity with fellow activists. Some indeed did know each other, while others knew that they were part of a far-flung community as they underscored when they assured distant friends that yes, indeed, they had passed on the books and pamphlets to other nearby activists.[43] In the post-Revolutionary years, many activists built local charitable institutions by drawing on ideas from far and

FIGURE 4.4 Portrait of Thomas Percival. Wellcome Library, London.

wide and they took steps to spread their own. Their approach came out of the customs, the bonds, and the outlooks of the British Atlantic community in which they had grown up. By continuing it after they had become foreigners to one another, they began laying the groundwork for worldwide philanthropy.

The Politics of Philanthropy

Besides the expectation that they would swap ideas with faraway friends, activists took another lesson about beneficence from the world of their younger years: that it had a political tenor. Their moral concern for suffering humanity sprang from many sources. Men who had grown up familiar with charities that sought to boost British population—and thereby its military might—and to buttress Britain's strategic interests in America, however, could not divorce their understanding of charitable activity from politics. As they conversed in the 1780s and early 1790s about saving drowning victims, ending the slave trade, improving prisons, and other causes, they imagined a new, cosmopolitan statecraft.

FIGURE 4.5 Portrait of Samuel Bard, by Samuel Waldo, 1816. Courtesy of Medical Center Archives of New York-Presbyterian/Weill Cornell.

The politics of empires and nations absorbed the attention of philanthropists who had lived through wars that changed the world, not once but twice within three decades. In the years after the Revolution, they filled their letters with opinions, news, and questions about the work of governments and societies around the Atlantic. Americans should attend to horticulture, not to "hanging Loyalists" or "expelling" blacks, counseled a Briton sympathetic to the American cause, in a reminder that even British supporters of the Revolution had misgivings about the effects of American independence. After the repeal of Pennsylvania's test laws—Revolutionary laws that disenfranchised many through a mandatory oath of allegiance that Quakers and others refused to take—a Philadelphian opposed to the policy and concerned about the new nation's reputation informed a British friend that the laws had been rescinded. Of less immediate concern, there were "rumours of war" brewing between the Holy Roman Empire and the Dutch Republic and now the French were mediating, reported a Londoner. "Liberty of the press" was improving in France, a Mancunian noted to one friend, asking another, an American, what came out of the "Convention . . . for the melioration

FIGURE 4.6 *Jeremy Belknap*. Oil on canvas by Henry Sargent, 1798. Collection of the Massachusetts Historical Society.

of your federal Government?" "My Constituents," concluded the letter of a Bostonian to a Philadelphian "are generally well pleased with the Convention" and hope Americans south of New England will support it.[44]

Activists not only offered their many thoughts on matters political but also wove them together with discussions of philanthropy. Typical in this regard was a 1788 letter from John Coakley Lettsom to Benjamin Rush. The information you sent me about the health of slaves—to help the antislavery cause—has been sent on to a newspaper and to the London Medical Society, the Londoner began. The other scientific information was also very interesting, Lettsom went on, sharing with Rush some more news from learned societies. The account you sent me about the federal union, he then noted, had been inserted in the *Gentleman's Magazine*. You mentioned that your abolition society was opening a correspondence with French abolitionists, Lettsom reminded Rush, and then offered his analysis of the revolutionary ferment in France. A couple of requests for friends came next. Then Lettsom returned to philanthropy. He was sending a medical essay, but essays on resuscitation for the Humane Society—a charity devoted to

FIGURE 4.7 *John Lathrop.* Mezzotint engraving by Gilbert Stuart pinxt.; C. E. Wagstaff & J. Andrews. Collection of the Massachusetts Historical Society.

saving the lives of drowning victims—would not be ready in time. Commenting then that the cause of abolition was gaining support in England, he explained the politics of abolition legislation. Apropos of seemingly nothing, Lettsom moved on to a discussion of new wars that had broken out in Europe. He then returned to French politics, followed those thoughts by boasting about the popularity of Britain's king, and finished the letter with observations about the likely ratification of the new American Constitution. Philanthropy had a political valence, this interlacing of the topics indicated.[45]

Like Lettsom, many American and British activists were engrossed by the "Convention, now held at Philadelphia," and they similarly intertwined their thoughts on the proposed federal union with discussions of beneficence. The former compatriots, however, made different associations between politics and philanthropy on this topic. When Americans thought about the Constitution and philanthropy together, they thought concretely. In a 1787 letter relating news of the Philadelphia prison and abolition societies, Benjamin Rush related plans to "petition our Convention" about "the suppression of the African trade in the United States." Similarly, a discussion of the abolition cause and, in particular, Pennsylvania Abolition Society strategy led Jeremy Belknap to comment on Quaker opposition to the Constitution based on its provision allowing the international slave trade to continue for twenty years. Bostonian Samuel Parker connected a different cause in his mind with the Constitution. Informing his Philadelphia friend that he was sending him materials from the new Massachusetts Humane Society prompted Parker to ruminate on the prospects for the federal union.[46] Unlike Belknap and Rush, Parker did not touch on the political tactics of a charitable movement, but like his fellow citizens he associated the Constitution with the specific workings of a cause—in his case, coupling interstate cooperation in the lifesaving movement with interstate political cooperation.

British activists, by contrast, connected the Convention or Constitution with the process of philanthropic work in general, not the specifics of a particular cause. These Britons paid close attention to American affairs and they favored the new federal union. Unlike their American friends, however, they would not be subject to the Constitution and were not privy to as much news about it. They therefore approached the topic somewhat more abstractly. As a result, the slippage in Britons' minds between discussions of philanthropy and the Constitution related to the how, not the what. After commenting on how pleased he was to hear of the "wisdom and zeal" of the men forming a new American government, Richard Price moved on to praising both Benjamin Rush's prison reform efforts and, in particular, English prison reformer John Howard's "assiduity and zeal to this Subject." Similarly, Thomas Percival's thinking moved from the intellectual process of writing—John Howard, he noted, had at "the Press an interesting Tract on the subject of Lazarettos and the Plague"—to the intellectual process of talking—he was eager "to hear result of the Convention … for the melioration of your federal Government."[47] The particular mental connections that Britons made between the Philadelphia convention and philanthropy differed from those of their American colleagues, but the former compatriots similarly married the topics in their minds.

Beyond the subject of the Constitution, Americans and Britons shared common ideas about the political tenor of philanthropy. Moreover, their way of thinking was not subconscious. Rather, their presumption that beneficence had political import was explicit and in the postwar years the meaning they gave it, and in particular gave to transatlantic cooperation, pertained to the forging of a new peaceable statecraft for the Atlantic world. Underlying activists' hopes was their belief that to pursue philanthropy was to "cultivate the arts of peace," as John Coakley Lettsom put it in 1783. Discussing the nascent antislavery movement, he developed his views further a few years later in two letters that must be read together to make full sense. Thanking a friend in 1789 for his thoughts on slavery, Lettsom hoped that "the jubilee of freedom is becoming more and more extended. France, England, and America," he commented, "may determine the fate and happiness of empires. Were freedom universal, man would be literally the citizen of the world." Instead, "the powers of man have been enfeebled by the laws of despots." No word there about activists or their organizations, but a letter the previous year sheds light on the thinking behind his comment. The Pennsylvania Abolition Society, he noted in 1788, was planning to "open a correspondence with France"—Lettsom elevated a handful of French abolitionists to the status of the nation—and this epistolary exchange, he suggested, belonged to an American effort "to inspire distant nations with the same liberal principles" undergirding American progress toward "extending freedom on every side, and to every colour."[48] In sum, activists' correspondence could help foster liberty, which, in turn, would render obsolete the baneful politics of empires and nations. That is, to pursue philanthropy was not now to advance the British interest but to challenge the emerging state system.

Lettsom was a passionate man, given to grandiosity, but his less effusive colleagues likewise imbued beneficence with irenic power. Some saw learned, philanthropic, and abolitionist societies as "among the most efficacious means of promoting . . . happiness on earth" while still expecting them to complement traditional political activity. Not only was warfare less devastating, but also "the rights of mankind, civil and religious, are much better understood and more fully enjoyed than heretofore," observed John Lathrop in the midst of a discussion lauding "literary societies, and societies which have the general happiness of mankind for their object." "The great revolutions among the states and kingdoms of men," he added, reining in his enthusiasm for voluntary associations' influence, were "also . . . necessary" to advance liberty. If some expected politics and associationalism to work together to lessen human misery, others placed millennial hopes in charitable activity to end the misuse of political power. We must "cultivat[e] in ourselves & others principles of philanthropy"—love of mankind—"& benevolence & encourag[e] every institution which tends to promote them," Jeremy Belknap told Benjamin Rush, to help bring forward the day "when War, tyranny, & other abuses of human liberty will cease."[49]

Millennialism flourished in the age of revolution and profoundly shaped ideas about beneficence, but Belknap and his fellow activists' way of thinking had another source also. They had grown up familiar with the idea that philanthropy might advance the interests of the state, and as they pursued abolition, prison reform, lifesaving, and other causes in the postwar years, they assumed their activities had a political tenor. In their youth, that tenor was British and Protestant. In the 1780s and '90s, when the goal of furthering British strength no longer made sense as the basis of transatlantic cooperation, as Americans were fashioning a new nation based on universal principles and as Britons were refashioning their empire as liberal and humanitarian, the tone was cosmopolitan.[50] As they trafficked in charitable knowledge after the Revolution, Americans and Britons were not only aiding strangers, but also pursuing a new, peaceable statecraft for the Atlantic world.

5

Circumnavigations of Charity

THE YEAR 1786 saw John Howard "sadly drooping" in a lazaretto in Venice. His room was "cold" and "dirty" and the smell so foul that he lost his appetite. He got sick too and had to spend ten days recuperating in Trieste before he could continue his travels. Howard was not really complaining, though. It was his own doing that he spent six weeks quarantined in the filthy plague hospital.[1]

The Englishman had arrived in Venice hoping to serve quarantine in the city whose lazaretto had reputedly been the model for others throughout Europe.[2] No ordinary traveler, Howard was visiting Europe and the Ottoman Empire to investigate plague hospitals. Thirteen years earlier he had begun touring prisons in England and then abroad in an effort to call attention to their shortcomings and to urge improvements. His philanthropic journeys, totaling tens of thousands of miles, were not for the faint-hearted. He had traveled in miserable weather and through long nights, eaten dry bread and drunk sour milk, and courted arrest in France.[3] On what would prove to be one of his last reform trips, he had risked even graver illness by entering "pestilential jails."[4]

The public admired Howard for his punishing travels and viewed him as puritanical. His Independent (Congregational) faith was his uppermost concern, as he often stressed. Howard himself thought he had "peculiaritys in diet"—he ate no meat—and he also thought of himself as having had peculiarities in his education. According to friends, he took the biblical patriarchs as his models for parenting.[5]

Famously ascetic, Howard actually had a passion for travel that he indulged to find solace for an unhappy life. Long before Howard began trekking through prisons, he had visited Europe several times, unlike most British tourists, who usually made only one continental journey. As a young man, he traveled in France and Italy funded by money he inherited from his father, a wealthy upholsterer and carpet warehouseman in Smithfield, London. On his first trip, he cultivated a taste for fine art. His next European trip came after the death of his first wife, a woman more than twice his age whom he had married after she had nursed him through an illness. To ease his melancholy after her death, Howard headed in 1756 to Portugal, where he particularly wanted to see the effects of the recent earthquake in Lisbon; on that trip, he was captured by French privateers. In 1758, Howard married again. His second wife shared his piety, although she belonged to the Church of England and he was a Dissenter. She also shared her husband's commitment to benevolent projects for their tenants and the local poor, and her death after giving birth to a son in 1765 devastated Howard. In the 1760s and 1770s, to cope with his sorrow, Howard spent more time exploring Europe as well as the British Isles.[6]

In 1773, Howard became sheriff of Bedfordshire, and that November he set off on the first of more than ten trips to inspect prisons and hospitals. As with his leisure travel, unhappiness or disappointment drove him to journey abroad. Not every trip came about because of distress, but he met all his distress with travel. Howard had visited jails around England in late 1773 and 1774 and had been examined by the House of Commons on his findings. His first prison inspection trip to Europe, in 1775, came several months after Howard lost both an election for Parliament and the investigation of alleged improprieties by the election officers. When he returned to England later that year, he continued appraising English prisons. Lingering sadness over the death of his second wife made Howard long to spend time away from his estate in Bedfordshire, and over the next decade and a half, he crisscrossed the British Isles repeatedly and went to Europe six more times. Influenced by his findings, Parliament passed a bill in 1779 to build a new penitentiary and named Howard and two others as supervisors. The three men could not agree on a site—an important issue due to concerns about salutary conditions for prisoners—and Howard resigned as supervisor. True to form, he reacted to this latest disappointment by setting off for Europe. Howard's son's madness and, according to a scandalized twentieth-century biographer, drug use and homosexual activity, created yet another source of unhappiness. His distress over his son spurred Howard to leave England one last time, in 1789–1790.[7] He died in Russia on that trip.

Howard's peregrinations made him the most celebrated philanthropist of his day. His journeys focused attention on and sparked debate over moral responsibility to strangers at the same time that Americans and Britons were grappling with the remaking of their shared world. Others on the move also encouraged the universal direction in charity. Through his migrations in the postwar decades, John Crawford, an esteemed philanthropist but no Howard, exemplified universal benevolence as he succored those in need in each of his new homes. Meanwhile, the itinerancy of members of the lower sorts gave urgency to the question of aiding strangers. Celebrity philanthropists, less well-known activists, and needy people alike furthered Americans' and Britons' reckoning with the boundaries of moral responsibility—that is, with the boundaries of community—in the reordered Atlantic world.[8]

The Patriot of the World

John Howard had not set out to be a philanthropist. His only aim, he told readers of his last book, had been "to collect what was good, with a view of a reform in [his] own country."[9] Love of country, not love of mankind, had taken him abroad, at least initially.

Howard had written several books to promote his reforms. Along with his ideas for improvements, these books contain descriptions of prisons around the British Isles and Europe, jail by jail, datum by picayune datum. A reader could learn, for instance, that at the county bridewell in Nottinghamshire, there was "a room, on the ground-floor, in which were two men: one of them sentenced for three years, the other for seven, in a damp dungeon, down 10 steps, 14 feet square, 7 ½ feet high . . . Apothecary, Mr. *Hutchinson*." Or that "The *Prison* at NICE has three stories, with four or five good rooms on each floor. . . . Their beds have mattresses and blankets. Their allowance is two pounds of bread per day." Contemporaries did not find this glut of minutiae tedious: Jeremy Bentham extolled Howard's books as "a model for method."[10]

While others—famously George Whitefield—had traveled with benevolent aims, the scale and single-minded focus of Howard's journeys were new for non-missionary philanthropy and captured the attention of contemporaries, not least Howard's fellow reformers. "You certainly must have heard of [Howard]," Bentham wrote to a friend in the spring of 1778, "on the occasion of the extraordinary tours he took all over England, and a considerable part of the continent, merely for the purpose of inspecting the state of the prisons, in order to suggest improvements in that branch of the police." By the time he died twelve years later, Howard had visited prisons and hospitals in Austria, Britain, Denmark, Flanders, France, Germany, Greece, Holland, Ireland, Italy, Malta, Poland, Portugal, Prussia, Russia, Spain, Sweden, Switzerland, and Turkey. The tens of thousands of miles he covered—over 42,000 by his reckoning after his first decade of travel—cost him, according to an early biographer, more than £30,000.[11]

Howard's travels were remarkable, but perhaps more impressive were his skills at self-promotion. Like other men and women of his day, from the highborn to social climbers, Howard appreciated the art of image making. Benjamin Rush captured contemporaries' shrewdness about publicity when he proposed in 1785 that the church bell be rung when the newly chosen president of Carlisle College arrived in town. "The news of these things will make a clever paragraph in our Philadelphia papers and help allure scholars to our College," Rush explained. That sort of publicity know-how came from living in a world in which a consumer economy was booming. Howard, for all his quirks, was a product of the era's culture of self-invention and self-promotion, as well he might be since his London home was right near the Foundling Hospital with its art gallery, one of the best examples of the innovative marketing of beneficence. He distributed his books gratis to opinion makers to advance prison reform. The side effect was promoting himself. In common with Washington and his celebrated retirement from public life after the Revolutionary War, Howard shaped his public image with his refusal of public honors.[12]

Like other well-known philanthropists, the great prison reformer presented himself as modest. In other words, he paid enough attention to public opinion to make sure he would be remembered for ignoring it. Most famously, he nixed the plans, under way in London 1786 and 1787, to erect a statue in his honor. Howard had already written to friends from his travels abroad in a fruitless effort to have them call off the statue planning. His character, he told several friends sincerely, recoiled from public praise. But he voiced his views more widely than just among close friends. "My private education natural Temper &c all conspire in prompting me to avoid parade & Shew," Howard told an acquaintance, and thus, he explained, he was trying to squelch the statue plan. Finally Howard wrote to the statue committee two more times to ask for the plans "to be laid aside for ever." Of course, the letter revealing that the "great Philanthropist" was humble soon made it into print first in the *Gentleman's Magazine* and then, within months, in newspapers in New York, Philadelphia, and Boston. Howard had not explicitly written the letter for public consumption, but he would have been extremely naïve not to know that the statue committee—peopled, as Howard knew, with media-savvy men like John Coakley Lettsom—would make his missive public. Indeed, Howard was not against using the press to make his views known. He had earlier urged friends to advertise, if need be, his opposition to public honors. That stance brought him accolades. "In refusing a statue," one fan commented, Howard "shewed that he doubly deserved one."[13]

Howard's reputation was the product of his efforts at self-fashioning, as his friends' off-message comments highlighted. He thought of himself as odd, and he liked to stress that image to others, but after his death Howard's friends were at pains to qualify that perception. The daughter of a close friend of Howard explained that he forewent " 'every comfort in the prosecution of his extensive schemes of benevolence' " but that those sacrifices did not reflect " 'any austerity which he practised at home.' " Likewise, a good friend and biographer commented

FIGURE 5.1 Portrait of John Howard, stipple engraving by E. Scott, 1789, after M[ather] Brown. Wellcome Library, London.

that "his peculiar habits of life, and the exclusive attention he bestowed in later years on a few objects, caused him to appear more averse to society than I think he really was."[14]

Besides making sure he would be remembered for not wanting to be remembered, Howard managed his image in other ways. His letters from his trips are filled with comments about the arduous and heroic nature of his labors, his various forms of self-abnegation (of pleasures, of honors), and his always "calm, steady spirits." He also made a point of insisting to friends how little he cared about meeting important people before giving detailed news about meeting important people. Since norms of the day called for letters to be read aloud or passed around, Howard's news—his punishing labors, his impact—would not be confined to a few intimates. Sure enough, excerpts from his letters made it into print. In spite of Howard's claims not to care about public opinion, he knew he was on display. According to a biographer, he had his gardener tend his grounds even when he was away in recognition that his celebrity brought many visitors to his estate (where visitors could see the cottages Howard built for his tenants).

Moreover, Howard paid heed to public interest in his work; he knew he needed it to carry out his goals. He could not leave London for about a week, Howard told his steward, because he was busy investigating London hospitals. "'The public know it,'" he added, "'and look for my free thoughts on those Institutions'" and, therefore, Howard could not be distracted by going home to Bedfordshire.[15]

Howard tended his image but could not control it. He avowedly had not set out on his reform travels from an impulse to help foreigners. His followers on either side of the Atlantic, however, made him a citizen of the world as they battled over claims to universal moral responsibility. By autumn 1786, the season that saw Howard languishing in his Venetian hospital room and his admirers in London planning a statue in his honor, expansive notions of moral responsibility were becoming common in Britain. Earlier in the century, Britons had been ambivalent about moral responsibility to people from different religious, racial, or national backgrounds or even to faraway British subjects. Those doubts had ebbed with the American Revolution. The conflict had left Britons eager to restore moral capital lost in the effort to quash Americans' liberty and had given them new experience caring for fellow, but still foreign, British subjects—that is, the Loyalists—suffering from the war and exile. Those forces had encouraged a consensus in favor of a paternalistic moral responsibility to British subjects throughout the empire, including slaves, and also encouraged liberal and humanitarian attitudes toward foreigners more generally.[16]

Howard's far-flung philanthropic travels fit that emerging sensibility perfectly, and his compatriots endlessly celebrated him as the paragon of liberal humanitarianism. To one, Howard was *a Friend to Every Clime, a Patriot of the World.* Another praised him for building cottages for tenants on his Bedfordshire estate with only the condition that the tenants "attend divine service every Sunday at CHURCH, at MASS, MEETING, or SYNAGOGUE. Thus you see"—here Howard's admirer stressed his point that he was a true citizen of the world—"his expanded and benevolent disposition is confined to no sect, nor any particular notion." (Never mind that Catholics and Jews were probably few and far between in Bedfordshire.) Edmund Burke, though, said it best when he hailed Howard in a 1780 speech for "visit[ing] all Europe . . . to dive into the depths of dungeons; to plunge into the infection of hospitals; to survey the mansions of sorrow and pain; to take the gage and dimensions of misery, depression, and contempt; to remember the forgotten, to attend to the neglected, to visit the forsaken, and to compare and collate the distresses of all men in all countries. His plan," Burke exulted, "is original; and it is as full of genius as it is of humanity. It was a voyage of discovery; a circumnavigation of charity."[17]

Celebrating Howard as a cosmopolite was not necessarily, however, a cosmopolitan endeavor. The *Consummate Philanthropist*['s]" fellow Englishmen sought to claim Howard as an exemplar of a unique English humanitarianism through the statue campaign. The idea of erecting a monument to Howard had first been proposed by Dr. John Warner, writing as Anglus—that is, English or Englishman—in the *Gentleman's Magazine* in May 1786. Open a subscription to fund a statue in homage to Howard, Warner suggested, and thanks to the "the glorious possibilities of the English character," the money would quickly be raised.[18] The statue would thereby not only honor Howard but also exalt "this glorious country which produced him." (Some of the rulers of the inglorious country across the English Channel, Warner felt compelled to mention, had considered arresting this "true vicar of the God of Mercy.")[19]

Warner's suggestion met a receptive audience and both subscriptions and letters of support flowed in, but the effort to claim an exclusive English humanitarianism through Howard did not go unchallenged. The first to contest it were Scottish admirers of Howard. Having read news of the statue fund in the London newspapers, gentlemen in Glasgow opened a subscription to raise money there. Their contributions were "a small testimony of our high veneration for uncommon merit," they explained. Moreover, their spokesman noted pointedly, they hoped "to see a monument . . . rise out of the hearts of the whole nation." The statue to Howard would be a British, not an English, project, the Scots' donations said.[20]

Howard scotched the statue plans in the winter of 1786—after his death a statue went up in St. Paul's Cathedral—and the committee instead put the money toward medals and prints to honor Howard and, they hoped, "diffuse widely the spirit of benevolence."[21] The great philanthropist could stop the plans for the statue but could not stanch the adulation. John Coakley Lettsom was particularly committed to promoting "public approbation" of Howard's virtue and thereby nurturing virtue more generally.[22] Besides helping lead the statue committee in London, Lettsom dispatched news of Howard's travels and copies of his books to friends in Philadelphia and Boston.[23] Thanks especially to the partnership between Lettsom and Benjamin Rush, American newspapers and periodicals carried news of Howard. Americans learned that his presence in Vienna had led to improvements in Austrian prisons and they read Burke's paean to Howard. They learned too that Thomas Clarkson, the advocate for the abolition of the slave trade, was modeling himself on Howard, and so were the members of the Philadelphia Society for Alleviating the Miseries of Public Prisons. Early 1790 brought a report that " 'Mr. Howard departed from London on a philanthropic expedition to our imprisoned fellow creatures in some parts of Holland, Germany, Constantinople, Cairo, Aleppo, and Barbary.' "[24]

Like their English and Scottish counterparts, Americans embraced Howard as the era's paramount philanthropist, but not as an example of a distinct British

benevolence. Instead, reformers in the United States helped foster an understanding of Howard as the paragon of a shared philanthropic sensibility. Even
as Britons cited him as an example of a unique British humanitarianism, and
especially because they did so, they paid heed to Americans' response to their
hero.[25] The *Gentleman's Magazine* burnished Howard's image by reprinting a letter about his recent lazaretto trip that had been sent by John Coakley Lettsom
to Benjamin Rush and printed in a Philadelphia newspaper. The accompanying introductory comments from the secretary of the Philadelphia Society for
Alleviating the Miseries of Public Prisons reflected well on Lettsom (of course,
the person who passed the excerpt on to the *Gentleman's Magazine*) and on
Rush. More important, in the context of the patriotic veneration of Howard, the
homage paid to him by the secretary's reference to the "celebrated Howard" told
Britons that foreigners also appreciated the exemplar of what they saw as a special
British benevolence to all.[26]

The men of the Philadelphia Society for Alleviating the Miseries of Public
Prisons did indeed esteem Howard, but not as an example of an exclusively British
phenomenon. In early 1788, the Society wrote to Howard to send him a copy of
the group's constitution and to ask, in return, for "Communications" from him
on prison issues. Like his English and Scottish admirers, the Americans lauded
Howard for his universal beneficence. May you "enjoy the pleasure of seeing the
Success of your Labours in the cause of humanity in every part of the Globe,"
the Society told him. Philadelphians saw Howard as a model of a transatlantic
cosmopolitan philanthropy. We "heartily concur with the Friends of Humanity
in Europe, in expressing [our] Obligations to you" for all you have done in our
shared cause, the Society told Howard.[27] The practice of humanitarianism knew
no country in the Americans' formulation.

Over time, the public response to Howard had an impact on the man himself.
His early foreign prison reform trips had been prompted by "love to my country." "The redress and investigation of foreign abuses," Howard told readers of his
first book, published in 1777, "was not my object."[28] Traveling changed Howard.
According to an early biographer, all the time Howard had spent in Europe "had
given him much the air and appearance of a foreigner."[29] Realizing that he was
being adulated on both sides of the Atlantic for trying to succor people without regard to nationality changed him too. Even the most famous example of
the British ethos of liberal humanitarianism in the 1780s, then, was not purely a
British creation. Howard would not leave Moscow until he had "made repeated
visits to the Prisons and Hospitals, as the first Man in the Kingdom assured him
that [his] publication would be translated into Russian," he told a friend as early
as 1781. As he increasingly heard—from Britons, Europeans, and Americans
alike—that his influence and fame went far beyond the British Isles, his sense of

his mission grew. By the end of his life, love of mankind, not just love of country, animated his travels. In the introduction to his last book, published posthumously, Howard explained to readers that he had set off on his final tour "to gain further knowledge" as well as—and here he slightly paraphrased a comment he had made in a letter to a friend—"with the hope that the torch of philanthropy might be conveyed into remote countries."[30]

Americans had contributed to the creation and self-creation of Howard and thereby to the emerging trend of universal beneficence. But were they, as some historians suggest, merely truckling to Britons by following their lead in beneficence, in this case by embracing both Howard and a cosmopolitan moral responsibility? Scholars who argue that American philanthropists sought the approval of their British friends and associates point to both their adoption of British practices and the deferential tone of Americans' correspondence to British counterparts.[31] The perception of Americans' subservience to European, especially British, cultural superiors, however, results from studying the American past within national traditions. Looking across borders tells a different story.

A case in point is Benjamin Rush's 1789 appeal to John Howard to visit the United States. There, Rush wrote, Howard could be particularly influential by helping make penal policy while the country was still "in a *forming* State." Telling Howard that American prison conditions were poor—"tho' perhaps in a less degree . . . than in Europe"—he closed his missive by urging him to "Come then Dear Sir, and direct [the troubled waters] into their proper channel."[32] Both Rush's entreaty and tone certainly sound like post-colonial insecurity. In neither, however, was the American unusual. Indeed, Rush's invitation was somewhere between a request and not quite a demand, but an expectation.

As Howard's fame had grown, his fellow philanthropists sought to use his celebrity toward their own ends, and not only for the cause of prison reform. The Chester, England, doctor, John Haygarth, hoped that Howard would mention in one of his books a pet project of Haygarth's, namely, a school for poor girls. Since Howard had approved of the girls' school when the two men had talked about it, his "silence on this head rather disappointed [Haygarth]." Howard's "recommendation" of the boys' schools, the doctor told the star reformer, "will probably have an extensive influence in exciting other towns to adopt like regulations," and Haygarth wanted to put Howard's clout to work in spreading the model of the girls' school. John Haygarth wanted only public backing of a project, but other people wanted more from the celebrity activist. Jeremy Bentham, who hoped his own penal reform ideas would be adopted in Russia and who saw Howard as an ally in the cause, "wish[ed]" Empress Catherine "would invite [Howard] to Petersburgh."[33] Members of the Irish Parliament evidently asked Howard to visit; he told a friend in 1786 that he planned to go to Ireland to "perform his promise to some Irish members."[34] Similarly, the *Barbados Mercury* reported, evidently inaccurately, that "the humane Mr. Howard is meditating a voyage to the West-Indies, in order to make the gaols in that part of the world objects of legislative concern and attention," as if he alone could spur action.[35] Howard's renown made him uniquely useful to other activists. He had "travers[ed] the globe" for the cause and they looked for him to go wherever needed to further the shared mission.[36] Benjamin Rush's invitation, then, reflected a common view among reformers on both sides of the Atlantic.

The tone of Rush's letter to Howard was likewise typical. In particular, Rush's defensive comments that prisons in the United States really were not so bad were similar to Britons' sensitivity to reproof. After having read the "Observations" about a jail in his jurisdiction that the influential reformer had just published, a magistrate in Wiltshire, England, wrote a letter of protest to Howard. The magistrate was "very much chagrined" with Howard's fault-finding after he and his colleagues had worked hard to improve the jail. True, there was more work to be done, but they had made real progress. He "was, if possible still more mortified at" Howard's criticisms of the local infirmary, where problems were "immediately corrected."[37] Touchiness, no less than humanitarianism, knew no country.

A final caution against the view of American insecurity in the post-Revolutionary years is that Americans not only followed, but they led also. After Howard had put an end to the plans for a statue in his honor, the organizers had debated what to do with the funds collected. Some, including John Coakley Lettsom, had suggested setting up a prison reform society. He was optimistic that such an organization would succeed, he told readers of the *Gentleman's Magazine*, based on "the successful formation of an institution of this kind in Philadelphia."[38] Howard was also impressed by the Philadelphia Society for Alleviating the Miseries of Public Prisons and cited it as the model of a charity his supporters might set up.[39]

Howard never visited the United States—he died before receiving Rush's invitation—but his travels had furthered the universal direction of philanthropy on both sides of the Atlantic. An expansive sense of moral responsibility appealed widely in the late eighteenth century for reasons beyond Britons' desire to re-establish lost moral capital and Americans' eagerness to assert themselves on the world stage. As Edmund Burke had suggested when he referred to Howard's travels as "a voyage of discovery," this was an era when James Cook and Louis-Antoine de Bougainville circumnavigated the globe and when many Britons and Americans participated in quests after useful knowledge, especially of natural history, from around the world. Knowledge meant power—to treat diseases better, to grow new crops, to settle and exploit new lands—and the apparent march of knowledge fostered confidence about capabilities to act at home and abroad.

Moreover, the new voyages of discovery and more mundane travels and migrations brought faraway places closer. Acting on the ideal of universal benevolence, then, seemed to be within reach, yet most charitable organizations operated close to home. By embracing John Howard, Britons and Americans laid claim to the accomplishments of a figure who transcended local boundaries. That is, they generally acted locally but they were thinking more and more globally.

"Universal Philanthropy . . . Marked the Character of Our Friend"

The year 1786, the same year that John Howard was languishing in a Venetian lazaretto, found another peregrinating philanthropist busy making plans for a new charity in Barbados. John Crawford had arrived on the island in 1779. He had moved there as a newlywed to take up a plum position as surgeon and agent to the naval hospital. It was not his first overseas experience. Born in 1746 in Northern Ireland to a Presbyterian minister and his wife, Crawford had studied medicine at Trinity College Dublin. By the early 1770s, he was serving in the East India Company as a ship's surgeon. He felt he had learned much during his time in Asia about "treating the disorders incident" to hot climates, so he probably considered himself well prepared for the post in Barbados.[40]

The job, however, proved trying. At the beginning, as he told it, the hospital could handle only one hundred "sick and wounded seamen" although, with the American Revolutionary War raging, many hundreds more were arriving in need of care. "The rest were obliged to lie on floors, and were generally so close together that there was scarcely room left to pass betwixt any two of them." Even after he and his colleagues brought some order to the situation, conditions at the hospital remained "wretched." Supplies were so inadequate that in early 1780, "not one" patient was on a full diet. The patients drank much too much rum (which they bought by selling hospital supplies) and "wander[ed] about the Town in the middle of the Day." Superiors accused Crawford of favoritism toward a hospital contractor and blamed him for the high rates of desertion and death in the hospital.[41]

As if that welcome were not bad enough, a ruinous hurricane hit Barbados in October of 1780. The "Great Hurricane" killed more than two thousand slaves, flattened buildings, and destroyed thousands of cattle and other property. It was like being in a war zone, reported one eyewitness, while another thought the apocalypse was upon him.[42] John Crawford was evidently still talking about the experience years later. At his funeral in Baltimore, his eulogist recounted, based on information from someone close to Crawford, how his "high souled and benevolent friend" had responded to the disaster. In his telling, Crawford's

FIGURE 5.2 Portrait of John Crawford. This image is provided by, and usage in this publication is authorized by, Historical and Special Collections, Health Sciences and Human Services Library, University of Maryland, Baltimore.

supply of medicine alone had survived the storm and, rather than "profit" from the situation, he had "dispensed [the medicines] with a liberal hand to all who needed them."[43]

The first year or so had taken its toll. "The labour, vexation, and disappointment I experienced," Crawford later wrote, had "materially injured my health," and in 1781, he, his wife, and their two young children headed for England so that he could recuperate. On the voyage out, Mrs. Crawford died. For "the remainder of his days," Crawford's eulogist recalled, "he never ceased to lament" her loss.[44]

How or where Crawford spent his time in England is a mystery, but after he recovered his health, he returned to Barbados. He resumed his post caring for sick and wounded seamen, and he and a partner also ran a business importing drugs from London.[45] Work was not the only thing filling his days. In 1786, he and others set up a new medical charity, the Barbados General Dispensary, with the governor as patron, and the following year, they added a humane society program to the charity. As a result, Barbados can lay claim to having the first or second dispensary in Anglophone America and the third humane society.

(Philadelphians were also busy establishing a dispensary in 1786. The same year, men in Boston organized a humane society, while Philadelphians had set up a humane society in 1780, which faded by 1784 and was revived in 1787.)[46]

Why were men in Barbados, and not in Jamaica or New York, at the very forefront of founding the new medical charities? After all, there were plenty of poor people who got sick and needed attention in other cities, and drowning was a familiar hazard everywhere. Over time, dispensaries and humane societies were established in many cities on both sides of the Atlantic, and in retrospect it may seem that those movements, like other philanthropic causes at other times, were just in the air at a certain time.

In the late eighteenth century, the seemingly impersonal process of the spread of charitable movements rested on the very personal itineraries, motives, and interests of people—usually people more typical than John Howard—on the move, often because the age of revolution had unsettled their lives. The contributions of these itinerants might be as simple as new ways of looking at situations. Thomas Bernard had been one of the first to have his life disrupted by the revolutionary era. After his father had been dismissed as royal governor of Massachusetts, he had returned home from New England, where poverty had been rising but remained low compared to its incidence in England. A tolerant, conservative man, he brought with him the expectations that laborers could improve their lots in life and that economic expansion did not have to be coupled with destitution. His views would find expression in the Society for Bettering the Condition and Increasing the Comforts of the Poor, a prominent English clearinghouse for ideas about poor relief, at the end of the century.[47]

Besides introducing fresh outlooks, migrants and sojourners brought improving resources from place to place. The exiled Loyalist Count Rumford brought his love for maize, a staple of the diet in his natal North America, to Europe, and during the hungry, revolutionary 1790s, when the well-to-do worried about the restive poor, he advocated it as a cheap, nutritious food for the lower sorts. Another Loyalist moved a philanthropic resource across the Atlantic the other way. A few years after his return to America, Dr. Elisha Poinsett, a Charlestonian who had spent five years in the mid-1780s in London, imported a Royal Humane Society lifesaving apparatus and gave it to the city's Medical Society "at cost and charges." Benevolent exchange played a special role in the Anglophone community, but ideas came from far and wide. A Scottish Anglican clergyman who served as the director of the Madras Male Asylum from 1789 to 1796 brought back to Britain the Indian educational techniques of teaching children to write by forming letters in sand and of having older children instruct younger ones (the monitorial system) that he had observed at a Malabar school. British and American charity schools adopted those ideas, though the English Quaker

Joseph Lancaster also developed a monitorial system of education around the same time.[48]

Besides using new resources in old undertakings, migrants also planted unfamiliar causes in their new homes, though this is often obscured in the historical record. The publications of associated charities generally stressed the association of individuals in support of a cause and did not single out individuals for recognition. (In later publications, when they looked back to their early years, organizations might acknowledge the role of particular individuals who had been crucial to their beginnings.) Often, however, when a novel charity was set up, someone was involved who had previous experience with the type of institution in question. As activists knew, before subscribing to a new charity many prospective supporters "keep back until they see, (to use their own phrase) *how it will work*."[49] Potential subscribers needed to be persuaded that if they parted with their money, it would be for worthwhile ends. In addition, the initial few people who came together to plan and launch a new charity had to be convinced that they would be devoting their time to a viable endeavor. Someone with firsthand knowledge of an intriguing, but locally untried, charity could allay doubts of other would-be organizers.

That role was often played by migrants, who had reasons beyond charity to found institutions in their new communities. Social integration was one motivation. Initiating the formation of charities helped migrants forge ties in their new homes. Newcomers might meet "persons of great respectability" thanks to their efforts, as did the London Humane Society supporter who moved to the Severn Valley in England and launched a lifesaving charity there.[50]

Professional reputation was another, especially in medical philanthropy. Medical charities, such as dispensaries and hospitals, gave doctors not only experience but also public visibility. Perhaps, then, it is no coincidence that after one young doctor, John R. B. Rodgers, decamped from Philadelphia, where he had trained under Benjamin Rush and served as an attending physician at the lone dispensary in the United States, to New York in late 1788, activists began organizing a dispensary there. It opened in early 1791, in the midst of a battle for control of the charity. The parties disputed who "first threw out" the idea of founding a dispensary in New York, with Dr. John Bard speaking up for himself and his anonymous antagonist championing the Reverend John D. Rodgers, father of John R. B. Rodgers. Either man is plausible; both had ties to the Philadelphia medical community and experience in voluntary associations. But Bard hurt his case when he commented that the city's Medical Society had drawn up plans for a dispensary that were "ever intended to be carried into execution as soon as it could conveniently be done." This is likely true but not proof that he took public steps toward founding the charity before the clergyman did. Indeed, the case for

Rodgers is stronger. Through his son, he would have had firsthand knowledge of the Philadelphia Dispensary, knowledge that either Rodgers could share with others. Moreover, the opportunities the charity would offer his son, who served as one of its initial physicians, to build his career in a new place gave Rodgers more reason to work toward setting up a dispensary.[51]

Just as individual newcomers' arrival spurred the establishment of new charities elsewhere, so did Crawford's return to Barbados lead to the founding of the General Dispensary and Humane Society there. Crawford had been in England, recuperating from his stressful first years in Barbados, when the dispensary and humane society movements were exciting new causes, much talked about in medical circles. His younger brother Adair, also a doctor, was in England at that time too. Adair was active in both of the new movements. Moving to London in 1780, Adair Crawford served as one of the physicians to the General Dispensary in Aldersgate Street (on which the Philadelphia Dispensary was modeled). Besides his dispensary work, Adair supported the Royal Humane Society and served as one of the Society's Medical Assistants—professionals who were called to the scene of an emergency to oversee resuscitation procedures—for London and Westminster in the early 1780s.[52] Perhaps during his sojourn in England, John Crawford had spent time with his brother and been exposed to the movements.

A few years after his return to Barbados, Crawford and his colleagues set up Anglophone America's first or second dispensary. As was typical in other cities, the charity had evidently begun seeing patients in makeshift quarters as it continued setting up operations. Once the dispensary had a building, Crawford proposed that "a proper shop should be fitted up for the medicines." His proposal was approved. In addition, he suggested, the charity should hire a woman as a midwife. Also approved. In addition, the Royal Humane Society in London had sent an apparatus for resuscitating drowning victims at his request—perhaps the managers felt some anticipation as "the apparatus . . . was now unpacked, and presented, and . . . found to be a very handsome present from the humane society." The managers then "resolved that the plan of the humane society should be annexed to the design of this Dispensary." The scant surviving evidence, from the July 1787 meeting, suggests that Crawford led the formation of the Dispensary and Humane Society in Barbados.[53] He was the driving force at that meeting and probably had proposed forming the institution, perhaps inspired by his brother's activities. His experience during the 1780 hurricane could also have convinced him of the need for an institution providing medical care to people in distress. These medical charities came to Barbados when they did because he did. Crawford was not a great man, but a good man with particular connections and motivations, the temperament to lead the founding of charitable organizations, and a life of migrations shaped by revolutionary wars.

A little more than a decade after setting up the charity in Barbados, Crawford, then living in Baltimore, was planning another dispensary. There had been a lot of "rainy weather" that spring of 1798. If "excessive heat" came next, he feared that "the poorer order of the People," who lived "in narrow dirty alleys" and near "filthy wharves" would suffer epidemic disease—namely, the yellow fever that had ravaged American port cities routinely throughout the 1790s. That was one reason he wanted to establish a dispensary in his new home, he told his friend Benjamin Rush. Would Rush please send him "a copy of the Rules" of the Philadelphia Dispensary? Also, he was "much concerned" about the "scism" in the College of Physicians, which had been the organization behind the dispensary. "Your kind advice, as to the means of our obviating so serious an evil will be peculiarly acceptable," he added.[54]

Crawford had reason to worry about what happened when "scism" beset a voluntary organization. The Barbados Dispensary had been doomed by just such unpleasantness. The charity had been off to a promising start. In its first two years, the dispensary had admitted 227 patients. Jews as well as Christians supported the dispensary, and the second anniversary report particularly noted the liberality of the Jewish community (not to mention the "decent and becoming" behavior of the Jews who had attended the anniversary church service in contrast to "the levity and ill-manners of some [Jewish] folks" that had been observed at synagogue services by (Christian) visitors, who were unsettled by the conduct of congregants at Jewish worship services).[55] In spite of its reported success, the Barbados Dispensary ceased to exist sometime after its second anniversary. According to a local historian writing two centuries later, financial difficulties had doomed the dispensary. But the factional political conflict that surfaced during a struggle between the dispensary and parish vestry over caring for patients in a particular Bridgetown parish presumably played a role.[56]

Several months after that brouhaha, in early 1788, Crawford decided to leave Barbados. His early experience there had been shaped by the American Revolutionary War. The course of his life over the next several years would be determined by war spawned by the French Revolution. After quitting his post in Barbados, Crawford moved in 1790 to the Dutch South American colony of Demerara, where he had been named garrison surgeon through the patronage of a British general. "No situation," he later recalled, "could have been more favourable for the acquisition of medical knowledge." With sixty to eighty patients typically under his care at a time, he had ample opportunity to study disease. Drawing on his research in Demerara and on his Asian voyages, he published his research in an Edinburgh medical journal, and he developed the early germ theory that was his first historical legacy.[57] Though he found his work gratifying, by 1794, he was in poor health and went to Europe to recover. Summer of

1794 found him in the United Provinces, where he received a medical degree in Leiden. While in Holland, he made plans for a bright future in Demerara. He successfully petitioned the Dutch council for colonial affairs to name him superintendent of the medical affairs of the Colony of Demerara and Essequibo and, vital to his medical research, he won permission to set up a botanical garden in Demerara where he could grow plants that "country practitioners" taught him had medicinal uses. He planned to send the plants to the botany professor at Leiden.[58] This happy life was not to be. At war with the Dutch as well as the French, the British took over Demerara. Crawford petitioned British officials to honor his position—the terms of the surrender required it and, after all, it was "in consequence of the revolution" that he had been stuck in Holland all those months—and, according to his eulogist, the new British governors of Demerara offered to reappoint him. But his later complaints to a friend about the many disappointments he had suffered in life and his pinched circumstances in Baltimore suggest that the vagaries of a revolutionary world, more than choice, had caused him to move again. In 1796, heeding his brother-in-law's suggestion, he moved to Baltimore.[59]

Even before setting foot in the city, Crawford was contemplating, with fellow philanthropist Benjamin Rush, the need for a dispensary there. The two men probably met for the first time when Crawford stopped in Philadelphia on his way to his new home, but they already had ties through medical circles. Thirteen years earlier Rush had begun a correspondence (evidently short-lived) with Crawford's brother Adair, who also happened to be an acquaintance of Rush's friend Lettsom.[60] During their visit, the two doctors "talked of the advantages that might result from establishing a Dispensary in" Baltimore.[61] Talking medical charity may have given the men a way to relate. Moreover, Rush had been one of the key founders of the Philadelphia Dispensary. He had retired from active public life in the City of Brotherly Love after his heroic, but probably often lethal, ministrations to patients in the 1793 yellow fever epidemic brought him local censure (but won him international acclaim). He remained eager, however, to be engaged in philanthropy and had tried to seed a dispensary in Boston a few years earlier.[62] Through his new friend, Rush could again help set philanthropic agendas. For his part, as they talked, Crawford may have been thinking about how to establish himself in a new place. He was heading to Baltimore with good connections: Not only was he a Freemason, but also he had kin and other ties from home there plus a letter of introduction from Rush. Working with others to set up a dispensary would further help him settle into a new community. Medical men understood well the advantages to themselves of medical charities, and for Crawford, long plagued by money woes, establishing a good practice was important.[63]

By 1798, he was talking up the idea. "Many of the principal Inhabitants" liked it "and have promised the institution their warmest support," and he sent the mayor a proposal "grounded upon" the Philadelphia Dispensary but "suitable to [Baltimore's] situation."[64] The idea, however, was not enough. Not until a disaster hit the city did concerted efforts to organize a dispensary begin. An outbreak of yellow fever, rather than a hurricane, focused attention on the need for better access to medical services. The crisis occurred in 1800 when an abandoned girl, ten or twelve years old, died from yellow fever after the city's health commissioner (and mayoral candidate), among other failings, forced the child to walk to the hospital. Angered by the health commissioner's "wretched management" and callous disregard toward the sick poor, Dr. James Smith proposed setting up a dispensary. In 1801, the charity opened, with Crawford—who by then was both chairman of the Medical Faculty of Baltimore and Grand Master of the Freemasons of Maryland—active in its organization and operation.[65] Three years later, just as he had in Barbados, he facilitated the addition of a humane society program to the dispensary's mission.[66]

None of this is to suggest that Crawford was the indispensable man, an apostle of medical charity without whom no dispensaries would ever have been founded in Bridgetown and Baltimore. He played leading roles in bringing dispensaries to two Anglophone Atlantic cities, but he could not and did not do it alone. Working with others, the globetrotting doctor helped sustain and renew a far-flung community of activists in the decades after the American Revolution. Did Crawford's associates in the West Indies or United States know about medical charities elsewhere because of him? The sources do not say. It strains the imagination, however, to think that Crawford, a man with a "talent for social conversation," did not talk about at least some of his earlier medical charity experience with fellow philanthropists.[67] In Barbados, when he offered his thoughts on how to set up the dispensary and suggested founding a humane society, presumably he gave his colleagues some background, perhaps from exposure through his brother in London, on the institutions elsewhere. In Philadelphia, when he talked with Benjamin Rush about founding a dispensary in Baltimore, he may have recounted his experience with the Barbados Dispensary. And in Baltimore, he could bring to his new colleagues both firsthand and secondhand knowledge of the two movements in three cities.

Did they know about this or that dispensary or humane society in another city? Maybe. What they did know, what they would remember, and what inspired them was the "universal philanthropy which so peculiarly marked the character of [their] friend."[68] When Crawford died, accomplished but with his last years burdened by the death of his son and son-in-law and inescapable indebtedness, his eulogist, a fellow Freemason, recounted how "a heart devoted to the cause of suffering humanity" had driven Crawford to spearhead the founding of the dispensary. He recalled Crawford's dedication to medical research—part of his effort to be "serviceable to his fellow-creatures"—and his leading roles in establishing the Maryland penitentiary and the Baltimore Bible Society. Benevolence, particularly an expansive benevolence, were hallmarks of Freemasons' self-image, so it is no surprise that his eulogist spoke of a "pure spirit of philanthropy," an "ardent zeal for the happiness of man," and an "ambition *to be good*" that, he said, Crawford shared with their fellow Freemason, "the immortal WASHINGTON" (with whom the doctor also was said to share a physical likeness). Invoking those ideals was not mere formulaic tribute. Crawford, his eulogist told his fellow-mourners, had ministered to sufferers during the "Great Hurricane" and been unstinting in his hospitality to strangers in Demerara. Once in Baltimore, "the active share he took in every work of benevolence," his eulogist remembered, had led to his rapid rise in Maryland's Masonic hierarchy. The Freemasons, like others in the era, embraced the ethos of universal philanthropy, but their perambulating friend had lived it. Not a celebrity like John Howard or Count Rumford, Crawford, like other locally known activists whose lives had made them citizens of the world, left a legacy for his brethren of a "great mind [that] embraced the needy of all countries."[69]

Strangers

What of the "needy of all countries?" Were the perambulations of the well-heeled, rather than the needs of people in distress, really the critical factor in activists' embrace of universal philanthropy in the post-Revolutionary era? Boston minister John Eliot might have answered yes to that question. "Another thing on the wind," he wrote in 1786 after having heard that fellow Bostonians had set up a new charity in response to the entreaties of a visiting Scot, "& of a very windy nature from what I know of it. The humane society [a group devoted to the rescue of drowning victims]." But, the charity's future treasurer added, "The Subscription only [six shillings, eight pence] & therefore I put down my name."[70]

As Eliot's jaundiced view suggested, need often was not the main impetus in the formation of new charities. Typical were the founders of New York Hospital who were aware of "the great Necessity there [was] for such an Institution," but they were also motivated by the desire to keep up with their counterparts in Philadelphia.[71] Staying current with charitable trends not only signaled to genteel activists and the world that they and their city were humane, worldly, and up-to-date but also gave them new opportunities to correspond with their fellow philanthropists abroad.

If far-flung trends, more than local social conditions, often impelled activists to set up novel charities, the same was not true with charities aiding the itinerant poor. Instead, through their presence, distressed wayfarers forced philanthropists to rethink the charitable infrastructure of their cities. In the 1770s and 1780s, John Murray and his colleagues in Norwich, England, had developed a charity to aid outsiders. The 1790s saw activists on both sides of the Atlantic taking up the issue.

Outsiders had long loomed large in the minds of managers of charities. Charged with the careful oversight of donors' money—and always eager to attract more—managers worried particularly that unknown people could take advantage of their largess. As Pennsylvania Hospital was being established, one of its founders fretted that the charity would "allure Strangers from" other parts of America.[72] Decades later, the leaders of the infirmary in Manchester, England, cautioned subscribers (who had to provide recommendations for would-be recipients to get aid) that they should not recommend strangers without "the most credible Testimony of their being in a necessitous Condition."[73]

One reason that charities' managers felt the need to warn subscribers against duplicitous outsiders preying on their benevolence was that, whatever the rules and regulations were, both individuals and organizations emulated the good Samaritan. As the scriptural parable told, the humane man had succored an injured stranger whom others had ignored and set the standard that Jesus urged his believers to follow. The "Samaritan Society" was an obvious name, then, for the new charity established by some governors of the London Hospital. Aware that the hospital was taking patients "whose relief was not within its general regulations," they established, in 1791, a new charity "for Convalescents from the London Hospital, and for Cases not within the Provision of Public Hospitals." The men were motivated in part by the worry that down-and-out strangers might turn to crime or beggary. But compassion for poor people far from home and an understanding that the charitable infrastructure often failed them played their parts too. The charity helped poor people from distant places in the British Isles as well as "destitute *foreigners*" "to reach their homes, and resume their occupations," and it provided those unable to return to their previous work "with a means of procuring a subsistence."[74]

The plights of poor strangers likewise moved a group of women in New York City to set up a new charity. The widowed Mrs. C. was an Irish native, "broken in spirits, and broken in health," with no other option for herself and her young child but "to seek an asylum in the Alms-House," typically the last resort of the poor. The suffering of women like her—destitute and uncared for by any of the city's private charities—came to the attention of Joanna Bethune through her husband's work with the St. Andrew's Society. In response, she, her mother

Isabella Graham, and Elizabeth Seton formed the Society for the Relief of Poor Widows with Small Children.[75]

It took no imagination for Graham and Bethune to sympathize with the trials faced by widowed women with young children. Like John Crawford and so many other philanthropic leaders of the post-Revolutionary decades, they had earned places in the Atlantic community through lives of mobility. Graham had been born Isabella Marshall to a gentry family in Lanark, Scotland, in 1742. In 1765, she married a British army physician, John Graham, and began a series of migrations. Following his regiment, the couple moved to Montreal and then to Fort Niagara. Three daughters, including Joanna, were born while they were in North America. In 1772, the brewing imperial crisis touched the family, including two Indian slaves. Worried about the loyalties of the many Americans in John Graham's regiment, the British army sent the regiment to Antigua. Two years later, Dr. Graham died. Left with three girls under six and another child on the way but little by way of "temporal property," Isabella Graham returned to Scotland. There she struggled for a couple years until well-placed patrons helped her establish a boarding school that was soon thriving. Nevertheless, after several years, Graham and her daughters moved to the United States. Years earlier, she had visited New York City and forged relationships with leading Scottish evangelicals there. She long "had indulged a secret expectation of returning" to America, and at the behest of John Witherspoon, she settled in New York in 1789 and set up another school that soon flourished. Well-connected and comfortable for much of their lives, Graham and Bethune had experienced and, more important, identified with the lot of "the widow and the fatherless ... in a foreign land."[76]

In 1797, Graham, Bethune, and Seton established the Widows Society at Bethune's initiative. The charity was among the earliest organizations established by women in the United States, and historians have rightly focused on the group's role in the emergence of women's activism, but it was also one of the first groups to give aid on a non-sectarian, non-ethnic basis.[77] Most of New York's charities gave aid based on religious or ethnic affiliation and the few that did not—New York Hospital and the New York Dispensary—provided medical care, not food, fuel, and raiment. (Moreover, the dispensary required a would-be recipient to get a recommendation from a subscriber, who could sponsor two patients at a time. Since access to that charity was based on personal ties, strangers were at a disadvantage.)[78] The Widows Society innovated by helping distressed women obtain the necessaries of daily life without "limitation," that is, without regard to their ethnic or religious background, though it did discriminate based on race. The women were not necessarily foreigners or newcomers to New York—those who were foreign born, however, were excused from the requirement of being resident in New York for a year before being eligible for aid—but they were outsiders to the city's other charities and they, as much as their benefactors, deserve credit for the rise of impartial philanthropy.[79] Joanna Bethune does not acknowledge the needy women's influence when she describes the formation of the Widows Society; instead, she explains that her husband was a "distributing manager" of the St. Andrew's Society and that she, Joanna, was concerned about "widows not entitled to the bounty of the" charity for Scots. But how did these needy women come to her attention in the first place? The most likely explanation is that, directly or indirectly, they approached Bethune with tales of woe and pleas for help. Probably strategically meek and suppliant, the indigent widows pushed their social superiors to expand the charitable infrastructure.[80]

Unlike some of their fellow activists, the governors of New York Hospital—which had been chartered in 1771 but only began admitting patients in 1791—had from the beginning anticipated caring for "poor sick people of every country and Denomination."[81] They really had no choice. The publicly chartered, and eventually substantially publicly financed, charity needed broad support. Ministers from all the denominations in the religiously polyglot city therefore served as ex-officio members of the board, and, similarly, the governors stressed from their earliest appeal for public funds that the hospital would admit patients "without the most distant regard to National, Civil, or Religious Distinction."[82] The need to fundraise was not the only reason for the governors' catholicity. As the governors noted in 1771, the city "ha[d] drawn a great number of poor people to it from Britain & Ireland, as well as far other parts of Europe," who lacked "sufficient" access to medical care.[83] The founders had expected that the hospital would care for poor strangers, and thirty years later they were proved right. Between 1797 and 1803, over half of the patients were foreign born. Most were from Ireland, England, Scotland, and Germany, but East Indians, Portuguese, a couple of Asians, and a lone Pole, among others, also received care.[84]

Ministering to these emigrants and wayfarers, many of whom were likely mariners, was a matter of realizing the "principles of Christianity and general benevolence," but doing so also contributed to making New York "a great sea port."[85] The health of newcomers and wayfarers mattered to the economy of the city, as the successful men who ran the hospital well understood. "The immense business carried on in [New York], in Navigation, Merchandize, Architecture, and in all the auxiliary Arts and Trades," often resulted in accidents that injured laborers. They then needed recourse to a "public Hospital," not a "poor-house." If the city and state wanted to continue attracting such useful people, the governors of the hospital thought the city's charitable infrastructure had to provide for them. The desire to draw "emigrants from the neighbouring States and from foreign countries" to their city convinced the governors that "maladies

FIGURE 5.3 View of the New-York Hospital, drawing by John R. Murray, early 1800s.
Courtesy of Medical Center Archives of New York-Presbyterian/Weill Cornell.

and extreme indigence," not "any political, civil, or religious distinction among
men," were the only criteria the hospital should care about.[86] Impecunious outsiders and globetrotting philanthropists alike not only moved contemporaries
toward universal philanthropy but also sustained the connections that made the
Anglophone Atlantic world a community even though its members were no longer compatriots.

6

The Common Cause of Humanity

WHILE JOHN HOWARD was crisscrossing Europe inspecting prisons and hospitals and John Crawford was planning for the dispensary and humane society in Barbados, another peregrinating philanthropist was busy pushing his pet cause. Dr. Henry Moyes, a Scotsman, had arrived in the United States in 1784. A celebrated itinerant lecturer on natural philosophy, Moyes attracted the attention of prominent Americans eager to end the intellectual and cultural isolation of the war years. He was feted in Providence, asked to settle in New York, and pleasantly surprised to find his lectures thronged in Charleston.[1]

In December of 1785, Moyes was back in Boston. One night, he invited a number of new friends, well-connected gentlemen, to dine with him. To later generations, the men's discussion seems to have been "chance." As one historian tells it, the "conversation turned" to the topic of charitable institutions and Moyes "mentioned" the Royal Humane Society, the London lifesaving group. As a result of their talk, his dinner companions organized one of the first of the groups set up in the post-Revolutionary charitable boom.[2] Happenstance, however, had nothing to do with the drift of conversation that night in Boston. Moyes had come to the United States with a mission to plant humane societies and thereby to court Americans' return to international philanthropic circles. Little could the British visitor have known that his American friends would use their new charity to challenge British pretensions to a unique humanitarian ethos. In time, they would make a shared commitment to universal benevolence the basis of a new relationship between the former compatriots.

Known as the "blind philosopher," Dr. Moyes was one of the "literary phaenomena of the . . . age." He had been born in Kinghorn, Fifeshire, Scotland, and had lost his sight after having smallpox as a young child. Reportedly having won the friendship of Adam Smith, he studied in the universities of Edinburgh and of Glasgow thanks to the older man's intervention. Sometime in the 1770s,

Moyes began giving lectures on chemistry and natural philosophy in Edinburgh. In 1779, he went to England where he made his name as an itinerant public lecturer. Five years later, he went to the United States. Contemporaries regarded Moyes as deeply knowledgeable about natural philosophy, but publics on both sides of the Atlantic found him especially fascinating because of his blindness.[3]

Sometime before he headed to the United States, Moyes met Alexander Johnson, a Londoner who was an ardent proponent of the resuscitation cause, a charitable movement that was relatively new in Britain and little known in the United States. The cause of resuscitation had begun in Amsterdam a few years earlier, in 1767, when a group of wealthy men had founded the Society for the

FIGURE 6.1 Portrait of Henry Moyes, etching by John Kay, 1796. Wellcome Library, London.

Recovery of the Drowned to cope with the common problem of people drowning in the city's canals. For decades before the founding of the group, the problem of how to restore apparently dead people to life had interested European physicians. But resuscitation from apparent death was a novel program, greeted with public skepticism in the late 1760s and early 1770s. Likewise, organizations to promote the rescue and resuscitation of drowned persons were a new type of charitable undertaking. The Amsterdam Society's program was twofold. It publicized its methods of resuscitation, which replaced older methods, now scorned by elite medical practitioners, for reviving people half-dead—though not apparently dead—from drowning, hanging, or other causes. In addition, the Society offered rewards to encourage lifesaving. Cities across the European continent soon followed suit. By the early 1770s, Hamburg, Milan, Padua, Paris, Venice, Vienna, and others had set up lifesaving programs, and the sovereigns of Hungary and Russia had encouraged the new lifesaving methods.[4]

A group of men in London launched the resuscitation movement in Britain when they founded the Society for the Recovery of Persons Apparently Drowned, as a typical subscription charity, in 1774. In 1776, the group changed its name to the Humane Society and in 1783 or '84 it received royal patronage and became the Royal Humane Society. The Society had as its mission "to restore such as have in an instant *been numbered amongst the dead*, by some dreadful disaster, or by some sudden impulse of phrensy." The Society focused on saving people from drowning, whether from accidents or suicide attempts, but the charity also aimed to revive people apparently dead from hanging, noxious vapors, freezing, and other causes of sudden death. Following the basic model of the Amsterdam group, the London charity operated by offering rewards to people who retrieved drowned bodies, who took the apparently dead bodies into their houses, who followed the Society's resuscitation procedures, and who fetched the Society's Medical Assistants to the scene of emergencies to oversee resuscitations.[5] The Royal Humane Society only gave rewards for lifesaving in London and its environs, but it distributed its materials far and wide to spread knowledge of resuscitation and to spur the organization of humane societies in places "too remote to be intimately connected" with the London charity. Meanwhile, Alexander Johnson—the man Henry Moyes befriended shortly before his trip to the United States—also kept busy in the 1770s, '80s, and into the '90s, sending "pamphlets and instructions" about the cause around the British Isles, the West Indies, and North America.[6]

Information about resuscitation had reached America quickly. In 1774, the (Boston) *Royal American Magazine* printed a Swiss doctor's instructions for recovering drowned persons, while a Philadelphia newspaper reported the successful resuscitation of a sailor based on the new method now in use "in many

Parts of Europe, particularly in Holland." Also in 1774, only a few months after the London Humane Society's founding, one New Yorker had received a Society pamphlet that he in turn gave to a surgeon friend who restored someone to life by following the group's precepts.[7] Activists did not, however, found the first humane society in America until several years later. The dislocations of the war years generally derailed Americans from keeping up with European philanthropic trends. In 1780, however, with life in the City of Brotherly Love relatively routine, a group of doctors and laymen organized the Humane Society of Philadelphia. The group limped along for a few years, but petered out in 1784.[8]

When Moyes arrived in the United States, Americans had not yet embraced the lifesaving movement. Although Philadelphians had already formed a humane society, the group had faded, having saved only one person. While Dr. Benjamin Waterhouse, a Rhode Island native who had received medical training in Leiden and London, had tried to promote knowledge of resuscitation techniques and had called for the formation of a humane society in Newport, his efforts had been to no avail. The movement, in short, had gone nowhere.[9]

At the behest of his friend Johnson, Moyes put lifesaving on the American charitable agenda. At his lectures, he handed out pamphlets with lifesaving directions. He also had the information printed in newspapers. "To render those Directions more extensively useful," the *Providence Gazette* emblazoned them on the front page.[10] Most important, in Boston and presumably in other cities, Moyes suggested to Americans that they might found humane societies. When "the blind philosopher" threw out the idea in Boston, some of the men already knew of the cause: One of his companions replied that another gentleman in town had received a Royal Humane Society pamphlet from a founder of the London group. Knowledge and action, however, were two different things, and it was Moyes's intervention that led the Boston men to set up a new charity. The Massachusetts Humane Society began operation in 1786.[11]

Moyes's good offices extended to Philadelphia too, where he seems to have provoked the revival of the Philadelphia Humane Society. The immediate impetus for the charity's resumption came at a February 1787 meeting of the Philadelphia Dispensary managers. The men, having dealt with money matters and the possibility of incorporation, were close to wrapping up business when one of the managers proposed that the group "engraft the Humane Society on the Dispensary." The dispensary managers rejected the proposal because in their view, their charity already served the same needs.[12] The incident, however, evidently worried members of the dormant Philadelphia Humane Society, because within two weeks, they decided to defend their turf and revived the charity. Moyes had left the United States by that point, but he had spent months in Philadelphia in early 1785 and the winter of 1785–1786; and his friends there included dispensary

physician and Humane Society member Benjamin Rush and a dispensary manager, merchant Thomas Clifford. Moyes aimed to spread the resuscitation movement, and he rubbed shoulders with men involved with Philadelphia medical
charities. Moreover, a friend later said he thought Moyes had planted a humane
society in Philadelphia. It is reasonable, then, to assume that he bandied about
the topic of humane societies on his visits to City of Brotherly Love and that,
as a result, a dispensary manager broached adding the lifesaving program to
that institution. Any knowledge the Philadelphia men might have had that a
humane society had been recently set up in Massachusetts—knowledge Moyes
could and likely would have provided—would probably have heightened the
Philadelphians' interest in reviving the humane society.[13]

In one way, it was not "the blind philosopher" himself, celebrity though he
was, who mattered so much. Rather, what mattered was that someone with firsthand knowledge of the little-known cause could make a novel undertaking seem
less abstract and more doable, as Alexander Johnson presumably had hoped when
he enlisted Moyes's help. In many cases, when new charities were set up, someone
with previous experience with a particular type of organization was involved.

In another way, however, it was Moyes himself—a British visitor with ties to
the metropolitan movement—who mattered. His efforts to encourage lifesaving
assured citizens of the new nation that their former compatriots welcomed the
participation of American organizations in the cause. The way he went about
promoting lifesaving also mattered. He encouraged the idea of forming new
humane societies but, different from John Murray's plans to expand the Society
of Universal Good-will, he did not try to set up branches of a British charity.
Americans wanted to keep up with European trends. When the Philadelphia
Humane Society was first being set up in 1780, its organizers noted that they were
forming it "in imitation of those in Paris, London, and Amsterdam."[14] But following the example of European counterparts was not enough. The Philadelphians
anticipated that they would correspond with their fellow members of the resuscitation movement, that is, that they would be their partners in a shared cause.
Correspondence to foster and disseminate knowledge was common in learned
circles, and, as the Philadelphians would have known from the pamphlets of the
Royal Humane Society, the London group received and printed scores of letters about resuscitation, primarily from friends of the cause within Britain. In
late 1782, therefore, the Philadelphia Humane Society resolved to write to the
Amsterdam group and, six months later, after the signing of a preliminary peace
treaty between the United States and Britain, to the London group.[15]

Those letters seem never to have been written or sent and it is clear that the
Philadelphia and London societies did not establish a relationship in the early
1780s.[16] When Moyes arrived, therefore, the Philadelphia Humane Society men

were primed to be drawn into British trends, but like their fellow Americans in Boston, they wanted to know they were wanted. Moyes's presence, entreaties, and presumably flattery of his hosts told Americans that Britons anticipated their partnership in the cause of humanity. Being wooed indeed made it easier for Americans to forge a relationship with their British counterparts. Not long after the Philadelphia Humane Society men had reorganized the group in 1787, they dispatched its publications to their London colleagues and asked for Royal Humane Society materials in return.[17] Americans did not fall into the humane society movement by the chance drift of conversation one winter's night nor did they join because of a servile attachment to British trends. Rather, they were welcomed in by would-be colleagues.

Humane Societies and Antislavery

The year that the Philadelphia Humane Society established ties with its London counterpart, 1787, is better known for another humanitarian milestone. Meeting in a London printing shop that May, twelve men established what became the Society for Effecting the Abolition of the Slave Trade. Slavery was an institution sanctioned by time and by Scripture, but here was an organization dedicated to dismantling one of its pillars.[18]

The resuscitation movement does not get the respect antislavery does. One scholar suggested that we today might "be more than a little mystified by the enthusiasm which it evoked," and indeed, people today—probably swimmers all—often are amused when first hearing of the cause to rescue and revive drowning victims.[19] For people who often could not swim but who routinely traveled, worked, or played on or by oceans, rivers, streams, and wells, however, watery deaths were an ever-present danger. The possibility of preventing those deaths was exhilarating—so exhilarating it called to mind Jesus's power to raise the dead.[20] "To restore suspended animation [i.e., vitality], to recover and call into action the latent powers of life, is working a miracle to preserve the devoted victim of inauspicious chance—It is saying to the motionless frame—'LAZARUS, *come forth!*,'" was how a newspaper report on the founding of a new humane society put it.[21] Contemporaries found the anti-drowning cause thrilling. On both sides of the ocean, in distinct ways, they also found in it possibilities for attacking the underpinnings of slavery and thereby imagining an Atlantic community defined not by racial hierarchy but by the shared humanity of all its members.

The humane society movement was widely known in the British Isles by the time the Society for Effecting the Abolition of the Slave Trade was formed and abolition began to emerge as a mass cause. By 1787, men had set up lifesaving institutions or programs (generally but not always with the words "humane society" in the name) in Bristol, Chester, Devon, and Cornwall, Hull, Norwich, the Severn Valley, and Whitehaven in England and in Cork and Dublin in Ireland. The London-based Royal Humane Society showered its rewards over a wide area, and in 1786 it had 204 medical assistants in Middlesex and surrounding counties. Besides overseeing resuscitations, these men were asked to hang the Society's lifesaving directions up in their "Shops or Surgerys."[22]

Public awareness of the cause went well beyond its supporters. The groups deposited equipment to facilitate lifesaving along waterways, often at public houses, or in other convenient places including merchants' counting houses. Activists and organizations disseminated masses of material far and wide. They posted resuscitation directions on broadsides in public houses and other high-visibility places. They printed and distributed annual reports, shorter pamphlets, and yet more compact versions of the methods of treatment to subscribers, medical men, sea captains, clergymen, and grand juries, and they left materials at coffeehouses and other relevant places. They also publicized the movement in newspapers and periodicals. People who received the movement's pamphlets commonly passed them on to others.[23]

People who did not encounter printed material could still learn about the movement. Clergymen in London and elsewhere gave fundraising sermons, which were sometimes preceded by the Humane Society hymn and heard by whoever was in the church. Moreover, clergymen preached ten times in favor of the Royal Humane Society in 1780 alone.[24] Furthermore, theaters sometimes held benefits for the Royal Humane Society. At one 1786 benefit at the Covent Garden Theatre, a performer read a poem about lifesaving before the show began. William Hawes, the Society's prime mover, gave an annual course of lectures "on the theory and practice of restoring animation to the human body" in London. Even those men and women who did not see a broadside, receive a pamphlet, hear a sermon, attend a benefit play, or watch a rescue or resuscitation—events that drew crowds—could learn about lifesaving methods by reading William Buchan's *Domestic Medicine*, one of the most popular books of the age.[25]

With all this attention on lifesaving, people who never contributed to a humane society still thought about the problem of watery deaths. A London debating society debated whom a man should save from drowning—his father, wife, or son (the audience voted for the wife). Clever people approached the societies with inventions, such as new life preservers, to enhance lifesaving. Poets extolled the movement in verse. Many, then, had come to think of preventing accidental deaths as both possible and as a moral imperative.[26]

In Britain, contemporaries used this preoccupation with the very real problem of drowning to help stoke opposition to the slave trade. To counter the belief that the slave trade was a nursery for British mariners—that is, that it provided the navy with a supply of men—and was thus beneficial, activists stressed instead that it was "a *grave*" for seamen, with drowning one of the prime causes of death.[27] Abolitionists also called attention to the watery ends of many captives' lives. During the Middle Passage, slaves routinely committed suicide by drowning, abolitionists informed the public. Activists also highlighted slave traders' commission of homicide by throwing Africans overboard to their deaths in the open water. John Newton, the former slave trader best known for writing "Amazing Grace," told of a sailor who, irritated by a crying baby, pitched the child into the sea. Others related the notorious 1781 *Zong* incident in which the crew of a slaver committed mass murder by throwing 123 Africans into the sea so that he could collect insurance on them. Abolitionists also spotlighted captives' deaths by suffocation, another cause of sudden death that the humane society movement targeted.[28]

Poets often used drowning to evoke the horror of the slave trade. In "The Desponding Negro," a poem first published in 1792, a slave trader "dash'd [a captive] overboard" because his "Value, compar'd with [his] Keeping, was light"—a reference presumably to the *Zong* case. In many poems, authors have slaves "plunge headlong in the deep" or obey "the brutal mandate to embrace / A watery death." Africans, these verses suggested, were self-respecting, preferring their own deaths to the loss of liberty. They also were desperate. The cruelty of the slave trade left captives "hopeless." Self-destruction was a dignified form of resistance in these portrayals, but poets also insisted that being kidnapped and trafficked made Africans "[sink] in despair." Slaves' attempts to drown themselves were thus heartbreaking as well as noble. In a few writers' telling, the ocean's (to wit, God's) "angry billows" endangered enslaving mariners too. One poet sent an entire crew to its death in a storm. In another poem, Africans, whose shipboard uprising was in the course of being put down, grabbed mariners, then all "rushed together to a watery death."[29] The pathos of the poetic depiction of drowning was that the trade turned a calamity into a mercy—or an act of justice if mariners were also killed. The existence of a movement dedicated to preventing drowning and other causes of sudden death made all the more reprehensible a trade that sent so many people to watery graves and that upended the meaning of those deaths. A few artists went so far as to counter-pose lifesaving and slave trading. In a 1788 poem entitled "The Slave Trade," William Collins taunted the slave-trading nation by asking if "by tempest's rage, on *Afric's* shore, / Your ship is driv'n, with her pallid crew / What help from Blacks! Dare you their aid implore? / Will they forget their foes, and save them too?" The answer was yes. "Dauntless they plunge amidst the waves, / And snatch from death" the Britons who might be their "future tyrants." Collins's moral drama came to view in a painting by George Morland entitled *African Hospitality*, which was first displayed in London in 1790 and later engraved for wider circulation. Britons, the poet and the painter insisted, should think about their expectations about moral responsibility by reference to lifesaving from drowning.[30]

The same year that Collins wrote his poem, Samuel Jackson Pratt—author of *Emma Corbett, or the Miseries of Civil War*—published a book-length poem on slavery throughout human history, with the African slave trade getting much of the attention. In introductory comments to *Humanity, or the Rights of Nature*, Pratt claimed that whether the slave trade continued was not what mattered. What did matter was that all people should enjoy the "RIGHTS OF NATURE" to be free from "insult, misery, and death." For him, it was possible to imagine that slavery and the slave trade could exist with protections for slaves against abuse, although in verse he does not describe such a state of affairs. Consistent with his concern to promote the humane treatment of people, Pratt condemned cruelty and lauded benevolence among people touched by the slave trade. "The slave-agent bending o'er his gold . . . Robber at once and butcher of his slaves" is an example of brutality. Later in the poem, by contrast, "Midst the wild waves HUMANITY appears" when Africans save shipwrecked Christian mariners from drowning on the coast. Collins and Morland leave us to wonder if the humane society movement inspired their work. Not Pratt. He opened his poem with a paean to a personified Humanity, who "Drag[s] the pale victim from the

FIGURE 6.2 *African Hospitality*, engraved by John Raphael Smith after George Morland. Courtesy National Museums Liverpool (Maritime Collection).

whelming wave,/And snatch[es] the body from the floating grave." The person who has been restored to life, after thanking God, blesses the proponents of "that glorious institution," the Humane Society.[31]

Historians have explained the crucial role that the dead played in antislavery politics and the humanitarian narrative beginning in the mid- to late eighteenth century. To account for how the dead came to influence antislavery and humanitarianism, they cite evangelicalism, sentimental literature, and humble people's insistence on being recognized at death.[32] Some of those same broad societal developments also shaped the lifesaving cause. One movement did not spur the other. Nonetheless, the lifesaving campaign put drowning—a cause of death endemic in the slave trade—on the philanthropic agenda and made those deaths preventable. Through the humane society movement, people were making their oceangoing world safer and more benign. To some, the enhanced ability to save lives made a trade that took those lives all the more horrific and demanded moral reckoning with it.

There was a dark side, however, to the connection between lifesaving and the slave trade. The same knowledge that could save lives as part of a charitable movement could save them for exploitation. One savvy Londoner recognized not only that advances in lifesaving could be a boon to slave traders, but also that he could make money from them. This inventive and entrepreneurial man was the tallow-chandler William White. In 1790, he patented an improved ventilator. The machine pumped "COOL FRESH AIR" into confined spaces, expelling "STAGNANT" and unhealthful air. It had "the Appearance of a very ornamental Piece of Furniture," White promised, and was available in a model from one foot, ten inches in size costing fifteen guineas to one that was four feet, two inches in diameter and cost thirty-six guineas. To assure would-be buyers of the ventilator's effectiveness, White included testimonials in his marketing materials from gentlemen in the coal-mining business and from voluntary associations including the Royal Humane Society, which had recently drawn attention to the problem of colliers suffocating in mines. In its endorsement, the Society wrote that White's air machine " 'ha[d] been experimentally ascertained to be an effectual destroyer of inflammable air in coal-mines, and other destructive vapours.' " The ventilator, therefore, was " 'the certain preservation of mankind.' " White's target buyers for this lifesaving machine included the owners or managers of "Mines, Ships, Hospitals, Prisons, Workhouses, Slave ships, &c. &c." As he and his contemporaries knew, contagious disease spread or inadequate oxygen killed people in all these spaces.[33]

Marketing lifesaving technology to slave traders made sense. As White recognized, they had great incentives to keep people alive and accordingly they pursued every means to that end. Slavers installed netting and carried larger crews in efforts to prevent captives from jumping overboard, they showed early interest in the new technology of inoculation for smallpox in the first decades of the eighteenth century, and they provided shipboard medical care to ensure that as many Africans as possible arrived at the colonial market alive. The humane society movement gave slave traders additional know-how for preserving lives. On occasion, slavers' crews recovered people from drowning. Witnesses testifying before a parliamentary investigation into the slave trade in 1790 and '91 recounted numerous incidents of captives who jumped overboard and were retrieved. Perhaps the rescuers used equipment invented at the instigation of humane societies and promoted by them. Moreover, as members of the medical profession, slavers' surgeons moved in the circles where the humane society movement disseminated its knowledge, and there are hints that they used the movement's resuscitation techniques on slaving ships. When an African woman hanged herself during the Middle Passage, the surgeon "used the proper means for her recovery," although the woman died. The phrase "proper means" was one used often by men who wrote to the Royal Humane Society to relate their efforts to resuscitate bodies based on the Society's methods. Here it may indicate that the slaver's surgeon tried to revive the woman with the up-to-date, lifesaving movement's methods.[34]

The Royal Humane Society reported one case in which a surgeon involved in the slave trade restored an African to life using the Society's techniques. The incident occurred at Cape Coast Castle, in what is now Ghana, in 1793 or '94. The surgeon at the slave-trading station was "called to visit a black girl of this town, [who was] apparently dead." On her, he "*successfully practised*" the Society's resuscitation method "to the surprise and satisfaction of the parents, and many other bye-standers." The Society later touted this incident, along with the resuscitation of an Indian youth at Hudson's Bay, to herald the likelihood that it would be responsible for the ability to "*sav[e] and preserv[e] life in* every country." Eager to trumpet its cosmopolitan nature, the Society again recounted the Cape Coast Castle case in 1795 and explained that at some unspecified time it had given resuscitation material to the Company of Merchants trading to Africa.[35] Through its efforts, the lifesaving movement helped to make the maritime world less deadly—although not always more humane.

Its technology and techniques could be used by slave traders, but the humane society movement had helped nurture antipathy toward the slave trade in Britain. The same was not true in the United States where antislavery had emerged (though not as a mass cause until the 1830s) before Americans embraced the lifesaving movement. By the time the Massachusetts and Philadelphia Humane Societies were formed, Americans from New England to Virginia were challenging slavery. In 1775, Pennsylvanians set up the world's first antislavery society. Vermont's

1777 constitution prohibited slavery, while judicial decisions in Massachusetts and New Hampshire in the early 1780s ended human bondage in those states. Meanwhile, in 1780, Pennsylvania adopted a gradual emancipation statute as did Connecticut and Rhode Island in 1784. The same year saw New Yorkers form a manumission society. And in Virginia, slaveholders, inspired by Revolutionary ideas and empowered by the 1782 law lifting legal impediments to manumission, freed thousands of their fellow humans during the republic's first two decades.[36]

Not only did antislavery precede humane societies in the United States, but American activists also grappled more with the problem of freeing slaves and the related issue of free blacks' role in society than with ending the slave trade. In this context, the anti-drowning cause would not foster moral revulsion at the slave trade. Instead, the relationship between the lifesaving and antislavery movements in the United States touched upon the central conundrum of antislavery for white Americans: How would free blacks fit into the new republic?[37] Few Northern whites accepted black social equality, but through their treatment of black rescuers and black would-be drowning victims, humane societies publicly endorsed the moral worth of Americans of African descent. They thereby suggested that African Americans might one day be full members of American society.

Like their Dutch and British counterparts, the Massachusetts and Philadelphia humane societies encouraged lifesaving by offering rewards to passersby who rescued or resuscitated victims of drowning or certain other causes of sudden death. A typical case, one that came before the Philadelphia Humane Society, went like this: In mid-January, 1793, two men were in a bateau—a shallow, flat-bottomed boat—on the Delaware when the boat "overset." The two "must inevitably [have] perished" but for the intervention of Benjamin Manly, a ferryman, and Ludwick Khun. In February, six men signed a certificate attesting that Manly and Khun had saved the two men from drowning. The certificate was presented at the March 4 meeting of the Philadelphia Humane Society managers, and Dr. Benjamin Say, one of the group's more active members, was "appointed to enquire into the Case & report to [the] next meeting." Two weeks later, Dr. Say duly reported that he had looked into the incident and verified that Manly and Khun had indeed rescued the two men from drowning. The Philadelphia Humane Society president, Benjamin Rush, was then instructed to "draw on the Treasurer for Six Pounds" and to present the reward to the rescuers.[38]

In Philadelphia, with its growing free black population, and no less in Massachusetts, African Americans were among the rescuers or rescued. The charities did not discriminate either in rewarding black rescuers or in valuing the lives of African Americans. Admittedly, the number of cases in which either rescued or rescuer was black is tiny. Of the eighty-three people rescued in Philadelphia

Humane Society cases, three were black, and of the more than seventy-four rescuers in these cases, two were black. Black or mulatto men also gave assistance in two cases in which the drowning victims died. In Massachusetts Humane Society cases, more than 397 people were aided, and at least six were black or mulatto (that is, six were identified as black or mulatto, but it is possible that people of African descent were among the groups identified, for instance, as "several people" or "39 people"). Two rescuers in Massachusetts cases were identified as black.[39]

"Prompt and spirited" was how observers described the "exertions" of Dolphin Garler. In 1795, the Plymouth, Massachusetts, African American man received the Massachusetts Humane Society's highest reward to an individual for the preceding year. (Three men shared a $17 reward, the highest payout that year.) Around the first of September of 1794, Garler had been at work at a store when there had been a call for help. Passing by a bridge in the town, a man by the name of Captain Churchill had been stopped by a young child who "told that a boy was in the water. Capt. Churchill looking from the wharf, observed a hat swimming on the water, but nothing more." He could get no more information from the child, so he "immediately made an outcry." Garler, a fellow worker, and their employer "repaired to the spot." Bystanders must have been close to despair because "it was nearly high water, and the bottom could not be discerned." Garler and his companions, however, evidently stayed focused because "while they were earnestly looking a bubble was perceived to rise from the bottom." "*Dolphin Garler*, a negro man . . . instantly dived down at the spot from whence the bubble ascended. He rose without the boy. He plunged again" and brought up the eight-year-old-child. "There were no signs of life in him when first brought on shore." Various resuscitation methods were used, including the folk technique of rolling a body on a barrel that humane societies deplored. The boy revived and was "*delivered to his mother.*"[40]

Impressed with his quick and able response to the emergency, Garler's fellow Plymouth residents thought he deserved a reward from the statewide lifesaving charity. Four leading townsmen wrote up the account and sent it in, and the Massachusetts Humane Society gave Garler $10. The size of the reward reflected the circumstances Garler had faced. Humane societies determined premiums based on the danger to the rescuer. The greater the effort and risk by the rescuer, the greater the reward. The status of the rescuer mattered too—somewhat. Gentlemen would not have been offered and would not have accepted monetary rewards. Unlike their British counterparts, American humane societies did not stress giving premiums as a means of inducing the unfeeling lower sorts to help people in distress.[41] With the exception that gentlemen would not be given pecuniary rewards, the American societies did not hammer home hierarchy rhetorically or monetarily. Garler received the biggest single reward one year. The following year, another black rescuer's premium was in the middle of the pack.[42]

Dolphin Garler's race did not affect the reward he received, but it did shape his public recognition. Each year, the Massachusetts Humane Society catalogued the premiums it paid in the appendices to its annual discourses. In general, the Society related little more than who was involved and how much the reward was. During the 1790s, the annual reports also sometimes carried letters that posed questions about resuscitation in cases where attempts had not been successful. Letters recommending rescuers for honors were typically not included, but in 1795, the account of the Garler case was printed with commentary. The Massachusetts Humane Society men assured their fellow members that the incident had been recounted "by some of the most respectable characters in *Plymouth*."[43] In other words, the story of the heroic black laborer was believable. This comment was as much about class as race. Rescuers were typically working men, and it was standard practice for humane societies—ever concerned, as were other charities, to allay worries about fraud—to note the respectability of the people who attested to rescues.[44] For their part, the Plymouth worthies who nominated Garler for a reward pointed out that he was black and thus different, and they indicated that he was not their social equal by referring to him merely as "Dolphin."[45] Yet the Society's outsized attention to him made a political statement.

At a time when many white Americans assumed that free blacks were debased and disorderly and therefore threats to the health of the republic, showcasing Garler's valor and humaneness said that African Americans could be worthy members of society.[46] In the post-Revolutionary years, Americans—white and black, men and women—invested great importance in philanthropy. They looked to benevolence to bind citizens to one another, to the republic, and to foreigners. American women, like their counterparts abroad, also carved out public roles through humanitarian activity. African Americans staked claims to full inclusion in American society by setting up aid societies to care for their own. They too were responsible, respectable, and charitable, their groups proclaimed. They belonged. Black leaders Richard Allen and Absalom Jones of Philadelphia had sought to underline that message by succoring victims, white and black alike, of the 1793 yellow fever epidemic in the City of Brotherly Love. Based on the mistaken belief that Africans were immune to yellow fever, Benjamin Rush had asked Allen to arrange for black Philadelphians to nurse fever patients. In hopes that African Americans' service would win white Americans' esteem and advance the cause of black equality, Allen and Jones agreed. Instead of being praised, however, African Americans were vilified. They stole things from homes in the deserted city, some said, and they asked too much for their nursing work to boot. The black lower sorts had prowled and looted the city, prominent printer Mathew Carey charged in a pamphlet about the city's experience of the epidemic. They were unsuited for citizenship.[47]

Richard Allen and Absalom Jones responded to Carey's slander with a pamphlet of their own. The black community, they maintained, had behaved altruistically during the crisis. Some African Americans had taken nothing for aiding fever victims while others had charged but little. Some had even given their lives caring for others. The public spirit and fellow feeling that Africans Americans had displayed in the epidemic, Allen and Jones suggested, showed that blacks were qualified for citizenship.[48]

The men who voted the ample reward to Dolphin Garler may or may not have known about the dispute over black Philadelphians' behavior during the yellow fever epidemic. (Allen and Jones's pamphlet was familiar to some activists on both sides of the Atlantic.)[49] Whether they knew about the controversy or not, the Massachusetts Humane Society trustees believed—with Carey, Allen, Jones, and many others—that they could judge people's civic fitness through their moral responsibility to others. As they understood it, a poor man who saved another was a "noble-spirited citizen."[50] By lavishing attention on Garler's heroism, then, the Massachusetts leaders were taking the stand that African Americans could meet the demands of republican citizenship.

Whatever the elite whites thought, what Dophin Garler thought about all the fuss is probably lost to time. For James Forten, the wealthy black Philadelphia sailmaker and antislavery leader, however, being honored by a humane society was a source of pride. In 1821, the Philadelphia Humane Society recognized Forten with a certificate—not a monetary reward, which would have been insulting given his status—for having saved the lives of twelve people in various incidents. Forten hung the certificate in his parlor and told one visitor he would not give it up for $1,000.[51]

Through the rewards they gave black rescuers, humane societies backed African American claims to be reliable members of republican society. Similarly, when African Americans were rescued from drowning, the charities valued black lives just as they did white lives. In 1809, thirteen-year-old Robert Anderson tumbled into the Delaware at the Vine Street wharf. Young Anderson was in grave danger because he had fallen "behind several tiers of corded wood which prevented his being seen by the people on the wharf. He could not swim." Thankfully, "his strugglings were seen by some boys at the end of a wharf below Vine street, who gave the alarm. Several men ran to the place pointed out by the boys, but the lad had sunk, the fingers of one hand were perceived just as he was sinking." People tried to help. "A young man who was bathing was at a distance swam to the place, & dove down, but missed him." Anderson "was searched for with a long pole, but could not be found." By now, the crowd must have been losing hope. But then, "George Muschert, sailmaker, heard the alarm while at work in his sail loft, & ran to the place, & dived under the water with all his clothes on, & also missed him, but observing some bubbles coming up he dove down a second time," and, finally, at long last, Muschert, "brought up the lad." He "was apparently lifeless, having been under the water as near as can be judged 8 or 10 minutes," but after bystanders and a doctor used various resuscitation methods, Anderson revived. The Philadelphia Humane Society, informed that "without [Muschert's] extraordinary & highly meritorious exertions the child must have died," voted the rescuer $10.[52]

Muschert received a large reward because of the danger he took in rescuing Robert Anderson, regardless of the boy's race. Likewise, in other cases where the rescued person was black or mulatto, race did not factor into the amount of the humane societies' rewards. The only criteria were the usual considerations of level of effort by and risk to the rescuer. In contrast to the dramatic Anderson case, a case of the mulatto infant in Massachusetts in 1803–04 is described as three men "taking a newborn mulatto Child out of the water." That phrase "taking a . . . Child out of the water" suggests the baby was near water's edge or somehow positioned to make the rescue easy; thus the men shared $4.[53] A cluster of Massachusetts Humane Society rewards in 1802–03 for the rescue of African Americans underscores that black and white lives were valued equivalently. A total of eighteen rewards were given that year. There were four $5 rewards, one for a black man and three for people were presumably white. There was only one $1 reward and it was for the rescue of a black man, but it was nearly matched by a $1.25 premium to someone who had saved a (presumably) white person's life. And there were matching $2 rewards to people who, in separate incidents, had saved the lives of a mulatto boy and a white boy. When African Americans were saved, humane societies used the rewards they gave to proclaim the equal worth of black and white lives.[54]

Humane societies' impartial approach to charity mattered deeply to their leaders and members. "It matters not if the Sufferer be remote, an Alien, an Outlaw, or even an Enemy. No difference of colour or climate, Nation, political arrangement of religion, or peculiar manners, form any obstacle to your benevolence," the speaker at the 1799 Massachusetts Humane Society festival reminded the group's members.[55] The leaders of other humane societies on both sides of the Atlantic echoed those views. All lives, they and the charities' supporters affirmed, deserved to be saved.

The Search for a Postwar Partnership

All lives deserved to be saved, but what did one do about that in practice? The Massachusetts Humane Society leaders pondered that question and also the implications of American independence as they sought to respond to a near-disaster that came to light in April 1788. The trouble began seven months earlier, in November of 1787, when a storm drove a vessel returning from Newfoundland to Newburyport, Massachusetts, onto the remote Sable Isle in the North Atlantic. Later in the month, another ship, the leaking and badly battered schooner *George* under a Captain Chadwell, sailing from Antigua to Ile St. Jean (later Prince Edward Island), had landed on the island. For months, neither party knew the other was there. Conditions were terrible. The men of the *George* were so near starvation that they were about ready to eat a dying companion. Finally, a month after landing, they caught and ate seals and had the strength to build a shelter. The other crew also had put up a shelter and, like their fellow sufferers, lived on seals, horses, and cranberries. In late January, the crews came upon each other and from then on cooperated in their survival efforts until American vessels rescued and relieved the men in April 1788.[56]

For the Massachusetts Humane Society, the sailors' plight created a golden opportunity. By providing for seamen shipwrecked on the island, the recently founded group could win public attention—if it could first win the help of the Royal Humane Society. In the mid-1780s, men like Benjamin Rush and John Coakley Lettsom had felt out the basis for their philanthropic partnership with now-foreigners. Cooperation between individuals, who often had met in person or had friends in common, differed from cooperation among organizations that in some way represented their state or nation. Starting in the late 1780s, as they sought to do something about Sable Isle, the Massachusetts Humane Society men wrestled with how the charity could work with a British counterpart. As they did, they found themselves grappling with the rupture in the British Atlantic community.

Shipwrecks on Sable Isle, actually a thirty-mile long, shifting sand dune, were a long-standing problem. As the Massachusetts government put it in 1738, the island was "so situated as it often happens, that Ships and other Vessels are unfortunately cast on said Island." In 1774, "a tea ship from London to Halifax, was lost on the isle of Sable, and every soul perished." The crew of the brig *Telemachus*, carrying a cargo of rice and tobacco from Georgia to Amsterdam in 1786, was luckier. The ship "was cast away" on the island and the vessel and cargo lost, but "the men were saved." Because of its remote location, people who were cast ashore on the island might die "for want of Food and other Necessaries there." To remedy that problem, Massachusetts had lent support in 1738 to a settlement on the island; the settlers were to provide "Subsistence and Relief" to anyone shipwrecked on the island. (The government's support consisted of approving the idea and forbidding Massachusetts residents from killing or stealing the livestock of settlers.) During the American Revolution, however, the families who lived on the island, "being plundered and harassed by the hostile parties," had left.[57]

In 1788, the problem of castaways on the island returned to public attention. News about the two crews' ordeals received widespread coverage in American newspapers and brought Sable Isle to the Massachusetts Humane Society's notice.[58] In the months before the near-calamity, the Society had already taken up the task of succoring shipwrecked mariners in Massachusetts. To shelter crews in distress, the Society had begun building huts along the state's coastline.[59] Finding a way to aid people marooned on Sable Isle, therefore, would not merely expand the geographic scope of the Society's work. It might also bring the young charity attention and accolades. What the Massachusetts Humane Society trustees seemed to have forgotten, or maybe it just took time to grasp all the implications of withdrawing from the British empire, was that Sable Isle was now foreign territory.

The Massachusetts Humane Society appointed a committee, chaired by merchant Thomas Russell, to consider how to go about settling families on the island to assist shipwrecked mariners. In October 1788, the committee issued its report. Sable Isle, the committee said, needed "several houses or families to answer the benevolent purposes intended by this Society." The young charity, however, lacked the necessary funds. Therefore, the committee urged "that [the project] ought to be made a governmental or national concern." John Hancock, then governor of Massachusetts, was thought to own much of the island, and so the Society asked him to intervene with the state or federal government to secure funds for the project. As requested, Hancock sent an appeal for help, drafted by Thomas Russell's committee, to Congress. The appeal inadvertently identified the stumbling block the Society would hit in its Sable Isle project. "Though this Island is situated in a foreign kingdom," it noted, "yet it would be no less advantageous to the navigation of the United States, than to that of other commercial nations" "to place a Light House, and a few families there."[60] True enough, but the fact that the island was now "situated in a foreign kingdom" made the Society's effort to aid mariners castaway there an international undertaking. Massachusetts and one of its most prominent families had long had close ties to Sable Isle, but American independence, the Society's trustees only belatedly realized, had entirely changed their relationship to the island, which remained British.[61]

Once the Massachusetts Humane Society men recognized the international dimensions of the project, they sought to collaborate on it with foreign partners. The trustees discussed the matter with the commander of a British naval vessel then in Boston harbor and with "some influential citizens of Halifax [Nova Scotia]." The appeal to the Nova Scotians must have seemed promising. A Halifax newspaper in July 1787, according to Massachusetts Humane Society records, had opined that due to the frequent shipwrecks on Sable Island, "some steps should be taken by government to settle a family or two there. . . . [T]here cannot be a doubt, that New England States would cheerfully join" an effort to protect property and lives. Nothing, however, came of either effort.[62]

The third party that the Massachusetts Humane Society turned to was the Royal Humane Society. The two societies had begun exchanging materials and publicizing each other's work soon after the founding of the Massachusetts group. Such communication was typical in the humane society movement with its mission of furthering knowledge of lifesaving. From its founding, the Royal Humane Society had published communications about lifesaving from far and wide and made itself a clearinghouse for information in the cause. Most common were letters from around the British Isles discussing rescues or resuscitations. But the London charity also included news of new societies and of innovations in lifesaving, poems, extracts of sermons, and more from the British Isles, Europe, and starting in the mid-1780s, America.[63] In its 1787 annual report, the Royal Humane Society for the first time incorporated material from a counterpart in the United States. Reprinting a passage from the Reverend John Lathrop's sermon at the Massachusetts Humane Society anniversary festival that year, the London group made the flattering comment that the American cleric's comments might lead to "Humane Societies being established in other parts abroad, as well as in many sea ports, &c. in Great Britain" that lacked lifesaving groups.[64]

With a relationship established, the Massachusetts Humane Society turned to the leading British humane society for help with Sable Isle. The Massachusetts men were sure that their London counterparts would agree that "the preservation of the lives of shipwrecked seamen" was as much part of the societies' shared mission as resuscitating apparently dead folks. Working together, the two societies would be able to redress a problem that affected not only Americans but also people from all maritime countries. In 1789, therefore, the Massachusetts Humane Society asked the Royal Humane Society for its "attention and assistance" on the Sable Isle problem.[65]

The Royal Humane Society ignored that request. Three years later, the Massachusetts Humane Society took advantage of the opportunity for one of its members, Amos Windship, to appeal for help in person when he visited London. While there for business, Windship attended the 1792 Royal Humane Society anniversary festival, held on March 1, and addressed the crowd. The Bostonian drew his listeners' attention to Sable Isle, where mariners, he explained, were cast away "with nothing left them, but the liberty of complaining." His group's funds were "small." But the Massachusetts Humane Society would "be highly gratified, to second a proposition" by the London Humane Society to care for seamen stranded on the island. In other words, the American charity expected the British group to lead.[66]

Again the Royal Humane Society ignored the Massachusetts group's request. To the New Englanders' thinking, aiding shipwrecked mariners was a natural extension of the lifesaving movement's mission, Sable Isle was problem shared by maritime nations, and the prominent London charity was in a position to take charge of the project. The Massachusetts Humane Society, however, had misjudged matters in several ways. First, by appealing to the Royal Humane Society to cooperate on Sable Isle, the Massachusetts men had tried to redefine the Londoners' program. The Royal Humane Society often boasted that it benefited Britain by saving the lives of drowning mariners. But, unlike the Massachusetts group, it did not understand its program as including sheltering shipwrecked seamen. The Massachusetts men assumed that their London counterparts would share the New Englanders' broad understanding of the mission of lifesaving. The Royal Humane Society, however, operated as part of the most highly elaborated charitable infrastructure in the Anglophone world. When, in 1782, the new Fire Company of London had donated one hundred guineas to pay rewards to rescuers of children or infirm people in "Danger of perishing by Fire," the Royal Humane Society resolved that that idea was "not consistent with the original plan of this Institution" and returned the Fire Company's money. In other parts of the Anglophone Atlantic world, charities added new programs to existing institutions, but in London the expectation was that new programs required separate institutions.[67]

The Massachusetts Humane Society trustees were also mistaken in thinking that the Royal Humane Society would fork over funds for the Sable Isle project. The London charity had spent thousands of pounds over the years to distribute printed materials and lifesaving equipment to found new societies. It only paid rewards for lifesaving efforts, however, within certain—changing, generally with donations—geographical limits, and each year it spent almost all of its income, including some investment income. When the Royal Humane Society decided to build receiving houses where half-dead bodies could be brought for resuscitation, it had to undertake a capital campaign for the new program. For the group to give financial support for settling families on Sable Isle was unlikely. Finally, if the Massachusetts men had hoped their London friends would lobby the British government for help with Sable Isle, it was wrong again. For years, the Royal Humane Society had hoped for parliamentary support to help it realize its goal of being established as a national institution. Parliament, however, did not accede to its requests on that count, and the group would presumably not have thought it wise to lobby Parliament, even if it wanted to, about a project that originated in the former colony that had been the hotbed of rebellion.[68]

It was as if that rebellion had never taken place, as if the United States had not declared independence. At first, it had not dawned on the Massachusetts men that Sable Isle, so long a part of their world, was now a foreign territory. That oversight was not the only way they had not yet fully adapted to independence. The Americans were also asking to cooperate with British colleagues in a way that was no longer possible. When American and British philanthropists had collaborated—as in the missionary charities—before the Revolution, Americans had run operations locally but Britons had held the power of the purse. Their cooperation rested on the presumption that Americans were junior partners in benevolent projects as they were in the empire. Americans had chafed at their inferior position to the point that as the imperial crisis deepened, they rejected a charity, the Society for the Promotion of Religious Knowledge, that had been increasing in support in the colonies because it had offered Americans an equal role. Now, however, the Massachusetts men were attempting to recreate that old colonial relationship. In part, they had no choice since Sable Isle was British. But Americans were also used to deferring to Britons—in science, fashion, and culture in general.[69] In their effort to address the Sable Isle problem, however, the Americans learned that the old model of transatlantic philanthropic partnership no longer applied. Americans were junior partners no more.

American Leadership, Transatlantic Reconciliation

Thomas Russell had resented Americans' subordinate position in the British empire. Before the Revolution, he had flourished as a merchant thanks to his strong relationship with an English firm. But the restrictions of the Navigation Acts still rankled, and he was an early supporter of the Patriot cause. Independence made it possible and, to Russell's mind, necessary for Americans to "explor[e] new channels of commerce." He therefore pioneered the United States' trade with Russia and he also traded with the East Indies. His mercantile leadership, one friend thought, set an example for other Americans.[70]

His fellow philanthropists recognized Russell as a leader too. The Bostonian's success in business enabled him to be "unbounded" in his charitable giving. The Massachusetts Humane Society, the American Academy of Arts and Sciences, the Boston Marine Society, the Massachusetts Congregational Charitable Society, and the Massachusetts Charitable Fire Society all received generous

FIGURE 6.3   Portrait of Thomas Russell by Edward Greene Malbone, c. 1796, water-color on ivory, after a portrait by John Trumbull. Courtesy, Yale University Art Gallery.

support from him. Fellow members rewarded his largess, and his investments of time, by electing him president of the Humane Society (in 1790), the Society for the Advice of Immigrants, the Massachusetts Agricultural Society, the Society for the Propagating the Gospel among Indians and Others in North America as well as the Boston Chamber of Commerce.[71]

All the organizations mattered to him, but it was the Humane Society he cherished most. He believed in the "godlike design of preserving life" and, in particular, this merchant who dispatched seamen across the globe and who knew "the precarious nature of property" favored the Society's efforts—the sheltering huts along the Massachusetts coast—to aid "the ship-wreck'd mariner." Extending the Society's aid to sailors stranded on Sable Isle moved him too. He had chaired the committee that had studied the Sable Isle issue and sought a way for the cash-strapped charity to "sav[e] the lives and property of those cast on shore on said Island."[72] The Royal Humane Society's refusal to assist in that project—to succor strangers as the Frenchman in Martinique had helped him—can only have been dismaying.

Perhaps Russell thought he could push the Royal Humane Society to collaborate on Sable Isle. Or perhaps by the summer of 1792, he had had enough
and wanted to declare, not independence, but equality with the British group.
That August, several months after Amos Windship's visit to the Royal Humane
Society festival, Russell sent the London charity a sizable donation of £100. He
was, he explained, "particularly interested in the encouragement of HUMANE
SOCIETIES *throughout the world*." In his letter accompanying the gift, Russell
was complimentary. Your group "does great honour to Human Nature," he said.
He also, following polite conventions, was deferential. "We shall," he hoped,
"imitate your virtues ... by establishing" a variety of charitable institutions
much as Britons had done. In addition, Russell was suitably modest; he was giving his "mite" and asked, moreover, that it be "little known." But by sending his
donation to the Royal Humane Society, Russell was also being assertive. A philanthropist from your former colonies, so long reliant on British financial support, can bestow a gift on you, his £100 said. His comment about encouraging
humane societies *"throughout the world"* emphasized one more thing. Even if you
are not interested in helping with Sable Isle, remember that lifesaving is a cause
that knows no borders. Russell was not trying to break ties with his assertiveness
but to build them. He wanted to build them, however, on the basis of mutual
respect. The Royal Humane Society had long worked to spread the resuscitation
movement. Now they would do it thanks to the largess of a citizen of an "infant
country."[73] An infant, *independent* country, that is.

Russell was not alone in his frustration that the Royal Humane Society had
rebuffed the request for help with Sable Isle. Around the same time that he made
his gift, the Massachusetts Humane Society trustees decided to take a new tack
with their London counterparts. In mid-1792, the Society named three leaders
of the Royal Humane Society—the Earl of Stamford, President; John Coakley
Lettsom, Treasurer; and William Hawes, Register—as honorary members. The
Massachusetts Humane Society's initial constitution had not provided for honorary members, but around 1792, the group amended its rules to allow them.
Honorary members could not live in Massachusetts, and three-quarters of the
trustees had to vote for their admission.[74]

Besides the Londoners, the Society named another honorary member, the
Reverend Andrew Brown, who the Massachusetts men probably hoped would
help address Sable Isle. Brown, a Scotsman who devoted years to writing but
never finishing a history of North America, served as a clergyman in Halifax,
Nova Scotia, from 1787 to 1795. In 1791, he visited Boston and spent time with
several leading Massachusetts Humane Society members. Two years later,
the Society made the Nova Scotia cleric an honorary member. In his letter of
thanks, he promised he would try to set up a humane society in Halifax, and the

prominent mention of Brown in the newspaper announcement of the 1794 formation of the Halifax Marine Humane Society suggests that he kept his word.[75]
It seems likely that by honoring Brown and the three Royal Humane Society
leaders, the Massachusetts Humane Society hoped to win their cooperation on
the Sable Isle project. The New Englanders never did undertake a joint Sable Isle
project with colleagues in London or Nova Scotia, but in 1801, the Nova Scotian
government established a lifesaving station called the Humane Establishment
on the island. (The Humane Establishment was in existence until 1959, by which
point new navigational technology had basically eliminated the danger of shipwrecks on the island.)[76]

The Massachusetts men had not been able to win the precise cooperation they
wanted, but they succeeded in changing the nature of the relationship between
the Massachusetts and London humane societies. No longer mere followers,
the Americans had become leaders too. Within months of Russell's gift and the
Massachusetts Humane Society's honoring of the three Royal Humane Society
leaders, the London group began naming honorary life governors of its own. In
its annual reports, the Royal Humane Society had previously recognized people
who had given generous gifts by noting "extraordinary donations." In emulation
of the Massachusetts group, the London charity distinguished its special friends
as honorary life governors, with Thomas Russell the first person to be named.
From 1793 on, the London group prominently listed honorary governors in its
annual reports. Over the years, the two groups would name other national and
foreign honorary governors, and other humane societies would follow suit.[77]

The Massachusetts Humane Society had initiated this new practice in part
out of frustration over their relationship with the Royal Humane Society, but
the Americans were also contesting exclusive British claims to universal philanthropy. Britons had embraced a liberal humanitarian ethos in the wake of
the American Revolution as they sought to burnish Britain's reputation and to
adapt to an even more heterogeneous empire. Abolitionism, paternalism toward
Loyalists and toward British subjects in India, and John Howard's prison reform
efforts told Britons that they and their empire were distinctly, if not uniquely,
benevolent, cosmopolitan, and responsible.[78] Americans had challenged that
outlook when they celebrated John Howard as a citizen of the world. Now they
more forcefully insisted on a shared culture of universal benevolence.

Honorary memberships were one part of that effort. So too were the messages
in the Massachusetts Humane Society's missives to the Royal Humane Society.
We would like to continue cooperating "in this common cause of humanity,"
noted the Society's first request for help with Sable Isle.[79] Best wishes in "*your*
endeavours*" (emphasis added) "in the common cause of philanthropic benevolence," said the letter announcing the naming of the three Royal Humane Society

leaders as Massachusetts Humane Society honorary members.[80] Similarly, the way the Massachusetts Humane Society presented itself publicly proclaimed equality in the pursuit of universal benevolence. The New Englanders—like their Philadelphia counterparts—had initially presented the Society as emulating European leaders. (Indeed, the men who founded the London humane society had likewise explained they were eager to keep up with continental peers.) In its earliest publications, the Massachusetts Humane Society had merely cited British and continental authorities. By honoring foreign and faraway friends and, starting in 1793, publishing letters it received from the London and Philadelphia humane societies along with the list of honorary members, the Massachusetts Humane Society publicly repositioned itself as allied with, not trailing, organizations and individuals elsewhere in a shared undertaking for the good of humanity.[81]

The Massachusetts Humane Society's new self-presentation was about more than the world of charity. Its shift belonged to a broader trend among Americans in the post-Revolutionary period as they positioned the new nation in the world. In the 1780s and '90s, Americans used voluntary organizations to espouse a cosmopolitan approach to their relations with foreigners. They did so by writing constitutions for some humanitarian organizations that explicitly envisioned and allowed for the participation of foreign members. Many groups did not address the issue of foreigners' eligibility for membership. Perhaps most assumed there was no need: Public subscription charities took money from all comers, and unlike the need to delimit recipients of charities, no purpose would be served by specifying the boundaries of eligibility for membership. Some groups, however, explicitly allowed for foreign members. The Pennsylvania and Delaware abolition societies provided that foreigners or people resident in other states could become corresponding members. They would not have to pay annual dues, but would be entitled to attend "the meetings of the society during their residence in the state." When the Humane Society of the State of New York was founded in 1794, it provided that both Americans and foreigners could become members.[82] Foreigners or out-of-state residents, all these groups took as given, would be aware of them, would feel a stake in their missions, would be interested in joining, and, in some cases, could have a role in governance.

This trend was not solely American. By 1780, the Scots Society of Norwich, England—later known as the Society of Universal Good-will—specified that people of all nations could join, as befitted its global mission. The Royal Humane Society, though it did not have a formal provision on the matter, allowed foreigners to become members: To a German supporter of the London group, this practice was notable and praiseworthy.[83] Not a uniquely American trend, then, but a cosmopolitan approach to philanthropic participation appealed especially to Americans in the late 1780s and 1790s for reasons beyond beneficence. During those years, Americans put in place a new structure, the federal Constitution, to govern relations among the states. Meanwhile, the new United States sought to build alliances with foreign nations. Moreover, once the French Revolution began, Americans watched it closely. Then once the French Revolutionary Wars had broken out in Europe, they debated fiercely what the young country's foreign policy should be, even forming political parties based on those views. In short, relations among states were of paramount importance to Americans in these years. By writing constitutions that allowed for participation without regard to nationality, they were attempting to remake the conduct of relations among peoples and nations on an open basis in pursuit of peace and human welfare.[84]

The Massachusetts Humane Society's naming of honorary members belonged to this post-Revolutionary trend of reimagining the nature of the Atlantic community. Like their fellow members of the British Atlantic world, the New Englanders had grown up familiar with the political valence of philanthropy. In the postwar years, they continued to assume that philanthropic activity had a political import, as they revealed in a 1792 letter to the French National Assembly. A Frenchman had saved the life of someone in Massachusetts and had been honored by the Massachusetts Humane Society. The French consul in Boston had forwarded the news to the National Assembly and the Assembly had then written to the Society exulting the honor done its citizen. The Massachusetts Humane Society responded with an ebullient letter that wove together politics and philanthropy and elevated the charity's relationship with the French Assembly to the level of diplomacy. "The Society" is working to "relieve the unfortunate" and is glad that the French nation is now too embracing pacific principles, it said. "We"—the Society—"behold, with rapture, the French and the American nations, inspired with the same ardour for human happiness," the charity went on, "and feeling the most intimate alliance with Frenchmen, we will only try to emulate them, in the glorious work of restoring the whole world to the situation of one great family, dwelling in peace, liberty, and safety." Along with the letter, the Society sent their pamphlets to give to the president of the National Assembly.[85]

The Massachusetts Humane Society trustees' approach to beneficence was shared by fellow Americans who otherwise differed greatly in politics and culture. The Quaker-influenced Pennsylvania Abolition Society, the short-lived Humane Society of the State of New York with its ties to the Democratic-Republicans, and the Massachusetts Humane Society in largely Federalist and Congregationalist Boston alike sought to model new transatlantic relationships through their ties to foreigners or foreign organizations. "The preservation of human life, and the advancement of useful knowledge, we trust," the Massachusetts Humane

Society told its London counterpart in 1795, "will ever unite our Societies"—
and, implicitly, our societies—"in the more permanent bonds of friendship."[86]
No longer based on imperial rule, the transatlantic community would now, in
the New Englanders' view, be united through amicable cooperation in the cause
of humanity.

The "more permanent bonds of friendship" were not what William Hawes, the
Royal Humane Society's founder and most energetic leader, had wanted. Certainly
he had a cosmopolitan bent. No one had done more to spread the humane society
movement far and wide than he had. But what his heart had long been set on was
a national lifesaving institution. He had broached the idea in a 1782 pamphlet.
Hawes's elaborate plan envisioned government-established receiving houses
in every parish where half-drowned people could be treated. He even pressed
Parliament to set up a school "for studying the Art of restoring Animation," with
classes for medical men and separate classes for the general public. There would be
no such school and no such national body.[87] Ignored by Parliament and pushed
by overseas counterparts, Hawes and his fellow Royal Humane Society supporters instead found themselves not only to be pursuing a universal mission but to be
pursuing it in partnership with their erstwhile compatriots.

    Like other humane societies founded before the late 1780s, the Royal Humane
Society had not started out with a worldwide mission. Yes, the Londoners and
the leaders of other humane societies had looked beyond their shores when they
emulated foreign peers. The Royal Humane Society had gone farther by trying to
found lifesaving groups around the British Atlantic, and the societies exchanged
information to advance knowledge of resuscitation. Nevertheless, the groups
aimed to save lives locally. With Britain at war much of its first decade, the
Royal Humane Society, in particular, stressed the goal of becoming established
throughout the kingdom.[88]

    The end of war itself did not change the Royal Humane Society's mission.
Rather, what changed it were the Society's interactions with new humane societies overseas and especially in the United States. The two decades following
the Peace of Paris saw a surge in the formation of new lifesaving charities. Nine
communities in the Anglophone world had established the groups (though the
charities did not always survive long) before 1783. Between 1784 and 1805, at least
thirty-two new humane societies were set up or re-established in the British Isles
and empire and the United States or were launched by Britons abroad, while
a few groups were established in Europe with Royal Humane Society help.
(A handful more were founded around 1807. The movement had a final growth
spurt around 1815.)[89]

FIGURE 6.4 This idealized image depicts a man recuperating in a Royal Humane Society receiving-house after being resuscitated by William Hawes and John Coakley Lettsom. Engraving by Robert Pollard, after Robert Smirke, 1787. Wellcome Library, London.

The new societies, particularly those in overseas British dominions and in the United States, taught the Royal Humane Society of its expanding reach. The Royal Humane Society's beneficence touched Portugal, Jamaica, and elsewhere, the energetic men who launched rescue and resuscitation groups in those places told the group. In many cases, the Society had sent lifesaving apparatuses and materials to help get the new charities started. The Royal Humane Society was, therefore, reasonably accurate when it boasted that new societies had "been established in consequence of every necessary assistance" provided by the London group.[90] The men, such as Charles Murray, who founded the faraway humane societies, did so on their own initiative. But when Murray, the British consul in Madeira (and a cousin of John Murray of the Society of Universal Good-will), introduced the movement to Portugal in 1787, he lauded William Hawes and, by implication, the Royal Humane Society for their charitable concern for the Portuguese along with the rest of mankind. Closing his letter with his hope "that the blessed effects of the labours of the Humane Society may be extended to all the human race," Murray underlined his view that the London charity's proper ambit was worldwide.[91]

Like Charles Murray and other Britons overseas, Americans also emphasized that the Royal Humane Society was pursuing a shared, universal mission
with far-flung, fellow philanthropists. Although the message was by and large
the same, it took on added meaning coming from former colonials. Before the
American Revolution, Protestant bonds had helped make the fractious British
Atlantic world a community. In the years following the war, Protestantism could
no longer serve that end because each party to the imperial crisis had betrayed
their common Protestantism during the conflict—the British with the Quebec
Act and the Americans by allying with the French. Protestant ecumenicalism,
however, had laid a base for the broader concept of universal benevolence, and
in the 1780s and '90s, Americans turned instead to cosmopolitan ideals—the
Massachusetts Humane Society's appeals to "the common cause of humanity" is
but one example—as they built a new relationship as foreigners of their former
fellow nationals.[92]

Among American humane societies, the Massachusetts group had an especially important effect on the Royal Humane Society, not only because of the
political import of its communication, but also because it was a reliable partner.
The London and Massachusetts groups exchanged letters, sermons, and pamphlets yearly. Both charities drew on each other's materials in their own publications and orations, but the Royal Humane Society took particular advantage of
this source of copy for its annual reports. Indeed, from the late 1780s to the early
1800s, the London charity quoted from the Massachusetts Humane Society's
materials more often than it did any other group. Transatlantic collaboration
filled the place of the Royal Humane Society's unattained national institution.

The emphasis on universal benevolence, and not only by other resuscitation
advocates, changed the Royal Humane Society. In 1788, the Society pointed to
the example of John Howard to make the point that philanthropy should be
expansive.[93] But the liberal ideals invoked by other members of the lifesaving
movement mattered more because they were coupled with other developments
such as the strong partnership with the Massachusetts Humane Society. The
London charity had not wholly shunned catholic concerns before the mid-1780s
but universalist terms had been used only occasionally. As it began to hear more
and more from distant collaborators, the Society's choice of language and focus
changed. By 1790, the Royal Humane Society began its annual report by hailing
each of its supporters as a "Philanthropist and [a] Citizen of the World." And in
1793, in response to Thomas Russell's gift, the prominent British charity endorsed
John Coakley Lettsom's view that "The good thus done by [the Society] is not
merely the saving life, . . . but the *diffusion of humanity* becomes an extended
focus of action, beyond the boundaries of province or kingdom, happily uniting
in mutual interests the stranger and the citizen."[94]

Uniting : . . . the stranger and the citizen. As the Royal Humane Society saw it, the movement was doing no less than rebuilding the transatlantic community as its members practiced universal benevolence. Humane societies gave rewards for lifesaving without regard to the background of the person rescued. That is, the societies and their members emulated the Good Samaritan by caring for people impartially. Moreover, because of the cooperation among humane societies, all humane societies and their members furthered each other's impact. By working within their own communities but cooperating as citizens of the world, activists meshed the traditional imperative to practice charity locally with the universal impulses that waxed strong in the wake of the Anglo-American crisis of community. But the importance of this cooperation went farther. After initial missteps in the relationship, the Massachusetts Humane Society men had established a strong partnership with the Royal Humane Society on the Americans' terms. They had successfully challenged the exclusive claims to universal humanitarianism that Britons made in their celebrations of John Howard. The London and Massachusetts humane societies' common aims, William Hawes acknowledged in an echo of the Americans' comment to him, would "ever unite our Societies in the most permanent bonds of friendship." Invited into the movement by a visiting Briton, Americans made universal philanthropy a force for reconciliation across the Atlantic.[95]

7

Ambivalent Cosmopolites

IN THE 1780s and '90s, men, and increasingly women, knit the pre-Revolutionary Atlantic community of their youth back together through philanthropy. Even as they did, a "storm . . . rage[d]" that threatened the amicable feelings. "Another fruitless, bloody, & most dangerous war" was how James Currie described the last conflict between the British and French empires. He hoped that the United States at least would stay "at peace." "No man can predict," he commented, how the French Revolutionary Wars would end.[1]

No one could predict the outcome, but Currie and his fellow philanthropists had seen turmoil coming. John Coakley Lettsom, thinking in 1791 that Britain might go to war against Russia, worried about the impact on the lower sorts. "The cry of the poor is not heard in the loud cry of the Minister for *Revenue, Revenue, Revenue*," he lamented. John Lathrop was more hopeful in his forecast of the coming years. In 1790, before Louis XVI was executed and before war or the Terror began, he expected that "an effort to . . . break the chains which had held the French in bondage for ages past, must shake the whole kingdom." If "those sufferings" were the price of liberty, however, he felt "reconciled" to them.[2]

Britons were not so sanguine. From the high-born to the lowly, most Britons opposed the French Revolution and feared that it could infect their country. British supporters of the Revolution were "proscribed and prosecuted," as one radical who emigrated to the United States put it. Their fellow subjects ostracized or, in the worst cases, attacked them, while the government repressed dissidents through the legal system. In spite of the widespread hostility to the Revolution, many Britons doubted the wisdom of the war.[3] To John Coakley Lettsom, the "present useless crusades" Britain was fighting "in favour of [its allies] Austria and Russia" were "unwise and impolitic."[4] As he had anticipated, the poor suffered from renewed fighting. Harvest failures in the mid-1790s conspired with the wartime disruptions to raise the price of wheat to prohibitive heights. Food rioting spiked with widespread hunger. Victories by Napoleon's armies in Europe in 1796–97 and fear of invasion added to Britons' anxieties. Moreover, mass meetings against the government, an attack on the king's coach in 1795, and naval mutinies in the spring of 1797 expressed the frustrations of the lower sorts, stoked fears among the well-off, and led to further repression. The abortive 1798 rebellion by United Irishmen who had expected French help deepened the sense of disorder throughout the British Isles.[5]

Like Britain, the United States was strained by the French Revolution and the resulting ferment throughout the Atlantic world. Americans initially had widely celebrated the French efforts "to break the yoke of oppression."[6] But as the Revolution's violence increased, the American consensus fractured along the emerging party lines. Federalists like John Lathrop—who wrote with "warmth" on the topic because he "knew some of the men who [were] disgraced and executed"—deplored the "the wild and extravagant conduct of the *Jacobins*," which they thought threatened social order throughout the interconnected Atlantic world.[7] Democratic-Republicans, by contrast, remained supportive of the Revolution. Yes, there were excesses, but France had joined the United States in the regenerative project of building republics in a world of monarchies.[8]

Americans' diverging perspectives were about more than faraway events. Rather, they reflected attitudes about the new nation's foreign policy, with Republicans concerned to honor the alliance with the French and Federalists eager to preserve trading ties with Britain. The war and American policy continued to set Americans at odds with each other throughout the 1790s, with tensions reaching fever pitch in 1798–99. French attempts to bribe Americans diplomats in the 1797 XYZ Affair—which united Americans in anger—were followed by the divisive Quasi-War with France and related persecution of dissidents under the Alien and Sedition Acts.[9] Meanwhile, the Haitian Revolution, which had begun in 1791, stoked fears of slave rebellion in the United States.[10] These foreign developments—repression in the British Isles, revolution and war in France and St. Domingue—and the dilemmas and anxieties they provoked were brought closer to Americans by the thousands upon thousands of immigrants who arrived in the United States in the 1790s, including English and Irish radicals, French aristocrats, and white, colored, and black St. Dominguens.[11]

Losing Faith in Universal Benevolence

By 1800, the decade of revolutionary upheaval in the Atlantic world was taking its toll on the cosmopolitan connections and worldwide aspirations Americans and Britons had used to rebuild their ties after the American Revolution. The most famous attack came from Edmund Burke, who had once lauded John Howard for his labors on behalf "of all men in all countries." In his 1790 *Reflections on the Revolution in France,* Burke denied that universal benevolence existed. Burke's *Reflections* came in response to Richard Price's 1789 speech, *A Discourse on the Love of Our Country,* which endorsed the French Revolution and argued that patriotism should be restrained by goodwill to humankind. Burke, opposed to the French Revolution and fearful of radicalism that the Revolution might unleash at home, assailed the idea of love of humankind as an existential threat to the familial and local ties that, in his view, were the bedrock of civilization. Earlier in the century, universal benevolence had been a morally strong position as a counterweight to selfish and potentially socially harmful attachments, such as patriotism in militaristic form. During the reactionary 1790s, Burke and his followers redefined the concept as the self-serving false idol of the opponents of family, society, and tradition.[12]

In the charged political atmosphere on both sides of the Atlantic, some activists echoed Burke in criticizing universal benevolence and in endorsing partial loyalties. The Chester, England, doctor John Haygarth urged readers in 1793 to embrace his national smallpox inoculation plan by arguing that Britons' sympathy "need not solely be excited by the inhabitants of the remote regions of the earth," that is, by enslaved Africans. Slaves, "objects of disgust," and criminals, "the most guilty," got too much attention in Haygarth's mind. British "acts of beneficence" should also be directed to "our neighbours and fellow-citizens."[13] With even more hostility, John Sylvester John Gardiner condemned "the specious veil of universal philanthropy" when he spoke at the Massachusetts Humane Society anniversary festival in 1803. The idea of universal philanthropy, he charged in Burkean tones, "conceal[ed] . . . indifference to the whole human species." "If we did not love those best with whom we are most nearly connected, who belong to the same community, dwell in the same town, worship at the same temple," he argued, "but were compelled by stern inflexible justice, to reserve our affections for the supposed superiority of merit in strangers, with whom we are but slightly acquainted, perhaps never saw, our situation would be truly deplorable, and men, of all creatures, would be most miserable." The search for ways to aid all humanity that had flourished in the wake of an earlier transatlantic crisis lost its force in the face of the new disorder in the Atlantic world.[14]

With their own and their supporters' interest in universal benevolence waning, activists focused more on the empire or nation. For Britons, new areas of the British empire captured humanitarian imaginations. Before the American Revolution, Britons had aimed to strengthen the British interest in North America through philanthropy. Immediately after the war, they took up abolition of the transatlantic slave trade as they came to terms with a changed Atlantic

empire. Next they began turning their attention eastward.[15] The Royal Humane
Society first highlighted ties to the East Indies in the mid-1790s (though there
were earlier references to the East India Company). The Society should extend
its reach to India, a Major Carroll urged in 1795. Not only would lives be saved,
but more importantly, he explained, "IDOLATRY would be done away [and]
hordes of Indians [would be] taught to worship the true GOD" as a result of
successful resuscitations. Moreover, Indians' trust in both Britons and British-
Indian commerce would grow.[16] Although they belonged to the same polity,
East Indians were strangers to Britons—not part of their community in the way
British Americans had been—so with his suggestion, Major Carroll urged an
expansive humanitarianism, but one increasingly inflected by imperialism.

Besides an imperial approach, some British reformers and their American
friends were reverting to the narrower bonds of a common Protestant identity
as the basis for philanthropic cooperation. In the 1780s and '90s, Americans
and Britons had used the language of cosmopolitanism to rekindle and redefine
transatlantic ties. Now they espoused a special Anglo-American Protestant civi-
lizing mission, in contrast to the French menace. Well-off British and Federalist
American philanthropists regularly denounced "those fierce and cruel passions"
of the French, which "threaten desolation, destruction, and misery far and wide,"
as Boston cleric John Lathrop put it in 1799. They also praised the goodness
shared by Britons and Americans. Some went farther. Patrick Colquhoun hoped
"that England and America will form a permanent union, as the best means of
preserving the peace of the world, and promoting the best interests of the human
species." Likewise, John Coakley Lettsom confided to Jedidiah Morse that he
thought the American purchase of Louisiana was "advantageous ... to the
human species" because it would "extend the English language, laws and religion." Not everyone spoke in those chauvinistic terms. That Lettsom, a man who
had been so taken with himself as a citizen of the world, did underscored the
changed climate.[17]

Americans too turned away from cosmopolitanism. Even as they had rebuilt
transatlantic ties through charitable cooperation, Americans had also built the
ties of nationhood through philanthropy. "I am, Sir, Your friend and fellow
citizen," the president of the Philadelphia Humane Society—Benjamin Rush—
wrote in closing a letter to the president of the Massachusetts Humane Society—
Thomas Russell—in 1793.[18] Cosmopolitanism and patriotism could coexist, but
in the 1790s and early 1800s, American activists increasingly used benevolence
to distinguish the United States from Europe. "Here," in the United States,
said Morgan Rhees, president of the Philadelphia Society for the Information
and Assistance of Persons Emigrating from Foreign Countries, "a great number of philanthropic citizens associate together and form committees to take the

stranger and the distressed *pilgrim* by the hand." In Europe, by contrast, poor newcomers to cities could expect to be "cheated . . . of the small pittance they had to subsist on."[19] Thomas Dunn, president of the New York Society for the Information and Assistance of Persons Emigrating from Foreign Countries, went further. Dunn, like Rhees, was a radical Dissenter, and in the face of British persecution he had recently emigrated to the United States. Also like Rhees, he enjoined his audience to emulate the Good Samaritan. Here, however, Dunn, unlike humane societies, did not couple the exhortation to universal benevolence with a message of transatlantic reconciliation. Indeed, quite the opposite. The British government's treatment of the United States, Dunn avowed, reminded him of nothing less than Pharaoh's treatment of the Israelites.[20]

Even those American activists who often borrowed ideas from British counterparts stressed the differences between the two countries. Americans held as an article of faith that their country's plenty meant that social ills were less severe in the United States than in Europe. "Many of the evils which afflict and deform the more populous societies of Europe, either do not exist among us, or appear only in a small degree," New Yorker Thomas Eddy assured Londoner Patrick Colquhoun in 1803. DeWitt Clinton likewise drew distinctions between the United States and Britain. In an 1809 speech to the Free School Society of New York, Clinton cited common urban problems and the use by both American and British philanthropists of the Lancastrian educational system (in which older pupils taught younger children) in response to those problems. He highlighted his concern for schooling all the world's "poor and distressed." He noted that personal contacts had played an important role in the spread of the Lancastrian method from England to New York. A decade earlier, Clinton had hoped for the establishment of an international university, where partial loyalties among the world's peoples would fade. In 1809, he remained morally and intellectually a citizen of the world, but now he emphasized political distinctions between the United States and Britain. "Here, no privileged orders—no factitious distinctions in society—no hereditary nobility—no established religion—no royal prerogatives exist." The American belief that "all men . . . enjoy[ed] an equality of rights," he explained, made the United States "more fertile soil" for educating children of all backgrounds than Britain, where some reformers had faced censure for upsetting the social order by schooling the children of the lower sorts.[21]

Even as the crises in the Atlantic world fostered national or imperial approaches to philanthropy, many activists continued to correspond with foreign colleagues. But the mood had changed even among those most cosmopolitan of philanthropists, the leaders of humane societies. In the early nineteenth century, the Massachusetts and London humane societies bumped their foreign friends from their places of preeminence in favor of imperial or national ties. The Royal Humane Society publicly downgraded its interest in foreign societies first. Starting with the 1787–89 report, the London charity had printed a list of the humane societies that, it boasted, had been established thanks to its help. For more than a decade, an overseas society always came first. Societies fell off or were added to the list and the order varied, but, with minor exceptions, the Royal Humane Society listed most of the overseas, Scottish, and Irish societies ahead of the societies in England. That custom changed in 1801. English societies were listed first, then Scottish societies, followed by the Dublin, North Wales, and Jamaica groups. Next came societies in Central Europe and St. Petersburg. Humane societies in the United States came last. The list remained more or less the same for several years. Then in 1809, the Royal Humane Society signaled even more explicitly that imperial ties and an imperial conception of Britain's place in the world were taking root. That year, the Society broke the list of societies out into three parts: "I. *BRITISH UNITED EMPIRE*"—societies in England, Scotland, Wales and Ireland. *"II. BRITISH FOREIGN SETTLEMENTS"*— societies in the East Indies, Nova Scotia, and Jamaica. And *"III. FOREIGN"*— societies in Central Europe, Russia, and the United States.[22]

The Massachusetts Humane Society changed its public face, too. In 1793, the Society had announced that it actively cooperated with other humane societies in a common cause by printing in its annual report extracts from letters sent by the Royal Humane Society. Every year from 1795 with the exception of 1799, the report of the Massachusetts group had included the annual letter it received from the Royal Humane Society. But in 1805, the Massachusetts men printed no missive from their London colleagues. Instead, they included a letter from the new Merrimack Humane Society, based in Newburyport, Massachusetts.[23] The Massachusetts and London charities had not broken off ties, although their correspondence lost its buoyant tone and became more businesslike.[24] After printing the Merrimack Humane Society letter, the Massachusetts Humane Society stopped inserting letters from other humane societies in its reports altogether. It did pay tribute to Royal Humane Society founder William Hawes when he died by including his obituary in the Massachusetts Humane Society report. The time when members of the humane society movement prized belonging to an international community, however, was past.[25]

The mood had changed, but activists did not lose faith in universal philanthropy entirely. The goal of impartial benevolence rested on the firm base of the parable of the Good Samaritan and had been widely considered morally desirable for decades. Even as philanthropists focused more on the empire or nation, they generally did not dispense with the catholic ideal completely. Instead, they hewed to the idea that love of mankind could grow from narrower bonds. John

Sylvester John Gardiner, for instance, followed up his attack on the "specious veil of universal philanthropy" by advising his listeners that "our charity, indeed, must begin at home, though it ought not to end there." Likewise, the London cleric Isaac Huntingford explained that people owed a greater moral duty to those close to them, but, he added, "every human Being, in every existing region, is considered by Christian Charity as entitled to that degree of assistance, which circumstances of prudence, and superior obligation, will fairly allow." From cler-gymen and charities alike, the message was as ambiguous as it had been in the 1760s. Nearer relations came first, and philanthropy helped build the empire or nation. Still, Christians must not forget their moral responsibility to all humanity.[26]

Global Action

Good feelings flowed at the first anniversary festival of the Royal Jennerian Society for the Extermination of the Small-pox. The three hundred men who met in London that May 17, 1803, at the Crown and Anchor Tavern had enjoyed an "elegant dinner." They had drunk toast after toast, to the king, queen, and other royals. They drank to Britain's navy and army, too, and then for good measure sang British naval tunes including "Rule Britannia." Then came a toast to Edward Jenner, and emotion reached fever pitch. The group repeated and repeated again the "plaudits" to the discoverer of vaccination until "the room was ready to burst."[27]

When Dr. Jenner rose to speak, he was so "overcome and opprest" by the acclaim "he confessed that he had not words to express the gratitude of his heart." He "wished," he added, that everyone there and "every friend of human-ity throughout the Universe" would share in his happiness. The next speaker, an Oxford don, did not need to "describe . . . the ravages of that horrid disease" they aimed to eradicate. The good news was "that its terrors are shortly to cease." Thanks to "Dr. Jenner, and to *every medical gentleman present, worthy associates in the cause*," smallpox vaccination had already reached "almost every civilized part of the globe." "This enlightened country, this glorious island (for glorious it will be, in spite of every effort of a proud and implacable foe)," he flattered his compatriots, "has given birth to a" lifesaving "blessing."[28]

The smallpox vaccination movement capped the philanthropic careers of the last generation to come of age in the pre-American Revolutionary British Atlantic community. They and the younger activists who were increasingly tak-ing over from them brought a patriotic, sometimes even martial, fervor to their benevolence in the war years. Yet they expected to cooperate with the friends of

FIGURE 7.1 Portrait of Edward Jenner. Pastel by John Raphael Smith, 18th century. Wellcome Library, London.

humanity everywhere and aspired to a global reach. They were ambivalent cosmopolites who looked forward to "rescuing from the grave more human beings than ever was" imagined "could possibly result, from the institution of any other Society, in the records of history or time."[29] They would build on the expansive practices of the humane society movement though its liberal spirit had waned.

It was Edward Jenner's discovery of vaccination that made the movement possible. The Berkeley, Gloucestershire, England, doctor had become interested in the folk knowledge that said exposure to cowpox, a disease that was generally milder than smallpox, gave milkmaids an immunity to smallpox. Human exposure to cowpox, however, was limited to places where cowpox occurred and to times when there were outbreaks of the livestock disease. Hoping to provide the immunity against smallpox more widely, Jenner experimented with person-to-person cowpox inoculation. His trial succeeded, and in 1798, Jenner announced his discovery to the world.[30]

Like knowledge of resuscitation, knowledge of vaccination procedures along with vaccine matter spread quickly through medical networks. By 1800, doctors from Vienna to New Hampshire had "obtained the [vaccine] matter . . . and [were] inoculating freely with it."[31] Unlike resuscitation operations, which were always charitable or civic undertakings, vaccination services were bought by those able to pay. Recognizing that good vaccine matter would attract paying patients, a group of New Hampshire and Massachusetts doctors agreed to control the supply of cowpox in their area. The entrepreneurial men also agreed to offer discounts for vaccinating a number of family members together.[32] On both sides of the Atlantic, those unable to pay might have access to the cowpox inoculation through the doctors, clergymen, and even some women who vaccinated poor neighbors gratis on their own. Or they might turn to the charitable programs that medical men and laypeople in both Britain and the United States set up in their effort to make cowpox inoculation universal.[33] (Europeans too participated in the cause by establishing vaccination programs that typically were government run.)[34]

When the Royal Jennerian Society was organized in at the end of 1802, it was not the first charity providing vaccination. Medical men at London's Smallpox and Inoculation Hospitals, which had long inoculated with the live smallpox virus, began experimenting with Jenner's discovery. At the end of 1799, one of the doctors prominent in the experiments led the formation of a vaccination charity, only consulting with Dr. Jenner once plans were under way.[35] Philanthropists in other cities took up the cause quickly. The Publick Dispensary in Edinburgh began providing free vaccination to children in early 1800.[36] Across the Atlantic, Dr. James Smith of Baltimore "performed [his] first successful Vaccination in . . . the alms House" in mid-1801, while New Yorkers established the Institution for the Inoculation of the Kine Pock in January 1802.[37]

Edward Jenner had been vexed that a London vaccination charity "had been set on foot and almost completely organized" without his involvement. He and he alone, he angrily told the leading doctor behind the charity, would "bear the odium" if there were problems with the still-new therapy. Spurred on by the presumptuous charity, which soon folded, Jenner joined with other London philanthropists at the end of 1802 to form the Royal Jennerian Society for the Extermination of the Small-pox.[38]

As its name proclaims, the Jennerian Society aimed at nothing less than "promoting universal Vaccination with a View to the extinction of the Small Pox."[39] The goal was ambitious, but Jenner and his colleagues had reason to think it could be met. In 1802, another medical charity movement—the humane society cause—stretched from America to the East Indies. It was now possible, contemporaries rejoiced, to restore the apparently dead to life anywhere that knowledge of resuscitation had spread. No one knew that better than founders of the Jennerian Society. The men who came together to organize the new charity included William Hawes, the Royal Humane Society founder; John Coakley Lettsom, besides Hawes, the London Humane Society's most energetic leader; and others such as humane society supporters John Julius Angerstein and William Wilberforce. Jenner himself had been a medical assistant for the humane society in his home region.[40]

The cause of vaccination appealed to these men in much the same way that resuscitation did. Jenner's discovery was further evidence that the world was improving. They believed in medical progress and their own roles in furthering it, whether they were medical men or laymen. Their support for vaccination was sincere, but it also underscored their superiority over the misguided lower sorts. The lower sorts had doubted the cause of resuscitation and lacked the benevolence, so humane society activists (especially in Britain) believed, to attempt life-saving without pecuniary inducements. Now the poor feared the new cowpox inoculation. A few early tragedies and anxiety about the efficacy and permanence of inoculation had stirred much greater opposition to vaccination than resuscitation had ever faced. But these philanthropists had overcome resistance to build the resuscitation movement, abolition, and other campaigns.[41] The evidence clearly showed that vaccination was safer than inoculation with the live smallpox virus, William Hawes affirmed in the 1803 Royal Humane Society report. He therefore urged "the support of [the Royal Jennerian] Society, whose success is so deeply interwoven with our very existence."[42]

When the Royal Jennerian Society was formed, the spread of cowpox inoculation was well under way. Just as the Royal Humane Society had formalized the exchange of knowledge of resuscitation that had begun through personal channels, the new charity did the same for vaccination. The Jennerian Society put much effort into building the infrastructure for cowpox inoculation throughout the United Kingdom. In London, where the Society was based, the charity ran stations around the metropolis for the free immunization of poor patients, who were largely children. In addition, the Society served as a hub for the movement worldwide in the same way the Royal Humane Society did for the resuscitation movement. From its Central House in Salisbury Square, off Fleet Street, the Jennerian Society disseminated vaccine matter and information. To facilitate the sending of matter and materials, the Society arranged franking privileges for its mailings (although in 1806 those privileges were revoked during a conflict that would bring down the Society two years later). A year after its founding, it had fourteen stations in operation, had vaccinated 5,987 people itself, had printed 4,500 copies of its pamphlets plus other materials, and had sent "6134 charges of matter to 2214 different persons . . . to almost every part of the empire and of the world." To advance its mission of eradicating smallpox, the Society asked the recipients of vaccine matter to inoculate poor patients at no charge and to send data on vaccinations to the Society.[43] "This gratuitous diffusion of Vaccine Virus," the Jennerian Society could therefore congratulate itself in 1805, "has been a principal means of spreading the Vaccine Inoculation through the British Empire, and the world."[44]

The Royal Jennerian Society did not boast idly about the building of a global movement. Like humane societies, most vaccination charities focused on their immediate communities, but they also participated in a worldwide effort. By vaccinating people locally, these organizations, the men and women who vaccinated poor neighbors on their own, and the doctors who vaccinated for profit took part in a global eradication effort. "It must . . . be pleasing to every friend of humanity to learn," New York doctor James Stringham wrote to an Edinburgh counterpart "that the physicians here [in the United States] are not behind the rest of their medical brethren in other parts of the world, in endeavouring to alleviate the pressure of human misery." Doctors appreciated that their local activities were part of a larger endeavor.[45]

Proponents of cowpox inoculation also cooperated as part of a global undertaking by helping to track progress in the cause. Just as humane societies reported their successes to the Royal Humane Society, vaccinators relayed data on the numbers vaccinated in their own communities to central institutions, in particular the Royal Jennerian Society, and to Edward Jenner himself. Seven thousand patients had been vaccinated in Swedish Pomerania between 1801 and 1804, two to three thousand in Bombay, and three thousand by one English cleric himself, correspondents informed Jenner—and, through his publicity channels, a broader audience. In addition, devotees of the cause shared their innovations for charting the course of the cowpox in patients and for organizing other patient information. Dr. James Smith of Baltimore, one of the foremost American vaccination activists, sent Jenner a copy of "the following Record . . . to convey to [Jenner] a more accurate Idea of [Smith's] data-tabulation method.

1807	Benjamin Carr born 6th Decr. 1806
April 15	Vaccinated in the left arm
19	taken effect . . .
24	a characteristic vaccine pustule
May 2	took off a perfect scab

Dismissed with Certificate No. 2701.[46]

Doctors also worked to make vaccination universal by experimenting with methods to send cowpox matter to faraway colleagues. Successful vaccination rested on inoculating patients with the infectious virus, so transmitting the cowpox matter was of paramount importance. Medical men tried preserving and transmitting the vaccine matter in quill pens, on glass, and in "many folds of Absorbent paper," and they communicated their successes and failures to one another.[47] James Smith paid particular attention to maintaining his supply of vaccine matter. Smith had been a medical student of Benjamin Rush and a founder of the Baltimore Dispensary with John Crawford. Through Dr. John Ring, a friend of Crawford who was also an avid supporter of Edward Jenner, Crawford had received some vaccine matter in summer 1800. Crawford's efforts at vaccination had failed. The following year, Smith acquired some vaccine matter from England and successfully vaccinated some pauper children.[48] Initially, he did subsequent vaccinations with "the vaccine Matter taken only on the 8th day [of the patient's cowpox virus] according to the Rule [Jenner] at first laid down." But he and other American doctors faced problems with the typical methods of preserving and transferring the virus "as well as with the almost insuperable difficulty of the keeping the matter active" in Baltimore's hot summers. In the summer of 1803, therefore, Smith adopted a new "method of preserving [his] vaccine Scabs" from patients undergoing inoculation. This technique not only kept the matter "active much longer," but also carried less risk of harming the patient.[49]

After explaining his methods to Edward Jenner—the namesake of his eldest son—James Smith closed his epistle by "Wishing [Jenner] many years of happiness to witness that [his] Discovery can encrease the Population of the World much faster than all the Rage of her numerous Tyrants can destroy [it.]"[50] Like the man he so admired, Smith dedicated himself to the cause of universal vaccination. In 1802, he and colleagues set up a Baltimore vaccination charity. Several years later, in 1809, he prevailed upon the Maryland legislature to name him vaccine agent for the state (a lottery-funded position). In the early 1810s, he became vaccine agent for the United States and also for Virginia. His duties included preserving vaccine matter and providing it, gratis or for a fee depending on whether he was acting in his capacity as Virginia or US agent, to people throughout the relevant jurisdictions. In his job as national agent, he oversaw twenty traveling agents, who had vaccinated an estimated 100,000 people by the early 1820s. Smith also dispatched vaccine matter to the West Indies and South America.[51]

Although the global eradication of smallpox was not achieved until the late twentieth century, the Royal Jennerian Society leaders believed that "so completely [was] the extermination of this destructive disease within [their] controul, that could inoculation begin at the same time over every part of the kingdom, a single year, a single month, almost a single week, would annihilate a pestilence which twelve centuries have been establishing." Saying smallpox could be exterminated within a week was in part publicity hyperbole. But proponents of vaccination, with their limitless zeal, did expect to conquer the world. Indeed in 1806, Thomas Jefferson congratulated Jenner for "hav[ing] erased from the calendar of human afflictions one of its greatest." The ability to destroy smallpox, contemporaries thought, meant that the disease would be eradicated soon, or even, to Jefferson's mind, that it already had been. By 1806, thousands upon thousands of people around the world—from Europe to the Americas to India to China—had been vaccinated. Vaccination supporters, then, had good reason to think global goals were viable. Governments sponsored or supported much of the diffusion of cowpox matter, but Royal Jennerian Society leaders assumed that a charity could direct an international humanitarian undertaking. Building on the structures of the humane society movement, early nineteenth-century medical philanthropists had achieved a worldwide reach.[52]

Britons, Americans, and Europeans cooperated in the cause of vaccination. They corresponded about methods, exchanged vaccine matter, encouraged each other in the face of setbacks, and shared news of their progress. They remained cosmopolitan in their practices. But the chaos in the Atlantic world had changed the public tone in beneficence. In a move that would have been unthinkable ten or so years earlier, in 1805 the Royal Jennerian Society vetoed almost all the prominent foreign medical men and statesmen who had been nominated to be honorary (non-medical) or corresponding (medical) members. John Adams, Thomas Jefferson, and the Reverend Dr. James Madison of Virginia were rejected. Even more surprising, so were Benjamin Rush, Benjamin Waterhouse, and three other American doctors. A few Frenchmen and other Europeans were voted in, but most honorary or corresponding members were Britons either at home or in the empire. (Some British nominees were also turned down, including Marquis Wellesley and numerous British doctors.)[53] Americans, for their part, established vaccine charities but did not, as they had with humane societies, use these groups to honor foreign friends.[54] Activists pursued a worldwide program, but their feelings were insular.

Epilogue

THE FRENCH AND Haitian Revolutions did what the American Revolution had not. The American Revolutionary War had disrupted many lives and left Americans and Britons initially unsure about how to relate to one another. But the activists who collaborated after American independence had used philanthropy to rebuild close ties. As the eighteenth century gave way to the nineteenth, years of war (both declared and Quasi), internal rebellions, political divisions, waves of refugees, and the suffering and tension wrought by dearth and epidemics undermined cosmopolitan sensibilities. Even before their countries fought each other again, Americans and Britons had grown more distant.

Time also played its role. The last generation of philanthropists to grow up before the American Revolution was dying off. Jeremy Belknap, Thomas Cogan, John Crawford, John Coakley Lettsom, Henry Moyes, Thomas Percival, Benjamin Rush, and Thomas Russell were all dead by 1820, most of them by 1815. "I once enjoyed a pretty wide range of professional correspondence, American as well as transatlantic," one of the survivors, Benjamin Waterhouse, wrote in 1813, "but alas! almost all my epistolary friends have gone down to the grave!"[1]

Waterhouse and his friends and friends of their friends had adapted to becoming foreigners by making the care of suffering strangers customary. They had built the practices that stretched charity—the love that could impel alms to the poor, ministrations to a sick friend, or words of wise counsel to a wayward neighbor—into philanthropy—the "love of mankind" that has led to institutions that aim to transform the lives of millions around the world.[2] Their efforts to adjust to the remaking of their shared world laid part of the foundation of later generations' increasingly robust efforts to remake the whole world.

As the Revolutionary-era activists aged and then passed from the scene, their children and protégés often carried on their elders' philanthropic missions. John Murray's Society of Universal Good-will had faded with his death, but his son

Charles Murray—not incidentally, Edward Jenner's right-hand man in the Royal Jennerian Society—and foreign Protestant clergy in London used the Society of Universal Good-will's leftover funds to seed the Society of Friends of Foreigners in Distress. Established in 1806, the charity pursued its mission of aiding "indigent Foreigners here, without distinction of country or religion" well into the twentieth century.[3] In Upper Canada, John Murray's daughter Anne Murray Powell continued the family tradition with the Society for the Relief of Strangers in Distress, formed in 1817.[4] Just as John Crawford's young colleague James Smith had emerged as a leader in the vaccination cause, students of Benjamin Rush were at the forefront of philanthropy in the next generation as were students of those students in later years.[5] Traditions across generations of charitable and reform activism were common in less well-known families also.[6] Their historical experience, and that of broader publics, included borrowing and offering charitable knowledge far and wide to improve the lot not just of neighbors or of fellow nationals, but of humankind.[7]

Like their eighteenth-century forebears, leading nineteenth-century activists often had overseas experience. Some nineteenth-century Americans, like their colonial predecessors, went abroad for education or for other personal reasons; while in foreign places, they explored welfare and civic institutions and forged connections. Americans at the forefront of Progressive social politics had commonly spent time in German universities. When they returned home, they often introduced new social policies to the United States.[8] Leisure travel exposed founders of American museums to European cultural institutions, while family took a pioneering Boston housing reformer to England.[9] Many activists, however, traveled abroad explicitly for philanthropic purposes. Proponents of education for the deaf sent an observer to Europe in the 1810s to gather information on schools there.[10] In 1838, an agent of the American Anti-Slavery Society went to Haiti to meet with the Haitian Abolition Society. Two years later, radical American abolitionists headed to London for a World's Antislavery Convention.[11] Black and white American abolitionists crisscrossed the British Isles on lecture tours, and women's rights advocates and temperance reformers did the same.[12] In the eighteenth century, a handful of activists had ventured the other way across the Atlantic, to North America to raise funds or promote causes. In the nineteenth century, European and Canadian "philanthropic tourists" added the United States to their itineraries. Some came to investigate American institutions, such as the up-to-date prisons in Pennsylvania, New York, and elsewhere. Others, like their American counterparts and friends, were on the transatlantic lecture circuits for abolition, social purity, and other causes.[13]

Citizens of the world like their predecessors, nineteenth-century reformers and humanitarians organized their efforts to work beyond their borders differently. Eighteenth-century philanthropists had worked not episodically, as some scholars have said, but routinely, through networks to achieve an expansive reach.[14] By encouraging distant peers to set up new charitable institutions or by exchanging information to further a common endeavor, they worked persistently to aid faraway sufferers. Nineteenth-century men and women also belonged to far-flung philanthropic communities, but they institutionalized their forebears' moral responsibility to strangers by founding international or world organizations to coordinate their efforts, often by pushing for governmental action, in causes from public health to the prevention of crime to the suppression of vice around the globe.[15] Thanks to faster communications and transportation, reformers could meet regularly in international gatherings.[16] Succoring faraway disaster victims also became more common, and by the late nineteenth century Americans and Britons traveled to oversee and publicize relief to people suffering from famines and from atrocities, with humanitarians departing for Russia, Ceylon, Turkey, and Cuba in the 1890s alone.[17] Aid to distant victims of natural disasters remained ad hoc but, beyond disaster relief, nineteenth-century men and women had formalized their predecessors' more personal approach to philanthropic cooperation.

The early twentieth century saw a new organizational form for improving the lot of suffering strangers. Wealthy Americans, such as John D. Rockefeller and the Scots-born Andrew Carnegie, set up foundations to do nothing less, in the words of the Rockefeller Foundation, than "promote the well-being of mankind throughout the world." Vast fortunes and legal changes made it possible for Americans to establish philanthropic foundations with broad aims and evolving charitable purposes: Until the late nineteenth century, the law of charity in the United States would not have protected trusts with such vaguely defined missions from the donors' heirs, and in Britain, the law continued to demand greater specificity than "the well-being of mankind" to uphold the validity of charitable gifts. American philanthropic foundations, then, were new in form. Moreover, they had the resources to undertake projects to improve the condition of humanity by promoting public health, fighting hunger, and supporting education, not through networks and not through international associations, but in their own right.[18] Novel in important ways, foundations furthered the philanthropic tradition of reaching across borders.

Universal moral responsibility within the Anglo-American world had developed in the wake of the crisis of community wrought by the American Revolution. Over the next century and half, reformers and philanthropists responded to improvements in communications and transportation, to the dilemmas of industrial capitalism, and, for the few, to the possibilities of great wealth to elaborate an evermore variegated eleemosynary infrastructure of local, national, and global charities and, increasingly, of local and state social welfare programs. Wars in the mid-nineteenth century also contributed to the growth of humanitarianism. In reaction to the horrors of the 1859 Battle of Solferino during the Italian Wars of Independence, leading Genevans founded, and many Europeans supported, an international movement to care for wounded soldiers and to regulate the conduct of war. Continuing the tradition of emulation and adaptation of charitable models, many nations joined what became the Red Cross and Red Crescent movement and ratified the initial Geneva Conventions. The origins of humanitarian law lie in that mid-nineteenth century conflict.[19] The vast suffering caused by the American Civil War also played its role in the expansion of philanthropy by nurturing a new generation of activists and by fostering "scientific" and more bureaucratic approaches.[20] A few decades later in the United States, organizations responding to the hardships of World War I and assisted by the new science of marketing, propelled mass giving to new levels, with Americans donating for fellow citizens and Europeans alike.[21]

By the early twentieth century, humanitarianism had grown markedly, but aiding suffering strangers remained the predominantly voluntary tradition it had been since former compatriots had sought to cultivate peace, liberty, and human welfare through their cooperative charitable endeavors. World War II transformed this tradition as universal moral responsibility became a facet of global governance. Faced with death and destruction on an unprecedented scale, many in the West sought to renew the world—and themselves—by building an international community based on the common humanity of all people.[22] Starting with efforts to relieve privation and to reconstruct societies in Europe, Western aid organizations expanded to all parts of the globe. They also became increasingly bureaucratic and professional. In addition, in the decades after World War II the work of the nominally voluntary groups was (and continues to be) substantially funded and coordinated by Western governments, which also established international humanitarian organizations, such as the United Nations High Commissioner for Refugees and the World Health Organization, and national agencies, such as the Peace Corps. Development and disaster relief for the world's poorest, many Western leaders came to believe during World War II and the Cold War, served their countries' national security interests.[23]

The end of the Cold War, with its loosing of new conflicts and threats, deepened the relationship between states and humanitarianism. To protect against the dangers of violent extremists, destabilizing wars, and flows of refugees, Western governments adopted explicit policies of state-building. That is, they sought through economic development, democratization, and the promotion of human rights to transform failing states and thwart their potential to breed global instability. Humanitarian organizations played central roles in pursuing these goals. Meanwhile, the earliest Geneva Conventions had burgeoned into a body of international humanitarian law designed to protect people in conflict zones. Humanitarianism came to encompass emergency relief, development aid, the securing of human rights, the promotion of democracy and civil society, and even armed intervention meant to prevent the slaughter of innocents.[24] The culture of universal moral responsibility had become a force for shaping world history.

Yet for many humanitarians, the seemingly ultimate realization of moral concern for suffering strangers provoked a crisis. In spite of—or because of—the close ties between humanitarian organizations and governments, aid organizations in the decades after World War II had insisted on their impartiality in their selection of aid recipients by need, not affinity; their neutrality in conflicts; and their independence from parties involved in conflicts (even indirectly as the superpowers were during the Cold War). Humanitarianism was apolitical, they maintained. Their ability to carry out their missions, they believed, depended on such a stance. If aid organizations were seen to be agents of one or another government, they worried, they might be denied access to sufferers by hostile leaders, face suspicion among would-be aid recipients, and even put aid workers at risk of attack.[25] The collapse of states, the armed conflicts, and the sense of possibility to reshape formerly closed societies following the fall of the Soviet empire, however, undermined the inherited principles. To meet their more ambitious goals, relief and development organizations were working ever more closely with Western states (including with their militaries) and with international agencies. In addition, the traditional distinctions between relief, development, and human rights groups were collapsing as aid workers and Western powers undertook multifaceted programs to remake vulnerable societies for the well-being of their members and the international community at large. As humanitarians grappled with these shifts, they had to face the reality that their efforts were political. For many, that process was uncomfortable. They had insisted that humanitarianism was apolitical not simply for pragmatic reasons but also to define their work as a challenge to conventional power politics. Confronting the political nature of what they did created uneasiness as they wrestled with their identity and with the moral basis of their activity.[26]

In recent years, the predicament that emerged after the fall of the Soviet Union has largely been resolved. No longer finding the "philanthropic paradigm" based on a desire to relieve suffering to make sense in the world they face, aid workers and activists have come to terms with an approach that roots their work in human rights, that is, in laws enacted through national and international governmental processes.[27] What an irony that the eclipse of the humanitarian tradition that emerged from the American Revolution, with its long-forgotten political dimensions, came about after the dissolution of another, more recent empire.

Abbreviations

HSP	Historical Society of Pennsylvania
LCP	Library Company of Philadelphia
MdHS	Maryland Historical Society
NHHS	New Hampshire Historical Society
NYAM	New York Academy of Medicine
NYH	New York-Presbyterian Hospital-New York Weill Cornell Medical Center Archives
NYHS	New-York Historical Society
MHS	Massachusetts Historical Society
PHA	Philadelphia Hospital Archives
PHS	Philadelphia Humane Society
RHS	Royal Humane Society
RHSA	Royal Humane Society Archives
RIHS	Rhode Island Historical Society
RJS	Royal Jennerian Society for the Extermination of Smallpox
SPCK	Society for Promoting Christian Knowledge
SPG	Society for the Propagation of the Gospel in Foreign Parts
SPRK	Society for Promoting Religious Knowledge among the Poor
SSPCK	Society for Propagating Christian Knowledge

Notes

INTRODUCTION

1. *An Account of the Scots Society in Norwich, from Its Rise in 1775, Until It Received the Additional Name of the Society of Universal Good-will in 1784*, 2nd ed. (Norwich, n.d.), 88, 91, 92.

2. *An Account of the Scots Society in Norwich, from Its Rise in 1775*, 83.

3. *An Account of the Scots Society in Norwich, from Its Rise in 1775*, 21.

4. On Americans' anger toward Britain in the lead-up to the war, see T. H. Breen, *American Insurgents, American Patriots: The Revolution of the People* (New York: Hill and Wang, 2010). On British alienation from Americans in the lead-up to and during the war, see Stephen Conway, "From Fellow-Nationals to Foreigners: British Perceptions of the Americans, circa 1739–1783," *William and Mary Quarterly* 59 (2002): 65–100. On Britons' conflicted feelings for Americans during the war, see Linda Colley, *Captives: Britain, Empire, and the World, 1600–1850* (New York: Anchor Books, 2002), 226; see also 225.

5. The questions that Revolutionary-era Americans and Britons grappled with are the flip side of the question asked by Daniel T. Rodgers in *Atlantic Crossing: Social Politics in a Progressive Age* (Cambridge, MA: Belknap Press of Harvard University Press, 1998). He investigates not how the fracturing of a transatlantic political community fostered humanitarianism but how economic developments fostered a transnational political culture. I am indebted to Rodgers's book for first stoking my interest in the transnational dimensions of reform, philanthropy, and social politics. My interest in imagined communities and in Americans' and Britons' adjustment to being foreigners owe to Benedict R. O'G. Anderson, *Imagined Communities: Reflections on the Origin and Spread of Nationalism* (London: Verso, 1983), Linda Colley, *Britons: Forging the Nation, 1707–1837* (New Haven, CT: Yale University Press, 1992), and Conway, "From Fellow-Nationals to Foreigners." The famous debate between David Brion Davis and Thomas Haskell on the origins of humanitarianism sparked my interest in

the subject. David Brion Davis, *The Problem of Slavery in the Age of Revolution, 1770–1823* (Ithaca, NY: Cornell University Press, 1975); Thomas L. Haskell, "Capitalism and the Origins of the Humanitarian Sensibility, Parts 1 & 2," *American Historical Review* 90 (1985): 339–361, 547–566. The crucial articles in the debate, plus responses and John Ashworth's contributions, have been collected in Thomas Bender, ed., *The Antislavery Debate: Capitalism and Abolitionism as a Problem in Historical Interpretation* (Berkeley: University of California Press, 1992). My curiosity in how the American Revolution reshaped philanthropy was piqued by Conrad Edick Wright, *The Transformation of Charity in Postrevolutionary New England* (Boston: Northeastern University Press, 1992). A recent book similarly points to a crisis of faith, which could be understood also as a crisis of community, as the impetus for the expansion of the humanitarian infrastructure, in that case after World War II. Michael Barnett, *Empire of Humanity: A History of Humanitarianism* (Ithaca, NY: Cornell University Press, 2011), 22.

6. Recent works about American nation-making include Sarah Knott, *Sensibility and the American Revolution* (Chapel Hill: Published for the Omohundro Institute of Early American History and Culture, Williamsburg, Virginia, by the University of North Carolina Press, 2009); Gordon S. Wood, *The Radicalism of the American Revolution* (New York: Vintage Books, 1991), esp. "Benevolence," 213–225; Andrew Burstein, "The Political Character of Sympathy," *Journal of the Early Republic* 21:4 (2001): 601–632; Catherine O'Donnell Kaplan, *Men of Letters in the Early Republic: Cultivating Forums of Citizenship* (Chapel Hill: Published for the Omohundro Institute of Early American History and Culture, Williamsburg, Virginia, by the University of North Carolina Press, 2008); Benjamin H. Irvin, *Clothed in Robes of Sovereignty: The Continental Congress and the People Out of Doors* (New York: Oxford University Press, 2011); Kariann Akemi Yokota, *Unbecoming British: How Revolutionary America Became a Postcolonial Nation* (New York: Oxford University Press, 2011); Sam W. Haynes, *Unfinished Revolution: The Early American Republic in a British World* (Charlottesville: University of Virginia Press, 2010); Eliga Gould, *Among the Powers of the Earth: The American Revolution and the Making of a New World Empire* (Cambridge, MA: Harvard University Press, 2012). Recent works examining British redefinition of its character and empire include Eliga Gould, "American Independence and Britain's Counter-Revolution," *Past and Present* 154 (1997): 107–141; Christopher Leslie Brown, *Moral Capital: Foundations of British Abolitionism* (Chapel Hill: Published for the Omohundro Institute for Early American History and Culture, Williamsburg, Virginia, by the University of North Carolina Press, 2006); Maya Jasanoff, *Liberty's Exiles: American Loyalists in the Revolutionary World* (New York: Alfred A. Knopf, 2011). In a new book, Peter Marshall similarly examines the remaking of the British Atlantic world after

American independence, with a focus on political leaders. He devotes some attention to humanitarian agendas in the 1780s, particularly antislavery, and views humanitarian cooperation as relatively limited, stressing instead Anglo-American "friction" over claims to righteousness. P. J. Marshall, *Remaking the British Atlantic: The United States and the British Empire after American Independence* (Oxford: Oxford University Press, 2012); on humanitarianism or lack thereof, see 205–206, 194 ("friction"). Michael Kraus surveys transatlantic cooperation in a range of humanitarian causes as evidence of an Atlantic civilization but does not treat the American Revolution as a problem for members of this shared culture. Michael Kraus, *The Atlantic Civilization: Eighteenth-Century Origins* (Ithaca, NY: Published for the American Historical Association by Cornell University Press, 1949). Meanwhile, Brent Sirota points to British commentators in the 1770s who rooted a defining national identification with benevolence in the Glorious Revolution. Brent S. Sirota, *Christian Monitors: The Church of England and the Age of Benevolence, 1680–1730* (New Haven, CT: Yale University Press, 2014), 7.

7. A universal approach to moral responsibility is often taken as the defining feature of humanitarianism. Michael Barnett, *Empire of Humanity*, 20, 77; Richard D. Brown, "Introduction," in Richard Ashby Wilson and Richard D. Brown, eds., *Humanitarianism and Suffering: The Mobilization of Empathy* (Cambridge: Cambridge University Press, 2009), 1–30, 3. On nineteenth-century objections to such an expansive idea of humanitarianism, see Margaret Abruzzo, *Polemical Pain: Slavery, Cruelty, and the Rise of Humanitarianism* (Baltimore: Johns Hopkins University Press, 2011).

8. Many scholars have explored the history of eighteenth- and early nineteenth-century humanitarianism and associationalism within the parameters of either distinct nations or movements. On English and British associated philanthropy, works include Donna T. Andrew, *Philanthropy and Police: London Charity in the Eighteenth-Century* (Princeton, NJ: Princeton University Press, 1989), esp. 4–49; Paul Langford, *A Polite and Commercial People: England, 1727–1783* (Oxford: Clarendon Press, 1989), 482–490; Peter Clark, *British Clubs and Societies 1580–1800: The Origins of an Associational World* (Oxford: Oxford University Press, 2000); Sirota, *Christian Monitors*; David Owen, *English Philanthropy 1660–1960* (Cambridge, MA: Belknap Press of Harvard University Press, 1964); Clare Midgley, *Women against Slavery: The British Campaigns, 1780–1870* (London: Routledge,1992); and on Scotland, see Rosalind Mitchison, *The Old Poor Law in Scotland: The Experience of Poverty, 1574–1845* (Edinburgh: Edinburgh University Press, 2000), 28–129. Works on the Thirteen Colonies/United States, include Sydney V. James, *A People among Peoples: Quaker Benevolence in Eighteenth-Century America* (Cambridge, MA: Harvard University Press, 1963), esp. "Private Societies to Do Good," 193–215; Wright, *The*

Transformation of Charity, esp. Part II, 49–111; Steven C. Bullock, *Revolutionary Brotherhood: Freemasonry and the Transformation of the American Social Order, 1730–1840* (Chapel Hill: Published for the Institute of Early American History and Culture, Williamsburg, Virginia, by the University of North Carolina Press, 1996); Anne M. Boylan, *The Origins of Women's Activism: New York and Boston, 1797–1840* (Chapel Hill: University of North Carolina Press, 2002); Johann N. Neem, *Creating a Nation of Joiners: Democracy and Civil Society in Early National Massachusetts* (Cambridge, MA: Harvard University Press, 2008); John K. Alexander, *Render Them Submissive: Responses to Poverty in Philadelphia, 1760– 1800* (Amherst: University of Massachusetts Press, 1980); Barbara L. Bellows, *Benevolence among Slaveholders: Assisting the Poor in Charleston 1670–1860* (Baton Rouge: Louisiana State University Press, 1993). Travis Glasson, while taking an Atlantic perspective, focuses on a particular organization. Travis Glasson, *Mastering Christianity: Missionary Anglicanism and Slavery in the Atlantic World* (New York: Oxford University Press, 2012). J. R. Oldfield and Francois Furstenberg also take transatlantic approaches to examinations of the abolitionism. J. R. Oldfield, *Transatlantic Abolitionism in the Age of Revolution: An International History of Anti-slavery, c. 1787–1820* (Cambridge: Cambridge University Press, 2013); Francois Furstenberg, "Atlantic Slavery, Atlantic Freedom: George Washington, Slavery, and Transatlantic Abolitionist Networks," *William and Mary Quarterly* 68:2 (April 2011): 247–286.

9. Works that make slavery and antislavery the focal point for examining debates about humanitarianism include Davis, *The Problem of Slavery in the Age of Revolution*; Haskell, "Capitalism and the Origins of the Humanitarian Sensibility"; Abruzzo, *Polemical Pain,* see 6–7 on victors in the debate over humanness defining the concept. In a recent article, Abigail Green notes that historians of nineteenth- and twentieth-century humanitarianism look particularly to antislavery to explain earlier humanitarianism. Abigail Green, "Humanitarianism in Nineteenth-Century Context: Religious, Gendered, National," *Historical Journal* 57 (2014): 1157–1175. As Travis Glasson has pointed out, before the emergence of an antislavery movement, members of the SPG sought to reform slavery. Such an effort is rightly not seen as humanitarian today (and Glasson rejects labeling it as such), but it reminds us that concepts of humanitarianism are historically contingent. Glasson, *Mastering Christianity,* 199–200, 7–8.

10. Works that take the American Revolution as a starting point of new trends include Wright, *The Transformation of Charity*; Bullock, *Revolutionary Brotherhood*; Neem, *Creating a Nation of Joiners.*

11. On the incomplete shift from charity to philanthropy, see Robert A. Gross, "Giving in America: From Charity to Philanthropy," in Lawrence J. Friedman and Mark D. McGarvie, eds., Charity, Philanthropy, and Civility in American History (Cambridge: Cambridge University Press, 2003). On medieval charity, see Miri

Rubin, *Charity and Community in Medieval Cambridge* (Cambridge: Cambridge University Press, 1987); Joel Rosenthal, *The Purchase of Paradise: Gift Giving and the Aristocracy, 1307–1485* (London: Routledge and Kegan Paul, 1972); see also Felicity Heal, *Hospitality in Early Modern England* (Oxford: Clarendon Press, 1990). On developments in sixteenth- and seventeenth-century welfare provision, see Ole Peter Grell and Andrew Cunningham, eds., Health Care and Poor Relief in Protestant Europe (London: Routledge, 1997); Joanna Innes, "The 'Mixed Economy of Welfare' in Early Modern England: Assessments of the Options from Hale to Malthus (c. 1683–1803)," in Martin Daunton, ed., *Charity, Self-Interest and Welfare in the English Past* (New York: St. Martin's Press, 1996), 139–140; Robert M. Kingdon, "Social Welfare in Calvin's Geneva," *American Historical Review* 76 (1971): 50–69; W. K. Jordan, *Philanthropy in England, 1480–1660* (New York: Russell Sage Foundation, 1959); Paul Slack, *Poverty and Policy in Tudor and Stuart England* (London: Longman, 1988); David Underdown, *Fire from Heaven: The Life of an English Town in the Seventeenth Century* (New Haven, CT: Yale University Press, 1992). On early moderns' consideration of their moral obligation to strangers and on expansive charitable undertakings, see Brian Pullan, "Catholics, Protestants, and the Poor in Early Modern Europe," *Journal of Interdisciplinary History* 35:3 (2005): 441–456, 445, 446, 448; Ole Peter Grell, *Brethren in Christ: A Calvinist Network in Reformation Europe* (Cambridge: Cambridge University Press, 2011); Peter Stamatov, *The Origins of Global Humanitarianism: Religions, Empires, Advocacy* (New York: Cambridge University Press, 2013).

12. On the expansion of moral responsibility within the English/British empire, see n. 21 below and Chapter 1 of this book. I am paraphrasing Eliga Gould's observation that the American Revolution marked "a crucial moment of the globalization of . . . the public law of European colonial powers." Gould, *Among the Powers of the Earth*, 7.

13. Conrad Edick Wright discusses early nineteenth-century New Englanders' worldwide aspirations, though he sees humanitarian activities only just beginning "to reach across international boundaries" in that era. Wright, *The Transformation of Charity*, 196–198, quotation 198. For his part, Brent Sirota argues for the importance of Anglican voluntary associations in the development of a global scope for British benevolence. The organizations he examines focused their activities within the English, then British, empire, which I characterize as imperial philanthropy. Sirota, *Christian Monitors*, 15.

14. The phrase "Age of Benevolence" emerged in Britain in the mid-eighteenth century, although observers had been hailing the development for several decades. Sirota, *Christian Monitors*, 6. On the meaning of "benevolence" and "beneficence" and the growing use of and meaning of the word "philanthropy," see Wright, *The Transformation of Charity*, 7, 120–121. The word "philanthropy" continued

to mean "love of mankind" throughout the nineteenth century. Merle Curti, *American Philanthropy Abroad* (New Brunswick, NJ: Rutgers University Press, 1963), viii.

15. "humanitarian, n. and adj.," OED Online. March 2015. Oxford University Press. http://www.oed.com/view/Entry/89276?redirectedFrom=humanitarian (accessed June 4, 2015). I am grateful to Travis Glasson for encouraging me to think carefully about my use of the term "humanitarianism." For his perspective on whether missionary organizations such as the Society for the Propagation of the Gospel in Foreign Parts should be deemed "humanitarian," see Glasson, *Mastering Christianity*, 7–8. In a recent book, Margaret Abruzzo examines the contested nature of the moral language of humanitarianism in the eighteenth- and nineteenth-century United States and defines humanitarianism as opposition to the "unnecessary infliction of pain." Abruzzo, *Polemical Pain*, quotation on 2. In the mid-twentieth century, Frank Klingberg used the term "humanitarianism" to refer to Anglican missionary activity. Frank J. Klingberg, *Anglican Humanitarianism in Colonial New York* (Philadelphia: Church Historical Society, 1940; rpt. 1971). Ford K. Brown, *Fathers of the Victorians: The Age of Wilberforce* (Cambridge, MA: Belknap Press of Harvard University Press, 1967), 106–115.

16. See, among others, Julia F. Irwin, *Making the World Safe: The American Red Cross and a Nation's Humanitarian Awakening* (Oxford: Oxford University Press, 2013); Keith David Watenpaugh, "Between Communal Survival and National Aspiration: Armenian Genocide Refugees, the League of Nations, and the Practice of Interwar Humanitarianism," *Humanity* 5:2 (2014); Gerard Daniel Cohen, *In War's Wake: Europe's Displaced Persons in the Postwar Order* (Oxford: Oxford University Press, 2012); Barbara Keys, *Reclaiming American Virtue: The Human Rights Revolution of the 1970s* (Cambridge, MA: Harvard University Press, 2014); Sarah B. Snyder, *Human Rights Activism and the End of the Cold War: A Transnational History of the Helsinki Network* (New York: Cambridge University Press, 2011).

17. On the importance of middling people's growing wealth for the expansion of charitable activity, see Langford, *A Polite and Commercial People*, 484; for a similar argument about how the expansion of a market economy facilitated church-building, see Mark A. Peterson, *The Price of Redemption: The Spiritual Economy of Puritan New England* (Stanford, CA: Stanford University Press, 1997). The most sophisticated statement of the social control thesis is Davis, *The Problem of Slavery in the Age of Revolution*. On the impact of commercial growth on cultural productions including novels, see John Brewer, *The Pleasures of the Imagination: English Culture in the Eighteenth Century* (New York: Farrar, Straus and Giroux, 1997); on the role of novels in nurturing humanitarian sensibilities, see Lynn Hunt, *Inventing Human Rights: A History* (New York: W.W. Norton, 2007); Thomas W. Laqueur, "Mourning, Pity, and the Work of Narrative in the Making of 'Humanity," in

Richard Ashby Wilson and Richard D. Brown, eds., *Humanitarianism and Suffering: The Mobilization of Empathy* (Cambridge: Cambridge University Press, 2009), 31–57; Haskell, "Capitalism and the Origins of the Humanitarian Sensibility, Parts 1 & 2."

18. Haskell, "Capitalism and the Origins of the Humanitarian Sensibility, Part 2," 556 ("explosive growth").

19. David Brion Davis and Christopher Leslie Brown, for examples, focus on religious communities. See Davis, *The Problem of Slavery in the Age of Revolution*; Brown, *Moral Capital*.

20. George W. Corner, ed., *The Autobiography of Benjamin Rush: His 'Travels through Life' together with His Commonplace Book for 1789–1813* (Princeton, NJ: Published for the American Philosophical Society by Princeton University Press, 1948), 44 ("republic of medicine"); John Morgan, *A Discourse Upon the Institution of Medical Schools in America; Delivered at a Public Anniversary Commencement, held in the College of Philadelphia May 30 and 31, 1765* (Philadelphia, 1765), 62 ("benefactors of mankind"). Thomas W. Laqueur briefly discusses the prevalence of doctors in eighteenth-century humanitarianism. Thomas W. Laqueur, "Bodies, Details, and the Humanitarian Narrative" in *The New Cultural History*, ed. and intro. by Lynn Hunt (Berkeley: University of California Press, 1989); on doctors' role in charitable and reform movements, see 182–191, esp. 184.

21. On the expanding practice of aiding distant sufferers within transatlantic religious communities or the British Atlantic world more generally, see James, *A People among Peoples*; P. J. Marshall, "Who Cared about the Thirteen Colonies? Some Evidence from Philanthropy," in *"A Free though Conquering People": Eighteenth-Century Britain and Its Empire* (Aldershot: Ashgate, 2003), 59–64; Matthew Mulcahy, *Hurricanes and Society in the British Greater Caribbean, 1624–1783* (Baltimore: Johns Hopkins University Press, 2006). On transatlantic missionary organizations, in particular, see Glasson, *Mastering Christianity*; Klingberg, *Anglican Humanitarianism in Colonial New York*; Laura M. Stevens, *The Poor Indians: British Missionaries, Native Americans, and Colonial Sensibility* (Philadelphia: University of Pennsylvania Press, 2004). On a new ecumenical approach to Protestantism that gave eighteenth-century New Englanders both a sense of belonging to a transatlantic British community and to the international Protestant community, see Thomas S. Kidd, *The Protestant Interest: New England after Puritanism* (New Haven, CT: Yale University Press, 2004). At the same time that a sense of a transatlantic British community was growing, so too, according to some scholars, were English and Scots developing a shared British identity. Colley, *Britons: Forging the Nation*. Religious fellowships that stretched across imperial boundaries also grew stronger in the eighteenth century. See Jon Sensbach, *Rebecca's Revival: Creating Black Christianity in the Atlantic World* (Cambridge, MA: Harvard University Press, 2005); Renate Wilson, *Pious Traders*

in Medicine: A German Pharmaceutical Network in Eighteenth-Century North America (University Park: Pennsylvania State University Press, 2000).

22. On the British Atlantic world in the eighteenth century, see, among many others, T. H. Breen, "An Empire of Goods: The Anglicization of Colonial America, 1690–1776," *Journal of British Studies* 25:4 (1986): 467–499; David J. Hancock, *Citizens of the World: London Merchants and the Integration of the British Atlantic Community, 1735–1785* (Cambridge: Cambridge University Press, 1995); Eve Tavor Bannet, *Empire of Letters: Letter Manuals and Transatlantic Correspondence* (Cambridge: Cambridge University Press, 2005); Sarah M. S. Pearsall, *Atlantic Families: Lives and Letters in the Later Eighteenth Century* (Oxford: Oxford University Press, 2010); Frank Lambert, *"Pedlar in Divinity": George Whitefield and the Transatlantic Revivals, 1737–1770* (Princeton, NJ: Princeton University Press, 1994); Peter Clark, "Overseas," in *British Clubs and Societies 1580–1800*, 388–429.

23. For a view of Anglican missionary activity agreeing that evangelizing non-Europeans in the British Atlantic world served imperial ends but making the case that in other ways the SPG either did not have political goals or undermined the British government's agenda, see Glasson, *Mastering Christianity*, 33. Meanwhile, in Margaret Abruzzo's view, humanitarianism "became politicized" as it developed in the nineteenth century, as opposed to having a political valence earlier. Abruzzo, *Polemical Pain*.

24. Scholars note the difficulty many Dissenting Protestant groups had in reestablishing ties after the war but have not focused on doctors. Marshall, *The Remaking of the British Atlantic*, 308. Katherine Carté Engel is working on a book project about the impact of the American Revolution on transatlantic Protestant ties. See Katherine Carté Engel, "The SPCK and the American Revolution: The Limits of International Protestantism," *Church History* 81:1 (2012): 77–103. On the crisis of confidence and lack of purpose in London charities during the 1770s, '80s, and '90s, see Andrew, *Philanthropy and Police*, 155–162; see also Joanna Innes and Arthur Burns, "Introduction," in *Rethinking the Age of Reform: Britain 1780–1850* (Cambridge: Cambridge University Press, 2003), 7–11.

25. Other recent scholars have examined eighteenth- and early nineteenth-century humanitarianism in light of political developments. Christopher Brown has recently explored the role of the American Revolution in fostering British abolitionism, while Maya Jasanoff credits the growth of British liberal humanitarianism in part to aid to exiled Loyalists. Brown, *Moral Capital*; Jasanoff, *Liberty's Exiles*. Meanwhile, focusing on a slightly later period, Caroline Shaw explores British humanitarianism to refugees in relation to political upheavals of the nineteenth century; in discussing the shift from the confessional model of the late seventeenth and early eighteenth centuries to the universal approach that emerged early in the 1790s, she does not give much attention to the impact of

the American Revolution on philanthropic traditions. Caroline Shaw, *Britannia's Embrace: Modern Humanitarianism and the Imperial Origins of Refugee Relief* (New York: Oxford University Press, 2015), 23–39. Two recent works have probed the impact of the French and Haitian Revolutions on American humanitarianism. Rachel Hope Cleves, *The Reign of Terror in America: Visions of Violence from Anti-Jacobinism to Antislavery* (Cambridge: Cambridge University Press, 2009); Ashli White, "The Dangers of Philanthropy," in *Encountering Revolution: Haiti and the Making of the Early American Republic* (Baltimore: Johns Hopkins University Press, 2010), 51–86. David Brion Davis too notes that important milestones in the growth of Quaker antislavery coincided with the Seven Years' War and the American Revolution, but he stresses the impact of those wars on the Atlantic economy. Davis, *The Problem of Slavery in the Age of Revolution*, 44, 48; see also 72–82. For his part, Peter Marshall thinks politics were of limited importance in the enduring cultural relationships between Americans and Britons after the war. Marshall, *Remaking the British Atlantic*, 321.

CHAPTER I

1. H. L. Thompson, *Thomas Bray* (London: SPCK, 1954).
2. Thompson, *Thomas Bray*, 36. On the animus by New Englanders outside Boston, see, for instance, Gillian Wagner, *Thomas Coram, Gent. 1688–1751* (Woodbridge: Boydell Press, 2004), 31, 36–37; Thompson, *Thomas Bray*, 57; Jon Butler, *Awash in a Sea of Faith: Christianizing the American People* (Cambridge, MA: Belknap Press of Harvard University Press, 1990), 99–108; Craig Rose, "The Origins and Ideals of the SPCK 1699–1716" in John Walsh, Colin Haydon, and Stephen Taylor, eds., *The Church of England c. 1689–c.1833: From Toleration to Tractarianism* (Cambridge: Cambridge University Press, 1993), 172–190, 187 ("Heathen Nation").
3. Margaret Connell Szasz, *Scottish Highlanders and Native Americans* (Norman: University of Oklahoma Press, 2007), 68–77.
4. Alan Taylor, *American Colonies* (New York: Viking, 2001), 276, chaps. 8–12, 158–272; Butler, *Awash in a Sea of Faith*, 99–108.
5. Taylor, *American Colonies*, 276–278. See also Steve Pincus, *1688: The First Modern Revolution* (New Haven, CT: Yale University Press, 2009).
6. Taylor, *American Colonies*, 278–288; Jacob M. Price, "The Imperial Economy, 1700 –1776," in P. J. Marshall, ed., *The Oxford History of the British Empire: The Eighteenth Century* (Oxford: Oxford University Press, 1998), 78–104, 78; Butler, *Awash in a Sea of Faith*, 99–108, 113–116.
7. T. M. Devine, "Union and Empire," in *Scotland's Empire 1600–1815* (London: Penguin Books, 2003), 49–68.

8. Rose, "The Origins of the SPCK." On the larger context of the efflorescence of Anglican voluntary organizations, see Brent S. Sirota, *Christian Monitors: The Church of England and the Age of Benevolence, 1680–1730* (New Haven, CT: Yale University Press, 2014).

9. Thompson, *Thomas Bray*, 72–73; Frank J. Klingberg, "Leading Ideas in the Annual S.P.G. Sermons, Particularly with Reference to Native Peoples," in *Anglican Humanitarianism in Colonial New York* (Philadelphia: Church Historical Society, 1940, rpt. 1971), 11–48. Another recent book stressing the Atlantic dimensions of the SPG's work is Travis Glasson, *Mastering Christianity: Missionary Anglicanism and Slavery in the Atlantic World* (New York: Oxford University Press, 2012).

10. Szasz, *Scottish Highlanders and Native Americans*, 71–77.

11. "Ignorance" quotation from *An Account of the Rise, Constitution and Management, of the Society in Scotland, for Propagating Christian Knowledge* (London, 1714), 6. On the political context in which the SSPCK was founded, see Szasz, *Scottish Highlanders and Native Americans*, 68–75, "extirpat[e]" quotation on 97; "true Christian religion" and "honest Imployment" quotations from *An Account of the Rise, Constitution and Management, of the Society in Scotland, for Propagating Christian Knowledge*, 7.

12. Philip Bisse, *A Sermon Preach'd Before the Incorporated Society for the Propagation of the Gospel in Foreign Parts; at their Anniversary Meeting in the Parish of St. Mary-le-Bow, on Friday, the 21st of February, 1717* (London, 1718), 11. On the ideas behind the SPG mission, see Klingberg, "Leading Ideas in the Annual S.P.G. Sermons," "civil unity" quotation on 30 from Thomas Secker, *A Sermon Preached Before the Incorporated Society for the Propagation of the Gospel in Foreign Parts* (London, 1741); "laying always in wait" quotation from George Berkeley, *A Sermon Preached Before the Incorporated Society for the Propagation of the Gospel in Foreign Parts* (London, 1732), 17; "every single *Indian*" quotation from Secker, *A Sermon Preached Before the Incorporated Society for the Propagation of the Gospel in Foreign Parts* in Klingberg, *Anglican Humanitarianism in Colonial New York*, 224.

13. Linda Colley, *Britons: Forging the Nation 1707–1837* (New Haven, CT: Yale University Press, 1992); Thomas S. Kidd, *The Protestant Interest: New England after Puritanism* (New Haven, CT: Yale University Press, 2004). On the anti-Catholic and anti-French motives in missions to North American Indians, see Laura M. Stevens, *The Poor Indians: British Missionaries, Native Americans, and Colonial Sensibility* (Philadelphia: University of Pennsylvania Press, 2004); Klingberg, "Some Leading Ideas in the Annual S.P.G. Sermons." Travis Glasson also stresses the importance of religious rivalry to missionary activity. Glasson, *Mastering Christianity*, 19.

14. *Pietas Hallensis: Or a Publick Demonstration of the Foot-steps of a Divine Being Yet in the World: In a Historical Narration of the Orphan-House, and Other Charitable Institutions, at Glaucha near Hall in Saxony* ... [trans. Josiah Woodward],

(London, 1705), i, xii. On the SPCK's role in the publication of *Pietas Hallensis*, see W. R. Ward, *The Protestant Evangelical Awakening* (Cambridge: Cambridge University Press, 1992), and Paul Slack, "Hospitals, Workhouses, and the Relief of the Poor in Early Modern England" in Ole Peter Grell and Andrew Cunningham, eds., *Health Care and Poor Relief in Protestant Europ, 1500–1700* (London: Routledge, 1997), 234–251, 244; Henry Mills, *Schools Commended. The Invaluable Blessing of a Sound, Useful, and Pious Education especially that of School Learning; with a Particular View to Archbp Whitgift's Foundation, in Croydon Surry* (London, 1732), 13, 14, 15.

15. Cotton Mather, *Bonifacius. An Essay Upon the Good, that Is to Be Devised and Designed, by Those who Desire the Great End of Life, and To Do Good While They Live.* (Boston, 1710), 175, vi.

16. Mather, *Bonifacius*, 175; *Pietas Romana et Parisiensis, or a Faithful Relation of the Several Sorts of Charitable and Pious Works Eminent in the Cities of Rome and Paris . . .* (Oxford, 1687), 8–12. See Stevens, *The Poor Indians*, 23; Solomon Stoddard, *Question Whether GOD Is Not Angry with the Country for Doing So Little Towards the Conversion of the Indians?* (Boston, 1723), 9.

17. Numerous scholars develop this point, among them Kidd, *The Protestant Interest*; Klingberg, *Anglican Humanitarianism in Colonial New York*, see esp. chap. 1; Rachel S. Wheeler, *To Live upon Hope: Mohicans and Missionaries in the Eighteenth-Century Northeast* (Ithaca, NY: Cornell University Press, 2008), 32–33; quotations Berkeley, *A Sermon Preached Before the Incorporated Society for the Propagation of the Gospel in Foreign Parts*, 20.

18. On Britons' and Americans' captivity and cultural assimilation, see James Axtell, "The White Indians," in *The Invasion Within: The Contest of Cultures in Colonial North America* (Oxford: Oxford University Press, 1985), 302–327; Linda Colley, *Captives: Britain, Empire, and the World, 1600–1850* (New York: Anchor Books, 2002); William Dalrymple, *White Mughals: Love and Betrayal in Eighteenth-Century India* (New York: Viking, 2003); John Demos, *The Unredeemed Captive: A Family Story from Early America* (New York: Alfred A. Knopf, 1994); Devine, *Scotland's Empire*, 10; Alison Games, *Web of Empire: English Cosmopolitans in an Age of Expansion, 1560–1660* (Oxford: Oxford University Press, 2008); Maya Jasanoff, *Edge of Empire: Lives, Culture, and Conquest in the East, 1750–1850* (New York: Alfred A. Knopf, 2005); quotation from Samuel Hopkins, *Historical Memoirs, Relating to the Housatunnuk Indians: Or, An Account of the Methods used, and Pains taken, for the Propagation of the Gospel among that Heathenish Tribe, and the Success Thereof, under the Ministry of the late Reverend Mr. John Sergeant* (Boston, 1753), 172.

19. Stoddard, *Question Whether God Is Not Angry*, 11. On Stoddard's family's first-hand experience with captivity, see Wheeler, *To Live upon Hope*, 19–20. On the various efforts to convert marginal groups, see below.

20. This sketch of Coram's life draws on Wagner, *Thomas Coram, Gent.* See also H. F. B Compston, *Thomas Coram Churchman, Empire Builder and Philanthropist* (London: SPCK,1918); John Brownlow,*Memoranda; or Chronicles of the Foundling Hospital, Including Memoirs of Captain Coram, &c. &c.* (London, 1847).

21. Taylor, *American Colonies,* 314, 318, 323, 324; on Huguenots, see Jon Butler, *The Huguenots in America: A Refugee People in New World Society* (Cambridge, MA: Harvard University Press, 1983), emigration statistic on 1.

22. Julie Flavell, *When London Was Capital of America* (New Haven, CT: Yale University Press, 2010).

23. Taylor,*American Colonies,* 302; David J. Hancock, *Citizens of the World: London Merchants and the Integration of the British Atlantic Community, 1735–1785* (Cambridge: Cambridge University Press, 1995); Taylor, *American Colonies,* 302. On the consumer revolution, see Maxine Berg, *Luxury and Pleasure in Eighteenth-Century Britain* (Oxford: Oxford University Press, 2005); T. H. Breen, "An Empire of Goods: The Anglicization of Colonial America, 1690–1776," *Journal of British Studies* 25:4 (1986): 467–499, see 486 on the 1740s take-off; John E. Crowley, *The Invention of Comfort: Sensibilities and Design in Early Modern Britain and Early America* (Baltimore: Johns Hopkins University Press, 2001); Neil McKendrick, John Brewer, and J. H. Plumb, *Birth of a Consumer Society* (Bloomington: Indiana University Press, 1982); on the colonial economy, see John J. McCusker and Russell R. Menard, *The Economy of British America, 1607–1789* (Chapel Hill: Published for the Institute of Early American History and Culture, Williamsburg, Virginia, by the University of North Carolina Press, 1985).

24. Ian K. Steele, *The English Atlantic 1675–1740: An Exploration of Communication and Community* (Oxford: Oxford University Press, 1986); Jeremy Black, *The English Press 1621–1861* (Thrupp, Stroud, Gloucestershire, 2001), 20, 9; 74, 110; Steele, *English Atlantic,* 165; Charles E. Clark, "Early American Journalism: News and Opinion in the Popular Press," in Hugh Amory and David Hall, ed., *A History of the Book in America,* Vol. I: *The Colonial Book in the Atlantic World* (Cambridge: Cambridge University Press, 2000), 347–366, 360–361.

25. Harry S. Stout, *The Divine Dramatist: George Whitefield and the Rise of Modern Evangelicalism* (Grand Rapids, MI: W. B. Eerdmans, 1991); Frank Lambert, *"Pedlar in Divinity": George Whitefield and the Transatlantic Revivals, 1737–1770* (Princeton, NJ: Princeton University Press, 1994); Susan O'Brien, "An Eighteenth-Century Publishing Network in the First Years of Transatlantic Evangelicalism," in Mark A. Noll, David W. Bebbington, and George A. Rawlyk, eds., *Evangelicalism: Comparative Studies of Popular Protestantism in North America, the British Isles, and Beyond, 1700–1990* (New York: Oxford University Press, 1994).

26. Wagner, *Thomas Coram, Gent.*

27. Szasz, "The Scottish Society and Native America," in *Scottish Highlanders and Native Americans*, 115–161. The Associates of Dr. Bray also worked to set up parochial libraries. John C. Van Horne, ed., Introduction in *Religious Philanthropy and Colonial Slavery: The American Correspondence of the Associates of Dr. Bray, 1717–1777* (Urbana: University of Illinois Press, 1985), 4–12; *London Magazine*, July 1732, 198; Wagner, *Thomas Coram, Gent.*, 46–52; Van Horne, ed., *Religious Philanthropy and Colonial Slavery*, 9–13; Verner W. Crane, "Philanthropists and the Genesis of Georgia," *American Historical Review* 27:1 (1921): 63–69; Verner W. Crane, "Dr. Thomas Bray and the Charitable Colony Project, 1730," *William and Mary Quarterly*, 3rd series, 19:1 (1962): 49–63; Ruth McClure, *Coram's Children: The London Foundling Hospital in the Eighteenth Century* (New Haven, CT: Yale University Press, 1981), 23–25; Wagner, *Thomas Coram, Gent.*, 91–100.

28. McClure, *Coram's Children*, 19–37.

29. McClure, *Coram's Children*, 55. For good studies of the connection between national policy goals and charity, see Donna T. Andrew, *Philanthropy and Police* (Princeton: Princeton University Press, 1989); James Stephen Taylor, *Jonas Hanway Founder of the Marine Society: Charity and Policy in Eighteenth-Century Britain* (London: Scolar Press,1985); *Gentleman's Magazine* 11 (1741), 163.

30. "Continuation of the Account and Progress &c. of the Orphan House" (1746) in *The Works of the Reverend George Whitefield*, vol. 3, 463. On the founding of Bethesda, see Edward J. Cashin, *Beloved Bethesda: A History of George Whitefield's Home for Boys, 1740–2000* (Macon, GA: Mercer University Press, 2001), esp. chap. 1, and Lambert, *"Pedlar in Divinity,"* 39, 58. "Continuation of the Account and Progress &c. of the Orphan House" (1746) in *The Works of the Reverend George Whitefield*, vol. 3, 463.

31. Lambert, *"Pedlar in Divinity,"* 139. On the Charleston schools founded by Whitefield's friends and by his opponents, see Glasson, *Mastering Christianity*, 121–125.

32. Besides Whitefield with his proposed Negro school and Huguenot refugee, Abel Tassin, Sieur D'Allone, whose bequest to Bray funded the Associates' outreach to people of African descent, the Italian Jewish-born Ottolenghe, the Huguenot-born Anthony Benezet, and the Frenchman Elias Neau were advocates of educating and/or Christianizing people of African descent. On D'Allone, see Van Horne, ed., *Religious Philanthropy and Colonial Slavery*, 3–6. On Ottolenghe, see below. On Benezet, see Maurice Jackson, *Let This Voice Be Heard: Anthony Benezet, Apostle of Atlantic Abolition* (Philadelphia: University of Pennsylvania Press, 2009). On Neau, see "The Society for the Propagation of the Gospel in Foreign Parts: Its Work for the Negroes in North America before 1783," *Journal of Negro History* 18:2 (April 1933): 171–212.

33. Hopkins, *Historical Memoirs*, 84, 97, 85, 119; Richard Brocklesby, *Private Vertue and Public Spirit Display'd: in a Succinct Essay on the Character of Capt.*

Thomas Coram, who Deceased the 29th of March and Was Inter'd in the Chapel of the Foundling Hospital (a Charity Established By His Solicitation) April 3d 1751 (London; Boston, 1751), 16. In his memoirs of John Sergeant, Samuel Hopkins provides some sketchy evidence on Coram's proposed boarding school, about which little is known; see Hopkins, *Historical Memoirs*, 133. For analyses of Sergeant's mission and the significance of his writings, see Wheeler, *To Live upon Hope*, esp. 56–63; Stevens, "The Sacrifice of Self: Emotional Expenditure and Transatlantic Ties in Brainerd's and Sergeant's Biographies," in *The Poor Indians*, 138–159.

34. Wagner, *Thomas Coram, Gent.*, 31–37, 187–188.

35. Lambert, *"Pedlar in Divinity,"* 176.

36. John Calam, *Parsons and Pedagogues: The S.P.G. Adventure in American Education* (New York: Columbia University Press, 1971), 32–33; Klingberg, *Anglican Humanitarianism in Colonial New York*, 6; Frank J. Klingberg, *Codrington Chronicle: An Experiment in Anglican Altruism on a Barbados Plantation, 1710–1834* (Berkeley: University of California Press, 1949), 9. " 'Mines of Wealth,' " " 'mother country,' " " 'creatures of God,' " and " 'possessions in their country,' " quotations in Klingberg, *Anglican Humanitarianism in Colonial New York*, 17, 24. On SPG finances, see the appendices to SPG sermons; on the circulation of annual sermons and fundraising, see Klingberg, *Codrington Chronicle*, 9; Glasson, *Mastering Christianity*, 25.

37. Thompson, *Thomas Bray*, 72–73; Jon Butler, *Power, Authority, and the Origins of the American Denominational Order: The English Churches in the Delaware Valley 1680–1730* (Philadelphia: American Philosophical Society, 1978), 25, 65. On the transatlantic Quaker community, see Frederick Tolles, *Quakers and the Atlantic Culture* (New York: Macmillan 1960), "one people" quotation on 14. On George Keith, the SPG missionary, see Butler, *Power, Authority, and the Origins of the American Denominational Order*, 32–39, 65–68; quotation about "reduction of the Quakers" in Thompson, *Thomas Bray*, 39.

38. On the New England Company, see William Kellaway, *The New England Company 1649–1776: Missionary Society to the American Indians* (New York: Barnes and Noble, 1962); on missionary groups founded in the eighteenth century, see Klingberg, *Anglican Humanitarianism in Colonial New York*; Calam, *Parsons and Pedagogues*; Szasz, *Scottish Highlanders and Native Americans*; John A. Grigg, "'How This Shall Be Brought About': The Development of the SSPCK's American Policy," *Itinerario* 3 (2008): 43–60.

39. Christine Leigh Heyrman, "A Model of Christian Charity: The Rich and the Poor in New England 1630–1730" (Ph.D. diss., Yale University, 1977), 115–116.

40. Whitefield was explicit about emulating Francke. See "An Account of the Orphan-House in Georgia" (dated 1741; published 1743), *The Works of the Reverend George Whitefield*, vol. 3, 432; "A Continuation of the Account of the Orphan-House

in Georgia" (dated 1742), in *The Works of the Reverend George Whitefield*, vol. 3, 451; "Continuation of the Account and Progress &c. of the Orphan House" (1746) in *The Works of the Reverend George Whitefield*, vol. 3, 466; compare the accounts of Bethesda to the accounts of Francke's institution in *Pietas Hallensis*. On Bethesda's shaky finances, see Lambert, *"Pedlary in Divinity,"* 207.

41. On the activities of the busy London philanthropist, John Percival, see the three volumes of his diaries covering 1730–1747 published as *Manuscripts of the Earl of Egmont* (London, 1920). On Colman, see Ebenezer Turell, *The Life and Character of the Reverend Benjamin Colman, D.D. late Pastor of a Church in Boston New-England. Who Deceased August 29th 1747* (Boston, 1749), see 145; Van Horne, ed., *Religious Philanthropy and Colonial Slavery*, 74–77, 82; *The Works of the Reverend George Whitefield*, vol. 3 (London, 1771), 449; "Letters of Thomas Coram," *Proceedings of the Massachusetts Historical Society* 56 (1923): 15–56; Heyrman, "A Model of Christian Charity," 116–120; Hopkins, *Historical Memoirs*, 84, 97, 85, 119.

42. On Bray, see Thompson, *Thomas Bray*. On Coram, see Wagner, *Thomas Coram, Gent*. On Whitefield, see Stout, *The Divine Dramatist*; Lambert, *"Pedlar in Divinity."* On Franklin, see Gordon S. Wood, *The Americanization of Benjamin Franklin* (New York: Penguin Press, 2004). On ambition in the eighteenth century, see J. M. Opal, *Beyond, the Farm: National Ambitions in Rural New England* (Philadelphia: University of Pennsylvania Press, 2008); Hancock, *Citizens of the World*.

43. On English associated philanthropy, see Andrew, *Philanthropy and Police*, esp. 44–49; Paul Langford, *A Polite and Commercial People: England, 1727–1783* (Oxford: Clarendon Press, 1989), 482–490; David Owen, *English Philanthropy, 1660–1960* (Cambridge, MA: Belknap Press of Harvard University Press, 1964), 11–68, 97–133. For the view that associationalism was nothing new in the eighteenth century, see Joanna Innes, "State, Church and Voluntarism" in Hugh Cunningham and Joanna Innes, eds., *Charity, Philanthropy and Reform from the 1690s to 1850* (New York: St. Martin's Press, 1998), 15–66, 37. On charitable trusts in Tudor and Stuart England, see Jordan, *Philanthropy in England*; Peter Clark, *British Clubs and Societies 1580–1800: The Origins of an Associational World* (Oxford: Oxford University Press, 2000); Jessica Choppin Roney, *Governed by a Spirit of Opposition: The Origins of American Political Practice in Colonial Philadelphia* (Baltimore: Johns Hopkins University Press, 2014).

44. Szasz, *Scottish Highlanders and Native Americans*, 74; Kellaway, *The New England Company*, 187–192; Grigg, "'How Shall This Be Brought About,'" 48–49. *Gentleman's Magazine* 9 (1739), 288. Roy Porter, "The Gift Relation: Philanthropy and Provincial Hospitals in Eighteenth-Century England," in Lindsay Granshaw and Roy Porter, eds., *The Hospital in History* (London: Routledge, 1989), 149–178; Adrian Wilson, "Conflict, Consensus and Charity: Politics and the Provincial

192 *Notes to Page 28*

Voluntary Hospitals in the Eighteenth Century," *English Historical Review* 111 (1996): 599–619; Adrian Wilson, "The Politics of Medical Improvement in Early Hanoverian England," in Andrew Cunningham and Roger French, eds., *The Medical Enlightenment of the Eighteenth Century* (Cambridge: Cambridge University Press, 1990).

45. *Manuscripts of the Earl of Egmont. Diary of the First Earl of Egmont (Viscount Percival),* vol. 2: *1734–1738* (London, 1920), 182 (June 25, 1735). See above on Colman's reaction to the SPG. "List of Books Sent to New England," [April 21, 1735], Van Horne, ed., *Religious Philanthropy and Colonial Slavery,* 76–77; Frank J. Klingberg, *Contributions of the S.P.G. to the American Way of Life* (Philadelphia: Church Historical Society, 1943), 40; *Diary of the First Earl of Egmont,* vol. 2, 256 (April 5, 1736), 170 (April 21, 1735); *New England Weekly Journal,* March 17, 1735. On the Bray Associates' ignorance about colonial slavery, see Van Horne, ed., *Religious Philanthropy and Colonial Slavery,* 36–38.

46. T. H. Breen, "Inventories of Desire: The Evidence," in *The Marketplace of Revolution: How Consumer Politics Shaped American Independence* (New York: Oxford University Press, 2004), 33–71. Franklin quotation from letter to Henry Homes, Lord Kames, January 3, 1760, in Alan Houston, *Benjamin Franklin and Politics of Improvement* (New Haven, CT: Yale University Press, 2008), 57; T. H. Breen, "'Baubles of Britain': The American and Consumer Revolutions of the Eighteenth Century," *Past and Present* 119 (1988): 73–104; Gary Nash, "Poverty and Poor Relief in Pre-Revolutionary Poor Relief," *William and Mary Quarterly,* 3rd series, 33:1 (1976): 3–30; Gary Nash, *The Urban Crucible: The Northern Seaports and the Origins of the American Revolution* (Cambridge, MA: Harvard University Press, 1986); Billy G. Smith, "Inequality in Late Colonial Philadelphia: A Note on Its Nature and Growth," *William and Mary Quarterly,* 3rd series, 41 (1984): 629–645; Billy G. Smith, "The Material Lives of Laboring Philadelphians, 1750-1800," *William and Mary Quarterly,* 3rd series, 38:2 (1981): 164–202; Billy G. Smith, ed., *Down and Out in Early America* (University Park: Pennsylvania University Press, 2004).

47. On the founding of the colleges, see Alan Tully, *Forming American Politics: Ideals, Interests, and Institutions in Colonial New York and Pennsylvania* (Baltimore: Johns Hopkins University Press, 1994), 134–159; on the desirability of stratification to well-off Americans, see Jack P. Greene, *Imperatives, Behaviors and Identities: Essays in Early American Cultural History* (Charlottesville: University of Virginia Press, 1992), 190–194. Allan Everett Marble, *Surgeons, Smallpox, and the Poor: A History of Medicine in Nova Scotia, 1749–1799* (Montreal: McGills-Queen's University Press, 1993), 32; Carl Bridenbaugh, *Cities in Revolt: Urban Life in America, 1743–1776* (New York: Alfred A. Knopf, 1955), 122–128; Stephen Edward Wiberly Jr., "Four Cities: Public Poor Relief in Urban America 1700–1775" (Ph.D. diss., Yale University, 1975); William H. Williams, "The 'Industrious

Poor' and the Founding of the Pennsylvania Hospital," *Pennsylvania Magazine of History and Biography* 97 (1973): 431–443.

48. Bridenbaugh, *Cities in Revolt*, 127; Peter Silver, *Our Savage Neighbors: How Indian War Transformed Early America* (New York: W.W. Norton, 2008), 100; Roney, *Governed by a Spirit of Opposition*; Clark, *British Clubs and Societies*; Tim Hitchcock, "Paupers and Preachers: The SPCK and the Parochial Workhouse Movement," in Lee Davison, et al., eds., *Stilling the Grumbling Hive: The Response to Social and Economic Problems in England, 1689–1850* (New York: St. Martin's Press, 1992), 145–166; John Woodward, *To Do the Sick No Harm: The British Voluntary Hospital Movement to 1875* (London: Routledge and Kegan Paul, 1974).

49. *Continuation of the Account of the Pennsylvania Hospital: From the First of May 1754, to the Fifth of May 1761* (Philadelphia, 1761), 62; Williams, " 'The Industrious Poor' and the Founding of the Pennsylvania Hospital."

50. Bridenbaugh, *Cities in Revolt*, 122, 126; Taylor, *Jonas Hanway Founder of the Marine Society*, 69–73, 15–16, 76–79; Andrew, *Philanthropy and Police*, esp. 110, 121–121; Hancock, *Citizens of the World*, 170, 310–312.

51. On prejudice against Germans, see Silver 12–13, 18–19, 98, 192–193; Houston, *Benjamin Franklin and the Politics of Improvement*, 138–139; *A Memorial of the Case of the German Emigrants Settled in the British Colonies of Pensilvania, and the Back Parts of Maryland, Virginia, &c.* (London, 1754), "considerable body" quotation, 6. On the schools, see Whitfield J. Bell, "Benjamin Franklin and the German Charity Schools," *Proceedings of the American Philosophical Society* 99: 6 (1955): 381–387; Carl and Jessica Bridenbaugh, *Rebels and Gentlemen: Philadelphia in the Age of Franklin* (New York: Reynal and Hitchcock, 1942), 52–53; Samuel E. Weber, "The Charity School Movement in Pennsylvania" (Ph.D. diss., University of Pennsylvania, 1905); William Smith, *A Brief History of the Rise and Progress of the Charitable Scheme, Carrying on by a Society of Noblemen and Gentlemen, for the Relief and Instruction of Poor Germans* (Philadelphia, 1755), and *A Memorial of the Case of the German Emigrants Settled in the British Colonies of Pensilvania, and the Back Parts of Maryland, Virginia, &c.* (London, 1754); *Gentleman's Magazine* 25 (1755), 103; "plain" and "no farther knowledge" quotations, *A Memorial of the Case of the German Emigrants*, 13.

52. On Wheelock's school, see Szasz, *Scottish Highlanders and Native Americans*, 136–150; Eleazar Wheelock, *A Plain and Faithful Narrative of the Original Design, Rise, Progress and Present State of the Indian Charity-School at Lebanon, in Connecticut* (Boston, [1763]); Van Horne, ed., *Religious Philanthropy and Colonial Slavery*, 20–25; John C. Van Horne, "Joseph Solomon Ottolenghe (ca. 1711–1775): Catechist to the Negroes, Superintendent of the Silk Culture, and Public Servant in Colonial Georgia," *Proceedings of the American Philosophical Society* 125:5 (1981): 398–409; Meetings of the Associates of Dr. Bray, July 10, 1752, June 8, 1753, June 21, 1754, Minute Book, vol. 1, 1735–1768; Manuscripts of Dr. Bray's

Associates, Facsimilies from English Archives, Society for the Propagation of the Gospel in Foreign Parts, Library of Congress, Washington, DC; John Waring to Benjamin Franklin, January 24, 1757, in Van Horne, ed., *Religious Philanthropy and Colonial Slavery*, 122; Frederick Cornwallis, *A Sermon Preached before the Incorporated Society for the Propagation of the Gospel in Foreign Parts* (London, 1756), 16.

53. *Gentleman's Magazine* 21 (1751), 86; *Gentleman's Magazine* 23 (1753), 539; *Gentleman's Magazine* 24 (1754), 552; *Gentleman's Magazine* 25 (1755), 103; Renate Wilson, *Pious Traders in Medicine: A German Pharmaceutical Network in Eighteenth-Century North America* (University Park: Pennsylvania State University Press, 2000); Sydney V. James, *A People among Peoples: Quaker Benevolence in Eighteenth-Century America* (Cambridge, MA: Harvard University Press, 1963); Jonas Hanway, *An Account of the Marine Society, Recommending the Piety and Policy of the Institution* (London, [1759]), 6, 39; "For the Encouragement of a Charitable Society," *New-York Gazette*, March 9, 1761; Matthew Mulcahy, "Sympathy in Distress," in *Hurricanes and Society in the British Greater Caribbean, 1624–1783* (Baltimore: Johns Hopkins University Press, 2006), 141–164. My thanks to Charlie Foy for pointing out the appeal to the New Yorkers by the London ladies' charity.

54. Benjamin Martyn, *Reasons for Establishing the Colony of Georgia, with Regard to the Trade of Great Britain, the Increase of Our People, and the Employment and Support It Will Afford to Great Numbers of Our Own Poor, as Well as Foreign Persecuted Protestants* (London, 1733), 31.

55. This discussion draws on Andrew, *Philanthropy and Police*, 38–40; Norman Fiering, "Irresistible Compassion: An Aspect of Eighteenth-Century Sympathy and Humanitarianism," *Journal of the History of Ideas* 37 (1976): 195–218; Karen Halttunen, "Humanitarianism and the Pornography of Pain in Anglo-American Culture," *American Historical Review* 100 (1995): 303–334; Albert Hirschman, *The Passions and the Interests: Political Arguments for Capitalism before Its Triumph* (Princeton, NJ: Princeton University Press, 1977); Sarah Knott, "Sensibility and the American War for Independence," *American Historical Review* 109 (2004): 19–40; John Mullan, *Sentiment and Sociability: The Language of Feeling in Eighteenth-Century* (Oxford: Clarendon Press, 1998); Evan Radcliffe, "Revolutionary Writing, Moral Philosophy, and Universal Benevolence in the Eighteenth Century," *Journal of the History of Ideas* 54 (1993): 221–240; Keith Thomas, *Man and the Natural World: Changing Attitudes in England 1500–1800* (Oxford: Oxford University Press, 1983); Janet Todd, *Sensibility: An Introduction* (London: Methuen 1986); Gordon S. Wood, "Benevolence," in *The Radicalism of the American Revolution* (New York: Vintage Books, 1991), 213–225. Quotation from Martyn, *Reasons for Establishing the Colony of Georgia*, 38.

56. Mandeville's pamphlet, *The Fable of the Bees, or Private Vices, Publick Benefits*, was first published in 1714. On his ideas and the reaction to them, see M. M. Goldsmith, "Mandeville, Bernard (bap. 1670, d. 1733)," in H. C. G. Matthew and Brian Harrison, eds., *Oxford Dictionary of National Biography* (Oxford: Oxford University Press, 2004), http://www.oxforddnb.com/view/article/17926 (accessed August 31, 2009); Andrew, *Philanthropy and Police*, 30–41; Hirschman, *The Passions and the Interests*, 18–19.

57. See note 55 above.

58. On medieval charity, see Miri Rubin, *Charity and Community in Medieval Cambridge* (Cambridge: Cambridge University Press, 1987); Joel Rosenthal, *The Purchase of Paradise: Gift Giving and the Aristocracy, 1307–1485* (London: Routledge and Kegan Paul, 1972); see also Felicity Heal, *Hospitality in Early Modern England* (Oxford: Clarendon Press, 1990). On changing ideas about charity, see Christine Heyrman, "A Model of Christian Charity"; Andrew, *Philanthropy and Police*, 12–20, Mandeville quotation on 33. On ideas about charity's benefits to donors, see Christine Leigh Heyrman, "The Fashion among More Superior People: Charity and Social Change in Provincial New England, 1700–1740," *American Quarterly* 34 (1982): 107–124; Carolyn Williams, "'The Luxury of Doing Good'": Benevolence, Sensibility, and the Royal Humane Society," in Roy Porter and Marie Mulvey Roberts, eds., *Pleasure in the Eighteenth Century* (New York: New York University Press, 1996), 77–107; Andrew, *Philanthropy and Police*, 20–22, 36 ("pleasant enjoyment"); Heyrman, "A Model of Christian Charity," 257 ("greatest pleasure").

59. On Hume, see Fiering, "Irresistible Compassion," 209–210; Radcliffe, "Revolutionary Writing, Moral Philosophy, and Universal Benevolence," 222. On Edwards, see Radcliffe, "Revolutionary Writing, Moral Philosophy, and Universal Benevolence," 222; Conrad Edick Wright, *The Transformation of Charity in Postrevolutionary New England* (Boston: Northeastern University Press, 1992), 42–45. On Adam Smith's views, see Fiering, "Irresistible Compassion," 210–212; Stevens, *The Poor*, 10–11; Adam Smith, *The Theory of Moral Sentiments* (1759; Prometheus books edition, New York, 2000), quotation 348. On the idea that universal benevolence was impractical, see Wright, "Our Powers Are Limitted" in *The Transformation of Charity*, 16–47; Radcliffe, "Revolutionary Writing," 222–226.

60. For mentions of the Good Samarian, see, for example, Mills, *Schools Commended. The Invaluable Blessing of a Sound, Useful, and Pious Education especially that of School Learning*, 6; Samuel Hopkins, *Historical Memoirs*, 181; John Gibson, *The Unlimited Extent and Final Blessedness of God's Spiritual Kingdom: A Sermon, Preached Before the Society for Propagating Christian Knowledge, At their Anniversary Meeting, In the High Church of Edinburgh, on Friday, June 3, 1768* (Edinburgh, 1768), 37.

61. *Gentleman's Magazine* 25 (1755), 521–522; on the Lisbon earthquake, see T. D. Kendrick, *The Lisbon Earthquake* (London: Methuen, 1956). Fred Anderson, *Crucible of War: The Seven Years' War and the Fate of Empire in North America* (New York: Vintage Books, 2001), 112–114; on the Acadian expulsion and the trials of the dispersed Acadians, see Christopher Hodson, *Acadian Diaspora: An Eighteenth-Century History* (Oxford: Oxford University Press, 2012); Silver, *Our Savage Neighbors*, 99–101; *Proceedings of the Committee Appointed to Manage the Contributions Begun at London Dec. XVIII MDCCLVIII for cloathing French Prisoners of War* (London, 1760), quotations in unpaginated preface.

62. A brilliant new book by Cornelia Dayton and Sharon Salinger brings to light the systems of public poor relief for strangers in Massachusetts and certain other New England colonies. Cornelia H. Dayton and Sharon V. Salinger, *Robert Love's Warnings: Searching for Strangers in Colonial Boston* (Philadelphia: University of Pennsylvania Press, 2014). Thomas Coram to Benjamin Colman, September 22, 1738, in "Letters of Thomas Coram," 48–51, quotation 48; Silver, *Our Savage Neighbors*, 100.

63. Draft of a letter from Benjamin Rush to the managers of Pennsylvania Hospital, September 24, 1810, Benjamin Rush Manuscripts, vol. 31, f. 53, Library Company of Philadelphia.

64. William Smith to Thomas Penn, August 3, 1762, William Smith Papers, Box 1, Folder 62, University of Pennsylvania Archives, Philadelphia; William Smith to Richard Peters, July 10, 1762, Box 2, Folder 40,William Smith Papers University of Pennsylvania Archives.

65. Benjamin Colman to the Bishop of Peterborough, November 1712, in Turell, *The Life and Character of the Reverend Benjamin Colman*, 123.

66. Kellaway, *The New England Company*, 194.

67. *Gentleman's Magazine* 36 (1766), 197, 425.

CHAPTER 2

1. Benjamin Rush to Ebenezer Hazard, September 27, [1762], Benjamin Rush to Ebenezer Hazard, October 22, 1768, in L. H. Butterfield, ed., *Letters of Benjamin Rush*, 2 vols. (Princeton, NJ: Published for the American Philosophical Society by Princeton University Press, 1951), vol. 1, 5 ("our forces"), 68 ("infernal scheme"); Fred Anderson, *Crucible of War: The Seven Years' War and the Fate of Empire in North America* (New York: Vintage Books, 2001), 500–501; Benjamin Rush to John Coakley Lettsom, May 18, 1787, in Butterfield, ed., *Letters of Benjamin Rush*, vol. 1, 417 ("empire of humanity"); John Morgan, *A Discourse Upon the Institution of Medical Schools in America; Delivered at a Public Anniversary Commencement, held in the College of Philadelphia May 30 and 31, 1765* (Philadelphia, 1765), 62 ("benefactors of mankind").

2. These men include Samuel Bard (1742–1821); Jeremy Belknap (1744–1798); Andrew Bell (1753–1832); Thomas Bernard (1750–1808); Thomas Cogan (1736–1818); Patrick Colquhoun (1745–1820); John Crawford (1746–1813); James Currie (1756–1805); Thomas Eddy (1758–1827); William Hawes (1736–1808); John Haygarth (1740–1827); John Howard (c. 1726–1790); John Lathrop (1740–1816); John Coakley Lettsom (1744–1815); John Murray (1721–1792); Thomas Percival (1740–1804); John D. Rodgers (1727–1811); Benjamin Rush (1746–1813); Thomas Russell (1740–1796); Benjamin Thompson, Count Rumford (1753–1814); Benjamin Waterhouse (1754–1846); and William White (1748–1836).

3. Albert Nicholson, "Percival, Thomas (1740–1804)," rev. John V. Pickstone, *Oxford Dictionary of National Biography* (Oxford: Oxford University Press, 2004), http://www.oxforddnb.com.proxy.lib.umich.edu/view/article/21921, accessed September 19, 2007; J. F. Payne, "Lettsom, John Coakley (1744–1815)," rev. Roy Porter, in *Oxford Dictionary of National Biography* (Oxford: Oxford University Press, 2004); "Jeremy Belknap" in *Sibley's Harvard Graduates* (Boston: Massachusetts Historical Society, 1970), vol. 15, 175–195; David Freeman Hawke, *Benjamin Rush Revolutionary Gadfly* (Indianapolis: Bobbs-Merrill, 1971), 163–164; David L. Cowen. "Crawford, John"; http://www.anb.org.proxy.lib.umich.edu/articles/12/12-00178.html; *American National Biography Online*, February 2000, accessed September 19, 2007; Philip Cash, "Waterhouse, Benjamin"; http://www.anb.org.proxy.lib.umich.edu/articles/12/12-00951.html; *American National Biography Online*, February 2000, accessed September 19, 2007; David Knight, "Thompson, Sir Benjamin, Count Rumford in the nobility of the Holy Roman empire (1753–1814)," *Oxford Dictionary of National Biography* (Oxford: Oxford University Press, 2004), http://www.oxforddnb.com.proxy.lib.umich.edu/view/article/27255, accessed September 19, 2007.

4. Basic biographical data on these men can be found in the following sources: On Samuel Bard, see J. Brett Langstaff, *Dr. Bard of Hyde Park* (New York: E. P. Dutton, 1942). On Jeremy Belknap, see "Jeremy Belknap" in *Sibley's Harvard Graduates*, 175–195. On Andrew Bell, see Jane Blackie, "Bell, Andrew (1753–1832)," *Oxford Dictionary of National Biography* (Oxford: Oxford University Press, 2004), http://www.oxforddnb.com.proxy.lib.umich.edu/view/article/1995, accessed September 19, 2007. On Thomas Bernard, see R. D. Sheldon, "Bernard, Sir Thomas, second baronet (1750–1818)," *Oxford Dictionary of National Biography* (Oxford: Oxford University Press, 2004), http://www.oxforddnb.com.proxy.lib.umich.edu/view/article/2251, accessed September 19, 2007. On Thomas Cogan, see Carolyn D. Williams, "Cogan, Thomas (1736–1818)," *Oxford Dictionary of National Biography* (Oxford: Oxford University Press, September 2004); online ed., May 2007, http://www.oxforddnb.com.proxy.lib.umich.edu/view/article/5813, accessed September 19, 2007. On Patrick Colquhoun, see Ruth Paley, "Colquhoun, Patrick (1745–1820)," in H. C. G. Matthew and Brian Harrison,

eds., *Oxford Dictionary of National Biography* (Oxford: Oxford University Press, 2004); online ed., ed. Lawrence Goldman, January 2008, http://www.oxforddnb.com/view/article/5992, accessed February 9, 2010. On John Crawford, see Cowen, "Crawford, John." On James Currie, see William Wallace Currie, *Memoir of the Life, Writings, and Correspondence of James Currie, M.D. F.R.S. of Liverpool* (London, 1831). On Thomas Eddy, see H. Larry Ingle, "Eddy, Thomas," http://www.anb.org.proxy.lib.umich.edu/articles/15/15-00200.html, *American National Biography Online*, February 2000, accessed September 19, 2007. On William Hawes, see Carolyn D. Williams, "Hawes, William (1736–1808)," in H. C. G. Matthew and Brian Harrison, eds., *Oxford Dictionary of National Biography* (Oxford: Oxford University Press, 2004), http://www.oxforddnb.com.proxy.lib.umich.edu/view/article/12648, accessed April 24, 2008. On John Haygarth, see Christopher Booth, *John Haygarth, FRS: A Physician of the Enlightenment* (Philadelphia: American Philosophical Society, 2005). On John Howard, see James Baldwin Brown, *Memoirs of the Public and Private Life of John Howard, the Philanthropist, Compiled from his own Diary ... His Confidential Letters; the Communications of his Surviving Relatives and Friends; and other Authentic Sources of Information*, 2nd ed. (London, 1823); D. L. Howard, *John Howard: Prison Reformer* (London: C. Johnson, 1958), http://www.oxforddnb.com.proxy.lib.umich.edu/view/article/57457, accessed September 19, 2007. On John Lathrop, see Francis Parkman, *A Sermon Delivered at the Interment of the Rev. John Lathrop, D.D., Pastor of the Second Church in Boston, who Died Jan. 4, 1816, in the Seventh-Sixth Year of His Age, and Forty-Eighth of His Ministry* (Boston, 1816). On John Coakley Lettsom, see Payne, "Lettsom, John Coakley (1744–1815)." On John Murray, see the obituary of Murray in *The Gentleman's Magazine* 62 (1792), 961. Patricia Cleary, *Elizabeth Murray: A Woman's Pursuit of Independence in Eighteenth-Century America* (Amherst: University of Massachusetts Press, 2000), 16; Nina Moore Tiffany, *Letters of James Murray Loyalist* (Boston, 1901), 1–2; John Burke, *Burke's Landed Gentry* (London, 1846), 903. On Thomas Percival, see Nicholson, "Percival, Thomas (1740–1804)." On John D. Rodgers, see Samuel Miller, *Memoir of the Rev. John Rodgers, D.D. Late Pastor of the Wall-Street and Brick Churches, in the City of New-York* (New York, 1813). On Benjamin Rush, see Goodman, *Benjamin Rush Physician and Citizen*; Hawke, *Benjamin Rush: Revolutionary Gadfly*. On Thomas Russell, see John Warren, *An Eulogy on the Honourable Thomas Russell, Esq.* (Boston, 1796). On Benjamin Waterhouse, see Cash, "Waterhouse, Benjamin"; Knight, "Thompson, Sir Benjamin, Count Rumford in the nobility of the Holy Roman empire (1753–1814)." On William White, see Bird Wilson, *Memoir of the Life of Bishop White* (Philadelphia, 1839).

5. John Crawford died in debt. Julia Wilson, "Dr. John Crawford, 1746–1813," *Bulletin of the School of Medicine, University of Maryland* 25 (1940): 116–132, 117.

6. David J. Hancock, *Citizens of the World: London Merchants and the Integration of the British Atlantic Community, 1735–1785* (Cambridge: Cambridge University Press, 1995), 280–281; John Bard to Samuel Bard, April 9, 1763, Bard Collection, New York Academy of Medicine (NYAM).

7. Gordon S. Wood, *The Radicalism of the American Revolution* (New York: Vintage Books, 1991), 19–24; Rhys Isaac, *The Transformation of Virginia 1740–1790* (Chapel Hill: Published for the Institute of Early American History and Culture, 1982), 104; John K. Alexander, *Render Them Submissive: Responses to Poverty in Philadelphia, 1760–1800* (Amherst: University of Massachusetts Press, 1980), 22–23; Gary Nash, "Poverty and Poor Relief in Pre-Revolutionary Poor Relief," *William and Mary Quarterly*, 3rd series, 33:1 (1976): 3–30; Billy G. Smith, "Inequality in Late Colonial Philadelphia: A Note on Its Nature and Growth," *William and Mary Quarterly*, 3rd series, 41 (1984): 629–645.

8. Neil McKendrick, John Brewer, and J. H. Plumb, *Birth of a Consumer Society* (Bloomington: Indiana University Press, 1982); Maxine Berg, *Luxury and Pleasure in Eighteenth-Century Britain* (Oxford: Oxford University Press, 2005). T. H. Breen, *The Marketplace of Revolution: How Consumer Politics Shaped the American Revolution* (New York: Oxford University Press, 2004), see esp. 53–59; John Brewer, *The Pleasures of the Imagination: English Culture in the Eighteenth Century* (New York: Farrar, Straus and Giroux, 1997); Jan Golinski, *Science as Public Culture: Chemistry and Enlightenment in Britain, 1760–1820* (Cambridge: Cambridge University Press, 1992); Sarah Lloyd, "Pleasing Spectacles and Elegant Dinners: Conviviality, Benevolence, and Charity Anniversaries in Eighteenth-Century London," *Journal of British Studies* 41 (2002): 23–57; Laura M. Stevens, *The Poor Indians: British Missionaries, Native Americans, and Colonial Sensibility* (Philadelphia: University of Pennsylvania Press, 2004), 4; Carolyn Williams, "'The Luxury of Doing Good': Benevolence, Sensibility, and the Royal Humane Society," in Roy Porter and Marie Mulvey Roberts, eds., *Pleasure in the Eighteenth Century* (New York: New York University Press, 1996), 77–107; Gordon S. Wood, *The Americanization of Benjamin Franklin* (New York: Penguin Press, 2004), esp. chap. 1; Harry S. Stout, *The Divine Dramatist: George Whitefield and the Rise of Modern Evangelicalism* (Grand Rapids, MI: W. B. Eerdmans, 1991); Donna T. Andrew and Randall McGowen, *The Perreaus and Mrs. Rudd: Forgery and Betrayal in Eighteenth-Century London* (Berkeley: University of California Press, 2001).

9. George W. Corner, ed., *The Autobiography of Benjamin Rush: His "Travels Through Life" together with His Commonplace Book for 1789–1813* (Princeton, NJ: Published for the American Philosophical Society by Princeton University Press, 1948), 28, 55, 56; Leigh E. Schmidt, "Finley, Samuel," *American National Biography* http://www.anb.org/articles/01/01-00284.html, *American National Biography Online*, February 2000, accessed January 3, 2013; John Coakley Lettsom, "Recollections

or Reminiscences [by Dr. J. C. Lettsom]," in Christopher Lawrence and Fiona A. MacDonald, eds., *Sambrook Court: The Letters of J. C. Lettsom at the Medical Society of London* (London: Wellcome Trust Centre for the History of Medicine at University College London, 2003), 17.

10. Ira Berlin, "The Emergence of Atlantic Creoles in the Chesapeake," in *Many Thousands Gone: The First Two Centuries of Slavery in North America* (Cambridge, MA: Belknap Press of Harvard University Press, 1998), 29–46; Cassandra Pybus, "Billy Blue: An African American Journey through Empire in the Long Eighteenth Century," *Early American Studies* 5 (2007): 252–288; Jon Sensbach, *Rebecca's Revival: Creating Black Christianity in the Atlantic World* (Cambridge, MA: Harvard University Press, 2005); on the delegates to the Constitutional Convention (compared to the Spanish American liberators), see J. H. Elliott, *Empires of the Atlantic World: Britain and Spain in America 1492–1830* (New Haven, CT: Yale University Press, 2006), 395–396.

11. Lawrence and MacDonald, *Sambrook Court*, 2. On American medical students abroad, see Whitfield J. Bell Jr., "Philadelphia Medical Students in Europe, 1750–1800," *Pennsylvania Magazine of History and Biography* 67 (1943): 1–29; Richard Harrison Shryock, *Medicine and Society in America 1660–1860* (Ithaca, NY: Cornell University Press, 1972), 7–18. John Bard to Samuel Bard, April 9, 1763, Bard Collection, NYAM; *The Autobiography of Benjamin Rush*, 43 ("several parts"); John M. O'Donnell, "Cullen's Influence on American Medicine," in A. Doig, J. P. S. Ferguson, I. A. Milne and R. Passmore, eds., *William Cullen and the Eighteenth Century Medical World* (Edinburgh: Edinburgh University Press, 1993), 236–237. The Anglican John Haygarth, for instance, went to Edinburgh. Christopher C. Booth, *John Haygarth, FRS (1740–1827): Physician of the Enlightenment* (Philadelphia: American Philosophical Society, 2005), 29; Lawrence and MacDonald, *Sambrook Court*, 2; Cash. "Waterhouse, Benjamin"; Knight, "Thompson, Sir Benjamin, Count Rumford in the nobility of the Holy Roman empire (1753–1814)."

12. Corner, ed., *The Autobiography of Benjamin Rush*, 52; Lettsom, "Recollections or Reminiscences," in Lawrence and MacDonald, *Sambrook Court*, 23–25; Benjamin Rush to John Morgan, July 27, 1768, in L. H. Butterfield, ed., *Letters of Benjamin Rush*, 2 vols. (Princeton, NJ: Published for the American Philosophical Society by Princeton University Press, 1951), vol. 1, 61; John Fothergill to Israel Pemberton, London, March 28, 1741, in Betsy C. Corner and Christopher C. Booth, eds., *Chain of Friendship: Selected Letters of Dr. John Fothergill of London, 1735–1780* (Cambridge, MA: Belknap Press of Harvard University Press, 1971), 57.

13. John Bard to Samuel Bard, New York, April 9, 1763, December 12, 1764, Bard Collection, NYAM; Samuel Bard to his parents, August 14, 1762, in John M'Vickar, *A Domestic Narrative of the Life of Samuel Bard, M.D. LL.D* (New York, 1822); Lettsom, "Recollections or Reminiscences" in Lawrence and MacDonald,

Sambrook Court, 15, 19, 22; Corner, ed., *The Autobiography of Benjamin Rush*, 53, 66–67, 54; John Coakley Lettsom, *Recollections of Dr. Rush* (London, 1815), 4–5; James Johnston Abraham, *Lettsom: His Life, Times, Friends and Descendants* (London: W. Heinemann, 1933), 360.

14. Lettsom, "Recollections or Reminiscences," in Lawrence and MacDonald, *Sambrook Court*, 24.

15. Corner, ed., *The Autobiography of Benjamin Rush*, 69; Benjamin Rush to Ebenezer Hazard, October 22, 1768, in Butterfield, ed., *Letters of Benjamin Rush*, vol. 1, 68.

16. Wilson, *Memoir of the Life of the Right Reverend Bishop White, D.D*, 31.

17. Currie, ed., *Memoir of the Life, Writings, and Correspondence of James Currie*, vol. 1, 10.

18. Hancock, *Citizens of the World*, 44–78; Thomas M. Doerflinger, *A Vigorous Spirit of Enterprise: Merchants and Economic Development in Revolutionary Philadelphia* (Chapel Hill: Published for the Institute of Early American History and Culture, Williamsburg, Virginia, by the University of North Carolina Press, 1986), 55–56; Warren, *An Eulogy on the Honourable Thomas Russell*, 11.

19. Warren, *An Eulogy on the Honourable Thomas Russell*, 13. Goodman, *Benjamin Rush*, 12; Lettsom, "Recollections or Reminiscences" in Lawrence and MacDonald, eds., *Sambrook Court*, 19, 22. Jonathan Allen Fowler, *Adventures of an 'Itinerant Institutor': The Life and Philanthropy of Thomas Bernard* (Ph.D. diss., University of Tennessee, 2003), 53. "Memoir of Thomas Cogan, M.D., One of the Founders of the Royal Humane Society," *The Annual Biography and Obituary, for the Year 1819* (London, 1819), 73–98, 76–77.

20. Benjamin Rush to Ebenezer Hazard, March 19, 1765, in Butterfield, ed., *Letters of Benjamin Rush*, vol. 1, 10.

21. For an overview of the English poor law in this period, see Paul A. Fideler, *Social Welfare in Pre-Industrial England: The Old Poor Law Tradition* (Basingstoke: Palgrave Macmillan, 2006); Steven King, *Poverty and Welfare in England 1700–1850: A Regional Perspective* (Manchester: Manchester University Press, 2000), 81, 79; Lynn Hollen Lees, *The Solidarities of Strangers: The English Poor Laws and the People, 1740–1948* (Cambridge: Cambridge University Press, 1998), 44–45; Rosalind Mitchison, *The Old Poor Law in Scotland: The Experience of Poverty, 1574–1845* (Edinburgh: Edinburgh University Press, 2000), 98, 102; Billy G. Smith, "Introduction: The Best Poor Man's Country," in Billy G. Smith, ed., *Down and Out in Early America* (University Park: Pennsylvania University Press, 2004), xiv–xviii; Gary B. Nash, "Poverty and Politics in Early American History," in Billy G. Smith, ed., *Down and Out in Early America* (University Park: Pennsylvania University Press, 2004), 2–9; Cornelia H. Dayton and Sharon V. Salinger, *Robert Love's Warnings: Searching for Strangers in Colonial Boston* (Philadelphia: University of Pennsylvania Press, 2014), esp. 4–21; Pedro L. V. Welch, *Slave Society in the*

City: Bridgetown, Barbados 1680–1834 (Kingston, Jamaica: J. Currey, 2003), 118–119.

22. Nash, "Poverty and Politics in Early American History," 9–14. Billy G. Smith, "The Material Lives of Laboring Philadelphians, 1750–1800," *William and Mary Quarterly*, 3rd series, 38:2 (1981): 164–202, 183, 178–179, 185; *Continuation of the Account of the Pennsylvania Hospital: From the First of May 1754, to the Fifth of May 1761* (Philadelphia, 1761), 62; George Parker, *A View of Society and Manners in High and Low Life* (1781), 117–118, quoted in Tim Hitchcock, *Down and Out in Eighteenth-Century London* (London: Hambledon and London, 2004), 119, 125.

23. *Continuation of the Account of the Pennsylvania Hospital: From the First of May 1754, to the Fifth of May 1761*, 62 ("many Mouths"); Billy G. Smith, *The "Lower Sort": Philadelphia's Laboring People, 1750–1800* (Ithaca, NY: Cornell University Press, 1990), 111; Hitchcock, "Pauper Professions," in *Down and Out in Eighteenth-Century London*, 49–74; "From Thomas Morse in [Great] Coggeshall to the churchwardens and overseers of St John Baptist, Hereford, 12 March 1750," in Thomas Sokoll, ed., *Essex Pauper Letters 1731–1837* (Oxford: Published for the British Academy by Oxford University Press, 2001), 290 ("some Friends" and "Bread"); Smith, *The "Lower Sort,"* 166; Hitchcock, *Down and Out in Eighteenth-Century London*, 26.

24. *Gentleman's Magazine* 25 (1755), 40.

25. Smith, "Material Lives of Laboring Philadelphians," 177, 188–189; "From Jane Cross in Canterbury to Austin Vailant, churchwarden of St Botolph, Colchester, 24 April 1755," in Sokoll, ed., *Essex Pauper Letters 1731–1837*, 292 ("must part"); Smith, "Material Lives of Laboring Philadelphians," 188–192; Hitchcock, *Down and Out in Eighteenth-Century London*, 115–119 ("cold victuals") 62, 77; Smith, *The "Lower Sort,"* 165; Hitchcock, *Down and Out in Eighteenth-Century London*, 80–82; Philip D. Morgan, "Slaves and Poverty," in Billy G. Smith, ed., *Down and Out in Early America* (University Park: Pennsylvania University Press, 2004), 93–131, 120, 121.

26. On the English and American poor law systems, see n. 21. "From Widow Camp in Widford [Essex] to Mr Humerson in Coopersale [Theydon Garnon], 12 July 1759," in Sokoll, ed., *Essex Pauper Letters 1731–1837*, 603; Robert Strettel to the Overseers of the Poor, Philadelphia, October 9, 1751, Stauffer Collection, #2146, quoted in Karin Wulf, "Gender and the Political Economy of Poor Relief in Colonial Philadelphia," in Billy G. Smith, ed., *Down and Out in Early America* (University Park: Pennsylvania University Press, 2004), 163–188, 167.

27. This paragraph draws on Hitchcock, "Begging from the Parish" in *Down and Out in Eighteenth-Century London*, 181–208; Lees, "Weekly Doles: Communal Support in the Eighteenth Century," in *The Solidarities of Strangers*, 42–81; Wulf, "Gender and the Political Economy of Poor Relief in Colonial Philadelphia."

28. Kevin Siena, *Venereal Disease, Hospitals, and the Urban Poor: London's "Foul Wards" 1600–1800* (Rochester: University of Rochester Press, 2004), 178; Joanna Innes, "The 'Mixed Economy of Welfare' in Early Modern England: Assessments of the Options from Hale to Malthus (c. 1683–1803)," in Martin Daunton, ed., *Charity, Self-Interest and Welfare in the English Past* (New York: St. Martin's Press, 1996), 139–180.

29. *Gentleman's Magazine* 30 (1760), 29 ("mad extravagance"). John Entick, *A New and Accurate Survey of London, Westminster, Southwark, and Places Adjacent*, 4 vols. (London, 1766), vol. 3, 273–274; Paul Slack, "Hospitals, Workhouses, and the Relief of the Poor in Early Modern England," in Ole Peter Grell and Andrew Cunningham, eds., *Health Care and Poor Relief in Protestant Europe, 1500–1700* (London: Routledge, 1997), 234–251, esp. 236.

30. Slack, "Hospitals, Workhouses, and the Relief of the Poor in Early Modern England," 245; John Entick, *A New and Accurate Survey of London, Westminster, Southwark, and Places Adjacent*, vol. 4 of 4 (London, 1766), 411, 413, 412.

31. David Owen, *English Philanthropy, 1660–1960* (Cambridge, MA: Belknap Press of Harvard University Press, 1964), 44; Benjamin Rush to John Morgan, October 21, 1768, in Butterfield, ed., *Letters of Benjamin Rush*, 66; David H. Solkin, *Painting for Money: The Visual Arts and the Public Sphere in Eighteenth-Century England* (New Haven, CT: Yale University Press, 1992), 165–173; Ruth McClure, *Coram's Children: The London Foundling Hospital in the Eighteenth Century* (New Haven, CT: Yale University Press, 1981), 68–72, 83–86, 87, 102–105; Richard Baldwin, *Baldwin's New Complete Guide to All Persons who Have Any Trade or Concern with the City of* London ([London], [1768]), 81; Entick, *A New and Accurate Survey of London, Westminster, Southwark, and Places Adjacent*, vol. 4, 432–433, 436, 239.

32. Entick, *A New and Accurate Survey of London, Westminster, Southwark, and Places Adjacent*, vol. 4, 311, 105; Entick, *A New and Accurate Survey of London, Westminster, Southwark, and Places Adjacent*, vol. 3, 342; Lisa Forman Cody, "Living and Dying in Georgian London's Lying-in Hospitals," *Bulletin of the History of Medicine* 78 (2004): 309–348; Owen, *English Philanthropy*, 50.

33. On the Bettering House, see Alexander, "Public Poor Relief, 1760–1776: Turbulent Innovation before the Revolution," in *Render Them Submissive*, 86–102; Clement Biddle, *The Philadelphia Directory* (Philadelphia, 1791), x. On Philadelphia's voluntary associations, see Carl Bridenbaugh, *Cities in Revolt: Urban Life in America, 1743–1776* (New York: Alfred A. Knopf, 1955), 127, 322, and Jessica Choppin Roney, "'First Movers in Every Useful Undertaking': Formal Voluntary Associations in Philadelphia, 1725–1775" (Ph.D. diss., Johns Hopkins University, 2008); Bridenbaugh, *Cities in Revolt*, 127, 323.

34. *Some Account of the Pennsylvania Hospital, from Its First Rise to the Beginning of the Fifth Month, Called May 1754* (Philadelphia, 1754), 30; Anne Boylan, *The Origins of Women's Activism: New York and Boston, 1797–1840* (Chapel Hill: University

of North Carolina Press, 2002); F. K. Prochaska, *Women and Philanthropy in Nineteenth-Century England* (Oxford: Oxford University Press, 1980).

35. James Boswell, *Life of Johnson*, ed. R. W. Chapman, intro. Pat Rogers (Oxford World's Classics ed., Oxford: Oxford University Press, 1998), 918; Bridenbaugh, *Cities in Revolt*, 216; *Gentleman's Progress: The Itinerarium of Dr. Alexander Hamilton 1744*, edited with an introduction by Carl Bridenbaugh (Chapel Hill: Published for the Institute of Early American History and Culture, Williamsburg, Virginia, by the University of North Carolina Press, 1948), quoted in Clark, *British Clubs and Societies*, 389; [Benjamin Franklin], "Reply to Coffee-House Orators," printed in the *London Chronicle*, April 7–9, 1767, www.franklinpapers.org ("talkers"); Clark, *British Clubs and Societies*, 41; David S. Shields, *Civil Tongues and Polite Letters in British America* (Chapel Hill: Published for the Institute of Early American History and Culture, Williamsburg, Virginia, by the University of North Carolina Press, 1997), 62; John Coakley Lettsom, "Hints on Tavern Feasts," in *Hints Designed to Promote Beneficence, Temperance, and Medical Science*, vol. 1 (of 1 vol.) (London, 1797), 205; *New-York Gazette*, August 3, 1767; Brewer, *The Pleasures of the Imagination*, 177–182; Sarah Knott, *Sensibility and the American Revolution* (Chapel Hill: Published for the Omohundro Institute of Early American History and Culture, Williamsburg, Virginia, by the University of North Carolina Press, 2009), 44–47.

36. Benjamin Rush to Ebenezer Hazard, March 19, 1765, in Butterfield, ed., *Letters of Benjamin Rush*, vol. 1, 10 ("usefulness and benevolence"); John Coakley Lettsom to Benjamin Rush, August 10, 1788, Benjamin Rush Manuscripts, vol. 28, f. 10, Library Company of Philadelphia (LCP) ("rational entertainment").

37. Eighteenth-century Britons and British Americans were torn about ambition. Often critical of it in concept, they nonetheless increasingly manifested the trait in practice. For an exploration of ambition in the early republican United States, see J. M. Opal, *Beyond the Farm: National Ambitions in Rural New England* (Philadelphia: University of Pennsylvania Press, 2008).

38. George B. Kirsch, *Jeremy Belknap* (New York: Arno Press, 1982), 9–10, 84, 87; "Memoir of Thomas Cogan, M.D.," 75–76.

39. Goodman, *Benjamin Rush*, 25; Cash, "Benjamin Waterhouse"; Booth, *John Haygarth*, 31; Edward Percival, ed., *Memoir of the Life and Writings of Thomas Percival M.D.* (London, 1807), xviii; Currie, ed., *Memoir of the Life, Writings, and Correspondence of James Currie*, 55–57.

40. Langstaff, *Dr. Bard of Hyde Park*, 99; Lawrence and MacDonald, *Sambrook Court*, 2; Francis M. Lobo, "John Haygarth, Smallpox and Religious Dissent in Eighteenth-Century England," in Andrew Cunningham and Roger French, eds., *The Medical Enlightenment of the Eighteenth Century* (Cambridge: Cambridge University Press, 1990), 223; *The Autobiography of Benjamin Rush*, 78–79.

41. Williams, "Hawes, William (1736–1808)"; Samuel L. Knapp, *The Life of Thomas Eddy* (1834; rpt. New York: Arno Press, 1976), 47–54.

42. John Coakley Lettsom and Thomas Cogan gained fortunes through their wives. Abraham, *Lettsom*, 100; "Memoir of Thomas Cogan, M.D.," 77; Clark, "Engines of Growth," in *British Clubs and Societies*, 141–193, quotation 155. John Crawford was a Freemason. Edward T. Schultz, *History of Freemasonry in Maryland, of all the Rites Introduced into Maryland, from the Earliest Times to the Present* (Baltimore: J. H. Medairy, 1884), vol. 2, 297–307.

43. Cleary, *Elizabeth Murray*, 16; Tiffany, *Letters of James Murray Loyalist*, 1–2; Cleary, *Elizabeth Murray*, 18, 19–20; *Gentleman's Magazine* 62 (1792), 961. [John Murray], *An Enquiry into the Origin, Progress, & Present State of Slavery: With a Plan for the Gradual, Reasonable, and Secure Emancipation of Slaves. By a Member of the Society of Universal GOODWILL in London and Norwich* (London, 1789), 3; Cleary, *Elizabeth Murray*, 20; [John Chambers], *A General History of the County of Norfolk* (Norwich, 1829), vol. 2, 1205; Tiffany, *Letters of James Murray Loyalist*, 101; *Gentleman's Magazine* 62 (1792), 961. (Receiving a degree did not necessarily mean that Murray had attended St. Andrew's. On receiving degrees without attending a university, see Wilson, "An Early Baltimore Physician and His Medical Library," 63.) On Murray's financial woes and Elizabeth's support, see Cleary, *Elizabeth Murray*, 90–91.

44. On James and Elizabeth Murray's lives, see Cleary, *Elizabeth Murray*; James Murray to John Murray, July 18, 1761, James Murray Papers, Reel 1, Massachusetts Historical Society, Boston (MHS). *Burke's Genealogical and Heraldic History of the Landed Gentry*, 903; David Hancock, *Oceans of Wine: The Emergence of American Taste and Trade* (New Haven, CT: Yale University Press, 2009), 144. On the children living in the Murray family, see James Murray to John Murray, February 26, 1755; James Murray to John Murray, August 5, 1760; John Murray to John Dubois, April 21, 1765, James Murray Papers, Reel 1, MHS; Cleary, *Elizabeth Murray*, 131, 187.

45. Parkman, *A Sermon Delivered at the Interment of the Rev. John Lathrop, D.D*, 21; Corner and Booth, eds., *Chain of Friendship*, 23, 287–288, 237; Thomas Joseph Pettigrew, *Memoirs of the Life and Writings of the late John Coakley Lettsom: with a Selection from his Correspondence*, 3 vols. (London, 1817), vol. 1, 87; Wilson, *Memoir of the Life of Bishop White*, 31.

46. *The Autobiography of Benjamin Rush*, 44, 53 ("republic of medicine," "conversation part[ies]"). Samuel Bard describes the rigor of medical society meetings. Samuel Bard to John Bard, September 1763, Bard Collection, NYAM; Hugh Ferguson to Benjamin Rush, September 30, 1793, Rush Manuscripts, vol. 23, f. 47, LCP ("literary correspondence"); John Morgan, *A Discourse upon the Institution of Medical Schools in America; Delivered at a Public Anniversary Commencement, Held in the College of Philadelphia May 30 and 31* (Philadelphia, 1765), 62; Amasa Dingley, *An*

Oration. On the Improvement of Medicine (New York, 1795), 39; Thomas Percival, *Essays Medical and Experimental* (1767), 4 ("benefactors of mankind"); Lettsom, *Recollections of Dr. Rush*, 5 ("soon after his return"), 5; Percival, *Essays Medical and Experimental*. On physicians and sensibility, see Knott, *Sensibility and the American Revolution*, 98–101.

47. See, for examples, Percival, *Memoir of the Life and Writings of Thomas Percival M.D*; Parkman, *A Sermon Delivered at the Interment of the Rev. John Lathrop*.

48. Benjamin Rush to Arthur Lee, May 4, 1774, in Butterfield, ed., *Letters of Benjamin Rush*, vol.1, 85.

49. Peter Kolchin, *American Slavery 1619–1877* (New York: Hill and Wang, 1993; 1st rev. ed. 2003), 252; Andrew Jackson O'Shaughnessy, *An Empire Divided: The American Revolution and the British Caribbean* (Philadelphia: University of Pennsylvania, 2000), 8–9.

50. "John Lathrop" in *Sibley's Harvard Graduates* (Boston: Massachusetts Historical Society, 1970), vol. 15, 428; William H. Robinson, *Phillis Wheatley and Her Writings* (New York: Garland, 1984), 14, 19, 50, 52; Hawke, *Benjamin Rush, Revolutionary Gadfly*, 361–362; Langstaff, *Dr. Bard of Hyde Park*, 176.

51. Christopher Leslie Brown, *Moral Capital: Foundations of British Abolitionism* (Chapel Hill: Published for the Omohundro Institute for Early American History and Culture, Williamsburg, Virginia, by the University of North Carolina Press, 2006), 284–285, 96–98, 283; Blackie, "Bell, Andrew (1753–1832)"; Currie, *Memoir of the Life, Writings, and Correspondence of James Currie*, 10; Paley, "Colquhoun, Patrick (1745–1820);" [Murray], *An Enquiry into the Origin, Progress, & Present State of Slavery*, 3, 29–31. The obituary for Murray in the Gentleman's Magazine names Murray as the author of the pamphlet. *Gentleman's Magazine* 62 (1792), 961. In that work, Murray related the incident with the enslaved nurse without identifying himself as the surgeon in charge of the naval hospital. Other evidence in the pamphlet suggests that Murray is the unnamed surgeon. James Murray to John Murray, c. March 1750/51, James Murray Papers, Reel 1, MHS. Fowler, "Itinerant Institutor," 49; Abraham, "Tortola" in *Lettsom*, 49–64; on Teresa, see John Coakley Lettsom to William Cuming, October 14, 1784, in Pettigrew, *Memoirs . . . of Lettsom*, vol. 1, 64–65; on the "heart [had] melted" comment, see John Coakley Lettsom to Sir Mordaunt Martin, January 20, 1791, in Pettigrew, *Memoirs . . . of Lettsom*, vol. 2, 36.

52. Isabel Rivers, "The First Evangelical Tract Society," *Historical Journal* 50:1 (2007): 1–22.

53. *An Account of the Society for Promoting Religious Knowledge Among the Poor* (London, 1759), 15, 7, 9, 11; *An Account of the Society for Promoting Religious Knowledge Among the Poor* (London, 1769), 7–36, 5 ("one guinea"), 6 ("parcel[s] of books"); *An Account of the Society for Promoting Religious Knowledge Among the Poor* (London, 1759), 3 ("poorer sort"), 4 ("aids"); *An Account of the Society for Promoting Religious Knowledge Among the Poor* (1769), 8; Jeffrey H. Richards, "Samuel Davies and

the Transatlantic Campaign for Slave Literacy in Virginia," *Virginia Magazine of History and Biography* 111:4 (2003): 333–378; *An Account of the Society for Promoting Religious Knowledge Among the Poor* (London, 1763), 34; *An Account of the Society for Promoting Religious Knowledge Among the Poor* (1769), 50.

54. Ron Chernow, *Washington: A Life* (New York: Penguin Press, 2010), 68; Anderson *Crucible of War*, 288.

55. Anderson, *Crucible of War*, 518; Eliga Gould, *The Persistence of Empire: British Political Culture in the Age of the American Revolution* (Chapel Hill: Published for the Omohundro Institute of Early American History and Culture, Williamsbug, Virginia, by the University of North Carolina Press, 2000), 110–119; Robert Middlekauff, *The Glorious Cause: The American Revolution, 1763–1789* (Oxford: Oxford University Press, 1982, 2005), chaps. 4–6, 74–141; Bernard Bailyn, *The Ideological Origins of the American Revolution*, enlarged edition (Cambridge, MA: Belknap Press of Harvard University Press, 1992), 233.

56. Benjamin Rush to Ebenezer Hazard, November 18, 1765, in Butterfield, ed., *Letters of Benjamin Rush*, vol. 1, 20; Benjamin Rush to Ebenezer Hazard, October 22, 1768, in Butterfield, ed., *Letters of Benjamin Rush*, vol. 1, 68.

57. Middlekauff, *The Glorious Cause*, 142–144.

58. Middlekauff, *The Glorious Cause*, chaps. 7–8, 142–178.

59. Gould, *The Persistence of Empire*, 116–119.

60. O'Shaughnessy, *An Empire Divided*, 88–89.

61. Benjamin Rush to —— ——, January 19, 1769, in Butterfield, ed., *Letters of Benjamin Rush*, vol. 1, 72; Linda Colley, *Britons: Forging the Nation* (New Haven, CT: Yale University Press, 1992), 139–141.

62. Benjamin Rush to Arthur Lee, May 4, 1774, in Butterfield, ed., *Letters of Benjamin Rush*, vol. 1, 68.

63. *An Account of the Society for Promoting Religious Knowledge Among the Poor* (London, 1786), 42.

64. William Kellaway, *The New England Company 1649–1776: Missionary Society to the American Indians* (New York: Barnes and Noble, 1962), 194. J[ohn] Rodgers to Benjamin Rush, March 20, 1771, Benjamin Rush Manuscripts, vol. 25, LCP.

65. Samuel Bard, *A Discourse Upon the Duties of a Physician, with Some Sentiments on the Usefulness and Necessity of a Public Hospital* (New York, 1769), 15, 16; *A Brief Account of the New York Hospital* (New York, 1804), 1, 7–20. For evidence about keeping up with Philadelphia as a motivation for founding New York Hospital, see Samuel Bard to John Bard, Edinburgh, December 29, 1762; John Bard to Samuel Bard, New York, April 9, 1763; Samuel Bard to John Bard, Bard Collection, NYAM.

66. Board of Governors' Meetings, November 13, 1771, February 11, 1772, March 27, 1772, February 2, 1774, March 10, 1773, July 2, 1773, New York Hospital Minutes, vol. 1, New York-Presbyterian Hospital-New York Weill Cornell Medical Center Archives.

CHAPTER 3

1. Betsy C. Corner and Christopher C. Booth, eds., *Chain of Friendship: Selected Letters of Dr. John Fothergill of London, 1735–1780* (Cambridge, MA: Belknap Press of Harvard University Press, 1971), 14–15; John Coakley Lettsom, *Memoirs of John Fothergill*, 4th ed. (London, 1786), 131; J. Brett Langstaff, *Dr. Bard of Hyde Park: The Famous Physician of Revolutionary Times, the Man Who Saved Washington's Life* (New York: E. P. Dutton, 1942), 112.

2. Historians have recently been examining the American Revolution as a civil war. See, among others, Maya Jasanoff, *Liberty's Exiles: American Loyalists in the Revolutionary World* (New York: Alfred A. Knopf, 2011).

3. William Wallace Currie, ed., *Memoirs of the Life, Writings, and Correspondence of James Currie, M.D. F.R.S. of Liverpool, Fellow of the Royal College of Physicians, Edinburgh, London Medical Society &c. &c.* (London, 1831), vol. 1, 18; John Murray to John B. Murray, July 31, 1774, photoduplicate of original letter, Murray Family Papers, Box 5, New-York Historical Society (NYHS); John Murray to James Murray, September 19, 1777, Murray Family Papers, Box 3, Folder 13, NYHS; John Murray to Gilbert Deblois, January 4, 1779, Murray Family Papers, Box 3, Folder 13, NYHS; Granville Sharp to Benjamin Rush, July 27, 1774, in John A. Woods, ed., "The Correspondence of Benjamin Rush and Granville Sharp, 1773–1809," *Journal of American Studies* 1 (1967): 1–38, 10; Benjamin Rush to Granville Sharp, July 9, 1774, in "The Correspondence of Benjamin Rush and Granville Sharp, 1773–1809," 9; Samuel Bard to John Bard, April 26, 1775, in John M'Vickar, *A Domestic Narrative of the Life of Samuel Bard, M.D. LL.D* (New York, 1822). Years later, Thomas Eddy also referred to the war as a civil war. Samuel L. Knapp, *The Life of Thomas Eddy* (1834; rpt. New York: Arno Press, 1976), 46.

4. James Currie and Benjamin Rush both used the phrase "horrors of a civil war." James Currie to Christian Duncan, September 1, 1775, in Currie, *Memoirs of the Life, Writings, and Correspondence of James Currie*, vol. 1, 23; Benjamin Rush to Granville Sharp, July 9, 1774, in "The Correspondence of Benjamin Rush and Granville Sharp, 1773–1809," 9; John Coakley Lettsom to Benjamin Rush, April 12, 1778, Rush Manuscripts, vol. 28, Library Company of Philadelphia (LCP).

5. Benjamin Rush to John Coakley Lettsom, November 15, 1783, in L. H. Butterfield, ed., *Letters of Benjamin Rush*, 2 vols. (Princeton, NJ: Published for the American Philosophical Society by Princeton University Press, 1951), vol. 1, 312; David J. Hancock, *Citizens of the World: London Merchants and the Integration of the British Atlantic Community, 1735–1785* (Cambridge: Cambridge University Press, 1995), 119–121; Thomas M. Doerflinger, *A Vigorous Spirit of Enterprise: Merchants and Economic Development in Revolutionary Philadelphia* (Chapel Hill: Published for the Institute of Early American History and Culture, Williamsburg, Virginia, by the University of North Carolina Press, 1986), 199–200; typescript copy of

letter from John Murray to John Murray, April 27, 1778, Murray Family Papers, Box 3, Folder 13, NYHS; John Warren, *An Eulogy on the Honourable Thomas Russell, Esq* (Boston, 1796), 14; James Currie to Christian Duncan, September 1, 1775, in Currie, *Memoirs of the Life, Writings, and Correspondence of James Currie*, vol.1, 25.

6. Currie, *Memoirs of the Life, Writings, and Correspondence of James Currie*, vol. 1, 29–42; Jonathan Allen Fowler, "Adventures of an 'Itinerant Institutor': The Life and Philanthropy of Thomas Bernard" (Ph.D. diss., University of Tennessee, 2003), 65–66, 68.

7. The synopsis of Thompson's life is drawn from W. J. Sparrow, *Knight of the White Eagle: A Biography of Sir Benjamin Thompson, Count Rumford* (London: Hutchinson, 1964); David Knight, "Thompson, Sir Benjamin, Count Rumford in the nobility of the Holy Roman empire (1753–1814)," *Oxford Dictionary of National Biography* (Oxford: Oxford University Press, 2004), http://www.oxforddnb.com.proxy.lib.umich.edu/view/article/27255, accessed September 19, 2007; Benjamin Thompson to Timothy Walker, December 24, 1774, and Benjamin Thompson to Timothy Walker, August 14, 1775, Rumford Papers, Folder 2, New Hampshire Historical Society (NHHS), Concord, New Hampshire.

8. Knapp, *The Life of Thomas Eddy*, 47–50, quotation 50.

9. Samuel Miller, *Memoir of the Reverend John Rodgers, D.D. Late Pastor of the Wall-Street and Brick Churches, in the City of New-York* (New York, 1813), 209–237; "John Lathrop" in *Sibley's Harvard Graduates* (Boston: Massachusetts Historical Society, 1970), vol. 15, 430; David Freeman Hawke, *Benjamin Rush Revolutionary Gadfly* (Indianapolis: Bobbs-Merrill, 1971), 174–175.

10. On Rush's time in Congress and his service as any army physician, see Hawke, *Benjamin Rush Revolutionary Gadfly*, 163–220. Benjamin Rush to Julia Rush, January 24, 1777, in Butterfield, ed., *Letters of Benjamin Rush*, vol. 1, 130–131; Benjamin Rush to Anthony Wayne, April 2, 1777, in Butterfield, ed., *Letters of Benjamin Rush*, vol. 1, 137.

11. On the odysesseys of Loyalists, see Jasanoff, *Liberty's Exiles*. On the often close ties among Patriots and Loyalists, see Judith L. Van Buskirk, *Generous Enemies: Patriots and Loyalists in Revolutionary New York* (Philadelphia: University of Pennsylvania Press, 2002); John Lathrop, *A Discourse Preached on the March the Fifth, 1778* (Boston, 1778), 13 ("pulled down and burnt," "torn.")

12. Lathrop, *A Discourse Preached on the March the Fifth, 1778*, 13 ("wanton destruction," "shocking manner"); Benjamin Rush in Richard Henry Lee, December 30, 1776, in Butterfield, ed., *Letters of Benjamin Rush*, vol. 1, 124 ("honors"), 123 ("particle of blood"); Benjamin Rush to Richard Henry Lee, January 14, 1777, in Butterfield, ed., *Letters of Benjamin Rush*, vol. 1, 128 ("savages"); on the identification of Britons with Indians during the American Revolutionary War, see Peter

Silver, "Barbarism and the American Revolution," in *Our Savage Neighbors: How Indian War Transformed Early America* (New York: W. W. Norton, 2008), 227–260.

13. Benjamin Rush to Richard Henry Lee, January 7, 1777, in Butterfield, ed., *Letters of Benjamin Rush*, vol. 1, 126; Hawke, *Benjamin Rush Revolutionary Gadfly*, 180.

14. John Murray to James Murray, September 19, 1777, Murray Family Papers, Box 3, Folder 13, NYHS; John Coakley Lettsom, *Some Account of the Late John Fothergill, M.D.* (London, [1783]), lix; Troy O. Bickham, *Making Headlines: The American Revolution as Seen through the British Press* (Dekalb: Northern Illinois University Press, 2009); Stephen Conway, "From Fellow-Nationals to Foreigners: British Perceptions of the Americans, circa 1739–1783," *William and Mary Quarterly* 59 (2002): 65–100.

15. Grant P. Cerny, "Pratt, Samuel Jackson (1749–1814)," in H. C. G. Matthew and Brian Harrison, eds., *Oxford Dictionary of National Biography* (Oxford: Oxford University Press, 2004); online ed., ed. Lawrence Goldman, January 2008, http://www.oxforddnb.com/view/article/22710, accessed March 30, 2010; Samuel Jackson Pratt, *Emma Corbett: Or the Miseries of Civil War* ([Bath] and London, 1780). The synopsis is based on reading Samuel Jackson Pratt, *Emma Corbett*, 2 vols., 5th ed. (London, 1783).

16. Pratt, *Emma Corbett*, vol. 1, 137, 138, 139, 140, 141–143.

17. Pratt, *Emma Corbett*, vol. 2, 100. On the word "philanthropy," see Samuel Johnson, *A Dictionary of the English Language*, vol. 2 (London, 1755); Conrad Edick Wright, *The Transformation of Charity in Postrevolutionary New England* (Boston: Northeastern University Press, 1992), 120.

18. Pratt, *Emma Corbett*.

19. John Coakley Lettsom to Benjamin Rush, April 12, 1778, Rush Manuscripts, vol. 28, LCP; Lettsom, *Some Account of the Late John Fothergill, M.D.*, cliv–clxii, clxxiii–clxxiv, clxxiv, clxxv.

20. Troy O. Bickham, *Savages within the Empire: Representations of American Indians in Eighteenth-Century Britain* (Oxford: Oxford University Press, 2005), 230–231, 238–240; Lettsom, *Memoirs of John Fothergill*, 4th ed., 96.

21. Bickham, *Making Headlines*, 109–112; [London] *Gazetteer and New Daily Advertiser*, January 12, 1778.

22. John Murray to Mrs. [Dorothy] Forbes, May 14, 1780 ("unnatural bustle"), James Murray Robbins Papers, Box 3, Massachusetts Historical Society (MHS), Boston; Patricia Cleary, *Elizabeth Murray: A Woman's Purusit of Independence in Eighteenth-Century America* (Amherst: University of Massachusetts Press, 2000), 130–131; John Murray to John B. Murray, Norwich, July 31, 1774, photo-duplicate of original letter, Murray Family Papers, Box 5; Anne Murray Powell to aunt [Elizabeth Murray] Inman, February 29, 1776, Murray Family Papers, Box 4, New-York Historical Society (NYHS); Mary Murray to cousin Elizabeth Murray,

Murray Family Papers, Box 4, NYHS; Cleary, *Elizabeth Murray*, 204–205; Elizabeth Murray Inman to John Innes Clark, January 4, 1777, in Nina Moore Tiffany, *Letters of James Murray Loyalist* (Boston, 1901), 261; typescript copy of letter from John Murray to John [B.] Murray, April 27, 1778, Murray Family Papers, Box 3, Folder 13, NYHS; on Murray's financial woes and Elizabeth's support, see also Cleary, *Elizabeth Murray*, 90–91.

23. "Autobiography of the Late Col. James B. Murray," Box 4, Murray Family Papers, NYHS; *An Account of the Scots Society in Norwich, in Great Britain. Founded in 1775* (Norwich, 1783), 33, 36; Mary Murray to cousin Elizabeth Murray, July 1, 1781, Murray Family Papers, Box 4 (NYHS); Gilbert Deblois, February 5, 1782, Gilbert Deblois Letterbooks, vol. 1, Rhode Island Historical Society (RIHS), Providence; Benjamin Cowell, *Spirit of '76 in Rhode Island: Or, Sketches of the Efforts of the Government and People in the War of the Revolution* (Boston, 1850); Francis B. Heitman, *Historical Register of Officers of the Continental Army During the War of the Revolution, April 1775, to December 1783* (revised ed. 1914; reprint Baltimore, 1982); Joseph Jencks Smith, *Civil and Military List of Rhode Island, 1647–1800* (Providence, 1900); personal communication from Lee Teverow, Reference Library, RIHS, March 5, 2010; Cleary, *Elizabeth Murray*, 204; typescript copy of letter from John Murray to John Murray, April 27, 1778, Murray Family Papers, Box 3, Folder 13, NYHS.

24. *An Account of the Scots Society in Norwich, in Great Britain. Founded in 1775* (Norwich, 1783), 3–9, 13, 17. The rules of the Society in the early 1780s provided that men married to Scotswomen could be full members, but whether that rule dated to 1776 or later is unknowable from the extant sources. For succinct overviews of the English poor law, see Paul Slack, *The English Poor Law, 1531–1782, Prepared for the Economic History Society*, 1st Cambridge ed. (Cambridge: Cambridge University Press, 1995); Paul A. Fideler, *Social Welfare in Pre-Industrial England: The Old Poor Law Tradition* (Basingstoke: Palgrave Macmillan, 2006).

25. P. Browne, *The History of Norwich, from the Earliest Records to the Present Time* (Norwich, 1814), 66, 160; *Gentleman's Magazine* 62 (1792), 961.

26. *An Account of the Scots Society in Norwich, from Its Rise in 1775, Until It Received the Additional Name of the Society of Universal Good-will in 1784*, 2nd ed. (Norwich, n.d.), 45–46. On the laws of settlement (including heated debate between Landau and Snell on their purpose), see Fideler, *Social Welfare in Pre-Industrial England*, 143–146; Norma Landau, "The Regulation of Immigration, Economic Structure and Definitions of the Poor in Eighteenth-Century England," *Historical Journal* 33 (1990): 541–571; Norma Landau, "The Laws of Settlement and the Surveillance of Immigration in Eighteenth-Century Kent," *Continuity and Change* 3 (1998): 391–420; K. D. M. Snell, *Annals of the Labouring Poor: Social Change and Agrarian England, 1660–1900* (Cambridge: Cambridge University Press, 1985), 17–18, 72–73, 146, 232; K. D. M. Snell, "Pauper Settlement and the Right to Poor

Relief in England and Wales," *Continuity and Change* 6 (1991): 375–416; James
Stephen Taylor, "The Impact of Pauper Settlement 1691–1834," *Past and Present* 73
(1976): 42–74. The best explication of the meaning to parish residents of the laws is
K. D. M. Snell, "Settlement, Parochial Belonging and Entitlement," in *Parish and
Belonging: Community, Identity and Welfare in England and Wales, 1700–1950*
(Cambridge: Cambridge University Press, 2006), 81–161. My understanding of
the laws of settlement follows Snell's. A distinct exception to the Anglo-American
norm of public poor relief being legally limited to people with settlements was
Massachusetts's system of provincial poor relief for strangers. See Cornelia H.
Dayton and Sharon V. Salinger, *Robert Love's Warnings: Searching for Strangers in
Colonial Boston* (Philadelphia: University of Pennsylvania Press, 2014).

27. *An Account of the Scots Society in Norwich, from Its Rise in 1775*, 56, 71; *An Account
of the Scots Society in Norwich, in Great Britain*, 27, 18.

28. *An Account of the Scots Society in Norwich, from Its Rise in 1775*, 68, 70–71.

29. *An Account of the Scots Society in Norwich, from Its Rise in 1775*, 37, 73; *An Account
of the Proceedings of the Society of Universal Good-will, from the Beginning of 1784.
To the End of the Year 1787* (Norwich, n.d.), 3–4.

30. *An Account of the Scots Society in Norwich, from Its Rise in 1775*, 89; [London]
Monthly Magazine 68 (1783).

31. *An Account of the Scots Society in Norwich, from Its Rise in 1775*, 32, 63.

32. On the importance of constitutions in eighteenth-century voluntary organiza-
tions, see Kathleen Wilson, "Urban Culture and Political Activism in Hanoverian
England: The Example of Voluntary Hospitals," in Eckhart Hellmuth, ed., *The
Transformation of Political Culture: England and Germany in the Late Eighteenth
Century* (London: German Historical Institute, 1990), 172–174 and Margaret
C. Jacob, *Living the Enlightenment: Freemasonry and Politics in Eighteenth-
Century Europe* (New York: Oxford University Press, 1991). See also Bruce Mann,
"A Shadow Republic" in *Republic of Debtors: Bankruptcy in the Age of American
Independence* (Cambridge, MA: Harvard University Press, 2002), 147–165; *An
Account of the Scots Society in Norwich, from Its Rise in 1775*, 29, 47–64, 20, 21; *An
Account of the Proceedings of the Society of Universal Good-will, from the Beginning
of 1784*, 4.

33. *Gentleman's Magazine* 62 (1792), 961; John Murray to [Elizabeth Murray
Campbell Smith], April 13, 1771, Box 3, Folder 13, Murray Family Papers, NYHS.
If Murray's colonial government plan is extant, it has not yet been found.

34. [John Murray], *An Enquiry into the Origin, Progress, & Present State of
Slavery: With a Plan for the Gradual, Reasonable, and Secure Emancipation
of Slaves. By a Member of the Society of Universal GOODWILL in London
and Norwich* (London, 1789), 3. The obituary for Murray in the *Gentleman's
Magazine* names Murray as the author of the pamphlet: *Gentleman's Magazine*
62 (1792), 961. On other British emancipation schemes of the 1770s and 1780s,

see Christopher Leslie Brown, "British Concepts of Emancipation in the Age of the American Revolution," in *Moral Capital: Foundations of British Abolitionism* (Chapel Hill: Published for the Omohundro Institute for Early American History and Culture, Williamsburg, Virginia, by the University of North Carolina Press, 2006), 209–258; quotation about "active engagement," 238.

35. [Murray], *An Enquiry into the Origin, Progress, & Present State of Slavery*, 29–31, 3, 31. In the pamphlet, Murray related the incident with the enslaved nurse without identifying the young surgeon at the Port Royal naval hospital in 1743. Elsewhere in the pamphlet, Murray says that he was in Spanish Town in 1744 and other evidence in the pamphlet suggests that Murray is the unnamed surgeon.

36. Brown, *Moral Capital*, 235–237; [Murray], *An Enquiry into the Origin, Progress, & Present State of Slavery*, 4–18, 41, 16. For a synopsis of the idea about Noah's curse, see David Brion Davis, *The Problem of Slavery in the Age of Revolution, 1770–1823* (Ithaca, NY: Cornell University Press, 1975), 539–541.

37. On the issue of language, see David Spadafora, *The Idea of Progress in Eighteenth-Century Britain* (New Haven, CT: Yale University Press, 1990), 194, 196–199. [Murray], *An Enquiry into the Origin, Progress, & Present State of Slavery*, 22, 19, 37, 22–23, 38, 22, 40, 31–41, 40.

38. *An Account of the Scots Society in Norwich, From its Rise in 1775*, 38. John Murray to Elizabeth Murray, November 9, 1771, in Tiffany, *Letters of James Murray*, 145.

39. *An Abstract of the Proceedings of the Scots Society in Norwich, November 30, 1780* (Norwich, n.d.), 11; John Murray to Gilbert Delbois, January 4, 1779 and John Murray to Gilbert Deblois, n.d. [received June 15, 1782], Murray Family Papers, Box 3, Folder 13, NYHS; John Murray to Gilbert Deblois, January 26, 1783, Murray Family Papers, Box 3, Folder 13, NYHS; *An Account of the Scots Society in Norwich, in Great Britain*, 36; *An Account of the Scots Society in Norwich, From its Rise in 1775*, 3; Tiffany, *Letters of James Murray Loyalist*, 287–288; Katherine M. J. McKenna, *A Life of Propriety: Anne Murray Powell and Her Family, 1755–1849* (Montreal: McGill-Queen's University Press, 1993).

40. *Proceedings at the Annual and Other Meetings of the Scots Society in Norwich, in 1778, 1779, and 1780* (Norwich, 1780), 9–10; *An Account of the Scots Society in Norwich, in Great Britain*, 33, 34, 29. *An Account of the Scots Society in Norwich, from Its Rise in 1775*, 82 ("pleasure to meet").

41. *An Abstract of the Proceedings of the Scots Society in Norwich, November 30, 1780*, 6, 7; *An Account of the Proceedings of the Society of Universal Good-will, from the Beginning of 1784*, 17; *An Account of the Scots Society, in Norwich, in Great Britain*, 31; *An Account of the Scots Society in Norwich, from Its Rise in 1775*, 3, 81–83, 50, 56–57.

42. *An Account of the Scots Society in Norwich, from Its Rise in 1775* 58, 59 ("send copies or abstracts," "deputies form the original society," "best and most proper").

43. *An Account of the Scots Society in Norwich, from Its Rise in 1775*, 20, 21; *An Account of the Proceedings of the Society of Universal Good-will, from the Beginning of 1784*, 4.

44. *An Account of the Scots Society in Norwich, from Its Rise in 1775*, 81 ("intrusted to his care"), 82 ("have heard nothing"), 82–83 ("present unfortunate situation"), 83 ("have not been able to render," "those who emigrate," "hostile parts"), 84 (no cause for despair").

45. *An Account of the Scots Society in Norwich, from its Rise in 1775*, 3; *Proceedings at the Annual and Other Meetings of the Scots Society in Norwich, in 1778, 1779, and 1780*, 6. On the marriage between Anne Murray and William Dummer Powell, see Cleary, *Elizabeth Murray*, 190–192 and John Murray to James Murray, November 22, 1775, Murray Family Papes, NYHS; Gilbert Deblois to Sterry and Murray, London, October 12, 1782, Gilbert Deblois Letterbook, vol. 1, RIHS.

46. Arthur Cash, *John Wilkes: The Scandalous Father of Civil Liberty* (New Haven, CT: Yale University Press, 2006), 379. *An Account of the Scots Society in Norwich, from its Rise in 1775*, 3. The Society's records show that Mrs. Hayley became a member on September 29, 1782, and her name on the membership list includes her title as Directress of the Society of Universal Good-will, N. America. The account in which that membership list is printed, however, was published in 1784 or later. Since the first mention I have found of Mrs. Hayley's plans to visit the United States dates from a letter from Gilbert Deblois in late 1783, I suspect she may have joined the Society in 1782 and been named as Directress later, once she planned to go to the United States. *An Account of the Scots Society, in Norwich, from Its Rise in 1775*, 3; Gilbert Deblois to William Deblois, Peckham, November 22, 1783, Gilbert Deblois Letterbooks vol. 1, RIHS; *Gentleman's Magazine* 51 (1781), 443; Sir Lewis Namier and John Brooke, *The History of the House of Commons*, vol. 2 (New York: Published for the History of Parliament Trust by Oxford University Press, 1964), 602; [London] *Gazetteer and New Daily Advertiser*, January 12, 1778. Letters from Gilbert Deblois establish the relationship between Mary Murray and the Hayleys. James Murray was a correspondent of George Hayley too. Gilbert Deblois to James Murray, Fulham, February 25, 1781, Box 3, James Murray Robbins Papers, MHS; *Norwich* [CT] *Packet*, January 15, 1784; *Pennsylvania Evening Post*, June 18, 1784; *Norwich* [CT] *Packet*, December 30, 1784; New York *Independent Journal*, October 23, 1784; Boston *Independent Ledger*, August 9, 1784.

47. *An Account of the Proceedings of the Society of Universal Good-will, from the Beginning of 1784*, 5, 18.

48. Tim Hitchcock, "Paupers and Preachers: The SPCK and the Parochial Workhouse Movement," in Lee Davison, et al., *Stilling the Grumbling Hive: The Response to Social and Economic Problems in England, 1689–1850* (New York: St. Martin's Press, 1992), 145–166.

49. *An Account of the Proceedings of the Society of Universal Good-will, from the Beginning of 1784*, 16.

50. *Articles and Regulations Proposed for the Society of Universal Good-will, in London, or Elsewhere, 1789* (Norwich, 1789), 6 ("all ranks and degrees," "all nations, religions and sects"), 11, 12, 13, 14 ("CREATOR"), 15, 3 ("fully established"). Because Murray was the key force behind the Society of Universal Good-will, because the tone is so similar to his speeches and his plan for the gradual abolition of slavery, and because the authors of both the proposed constitution and the abolition plan (both published in 1789) pay particular attention to the issue of language, I assume Murray is the unnamed author of the proposed constitution.

CHAPTER 4

1. John Sims to Thomas Parke, August 9, 1783, Etting Collection, "Scientists" folder, f. 79, Historical Society of Pennsylvania; Benjamin Rush to John King, April 2, 1783, in L. H. Butterfield, ed., *Letters of Benjamin Rush*, 2 vols. (Princeton, NJ: Published for the American Philosophical Society by Princeton University Press, 1951), vol. 1, 300; Richard Price to Rush, January 1, 1783, Rush Manuscripts Dickinson College, Part I, Library Company of Philadelphia (LCP); Benjamin Rush to John Coakley Lettsom, April 8, 1785, in Butterfield, ed., *Letters of Benjamin Rush*, vol. 1, 351; John Coakley Lettsom to Benjamin Rush, July 1788, Rush Manuscripts, vol. 28, LCP; Benjamin Rush to John Montgomery, February 20, 1786, in Butterfield, ed., *Letters of Benjamin Rush*, vol. 1, 379.

2. William Kellaway, *The New England Company 1649–1776: Missionary Society to the American Indians* (New York: Barnes and Noble, 1962), 277–281.

3. Beilby Porteus, *A Sermon Preached before the Incorporated Society for the Propagation of the Gospel in Foreign Parts; at their Anniversary Meeting . . . on Friday, February 21, 1783* (London, 1783), 25; John Butler, *A Sermon Preached before the Incorporated Society for the Propagation of the Gospel in Foreign Parts; at their Anniversary Meeting . . . on Friday, February 20, 1784* (London, 1784), 12; Boyd Stanley Schlenther, "Religious Faith and Commercial Empire" in P. J. Marshall, ed., The Oxford History of the British Empire: The Eighteenth Century (Oxford: Oxford University Press, 1998–1999), 128–150, 147; on the impact of the American Revolution on the SPG, see also Travis Glasson, *Mastering Christianity: Missionary Anglicanism and Slavery in the Atlantic World* (New York: Oxford University Press, 2012), 233, 207–209.

4. *An Account of the Expenditure, and General Management of the Affairs, of the Society in Scotland for Propagating Christian Knowledge: Contained in a Report Drawn up by a Committee of their Number, Appointed for that Purpose* (Edinburgh, 1796), 59–62; *Summary Account of the Rise and Progress of the Society in Scotland for Propagating Christian Knowledge* (Edinburgh, 1783), 47. On the bequest

that funded the Bray Associates' work in Philadelphia, see John C. Van Horne, ed., Introduction in *Religious Philanthropy and Colonial Slavery: The American Correspondence of the Associates of Dr. Bray, 1717-1777* (Urbana: University of Illinois Press, 1985), 5–9. Edgar Legare Pennington, "The Work of the Bray Associates in Pennsylvania," *Pennsylvania Magazine of History and Biography* 58:1 (1934): 1–25, 13, 17–18, 19. At the end of the eighteenth century, the SSPCK stopped funding its missionary in the United States: Henry Warner Bowden, *American Indians and Christian Missions: Studies in Cultural Conflict* (Chicago: University of Chicago Press, 1981), 150.

5. Troy O. Bickham, *Making Headlines: The American Revolution as Seen through the British Press* (Dekalb: Northern Illinois University Press, 2009), 235–236, 246; Benjamin Rush to James Currie, December 11, 1787, in Butterfield, ed., *Letters of Benjamin Rush*, vol. 1, 445.

6. Thomas Paine, *Letter to Abbe Raynal*, quoted in Gordon S. Wood, *Creation of the American Republic, 1776–1787* (Chapel Hill: Published for the Institute of the Early American History and Culture at Williamsburg, Virginia, by the University of North Carolina Press, 1969), 48 ("new era and new turn"); see also W. Caleb McDaniel, "Philadelphia Abolitionists and Antislavery Cosmopolitanism" in Richard Newman and James Mueller, eds., *Antislavery and Abolition in Philadelphia: Emancipation and the Long Struggle for Racial Justice in the City of Brotherly Love*, 149–173 (Baton Rouge: Louisiana State University Press, 2011), 157–158; Kariann Akemi Yokota, *Unbecoming British: How Revolutionary America Became a Postcolonial Nation* (New York: Oxford University Press, 2011); Sam W. Haynes, *Unfinished Revolution: The Early American Republic in a British World* (Charlottesville: University of Virginia Press, 2010); Eliga Gould, "American Independence and Britain's Counter-Revolution," *Past and Present* 154 (1997): 107–141.

7. T[obias] Watkins, *An Eulogium on the Character of Brother John Crawford, M.D. Late R.W.G.M. of Masons in Maryland. Delivered in the First Presbyterian Church, on the 24th June, 1813, In Obedience to a Resolution of the R.W.G. Lodge of Maryland* (Baltimore, 1813), 21.

8. On the *philosophes*, see Thomas J. Schlereth, *The Cosmopolitan Ideal in Enlightenment Thought* (Notre Dame, IN: University of Notre Dame Press, 1977), xiii.

9. *New York Daily Advertiser*, August 7, 1786; *An Account of the Scots Society, in Norwich, from Its Rise in 1775, Until It Received the Additional Name of the Society of Universal Good-will, in 1784*, 2nd ed. (Norwich, n.d.), 94; John Coakley Lettsom to James Madison, December 12, 1804, in Thomas Joseph Pettigrew, *Memoirs of the Life and Writings of the late John Coakley Lettsom: with a Selection from his Correspondence*, 3 vols. (London, 1817), vol. 2, 580; George W. Corner, ed., *The Autobiography of Benjamin Rush: His "Travels Through Life" together with his Commonplace Book for 1789–1813* (Princeton, NJ: Published for the American

Philosophical Society by Princeton University Press, 1948), 140, 145, 146, 151, 152, 161.

10. John Fothergill to Israel Pemberton, March 28, 1741, in Betsy C. Corner and Christopher C. Booth, eds., *Chain of Friendship: Selected Letters of Dr. John Fothergill of London, 1735–1780* (Cambridge, MA: Belknap Press of Harvard University Press, 1971), 57; on his anti-French prejudice, see 23; Corner, ed., *The Autobiography of Benjamin Rush*, 79; *An Account of the Scots Society in Norwich, from Its Rise in 1775,* 94.

11. John Bard to Samuel Bard, April 9, 1763, Bard Collection, New York Academy of Medicine (NYAM); Benjamin Rush to William Claypoole, July 29, 1782, in Butterfield, ed., *Letters of Benjamin Rush,* vol. 1, 284.

12. Photoduplicate of a letter from Dr. John Murray to John B. Murray, July 31, 1774, Murray Family Papers, Box 5, New-York Historical Society, New York.

13. John Lathrop to John Coakley Lettsom, November 13, 1799, in Pettigrew, *Memoirs of . . . John Coakley Lettsom,* vol. 2, 452.

14. Benjamin Rush to Richard Price, June 2, 1787, in Butterfield, ed., *Letters of Benjamin Rush,* vol. 1, 419; John Coakley Lettsom to William Cuming, March 2, 1785, in Pettigrew, *Memoirs of . . . Lettsom,* vol. 1, 96.

15. John Coakley Lettsom to Sir Mordaunt Martin, April 27, 1792, in Pettigrew, *Memoirs of . . . Lettsom,* vol. 2, 62–63; Pettigrew, *Memoirs of . . . Lettsom,* vol. 1, 155; John Coakley Lettsom to Sir Mordaunt Martin, June 6, 1790, in Pettigrew, *Memoirs of . . . Lettsom,* vol. 1, 27.

16. Jeremy Belknap, Journal of a Trip to Philadelphia in 1785, Jeremy Belknap Papers, Massachusetts Historical Society (MHS), Boston. On Protestant ideas about sacred space and about disorderly speech that would have conditioned Belknap's reaction to whispering at the Philadelphia synagogue, see Susan Juster, *Disorderly Women: Sexual Politics & Evangelicalism in Revolutionary New England* (Ithaca, NY: Cornell University Press, 1994), 18–26, 86, 88–96; see also Edwin Scott Gaustad, *The Great Awakening in New England* (1957; rpt. Chicago, 1968), 6, 70–73. Christian visitors to synagogues were not unusual. Similar to, but harsher than, Belknap's reaction, members of the German Reformed Church in Philadelphia referred to the "clamor" of Jewish services (and thus did not want a synagogue next to the church). William Pencak, *Jews and Gentiles in Early America* (Ann Arbor: University of Michigan Press, 2005), 95–96, 129, 222.

17. "A Letter Addressed to Lieutenant General Mathew on the means of preventing the method of treating and origins of the Diseases most prevalent and which prove most destr[uctive] to the Natives of Cold Climates visiting or residing in Warm Countries by John Crawford, M.D," Box 130, Manuscript Collections of the Medical and Chirurgical Faculty of Maryland (MS 3000), 73, Maryland Historical Society, Baltimore (MdHS). The Maryland Historical Society gives a tentative date of 1793 for Crawford's letter to Mathew, but Julia Wilson's date

of 1795 seems more likely. See Julia Wilson, "Dr. John Crawford, 1746–1813," *Bulletin of the School of Medicine University of Maryland* 25 (1940): 116–132, 129.

18. John Lathrop, *A Discourse Before the Humane Society, in Boston: Delivered On the Second Tuesday of June, 1787* (Boston, 1787), 12; John Coakley Lettsom to Benjamin Rush, September 8, 1783, Rush Manuscripts, vol. 28, f. 3, LCP; John Coakley Lettsom to Thomas Parke, February 3, 1789, Scientists, Etting Collection, Historical Society of Pennsylvania (HSP); John Coakley Lettsom to Sir Mordaunt Martin, July 11, 1791, in Pettigrew, *Memoirs of . . . Lettsom*, vol. 2, 53; Corner, ed., *The Autobiography of Benjamin Rush*, 209–210, 220, 243, 245, 258.

19. Benjamin, Count Rumford, *Essays, Political, Economical, and Philosophical*, 3 vols., vol. 1 (London, 1796), 246, 247.

20. On improvement, see, John Brewer, *The Pleasures of the Imagination: English Culture in the Eighteenth Century* (New York: Farrar, Straus and Giroux, 1997), 56–57; Richard L. Bushman, *The Refinement of America: Persons, Houses, Cities* (New York: Alfred A. Knopf, 1992); Joyce E. Chaplin, *An Anxious Pursuit: Agricultural Innovation and Modernity in the Lower South, 1730–1815* (Chapel Hill: Published for the Institute of Early American History and Culture, Williamsburg, Virginia, by the University of North Carolina Press, 1993), esp. 92–93, 106–128; John E. Crowley, *The Invention of Comfort: Sensibilities and Design in Early Modern Britain and Early America* (Baltimore: Johns Hopkins University Press, 2001); Richard Drayton, *Nature's Government: Science Imperial Government, and the "Improvement" of the World* (New Haven, CT: Yale University Press, 2000); John Gascoigne, *Science in the Service of Empire* (Cambridge: Cambridge University Press, 1998), 65–66; Jack P. Greene, *Pursuits of Happiness: The Social Development of Early Modern British Colonies and the Formation of American Culture* (Chapel Hill: University of North Carolina Press, 1988), 109–111, 197–198; David J. Hancock, *Citizens of the World: London Merchants and the Integration of the British Atlantic Community* (Cambridge: Cambridge University Press, 1995), esp. chap. 9, 279–319; Alan Houston, *Benjamin Franklin and the Politics of Improvement* (New Haven, CT: Yale University Press, 2008); Roy Porter, "Cleaning up the Great Wen: Public Health in Eighteenth-Century London," in W. F. Bynum and Roy Porter, eds., *Living and Dying in London (Medical History Supplement* No. 11, 1991), 61–75; Roy Porter, *The Creation of the Modern World: The Untold Story of the British Enlightenment* (New York: W.W. Norton, 2000), esp. chap. 19, 424–445; James C. Riley, *The Eighteenth-Century Campaign to Avoid Disease* (New York: St. Martin's Press, 1987); David Spadafora, *The Idea of Progress in Eighteenth-Century Britain* (New Haven, CT: Yale University Press, 1990); David Turley, "British Antislavery Reassessed," in Arthur Burns and Joanna Innes, eds., *Rethinking the Age of Reform: Britain 1750–1850* (Cambridge: Cambridge University Press, 2003), 182–199, 182–184; Jenny Uglow, *The Lunar Men: Five Friends Whose Curiosity*

Changed the World (New York: Farrar, Straus and Giroux, 2002); Houston, *Benjamin Franklin and the Politics of Improvement*, 16 ("set of priorities").

21. This analysis draws on extensive reading in sources related to philanthropy. See, for example, "Observations Recommendatory of the Philadelphia Society for Ameliorating the Miseries of Public Prisons," *American Museum* (1787), 1, 457; [John Murray], *An Enquiry into the Origin, Progress, & Present State of Slavery: With a Plan for the Gradual, Reasonable, & Secure Emancipation of Slaves. By a Member of the Society of UNIVERSAL GOODWILL in London and Norwich* (London, 1789), esp. 17, 22; John Howard, *The State of the Prisons in England and Wales, with Some Preliminary Observations, and an Account of Some Foreign Prisons* (London, 1777), 40–75, 488; John Lathrop to John Coakley Lettsom, November 9, 1790, in Pettigrew, *Memoirs of . . . Lettsom*, vol. 2, 444–445; John Coakley Lettsom, *Hints Designed to Promote Beneficence, Temperance, and Medical Science*, 3 vols., vol. 1 (London, 1801), 101; "Papers Relative to a Sick & Lying-in Patients by the Humane Society," Belknap Papers, Reel 161.A. (Reel 4), MHS; *Royal Humane Society, Instituted 1774: The Annual Report Published for the Anniversary Festival 1795 by William Hawes, M.D.* (London, 1795), 1; Benjamin Rush to Jeremy Belknap, August 19, 1788, in Butterfield, ed., *Letters of Benjamin Rush*, vol. 1, 447. On reasons activists prioritized ending the slave trade, see Christopher Leslie Brown, *Moral Capital: Foundations of British Abolitionism* (Chapel Hill: Published for the Omohundro Institute for Early American History and Culture, Williamsburg, Virginia, by the University of North Carolina Press, 2006), 257– 258, 321, 375–376, 386–388. John Coakley Lettsom to Sir Mordaunt Martin, April 4, 1791, in Pettigrew, *Memoirs of . . . Lettsom*, vol. 2, 42 ("gradually [prepar[ing]"). On the use of incentives, see [Murray], *An Enquiry into the Origin, Progress, & Present State of Slavery: With a Plan for the Gradual, Reasonable, & Secure Emancipation of Slaves*, 35; *Society for the Recovery of Persons Apparently Drowned, Instituted M.D.CC.L.XXIV* ([London, 1774]), 7; Benjamin Say, *An Annual Oration Pronounced Before the Humane Society of Philadelphia, on the Objects & Benefits of Said Institution; the 28th Day of February, 1799* (Philadelphia, 1799), 20; Benjamin, Count Rumford, *Essays, Political, Economical, and Philosophical*, vol. 1, 69.

22. Samuel Bard to John Bard, April 26, 1775, John M'Vickar, *A Domestic Narrative of the Life of Samuel Bard, M.D., LL.D.* (New York, 1822), 97 ("happy days"); John Howard to John Prole, March 28, 1778 ("Poverty & Misery"), Am. 08525, Howard Edwards Collection, Historical Society of Pennsylvania.

23. On John Howard, see James Baldwin Brown, *Memoirs of the Public and Private Life of John Howard, the Philanthropist, Compiled from his own Diary . . . His Confidential Letters; the Communications of his Surviving Relatives and Friends; and other Authentic Sources of Information*, 2nd ed. (London, 1823), 19. John Warren, *An Eulogy on the Honourable Thomas Russell, Esq., Late President of the*

Society for Propagating the Gospel Among the Indians and Others, in North America; the Humane Society of the Commonwealth of Massachusetts; the Agriculture Society; the Society for the Advice of Immigrants; the Boston Chamber of Commerce; and the National Bank in Boston (Boston, 1796), 11–12 "(severity")"; John Howard, *The State of the Prisons in England and Wales, with Some Preliminary Observations, and an Account of Some Foreign Prisons* (London, 1777), 23 ("perhaps . . . increased").

24. John Lathrop to John Coakley Lettsom, January 3, 1789, in Pettigrew, *Memoirs of . . . Lettsom*, vol. 2, 443 ("desolates"); John Coakley Lettsom to Sir Mordaunt Martin, March 13, 1790, in Pettigrew, *Memoirs of . . . Lettsom*, vol. 2, 25.

25. Benjamin Rush to Jeremy Belknap, April 5, 1791, in Butterfield, ed., *Letters of Benjamin Rush*, vol. 1, 578; "Extract of a Letter from Boston," *Federal Gazette and Philadelphia Daily Advertiser*, April 11, 1791.

26. On Britons' (including British Americans') familiarity with captivity, see Linda Colley, *Captives: Britain, Empire, and the World, 1600–1850* (New York: Anchor Books, 2002); on the conventions of caring for prisoners and reasons for public support of those norms, see Erica Charters, *Disease, War and the Imperial State* (Chicago: University of Chicago Press, 2014), 176, 177, 187, 188; Daniel Krebs, *A Generous and Merciful Enemy: Life for German Prisoners of War during the American Revolution* (Norman: University of Oklahoma Press, 2013), 121–132.

27. John Coakley Lettsom, *Memoirs of John Fothergill, M.D. &c.*, 4th ed. (London, 1786), 95 ("peace and amity"); Charters, *Disease, War and the Imperial State*, 183; Krebs, *A Generous and Merciful Enemy*, 173; John Lathrop, *A Discourse Preached on the Fifth of March, 1778* (Boston, 1778), 14–15; John Lathrop to John Coakley Lettsom, November 9, 1790, in Pettigrew, *Memoirs of . . . Lettsom*, vol. 2, 444 ("not carried on").

28. *An Account of the Scots Society in Norwich, from Its Rise in 1775*, 94.

29. Warren, *An Eulogy on the Honourable Thomas Russell, Esq*, 11–12.

30. John Howard to Reverend Smith, April 17, 1783, in Brown, *Memoirs of . . . Howard*, 375.

31. Thomas Percival to Benjamin Rush, March 29, 1790, Rush Manuscripts, vol. 28, f. 60, LCP. On Clerke, see Mark Smith, "Clerke, Sir William Henry, eighth baronet (1751–1818)," in Lawrence Goldman, ed., *Oxford Dictionary of National Biography*, online ed., (Oxford: Oxford University Press), http://www.oxforddnb.com/view/article/5633, accessed July 7, 2010.

32. Sir William Clerke, *Thoughts upon the Means of Preserving the Health of the Poor, by Prevention and Suppression of Epidemic Fevers. Addressed to the Inhabitants of Manchester, and the Several Populous Trading Towns, Surrounding and Connected with It* (London, 1790), 3.

33. John Lathrop, *A Discourse Before the Humane Society, Delivered on the Second Tuesday on June, 1787* (Boston, 1787), 22; *Account of the Dublin General Dispensary and Humane Society; Established at the Dispensary Court, No. 28, Temple-Bar, for*

the *Purpose of Administering Medical and Surgical Assistance to the Sick Poor of the City, and of Recovering Persons Apparently Dead from Drowning, Suffocating, or Other Accidents* (Dublin, 1793), 6; Amanda Bowie Moniz, "Saving the Lives of Strangers: Humane Societies and the Cosmopolitan Provision of Charitable Aid," *Journal of the Early Republic* 29 (Winter 2009): 607–640.

34. Thomas Percival to John Haygarth, 1787, in Edward Percival, ed., *Memoir of the Life and Writings of Thomas Percival M.D.* (London, 1807), cxix.

35. John Coakley Lettsom, *Hints Designed to Promote Beneficence, Temperance, and Medical Science* (London, 1797), 159–160; W. Waldgreave to John Coakely Lettsom, August 16, 1792, in Pettigrew, *Memoirs of . . . Lettsom*, vol. 2, 378–381. "Papers Relative to Sick & Lying-in Patients by the Humane Society," Jeremy Belknap Papers, Reel 161.A. (Reel 4), MHS; Clerke, *Thoughts upon the Means of Preserving the Health of the Poor, by Prevention and Suppression of Epidemic Fevers*, 23; John Haygarth, *An Inquiry How to Prevent the Small-Pox. And Proceedings of a Society for Promoting General Inoculation at stated periods, and preventing the Natural Smallpox in Chester* (Chester, 1784), 137–145.

36. Clerke, *Thoughts upon the Means of Preserving the Health of the Poor, by Prevention and Suppression of Epidemic Fevers*.

37. John Coakley Lettsom to Benjamin Rush, September 8, 1783, Rush Manuscripts, vol. 28, fl. 3, LCP; Thomas Arnold to Jeremy Belknap, 10th of 8th Month [August 10, 1789, Belknap Papers, 161.B (Reel 5), MHS; Thomas Percival to Benjamin Rush, July 20, 1790, Rush Manuscripts, vol. 28, f. 59, LCP; John D. Rodgers to Ashbel Green, November 6, 1797, Gratz Collection, John Rodgers Folder, HSP; Sir Mordaunt Martin to John Coakley Lettsom, April 6, 1789, in Pettigrew, *Memoirs of . . . Lettsom* vol. 2, 19; Jeremy Belknap to Benjamin Rush, Benjamin September 29, 1787, Rush Manuscripts, vol. 30, f. 1, LCP; John Halliburton to Benjamin Waterhouse, October 26, 1790, Benjamin Waterhouse Papers, Box 16.2, Countway Library; John Coakely Lettsom to [Benjamin Franklin], March 31, 1789, Dreer Collection, Physicians, Surgeons, and Chemists, vol. 2, HSP. In a recent book, J. R. Oldfield impressively reconstructs the communications strategies of the abolitionist movement. Similar to the communications strategies within humanitarian networks more broadly, the abolitionist movement differed in pursuing legislative goals. J. R. Oldfield, *Transatlantic Abolitionism in the Age of Revolution: An International History of Anti-slavery, c. 1787–1820* (Cambridge: Cambridge University Press, 2013), see esp. chap. 2. On one prominent person's engagement with transatlantic humanitarian, specifically abolitionist, conversations, see Francois Furstenberg, "Atlantic Slavery, Atlantic Freedom: George Washington, Slavery, and Transatlantic Abolitionist Networks," *William and Mary Quarterly* 68:2 (April 2011): 247–286.

38. On the practice of reading aloud or passing around letters, see Eve Tavor Bannet, *Empire of Letters: Letter Manuals and Transatlantic Correspondence, 1688–1820*

(Cambridge: Cambridge University Press, 2005), 47, 89–94; Benjamin Rush to Granville Sharp, June 5, 1785, in John A. Woods, "The Correspondence of Benjamin Rush and Granville Sharp, 1773–1809," *Journal of American Studies* 1 (1967), 1–38, 26; John Coakley Lettsom to Benjamin Rush, September 17, 1789, Rush Manuscripts, vol. 28, f. 14, LCP; Jeremy Belknap to Benjamin Rush, September 8, 1788, Rush Manuscripts, vol. 30, f. 6, LCP; Travis Glasson similarly finds that the eighteenth-century practices brought the SPG's views to a broader public than simply those involved with the organization. Glasson, *Mastering Christianity*, 37, 72.

39. John Morgan, *A Discourse Upon the Institution of Medical Schools in America; Delivered at a Public Anniversary Commencement, held in the College of Philadelphia May 30 and 31, 1765* (Philadelphia, 1765), 62 ("benefactors of mankind); Amasa Dingley, *An Oration. On the Improvement of Medicine: Pronounced before a Respectable Auditory of Citizens, in the Federal Hall in the City of New York; ... on the 16th January, 1794* (New York, 1795), 34 ("useful"), 39 ("active benevolence"); John Aitken, *Medical Improvement: An Address Read to the Medical Society* (Edinburgh, 1777), 13 ("unexplored regions"). On doctors' reputations, see John Eliot to Jeremy Belknap, January 24, 1786, Jeremy Belknap Papers, Reel 161.D, MHS. Dorothy Porter and Roy Porter, *Patients' Progress: Doctors and Doctoring in Eighteenth-Century England* (Stanford: Stanford University Press, 1989); Richard Harrison Shryock, "Origins of a Medical Profession," in *Medicine and Society in America, 1660–1860* (Ithaca, NY: Cornell University Press, 1960), 1–43. On the importance of communication and cosmopolitanism to medical men, see *Reports of the Royal Humane Society instituted in the Year 1774, for the Recovery of Persons Apparently Drowned for the Years MDCCLXXXI and MDCCLXXXII*, v. Adair Crawford to Benjamin Rush, London, July 4, 1783, Rush Manuscripts, vol. 25, f. 74, LCP; John Bard to Samuel Bard, New York, April 9, 1763, Bard Collection, NYAM; Benjamin Rush to William Claypoole, Philadelphia, July 29, 1782, in Butterfield, ed., *Letters of Benjamin Rush*, vol. 1, 284; Dingley, *An Oration. On the Improvement of Medicine*, 9, 39. See chapter 2 on far-flung future doctors meeting as medical students.

40. *The Autobiography of Benjamin Rush*, 44 ("republic of medicine"). The main caches of Lettom's letters are the correspondence printed in Pettigrew's *Memoirs of ... Lettsom*, the correspondence held by the Medical Society of London and printed in Lawrence and MacDonald's *Sambrook Court*, and the John Coakley Lettsom Papers at the Wellcome Library.

41. Benjamin Rush to John Coakley Lettsom, May 18, 1787, in Butterfield, ed., *Letters of Benjamin Rush*, vol. 1, 417 ("empire of humanity"); *Reports of the Royal Humane Society Instituted in the Year 1774; with an Appendix of Miscellaneous Observations on the Subject of Suspended Animation. For the Years MDCCLXXXVII, MDCCLXXXVIII and MDCCLXXXIX* [London, 1790], 87–88, 398–399,

400–401; Benjamin Waterhouse to Benjamin Rush, September 22, 1808, Rush Manuscripts, vol. 30, f. 113, LCP. On Waterhouse, see Phiilip Cash, "Setting the Stage: Dr. Benjamin Waterhouse's Reception in Boston, 1782–1788," *Journal of the History of Medicine and Allied Science* 1992 (47): 5–28; Benjamin Waterhouse to Eliphalet Pearson, November 11, 1795, American Academy of Arts and Sciences Letters, vol. 2, f. 41, Boston Athenaeum; William Tudor, *A Discourse Delivered Before the Humane Society, at their Anniversary, May, 1817* (Boston, 1817), 30; on Waterhouse, see John B. Blake, *Benjamin Waterhouse and the Introduction of Vaccination: A Reappraisal* (Philadelphia: University of Pennsylvania Press, 1957); Philip Cash, "Setting the Stage: Dr. Benjamin Waterhouse's Reception in Boston, 1782–1788," *Journal of the History of Medicine and Allied Science* 1992 (47): 5–28.

42. John Redman Coxe to Benjamin Rush, September 15, 1794, Rush Manuscripts, vol. 27, f. 26, LCP; Nicholas Pike to Jeremy Belknap, November 8, 1790, Belknap Papers 161.B (Reel 5), MHS.

43. John Lathrop to John Coakley Lettsom, November 16, 1791, in Pettigrew, *Memoirs of . . . Lettsom,* vol. 2, 446; Samuel Parker to William White, November 14, 1789, Gratz Collection, Protestant Episcopal Bishops of the US (Case 8, Box 34), HSP.

44. John Coakley Lettsom to Dr. Parke, July 21, 1785, Etting Collection, Scientists, f. 56, HSP ("hanging" and "expelling"); Benjamin Rush to Richard Price, April 22, 1786, in Butterfield, *Letters of Benjamin Rush,* vol. 1, 385; John Coakley Lettsom to Benjamin Rush, October 9, 1784, Rush Manuscripts, vol. 28, f. 6, LCP ("rumours of war"); Thomas Percival to unknown, February 4, 1787, in Percival, ed., *Memoirs of the Life and Writings of Thomas Percival,* cxvi ("liberty of the press"); Thomas Percival to Benjamin Rush, October 16, 1787, Rush Manuscripts, vol. 28, f. 71, LCP ("Convention"). Samuel Parker to William White, November 14, 1789, Gratz Collection, Protestant Episcopal Bishops of the U.S. (Case 8, Box 34), HSP ("generally well pleased").

45. John Coakley Lettsom to Benjamin Rush, August 10, 1788, Rush Manuscripts, vol. 28, f. 10, LCP.

46. Thomas Percival to Benjamin Rush, October 16, 1787, Rush Manuscripts, vol. 28, f. 71, LCP ("Convention"); Benjamin Rush to John Coakley Lettsom, May 18, 1787, in Butterfield, ed., *Letters of Benjamin Rush,* vol. 1, 417 ("petition our Convention"); Jeremy Belknap to Benjamin Rush, February 12, 1788, Rush Manuscripts, vol. 30, f. 2, LCP; Samuel Parker to William White, November 14, 1789, Gratz Collection, Protestant Episcopal Bishops of the US (Case 8, Box 34), HSP.

47. Richard Price to Benjamin Rush, September 24, 1787, Rush Manusripts, vol. 43, f. 118, LCP; Thomas Percival to Benjamin Rush, October 16, 1787, Rush Manuscripts, vol. 28, f. 71, LCP.

48. John Coakley Lettsom to Benjamin Rush, September 8, 1783, Rush Manuscripts, vol. 28, f. 3, LCP; John Coakley Lettsom to James Johnstone, September 4, 1789, in Pettigrew, *Memoirs of . . . Lettsom*, vol. 2, 372; John Coakley Lettsom to Benjamin Rush, August 10, 1788, Rush Manuscripts, vol. 28, 10, LCP.

49. John Lathrop to John Coakley Lettsom, November 9, 1790, in Pettigrew, *Memoirs of . . . Lettsom*, vol. 2, 444–445; Jeremy Belknap to Benjamin Rush, July 18, 1792, Rush Manuscripts, vol. 30, f. 22, LCP.

50. On the liberal paternalist approach to empire in the post-Revolutionary years, see Maya Jasanoff, *Liberty's Exiles: American Loyalists in the Revolutionary World* (New York: Alfred A. Knopf, 2011). That approach took some time to develop. Donna Andrew notes that the London charitable community in the 1770s and 1780s lacked direction, particularly in terms of its contribution to the nation. Donna T. Andrew, *Philanthropy and Police: London Charity in the Eighteenth Century* (Princeton: Princeton University Press, 1989), 162.

CHAPTER 5

1. John Howard to Samuel Whitbread, November 26, 1786, December 16, 1786, and July 22, 1786, in John Field, *Correspondence of John Howard, the Philanthropist, Not Before Published* (London, 1855), 127 ("sadly drooping"), 129 ("cold" and "dirty"), 114.

2. John Howard, *An Account of the Principal Lazarettos of Europe: With Some Papers Relative to Plague* (Warrington, 1789), 12.

3. John Howard to Joshua Symonds, June 20, 1775, John Howard to Thomas Smith, September 7, 1781, in James Baldwin Brown, *Memoirs of the Public and Private Life of John Howard, the Philanthropist, Compiled from his own Diary . . . His Confidential Letters; the Communications of his Surviving Relatives and Friends; and other Authentic Sources of Information*, 2nd ed. (London, 1823), 178–179, 332, 414–417.

4. Brown, *Memoirs of . . . Howard*, 204 ("pestilential jails").

5. For a scholarly view of Howard that stresses his asceticism, anxious spirituality, and severity as a parent, see Michael Ignatieff, *A Just Measure of Pain: The Penitentiary in the Industrial Revolution, 1750–1850* (New York: Pantheon, 1978), 47–52; John Howard to William Seward, October 24, 1786 ("pecuilaritys"), Add. MS 5418, British Library, London.

6. Jeremy Black, *The British Abroad: The Grand Tour in the Eighteenth Century* (Gloucester, England: Sutton, 1992), 4. This sketch of Howard's life comes from Brown, *Memoirs of . . . Howard*, 2–21, 22–7, 99–100; on his wife's death as a factor inclining him to travel, see 18.

7. For details of Howard's trips, see Brown, *Memoirs of . . . Howard*; on his parliamentary bid, see Brown, *Memoirs of . . . Howard*, 147–150; on his wife's death as

an impetus to travel see, Brown, *Memoirs of . . . Howard,* 241; on Howard's short-lived involvement with the proposed penitentiary, see Brown, *Memoirs of . . . Howard,* 307–309. On nonconformist doctors' belief in the importance of healthful conditions for the moral reform of prisoners, see Ignatieff, *A Just Measure of Pain,* 59–61. On the penitentiary project, see Ignatieff, *A Just Measure of Pain,* 59–61, 93–96. D. L. Howard, *John Howard: Prison Reformer* (New York: C. Johnson, 1958), 114–115. Brown, *Memoirs of . . . Howard,* 551.

8. Peter Clark explains the importance of membership in voluntary organizations for migrants and the importance of migrants to voluntary organizations' memberships, but he does not explore migrants' role in the formation of voluntary associations. Peter Clark, *British Clubs and Societies 1580–1800: The Origins of an Associational World* (Oxford: Oxford University Press, 2000), 158–161.

9. John Aikin, ed., *Appendix; Containing Observations Concerning Foreign Prisons and Hospitals: Collected by Mr. Howard, in his Concluding Tour* [London, 1791], 11 ("collect what was good").

10. John Howard, *Appendix to the State of the Prisons in England and Wales, &c. Containing a Farther Account of Foreign Prisons and Hospitals, with Additional Remarks on the Prisons of This Country* (Warrington, England, 1780), 282 ("room, on the ground-floor"). John Howard, *An Account of the Principal Lazarettos of Europe: With Some Papers Relative to Plague* (Warrington, 1789), 56 ("*Prison* at NICE"). Jeremy Bentham to John Forster, April/May 1778, in Timothy L. S. Sprigge, ed., *The Correspondence of Jeremy Bentham,* vol. 3 (London: Athlone, 1968), 106 ("model for method").

11. Jeremy Bentham to the Reverend John Forster, April/May 1778, Sprigge, ed., *The Correspondence of Jeremy Bentham,* vol. 3, 105–106 ("certainly must have"). On his travels, see Brown, *Memoirs of . . . Howard.* Field, *Correspondence of John Howard, Not Before Published,* 87; Brown, *Memoirs of . . . Howard,* 604.

12. Benjamin Rush to John Montgomery, June 8, 1785, in L. H. Butterfield, ed., *Letters of Benjamin Rush,* 2 vols. (Princeton, NJ: Published for the American Philosophical Society by Princeton University Press, 1951), vol. 1, 356 ("news of these things"); David H. Solkin, *Painting for Money: The Visual Arts and the Public Sphere in Eighteenth-Century England* (New Haven, CT: Yale University Press, 1992), 159–174. Paul K. Longmore, *The Invention of George Washington* (Charlottesville: University Press of Virginia, 1999); David Waldstreicher, *In the Midst of Perpetual Fetes: The Making of American Nationalism, 1776–1820* (Chapel Hill: Published for the Omohundro Institute for Early American History and Culture, Williamsburg, Virginia, by the University of North Carolina Press, 1997), 118–121; Francois Furstenberg, "Atlantic Slavery, Atlantic Freedom: George Washington, Slavery, and Transatlantic Abolitionist Networks," *William and Mary Quarterly* 68:2 (April 2011): 247–286, 249.

13. Paul Langford, *A Polite and Commercial People: England, 1727–1783* (Oxford: Clarendon Press, 1989), 482. The statue campaign documents can be found collected in John Coakley Lettsom, "Hints Respecting the Monument Erected to John Howard," in *Hints on Beneficence, Temperance, and Medical Science*, 3 vols. (London, 1801), vol. 2, 142–228, and in "Papers Relative to a Monument to John Howard," Add. 26055, British Library, London. John Howard to Reverend Smith, December 17, 1786, Howard Edwards Collection, Historical Society of Pennsylvania (HSP), Philadelphia; John Howard to Samuel Whitbread, January 18, 1787, in Field, *Correspondence of John Howard*, 135; copy of a letter from John Howard to Mr. Dilly, October 23, [1786], Add. 26055, British Library; copy of Part of a Letter from John Howard to Richard Price, October 13, 1786, inserted in a letter from Richard Price to John Coakley Lettsom, November 3, 1786, Howard Edward Collection, HSP; John Howard to Sir Robert Murray Keith, October 25, 1786 ("private education"), Hardwicke Papers, Add. 35537, f. 187, British Library; John Howard to the Statue Committee, December 15, 1786, in *Gentleman's Magazine* 57 (1787), 101 ("laid aside"); Lettsom, "Hints Respecting the Monument Erected to John Howard" in *Hints on Beneficence, Temperance, and Medical Science*, vol. 2, 200 ("great Philanthropist"); (New York) *Independent Journal*, April 21, 1787; *Pennsylvania Packet*, April 27, 1787; [Boston] *American Herald*, May 7, 1787; copy of part of a letter from John Howard to Richard Price, October 13, 1786, inserted in letter from Richard Price to John Coakley Lettsom, November 3, 1786, Howard Edward Collection, HSP; Thomas Coombe, *The Influence of Christianity on the Condition of the World: A Sermon, Preached in Trinity Chapel, Conduit Street, on Sunday, December 13, 1789* (London, 1790), 14 ("refusing a statue").

14. Brown, *Memoirs of . . . Howard*, 397 ("every comfort"); John Aikin, *A View of the Life, Travels, and Philanthropic Labors of the Late John Howard* (Philadelphia, 1794), 148 ("peculiar habits").

15. For examples of his letters about his trips, see John Howard to Samuel Whitbread, February 13, 1786; July 22, 1786; May 12, 1788, in Field, *Correspondence of John Howard*, 101–103, 113–115, 147–148 ("calm steady spirits"); Eve Tavor Bannet, *Empire of Letters: Letter Manuals and Transatlantic Correspondence, 1688–1820* (Cambridge: Cambridge University Press, 2005), 47; *Gentleman's Magazine* 57 (1787), 178, 1150–1151; Brown, *Memoirs of . . . Howard*, 395–396; John Howard to John Prole [n.d.] in Brown, *Memoirs of . . . Howard*, 513–514 ("public know it").

16. Eliga Gould, "American Independence and Britain's Counter-Revolution," *Past and Present* 154 (1997): 107–141; Maya Jasanoff, *Liberty's Exiles: American Loyalists in the Revolutionary World* (New York: Alfred A. Knopf, 2011); Christopher Leslie Brown, *Moral Capital: Foundations of British Abolitionism* (Chapel Hill: Published for the Omohundro Institute for Early American History and Culture, Williamsburg, Virginia, by the University of North Carolina Press,

2006); P. J. Marshall, "The Moral Swing to the East: British Humanitarianism, India and the West Indies" in *"A Free though Conquering People": Eighteenth-Century Britain and Its Empire* (Aldershot: Ashgate, 2003), 69–95.

17. "Observations on the Statue for John Howard, and Howardian Fund for Prison-Charities and Reforms. Written by Dr. Warner" (*"Friend to Every Clime"*) in Lettsom, "Hints Respecting the Monument Erected to John Howard" in *Hints Designed to Promote Beneficence, Temperance, and Medical Science*, vol. 2, 172; *Gentleman's Magazine* 56 (June 1786), 485 ("attend divine service"); Edmund Burke, "Speech at Bristol Previous to the Election 6 September 1780," in Warren M. Elofson and John A. Woods, eds., *The Writings and Speeches of Edmund Burke*, vol. 3 (New York: Oxford University Press, 1996), 637–638 ("visit[ing] all Europe").

18. Letter from Anglus to Mr. Urban, *Gentleman's Magazine* 56 (1786), 359 (*"Consummate Philanthropist"*), 360 ("glorious possibilities"). John Coakley Lettsom identified Anglus as the Reverend Dr. John Warner. Lettsom, "Hints Respecting the Monument Erected to John Howard" in *Hints Designed to Promote Beneficence*, vol. 2, 155.

19. Letter from Anglus to Mr. Urban, *Gentleman's Magazine* 56 (1786), 360 ("true vicar").

20. Thomas Reid to the Howardian Committee, August 20, 1786, in Lettsom, "Hints Respecting the Monument Erected to John Howard," in *Hints Designed to Promote Beneficence*, vol. 2, 172.

21. Lettsom, "Hints Respecting the Monument Erected to John Howard," in *Hints Designed to Promote Beneficence*, vol. 2, 149–150, 147–148, 198–207, 204 ("diffus[ing] widely").

22. John Coakley Lettsom to Mr. Urban, June 20, 1786, *Gentleman's Magazine* 56 (1786), 447 ("public approbation").

23. John Coakley Lettsom to Benjamin Rush, July 15, 1787, March 31, 1789, September 17, 1789, Rush Manuscripts, vol. 28, Library Company of Philadelphia.

24. *Pennsylvania Packet*, April 27, 1787; [Boston] *American Herald*, May 7, 1787; *American Museum* 1 (May 1787), 458; [New York] *Daily Advertiser* April 21, 1787; October 20, 1787; January 14, 1790 ("imprisoned fellow creatures").

25. Daniel Appleton White, *An Address to the Members of the Merrimack Humane Society, at their Anniversary Meeting, in Newburyport, Sept. 3, 1805* (Newburyport, 1805), 20.

26. *"From the* Pennsylvania Packet," *Gentleman's Magazine*, Supplement, for the Year 1787, 1150.

27. John Swanwick and William White, secretary and president, respectively, of the Philadelphia Society for Alleviating the Miseries of Public Prisons, to Howard, January 14, 1788, Letters to John Howard, MS English Misc. c. 332, f. 15 Bodleian Library, Oxford.

28. Howard, *The State of the Prisons in England and Wales,* 4 ("love to my country"), 78 ("not my object").

29. Brown, *Memoirs of . . . Howard,* 516 ("air and appearance").

30. Howard, *State of the Prisons,* 4, 78; John Howard to Reverend Smith, September 7, 1781, in Brown, *Memoirs of . . . Howard,* 331 ("first Man in the Kingdom"); Aikin, ed., *Appendix; Containing Observations Concerning Foreign Prisons and Hospitals,* 3 ("gain further knowledge"). In a letter to his friend Whitbread from Moscow in 1789, Howard wrote, "I labour to convey the Torch of Philanthropy in these distant regions." John Howard to Samuel Whitbread, September 22, 1789, Letters to John Howard, MS English Misc. c. 332, f. 15 Bodleian Library.

31. Comments by Johann Neem, Conference of the Society for Historians of the Early American Republic, July 2010; Kariann Akemi Yokota, *Unbecoming British: How Revolutionary America Became a Postcolonial Nation* (Oxford: Oxford University Press, 2011), 11, 16, 161, 163.

32. Benjamin Rush to John Howard, October 14, 1789, in Butterfield, ed., *Letters of Benjamin Rush,* vol. 1, 528.

33. John Haygarth to John Howard, May 30, 1789, ff. 24–34 ("rather disappointed"), Letters to John Howard, MS English Misc. c. 332, Bodleian Library; Jeremy Bentham to John Forster, April/May 1778, in Sprigge, ed., *The Correspondence of Jeremy Bentham,* vol. 3, 106 ("Empress Catherine").

34. John Howard to Samuel Whitbread, October 26, 1786, in Field, *Correspondence of John Howard,* 124 ("perform his promise").

35. *Barbados Mercury,* August 21, 1787 ("humane Mr. Howard").

36. Erasmus Darwin, *The Botanic Garden,* vol. 2 (1791; rpt. Merton, Yorkshire), 81 ("travers[ed] the globe").

37. Radnor to John Howard, April 20, 1789, Letters to John Howard, MS English Misc. c. 332, f. 18 ("very much chagrined," "mortified"), Bodleian Library.

38. Lettsom, "Hints Respecting the Monument Erected to John Howard" in *Hints Designed to Promote Beneficence,* vol. 2, 205 ("successful formation").

39. Brown, *Memoirs of . . . Howard,* 522.

40. Julia Wilson, "An Early Baltimore Physician and His Medical Library," *Annals of Medical History* 4 (1942): 63–80, 63; "A Letter Addressed to Lieutenant General Mathew on the means of preventing the method of treating and origins of the Diseases most prevalent and which prove most destr[uctive] to the Natives of Cold Climates visiting or residing in Warm Countries by John Crawford, M.D," Box 130, Manuscript Collections of the Medical and Chirurgical Faculty of Maryland (MS 3000), p. 73, Maryland Historical Society, Baltimore (MdHS), 1.

41. "A Letter Addressed to Lieutenant General Mathew . . . by John Crawford, M.D," 103 ("sick and wounded"), 104 ("obliged to lie"), 109 ("wretched"), 108 ("not one"), 111 ("wander[ed] about"), 109, 113, Box 130, Manuscript Collections of the Medical and Chirurgical Faculty of Maryland (MS 3000), MdHS.

42. Matthew Mulcahy, *Hurricanes and Society in the British Greater Caribbean, 1624–1783* (Baltimore: Johns Hopkins University Press, 2006), 76–82, 24, 81.

43. Tobias Watkins, *An Eulogium on the Character of Brother John Crawford* (Baltimore, 1813), 10 ("high souled," "profit," "dispensed").

44. "A Letter Addressed to Lieutenant General Mathew . . . by John Crawford, M.D," 125, Box 130, Manuscript Collections of the Medical and Chirurgical Faculty of Maryland (MS 3000), MdHS; Watkins, *An Eulogium on the Character of Brother John Crawford*, 10–11. Crawford's eulogist and a later historian give 1782 as the year Crawford headed to England to recuperate, but the *Hibernian Magazine* for December 1781 reports the death of "the lady of Dr. John Crawford of Barbadoes" on the passage from the Leeward Islands. *Hibernian Magazine*, December 1781, 672; Wilson, "An Early Baltimore Physician," 64.

45. On his business importing drugs, see the advertisements in the *Barbados Mercury*, for instance, April 17, 1783 and July 24, 1784.

46. *Reports of the Royal Humane Society instituted in the Year 1774, for the Recovery of Persons Apparently Drowned for the Years MDCCLXXXV and MDCCLXXXVI* [London, 1787], 170; *Barbados Mercury*, July 21, 1787. See Chapter 6 on the Philadelphia Dispensary and the Philadelphia and Massachusetts Humane Societies.

47. *The Reports of the Society for Bettering the Condition and Improving the Comforts of the Poor* (*SBCP Reports*), vol. 2, 4th ed. (London, 1805), 7; Jonathan Allen Fowler, *Adventures of an "Itinerant Institutor": The Life and Philanthropy of Thomas Bernard* (Ph.D. diss., University of Tennessee, 2003), 88–89, 164.

48. Benjamin, Count Rumford, *Essays, Political, Economical, and Philosophical*, 3 vols. (London, 1796), vol. 1, 248–277; Joseph Ioor Waring, *A History of Medicine in South Carolina* ([Charleston?]: South Carolina Medical Association, 1964), 121; Andrew Bell, *An Analysis of the Experiment in Education, Made at Egmore, Near Madras*, 3rd ed. (London, 1807), 49, 26, 53, 81–86. On the adoption in Britain of the practice of making letters in sand to teach writing, see Bell, *An Analysis of the Experiment in Education*, 86. *The Report of the Society for Bettering the Condition and Increasing the Comforts of the Poor*, vol. 3 (London, 1802), 254; Patrick Colquhoun, *A New and Appropriate Education for the Labouring People* (London, 1806), 14, 24. On the adoption of educational practices from Joseph Lancaster's and Andrew Bell's methods by the New York City Free School Society and the influence of the New York charity school on charity schools in Philadelphia, see DeWitt Clinton, *An Address to the Benefactors and Friends of the New York Free School Society, Delivered at the Opening of that Institution, in their New and Spacious Building* (New York, 1809), 11–12, 15. For more on British charity schools, see M. G. Jones, *The Charity School Movement: A Study of Eighteenth-Century Puritanism in Action* (London, 1938); on the controversy between Lancaster and Bell and their camps, see 333–339.

49. "Thoughts of a Public Dispensary," *New York Daily Advertiser*, January 24, 1791 ("how will it work").

50. *Reports of the Humane Society Instituted in the Year 1774, for the Recovery of Persons Apparently Drowned for the Years MDCCLXXXV and MDCCLXXXVI*, vii, 157, 158 ("great respectability"), 161, vi, 160.

51. John Bard was another of the twelve physicians first chosen. On John R. B. Rodgers, see Richard Harrison, *Princetonians 1769–1775: A Biographical Dictionary* (Princeton, NJ: Princeton University Press, 1980), 518–520; *Plan of the Philadelphia Dispensary for the Medical Relief of the Poor* (Philadelphia, 1787), 4. On the organization and opening of the dispensary in New York, see *New York Daily Advertiser* August 30, 1790, October 20, 1790, November 9 and 18, 1790, January 4, 1791; *New York Journal*, September 7, 1790, October 26, 1790; *New York Daily Gazette*, November 4, 1790, November 11, 1790, November 18, 1790, December 28, 1790, January 1, 1791, January 15, 1791. *Rules of the City Dispensary, for the Medical Relief of the Poor* [n.d., c. 1792]. On the dispute over the dispensary, see "Thoughts of a Public Dispensary," *New York Daily Advertiser*, January 24, 1791 ("first threw out"); *A Letter from John Bard, . . . to the Author of Thoughts on the Dispensary* (New York, 1791), 6 ("ever intended"); *A Letter from Doctor Richard Bayley, to Doctor John Bard. . . An Answer to a Part of his Letter Addressed to the Author of Thoughts on the Dispensary* (New York, 1791); "The Author of Thoughts on the Public Dispensary, to Dr. John Bard, President of the Medical Society," *New York Daily Advertiser*, May 31, 1791; *New York Daily Advertiser*, January 15, 1791.

52. On the dispensary movement, see I. S. L. Loudon, "The Origins and Growth of the Dispensary Movement in England," *Bulletin of the History of Medicine* 55 (1981): 322–342; Robert Kilpatrick, "'Living in the Light': Dispensaries, Philanthropy and Medical Reform in Late Eighteenth-Century London," in Andrew Cunningham and Roger French, eds., *The Medical Enlightenment of the Eighteenth Century* (Cambridge: Cambridge University Press, 1990); Charles E. Rosenberg, *Caring for the Working Man: The Rise and Fall of the Dispensary Movement* (New York: Garland, 1989). On the humane society movement, see Luke Davidson, "Raising Up Humanity: A Cultural History of Resuscitation and the Royal Humane Society of London, 1774–1808" (Ph.D. diss., University of York, 2001); Elizabeth Thomson, "The Role of Physicians in the Humane Societies of the Eighteenth Century," *Bulletin of the History of Medicine* 37 (1963): 43–51; Claire L. Nutt, "Crawford, Adair," *Oxford Dictionary of National Biography*, vol. 14, 68–69; *Medical Register* for 1780 (London, 1780), 54; *Medical Register* for 1783, 35. The *Medical Register* for 1783 listed Adair Crawford in the List of Physicians Resident in London and gave his address as Lamb-Conduits Street. *Medical Register* for 1783 (London, 1783), 11. That address is the same as the address given for the Dr. Crawford named in the Royal Humane Society reports.

Reports of the Royal Humane Society instituted in the Year 1774, for the Recovery of Persons Apparently Drowned for the Years MDCCLXXIX and MDCCLXXX ([London, 1781]), 141; Reports of the Royal Humane Society instituted in the Year 1774, for the Recovery of Persons Apparently Drowned for the Years MDCCLXXXI and MDCCLXXXII ([London, 1782/83]), 124–134; John Hadley Swain, A Sermon Preached at St. Martin's in the Fields, London, on Sunday, March 30, and at Hampstead Church, Middlesex, on Sunday, May 25, 1783, for the Benefit of the Humane Society (London, 1783), 45.

53. *Reports of the Royal Humane Society instituted in the Year 1774, for the Recovery of Persons Apparently Drowned for the Years MDCCLXXXV and MDCCLXXXVI*, 170; *Barbados Mercury*, July 21, 1787 ("proper shop," "now unpacked").

54. John Crawford to Benjamin Rush, June 13, 1798, Rush Manuscripts, vol. 3, LCP. On the College of Physicians' role in the Dispensary, see Simon Finger, *The Contagious City: The Politics of Public Health in Early Philadelphia* (Ithaca, NY: Cornell University Press, 2012), 114–118.

55. *Barbados Mercury*, October 21, 1788 ("decent and becoming," "levity and ill manners").

56. Warren Alleyne, "It So Happened," [Barbados] *Sunday Sun of the Nation*, May 31, 1998; *Barbados Mercury*, July 21, 1787; *Barbados Gazette*, July 18 to 21, 1787.

57. Wilson, "An Early Baltimore Physician," 64; "A Letter Addressed to Lieutenant General Mathew . . . by John Crawford, M.D," 2, Box 130, Manuscript Collections of the Medical and Chirurgical Faculty of Maryland (MS 3000), MdHS; *The* [Baltimore] *Observer*, September 19, 1807, 181; Wilson, "An Early Baltimore Physician," 64, 68.

58. *The* [Baltimore] *Observer*, September 19, 1807, 182; Wilson, "An Early Baltimore Physician," 64; "Memorial of Doctor [John] Crawford (the Chief Surgeon of the Colony of Demerary) to the Lord of the Treasury," (n.d.), Wellcome Library ("country practitioners"). Wilson says that Crawford went to England in 1794, but in his memorial to the Lords of the Treasury, Crawford says he received permission to leave Demerara in April 1794 and arrived in Holland in July. I think his mid-1790s trip to England came after his time in the United Provinces based on his memorial to the Lords of the Treasury.

59. "Memorial of Doctor [John] Crawford (the Chief Surgeon of the Colony of Demerary) to the Lord of the Treasury," (n.d.), Wellcome Library ("in consequence"); Watkins, *An Eulogium on the Character of Brother John Crawford*, 11; John Crawford to Hugh McCalmont, December 19, 1798, December 21, 1799, February 18, 1802, Correspondence of John Crawford (MS 1246), MdHS. Another historian who has studied Crawford is also skeptical that he left Demerara purely out of a desire to move to the United States and thinks "there must have been some definite period of rebellion or of disappointment." John Rathbone Oliver, "An Unpublished Autograph Letter from Dr. John Crawford (1746–1813) to General

William Henry Winder (1755–1824)," *Bulletin of the Institute of the History of Medicine* 4 (1936): 145–151, 146; Watkins, *An Eulogium on the Character of Brother John Crawford*, 11; Wilson, "An Early Baltimore Physician," 64.

60. John Crawford to Benjamin Rush, January 4, 1797, Rush Manuscripts vol. 3, LCP; Adair Crawford to Benjamin Rush, July 4, 1783, Rush Manuscripts, vol. 25, LCP; John Coakley Lettsom to Benjamin Rush, September 8, 1783, Rush Manuscripts, vol. 28, LCP. Wilson says Rush and Crawford "had long been acquainted through mutual exchange of letters and ideas." Wilson, "An Early Baltimore Physician," 64.

61. John Crawford to Benjamin Rush, June 13, 1798, Rush Manuscripts, vol. 3, LCP ("talked of the advantages").

62. David Freeman Hawke, *Benjamin Rush Revolutionary Gadfly* (Indianapolis: Bobbs-Merrill, 1971), 321–322; J. H. Powell, *Bring Out Your Dead: The Great Plague of Yellow Fever in Philadelphia in 1793* (Philadelphia, 1949; rpt. 1993), esp. "This Excellent Physician," 114–139; Dr. Zimmerman to John Coakley Lettsom, May 27, 1794, in Thomas Joseph Pettigrew, *Memoirs of the Life and Writings of the late John Coakley Lettsom: with a Selection from his Correspondence*, 3 vols. (London, 1817), vol. 1, 167; Benjamin Rush to Jeremy Belknap, May 5, 1790, in Butterfield, ed., *Letters of Benjamin Rush*, vol. 1, 565–566.

63. Watkins, *An Eulogium on the Character of Brother John Crawford*, 19–20; John Crawford to Benjamin Rush, January 4, 1797, Rush Manuscripts vol. 3, LCP; John Crawford to Hugh McCalmont, December 19, 1798, Correspondence of John Crawford (MS 1246), MdHS.

64. John Crawford to Benjamin Rush, June 13, 1798 ("principal Inhabitants," "warmest support"), January 27, 1799 ("grounded upon," "suitable"), Rush Manuscripts, vol. 3, LCP. Wilson too cites the correspondence between Rush and Crawford and implies their plans led directly—if slowly—to the establishment of the Baltimore Dispensary. Wilson, "An Early Baltimore Physician," 66.

65. James Smith, *The Additional Letters of Humanitas* ([Baltimore], 1801), 30 ("wretched management"); see also *One Hundred Years of History of the Baltimore General Dispensary* (Baltimore, 1901). On Crawford's Masonic role, Edward T. Schultz, *History of Freemasonry in Maryland, of all the Rites Introduced into Maryland, from the Earliest Times to the Present*, 2 vols. (Baltimore: J. H. Medairy, 1884), vol. 2, 297–307.

66. John Crawford to Benjamin Rush, February 15, 1804, Rush Manuscripts, vol. 3, LCP; *An Address to the Citizens of Baltimore and its Vicinity, Containing a Concise Account of the Baltimore General Dispensary, Its By-laws, and Other Matters Worthy of Notice* (Baltimore, 1812), 8.

67. Watkins, *An Eulogium on the Character of Brother John Crawford*, 21 ("universal philanthropy").

68. Watkins, *An Eulogium on the Character of Brother John Crawford*, 11.

69. On the deaths of Crawford's son and son-in-law and his dying in debt, see Julia Wilson, "Dr. John Crawford, 1746–1813," *Bulletin of the School of Medicine, University of Maryland* 25 (1940): 116–132, 117; Watkins, *An Eulogium on the Character of Brother John Crawford*, 18 ("heart devoted"), 16 ("fellow-creatures"), 17, 19. On the Freemasons' universal philanthropy, see Steven C. Bullock, *Revolutionary Brotherhood: Freemasonry and the Transformation of the American Social Order, 1730–1840* (Chapel Hill: University of North Carolina Press, 1996), 71–72, 186–198; Margaret C. Jacob, *Living the Enlightenment: Freemasonry and Politics in Eighteenth-Century Europe* (Oxford: Oxford University Press, 1991), 56–57; Watkins, *An Eulogium on the Character of Brother John Crawford*, 12 ("pure spirit," "ardent zeal," "ambition," "WASHINGTON"), 10, 11, 19 ("active share") 20 ("needy of all countries").

70. John Eliot to Jeremy Belknap, January 24, 1786, Jeremy Belknap Papers, Reel 161.D, pp. 50–69, Massachusetts Historical Society (MHS), Boston.

71. Samuel Bard to John Bard, Edinburgh, December 29, 1762; John Bard to Samuel Bard, New York, April 9, 1763; Samuel Bard to John Bard, Bard Collection, New York Academy of Medicine (NYAM); Auchmuty Sermon, November 3, 1771, 11, Box 1, New York-Presbyterian Hospital-New York Weill Cornell Medical Center Archives (NYH).

72. Draft of a letter from Benjamin Rush to the Managers of the Pennsylvania Hospital, September 24, 1810, Rush Manuscripts, vol. 31, LCP ("allure Strangers").

73. *Infirmary, Dispensary, Lunatic Hospital and Asylum, in Manchester, From the 24th of June, 1791, to the 24th of June, 1792*, 1, [Manchester, 1794] ("credible Testimony").

74. John Coakley Lettsom, "Hints Respecting a Samaritan Society," in *Hints on Beneficence, Temperance and Medical Science*, vol. 2, 3–27, 5 ("whose relief"), 3 ("for Convalescents"), 17 ("destitute *foreigners*"), 18 ("reach their homes," "means of procuring").

75. *The Power of Faith: Exemplified in the Life and Writings of Mrs. Isabella Graham of New-York* (New York, 1816), 400 ("broken in spirits," "seek an asylum"), 47. The fullest exploration of Graham, Bethune, Seton, and the Widows Society is in Anne M. Boylan, *The Origins of Women's Activism: New York and Boston, 1797–1840* (Chapel Hill: University of North Carolina Press, 2002).

76. *The Power of Faith*, 10–40, 17 ("temporal property"), 38 ("secret expectation"), 17 ("the widow and the fatherless"). Boylan notes that Graham imagined her experience as similar to those of the widows aided by her charity but highlights the advantages she had that allowed both Graham's schools and the Widows Society to thrive. Boylan, *The Origins of Women's Activism*, 98–100.

77. Boylan briefly discusses the Widows Society's impartiality, but it is not her focus. Boylan, *The Origins of Women's Activism*, 100.

78. See below on New York Hospital. On the Dispensary, see "City Dispensary" in William Duncan, *The New-York Directory and Register for the Year 1791* (New York, 1791), 45.

79. *The Power of Faith*, 47; Boylan, *The Origins of Women's Activism*, 108; Charlotte Parkinson, ed., *The Society for the Relief of Women and Children: 1797–1997: An Exploration of the Minutes and Records from 1797–1997 of the The Society for the Relief of Women and Children* ([New York], 2000), 13.

80. *The Power of Faith*, 46 ("distributing manager"), 47 ("widows not entitled").

81. On the early years of New York Hospital, see Eric Larabee, *The Benevolent and Necessary Institution: The New York Hospital 1771–1971* (Garden City, NY: Doubleday, 1971), chaps. 1–5, 1–136; NYH Board of Governors' Minutes, vol. 1, November 13, 1771, NYH.

82. Larabee, *The Benevolent and Necessary Institution*, 17; NYH Board of Governors' Minutes, vol. 1, October 28, 1771, NYH ("without the most distant regard").

83. NYH Board of Governors' Minutes, vol. 1, November 13, 1771, NYH.

84. *A Brief Account of the New York Hospital* (New York, 1804), 65.

85. *A Brief Account of the New York Hospital* (1804), 1 ("Christianity and general benevolence"); Annual Report for 1799 in NYH Board of Governors' Minutes, vol. 1, February 4, 1800 ("great sea port"), NYH.

86. *A Brief Account of the New York Hospital* (1804), 6 ("immense business," "public Hospital"), 5 ("emigrants"), 1 ("maladies," "political, civil, or religious").

CHAPTER 6

1. Conrad Edick Wright, *The Transformation of Charity in Postrevolutionary New England* (Boston: Northeastern University Press, 1992), 49; J. Brett Langstaff, *Dr. Bard of Hyde Park: The Famous Physician of Revolutionary Times, the Man Who Saved Washington's Life* (New York: E. P. Dutton, 1942), 154; Henry Moyes to Benjamin Rush, May 6, 1786, Rush Manuscripts, v. 10, Library Company of Philadelphia (LCP).

2. Wright, *The Transformation of Charity in Postrevolutionary New England*, 50 ("chance," "conversation turned," "mentioned").

3. *Providence Gazette*, September 11, 1784, from the *Gentleman's Magazine*, May 1784, ("literary phaenomena"); John Anthony Harrison, "Blind Henry Moyes, 'An Excellent Lecturer in Philosophy,'" *Annals of Science* 13 (1957): 109–125, 110–111; A. D. Morrison-Low, "Moyes, Henry (1749/50–1807)," in H. C. G. Matthew and Brian Harrison, eds., *Oxford Dictionary of National Biography* (Oxford: Oxford University Press, 2004); online ed., ed. Lawrence Goldman, October 2006, http://www.oxforddnb.com/view/article/53551, accessed July 19, 2010; Eva V. Armstrong and Claude K. Deischer, "Dr. Henry Moyes, Scotch Chemist," *Journal of Chemical Education* 24 (1947): 169–174; "Anecdotes of Dr. Moyes, the

Blind Philosopher" by George Bew, *Gentleman's Magazine* 56 (1786), 103–104; *New York Daily Advertiser*, April 17, 1786, and August 27, 1790.

4. Letter by Dr. Alexander Johnson, March 15, 1786, *Gentleman's Magazine* 57 Supplement (1787), 1154 ("benevolent offices"). On Johnson, see Carolyn D. Williams, "Johnson, Alexander (*bap.* 1716, *d.* 1799)," *Oxford Dictionary of National Biography* (Oxford: Oxford University Press, 2004); Alexander Johnson, *A Short Account of a Society at Amsterdam Instituted in the Year 1767 for the Recovery of Drowned Person; With Observations Shewing the Utility and Advantage that Would Accrue to Great Britain from a Similar Institution Extended to Cases of Suffocation by Damps in Mines, Choaking, Strangling, Stifling, and other Accidents* (London, 1773), 3–4; Martin Pernick, "Back from the Grave: Recurring Controversies over Defining and Diagnosing Death in History," in Richard M. Zaner, ed., *Death: Beyond Whole-Brain Criteria* (Dordrecht: Kluwer Academic, 1988), 20–23; Luke Davidson, "Raising Up Humanity: A Cultural History of Resuscitation and the Royal Humane Society of London, 1774–1808" (Ph.D. diss., University of York, 2001), 17–22, 132–139; Johnson, *A Short Account of a Society at Amsterdam Instituted in the Year 1767 for the Recovery of Drowned Person*, 3–7; Thomas Cogan, *Memoirs of the Society Instituted at Amsterdam in Favour of Drowned Persons, for the Years 1767, 1768, 1769, 1770, and 1771. Translated from the original by Thomas Cogan, M.D.* (London, 1773), ii, iv–v. For an overview of the movement, see Elizabeth Thomson, "The Role of Physicians in the Humane Societies of the Eighteenth Century," *Bulletin of the History of Medicine* 37 (1963): 43–51. For an analysis of American humane societies that stresses their role as the first suicide prevention organizations, see Richard Bell, *We Shall Be No More: Suicide and Self-Government in the Newly United States* (Cambridge, MA: Harvard University Press, 2012).

5. Davidson, "Raising Up Humanity," vii–ix; *Society for the Recovery of Persons Apparently Drowned. Instituted MDCCLXXIV* (1) (London, 1774]), 6 ("restore such as have"); *Society for the Recovery of Persons Apparently Drowned. Instituted MDCCLXXIV* (2) (London, 1774]), 14; Davidson, "Raising Up Humanity," 33–106.

6. *Reports of the Humane Society Instituted in the Year 1774, for the Recovery of Persons Apparently Drowned. For the Year MDCCLXXVI* ([London, 1776]), 107 ("too remote"); Meetings June 1, 1774, May 19, 1774, December 14, 1774, May 7, 1776, August 16, 1776, July 15, 1777, March 13, 1773, First Minute Book of the Society 1774–1784, Royal Humane Society Archives, London; *Gentleman's Magazine* 53 (1783), 626; *Gentleman's Magazine* 56 (1786), 538–540. On the distribution of materials, see also letters to William Hawes in the Society's annual reports. On Alexandar Johnson's efforts to spread the cause of resuscitation, see letter by Verus, September 12, 1791, *Gentleman's Magazine* 61 (1791), 821–824 ("pamphlets and instructions"); Alexander Johnson to Sir

Robert Murray Keith, May 28, 1773, Hardwicke Papers (Add. 35505), f. 280, British Library, London. Alexander Johnson to Benjamin Rush, April 3, 1790, Rush Manuscripts, vol. 25, LCP; "Directions for an Extension of the Practice of Recovering Persons Apparently Dead: Taken from the Instructions at Large Published by Alexander Johnson, M.D. (Introducer of the Practice in England) And Confirmed by Reporters Received from Abroad," published in the *Burlington* [NJ] *Advertiser,* June 22 and 29, 1790; the *Norwich* [CT] *Packet & Country Journal,* August 13 and 20, 1790; and the [Savannah] *Georgia Gazette,* September 23, 1790.

7. *Royal American Magazine,* March 1774, 100; *Pennsylvania Gazette,* December 7, 1774 ("in many Parts of Europe"); *Plan and Reports of the Society Instituted at London . . . for the Recovery of Persons Apparently Drowned* [London, 1775], 38. Information on resuscitation continued to circulate in America during the war. Daniel George, *An Almanack for the Year 1780* (Newbury, 1780).

8. *Pennsylvania Packet, September 2, 1780* ("in imitation"). Philadelphia Humane Society (PHS) meeting, September 5, 1780, Philadelphia Humane Society Minutes vol. 1, Pennsylvania Hospital Archives (PHA), Philadelphia. PHS managers' meetings, September 7, 1780, September 11, 1780, January 1, 1781, February 5, 1781, September 14, 1784, March 2, 1787, PHS Minutes, vol. 1, Pennsylvania Hospital Archive, Philadelphia (PHA).

9. Benjamin Waterhouse's draft memoirs, n.d., Box 16.4, Benjamin Waterhouse Papers (H MS c. 16), Francis A. Countway Library, Boston; *Newport Mercury,* July 20, 1782.

10. "Relief from Accidental Death; or Summary Instructions for the General Institution Proposed in the Year 1773, by Alexander Johnson, M.D.," *Providence Gazette,* October 2, 1784 ("more extensively useful"); "Relief from Accidental Death; or Summary Instructions for the General Institution Proposed in the Year 1773, by Alexander Johnson, M.D.," *Boston Magazine,* November 1785, 405–408, 449–454; "To the Printers of the Columbian Herald" [Charleston] *Columbian Herald,* May 29, 1786; "Relief from Accidental Death; or Summary Instructions for the General Institution Proposed in the Year 1773, by Alexander Johnson, M.D.," [Charleston] *Columbian Herald,* June 1, 1786.

11. William Tudor, *A Discourse Delivered Before the Humane Society, at their Anniversary, May, 1817* (Boston, 1817), 29, 30, 31. Benjamin Waterhouse gives a competing account in Benjamin Waterhouse's draft memoirs, n.d., Box 16.4, Benjamin Waterhouse Papers (H MS c. 16), Countway Library. See also Mark A. DeWolfe Howe, *The Humane Society of the Commonwealth of Massachusetts: An Historical Review, 1785–1916* (Boston: Printed for the Humane Society at the Riverside Press, 1918); Wright, *The Transformation of Charity,* 49–50.

12. Philadelphia Dispensary Managers' Meeting, February 19, 1787 ("engraft"), Philadelphia Dispensary Minute Book 1786–1806, PHA.

13. PHS Managers' Meeting, March 2, 1787, PHS Minute Book 1780–1805, PHA; Armstrong and Deischer, "Dr. Henry Moyes," 172; Henry Moyes to Thomas Clifford, October 3, 1785, Clifford Correspondence, vol. 7, Historical Society of Pennsylvania, Philadelphia; Alexander Johnson to Rush, April 3, 1790, Rush Manuscripts, vol. 25, LCP.

14. *Pennsylvania Packet*, September 5, 1780 ("in imitation").

15. PHS Managers' Meeting, December 2, 1782, May 5, 1783, PHS Minute Book 1780–1805, PHA.

16. The PHS records reveal dilatoriness, at best, with the letter to the Amsterdam group and do not report that the 1782–1783 letters were ever sent and Royal Humane Society (RHS) minutes and reports do not mention receiving a letter from the Philadelphians, whereas the RHS did note receiving a letter from the Amsterdam group. PHS Managers' Meetings, 1782–1784, PHS Minute Book 1780-1805; First Minute Book of the Society 1774–1784, Royal Humane Society Archives (RHSA), London; on the correspondence and gift from the Amsterdam group, see the minutes for May 7, 1783.

17. PHS Managers' Meeting, August 22, 1787, October 10, 1787, PHS Minute Book 1780–1805, PHA.

18. Adam Hochschild, *Bury the Chains: Prophets and Rebels in the Fight to Free an Empire's Slaves* (Boston: Houghton Mifflin, 2005), 3; see also Christopher Leslie Brown, *Moral Capital: Foundations of British Abolitionism* (Chapel Hill: Published for the Omohundro Institute for Early American History and Culture, Williamsburg, Virginia, by the University of North Carolina Press, 2006). On the Pennsylvania Abolition Society, the world's first anti-slavery organization, see Richard S. Newman, *The Transformation of American Abolitionism: Fighting Slavery in the Early Republic* (Chapel Hill: University of North Carolina Press, 2002).

19. David Owen, *English Philanthropy 1660–1960* (Cambridge, MA: Belknap Press of Harvard University Press, 1964), 60 ("more than a little mystified"). Luke Davidson points out Owen's comment. Davidson, "Raising up Humanity," 1.

20. Amanda Bowie Moniz, "Saving the Lives of Strangers: Humane Societies and the Cosmopolitan Provision of Charitable Aid," *Journal of the Early Republic* 29 (Winter 2009): 607–640.

21. Never mind that Lazarus had not drowned but expired from an illness before Jesus revived him. John 11:1–17, 38–43. "Jamaica," [Philadelphia] *Independent Gazette*, August 11, 1789.

22. Amanda Bowie Moniz, "'Labours in the Cause of Humanity in Every Part of the Globe': Transatlantic Philanthropic Collaboration and the Cosmopolitan Ideal, 1760–1815" (Ph.D diss., University of Michigan, 2008), 359–360; *Reports of the Royal Humane Society Society instituted in the Year 1774, for the Recovery of Persons Apparently Drowned For the Years MDCCLXXXV and MDCCLXXXVI*

(London, 1787), 247–250; Meeting, May 19 1774, First Minute Book of the Society 1774-1784, RHSA. N.B. The minute book covering 1784 to 1820 is missing.

23. Meetings, May 19, 1774, June 1, 1774, May 9, 1782 and September 10, 1783, First Minute Book of the Society 1774–1784, RHSA; *Plan and Reports of the Society Instituted at London . . . for the Recovery of Persons Apparently Drowned* [London, 1775], 39; *Reports of the Royal Humane Society . . . For the Year MDCCLXXVI*, 107–118; *Reports of the Royal Humane Society . . . For the Years MDCCLXXXV and MDCCLXXXVI*, 157–178; *Reports of the Royal Humane Society . . . For the Year MDCCLXXVI*, 94; Meetings, December 14, 1774, May 19, 1774, First Minute Book of the Society 1774–1784, RHSA; Meetings, May 7, 1776, May 19, 1774, August 16, 1774, July 15, 1777, March 13, 1783, First Minute Book of the Society 1774–1784, RHSA; *Gentleman's Magazine* 53 (1783), 626; *Gentleman's Magazine* 56 (1786), 538–540; *Plan and Reports of the Society Instituted at London . . . for the Recovery of Persons Apparently Drowned* [London, 1775], 38.

24. *Reports of the Royal Humane Society . . . For the Years MDCCLXXXV and MDCCLXXXVI*, 256; *Reports of the Humane Society instituted in the Year 1774, for the Recovery of Persons Apparently Drowned for the Years MDCCLXXIX and MDCCLXXX* [London, 1781], 127.

25. *Reports of the Royal Humane Society . . . For the Years MDCCLXXXV and MDCCLXXXVI*, 254–255, 264. William Buchan, *Domestic Medicine: Or A Treatise on the Prevention and Cure of Diseases by Regimen and Simple Medicines* (London, 1784), 671–676, 696. On Buchan, see Charles E. Rosenberg, "Medical Text and Social Context: Explain William Buchan's *Domestic Medicine*" in *Explaining Epidemics and Other Studies in the History of Medicine* (Cambridge: Cambridge University Press, 1992), 32–56, esp. 32–34.

26. Donna T. Andrew, comp., *London Debating Societies, 1776–1799* (London: London Record Society, 1994), 16; Meeting, September 24, 1783, First Minute Book of the Society 1774–1784, RHSA; Treatise on Medical Electricity by Moses Willard, September 1789, Benjamin Rush Manuscripts, Box 8/Yi2, 7401, f. 22, Library Company of Philadelphia; *Reports of the Royal Humane Society . . . For the Years MDCCLXXXV and MDCCLXXXVI*, 259–262; Edward Burnaby Greene, *Ode to the Humane Society* (London, 1784).

27. Thomas Clarkson, *An Essay on the Impolicy of the Slave Trade. In Two Parts.* (London, 1788), 59.

28. Thomas Clarkson, *An Essay on the Slavery and Commerce of the Human Species, Particularly the African* (London, 1786), 130; *The Interesting Narrative of Oulaudah Equiano, or Gustavus Vassa, the African. Written by Himself* (London, [1789], 81–82; *Abstract of the Evidence Delivered Before a Select Committee of the House of Commons, in the Years 1790 and 1791; on the Part of the Petitioners for the Abolition of the Slave Trade* (London, 1791), 39, 40, 41; John Newton, *Thoughts Upon the African Slave Trade* (London, 1788), 18–19; Clarkson, *An Essay on the Slavery*

and Commerce of the Human Species, 131; *Thoughts and Sentiments on the Evil and Wicked Traffic and Slavery of the Human Species, Humbly Submitted to the Inhabitants of Great-Britain by Ottobah Cugoano* (London, 1787), 111–1112. Ten of the 132 people who died in the *Zong* massacre leaped overboard to wrest control of their deaths from their captors; one who was thrown climbed back aboard the ship. On the *Zong* case and on the *Zong* and death more generally in the antislavery campaign, see Vincent Brown, *The Reaper's Garden: Death and Power in the World of Atlantic Slavery* (Cambridge, MA: Harvard University Press, 2008), esp. 158–160, 173–175; *Abstract of the Evidence Delivered Before a Select Committee of the House of Commons*, 35–36.

29. John Collins, "The Desponding Negro" in James G. Basker, ed., *Amazing Grace: An Anthology of Poems about Slavery* (New Haven, CT: Yale University Press, 2002), 453; James Field Stanfield, *The Guinea Voyage. A Poem. In Three Books.* (London, 1789), 34; John Jamieson, *The Sorrows of Slavery, a Poem. Containing a Faithful Statement of Facts Respecting the African Slave Trade* (London, 1789), 46; Helen Maria Williams, *A Poem on the Bill Lately Passed for Regulating the Slave Trade* (London, 1788), 22; James Grahame, "To England, on the Slave Trade" in Basker, *Amazing Grace*, 458; William Julius Mickle, from Book V of "Camoes's *Lusiad*," in Basker, *Amazing Grace*, 278; William Roscoe, from "The Wrongs of Africa" in Basker, *Amazing Grace*, 199.

30. [William Collins], *The Slave Trade; a Poem. Written in the Year 1788. Dedicated to the Gentlemen, who Compose that Truly Noble, Generous, and Philanthropic Society for the Abolition of the Slave Trade* (London, 1793), 12, 13; on Collins's poem and Morland's painting, see also J. R. Oldfield, *Popular Politics and British Anti-slavery: The Mobilisation of Public Opinion Against the Slave Trade 1787–1807* (Manchester: Manchester University Press, 1995), 170–171; on the painting, see also Hugh Honour, *The Image of the Black in Western Art*, vol. 4:1 (Cambridge, MA: Belknap Press of Harvard University Press, 1989), 68–72.

31. [Samuel Jackson Pratt], *Humanity, or The Rights of Nature, A Poem; In Two Books. By the Author of Sympathy* (London, 1788), ii, iii, 45, 71, 4.

32. Brown, *The Reaper's Garden*; Thomas W. Laqueur, "Mourning, Pity, and the Work of Narrative in the Making of 'Humanity'" in Richard Ashby Wilson and Richard D. Brown, eds., *Humanitarianism and Suffering: The Mobilization of Empathy* (Cambridge: Cambridge University Press, 2009), 31–57.

33. *Extracts from the Reports of the Royal Humane Society, Which Fully Evince the Utility of an Air Machine, Invented by Mr. White* ([London?], 1790), 3, 7, 14–19, 22, 8–11; *Extracts from the Reports of the Royal Humane Society, Which Fully Evince the Utility of an Air Machine, Invented by Mr. White* ([London?], 1794), 31.

34. David Richardson, "Shipboard Revolts, African Authority, and the Atlantic Slave Trade," *William and Mary Quarterly*, 3rd series, 58:1 (2001): 69–92, 73; Larry Stewart, "The Edge of Utility: Slaves and Smallpox in the Early Eighteenth

Century," *Medical History* 29 (1985): 54–70; Richard B. Sheridan, "The Guinea Surgeons on the Middle Passage: The Provision of Medical Services in the British Slave Trade," *Interdisciplinary Journal of African Historical Studies* 14:4 (1981): 601–625; *Abstract of the Evidence Delivered Before a Select Committee of the House of Commons*, London, 1791, 40; Sheila Lambert, ed., *House of Commons Sessional Papers*, vol. 69 (Wilmington, DE: Scholarly Resources, 1975), 143; *Abstract of the Evidence Delivered Before a Select Committee of the House of Commons*, 40, 41. *Reports of the Royal Humane Society . . . For the Years MDCCLXXXV and MDCCLXXXVI*, 13.

35. *Royal Humane Society, Instituted 1774: The Annual Report. Published for the Anniversary Festival 1794 by W. Hawes M.D. Register* ([London, 1794?]), 62–63; *Royal Humane Society. Instituted 1774. The Annual Report Published for the Anniversary Festival 1795 by William Hawes M.D.* [London, 1795?], 21.

36. On the development of antislavery as a mass cause in the United States, see Newman, "The New Abolitionist Imperative: Mass Action Strategies" in *The Transformation of American Abolitionism*, 131–151; on the formation of the group, see "Republican Strategies: The Pennsylvania Abolition Society," in Newman, *The Transformation of American Abolitionism*, 16–38; David Brion Davis, *The Problem of Slavery in the Age of Revolution* (Ithaca, NY: Cornell University Press, 1975), 313, 314; David Brion Davis, *Inhuman Bondage: The Rise and Fall of Slavery in the New World* (Oxford: Oxford University Press, 2006), 152, 154; Newman, *The Transformation of American Abolitionism*, 18; Eva Sheppard Wolf, *Race and Liberty in the New Nation: Emancipation in Virginia from the Revolution to Nat Turner's Rebellion* (Baton Rouge: Louisiana State University Press, 2006), esp. chap. 2. Wolf stresses that manumitters were not necessarily motivated by antislavery sentiments.

37. James Oliver Horton and Lois E. Horton, *In Hope of Liberty: Culture, Community, and Protest among Northern Free Blacks, 1700–1860* (New York: Oxford University Press, 1997); Gary Nash, *Forging Freedom: The Formation of Philadelphia's Black Community 1720–1840* (Cambridge, MA: Harvard University Press, 1988); Richard S. Newman, *Freedom's Prophet: Bishop Richard Allen, the AME Church, and the Black Founding Fathers* (New York: New York University Press, 2008).

38. PHS Managers' Meeting, March 21, 1793 ("overset," "inevitably"), March 4, 1793 ("enquire into"), March 21, 1793 ("draw on the Treasurer"), PHS Minute Book 1780–1805, PHA.

39. Moniz, "Saving the Lives of Strangers," 629, 630.

40. John Brooks, *A Discourse Delivered Before the Humane Society of the Commonwealth of Massachusetts, June 9th, 1795* (Boston, 1795), 16 ("prompt and spirited," "exertions"), 25, 15 ("a boy was in the water"), 16 ("outcry," "repaired," "nearly high water," "earnestly looking," "*Dolphin Garler*," "no signs of life," "*his mother*"). On the skills of people of African descent as swimmers and divers, see Kevin Dawson,

"Enslaved Swimmers and Divers in the Atlantic World," *Journal of American History* 92 (2006): 1327–1355.

41. On honors, not monetary rewards, for genteel rescuers, see Davidson, "Raising Up Humanity," 254–258; on the same issue in the American context, see Moniz, "Saving the Lives of Strangers," 632–633. On the Royal Humane Society view that the lower sorts needed to be motivated by incentives, see Davidson, "Raising Up Humanity," 258–263.

42. Moniz, "Saving the Lives of Strangers," 630.

43. Brooks, *A Discourse Delivered Before the Humane Society of the Commonwealth of Massachusetts*, 16 ("respectable characters").

44. Moniz, "Saving the Lives of Strangers," 618, 621.

45. Brooks, *A Discourse Delivered Before the Humane Society of the Commonwealth of Massachusetts*, 16.

46. On white attitudes about free blacks' place in the republic, see Davis, *The Problem of Slavery in the Age of Revolution*, 304–306; Horton and Horton, *In Hope of Liberty*, 101.

47. Newman, *Freedom's Prophet*, 87–95.

48. Newman, *Freedom's Prophet*, 95–98.

49. Newman, *Freedom's Prophet*, 105.

50. Thomas Thacher, *A Discourse Delivered at Boston, Before the Humane Society of the Commonwealth of Massachusetts, June 10th, 1800* (Boston, 1800), 16 ("noble-spirited").

51. Julie Winch, *A Gentleman of Color: The Life of James Forten* (Oxford: Oxford University Press, 2002), 86.

52. Managers' meeting, October 11, 1809 ("corded wood," "strugglings," "young man," "long pole" "George Muschert, sailmaker," "brought up the lad," "apparently lifeless," "extraordinary & highly meritorious"), PHS Minutes, vol. 2, PHA.

53. John Clark Howard, *A Discourse Delivered Before the Humane Society of the Commonwealth of Massachusetts, at their Semiannual Meeting, June 12, 1804* (Boston, 1804), 46 ("newborn").

54. John Sylvester John Gardiner, *A Sermon Delivered Before the Humane Society, of the Commonwealth of Massachusetts, at their Semiannual Meeting, June 14, 1803* (Boston, 1803), 35–36.

55. Isaac Hurd, *A Discourse Delivered in the Church in Brattle Street, in Boston, Tuesday, June 11th, 1799, Before the Humane Society of the Commonwealth of Massachusetts* (Boston, 1799), 8.

56. One of the crews did not leave with the rescuers but finished building a boat to get off the island. The account given by Captain Gerrish of the unnamed vessel appeared in the Middletown, Connecticut, *Middlesex Gazette*, May 12, 1788; the New York *Impartial Gazetteer*, May 17, 1788; the Philadelphia *Independent Gazetteer*, May 22, 1786; the *Worcester Magazine*, May 22, 1788; the *Fairfield*

[CT] *Gazette,* May 28, 1788, plus other newspapers. The account given by the crew of the *George* appeared in the *New York Packet,* August 8, 1788; the Philadelphia *Independent Gazetteer,* August 12, 1788; the *New Haven Journal,* August 13, 1788; the *Columbian Herald,* August 21, 1788; the *Middlesex Gazette,* August 25, 1788; and the Windsor *Vermont Journal,* September 22, 1788, plus other newspapers.

57. [Proclamation, September 4, 1738], By His Excellency Jonathan Belcher ("so situated"); *Pennsylvania Packet,* May 30, 1774 ("tea ship"); *New York Independent Journal,* July 29, 1786 ("cast away," "men were saved"); [Proclamation, September 4, 1738] ("Subsistence and Relief"); *A Continuation of the Proceedings of the Humane Society of the Commonwealth of Massachusetts, from the second Tuesday in June 1788, to the second Tuesday in June 1789* (Boston, 1789), 2 ("plundered and harassed"). For more on the efforts to settle *Sable Island,* see Lyall Campbell, *Sable Island, Fatal and Fertile Crescent* (Windsor, Nova Scotia: Lancelot Press, 1974), 30–36.

58. See n. 56.

59. On the huts, see Wright, *The Transformation of Charity,* 49–50, 138–139.

60. *A Continuation of the Proceedings of the Humane Society of . . . Massachusetts,* 1, 2 ("several houses or families," "ought to be made"), 3, 4 ("Though this Island," "Light House").

61. Similarly, Peter Marshall notes that American political leaders were aggravated to be deemed "aliens" for trading purposes by the British in 1783. Marshall, *The Remaking of the British Atlantic,* 103.

62. *A Statement of the Premiums Awarded by the Trustees of the Humane Society of Massachusetts, from July 1817, to April 1829,* 46;*History of the Humane Society of Massachusetts* (Boston, 1845), 7 ("influential citizens," "some steps should be taken").

63. See the reports of the Royal Humane Society.

64. For the Benjamin Rush citation, see *Reports of the Royal Humane Society instituted in the Year 1774, for the Recovery of Persons Apparently Drowned for the Years MDCCLXXXV and MDCCLXXXVI,* 188; *Reports of the Royal Humane Society instituted in the Year 1774, for the Recovery of Persons Apparently Drowned for the Years MDCCLXXXVII, MDCCLXXXVIII, and MDCCLXXXIX* [London, 1790], 72–74, ("Humane Societies" quotation on 72).

65. Samuel Parker to William Hawes, July 6, 1789, in *Reports of the Royal Humane Society instituted in the Year 1774, for the Recovery of Persons Apparently Drowned for the Years MDCCLXXXVII, MDCCLXXXVIII, and MDCCLXXXIX,* 352, 353 ("preservation of the lives," "attention and assistance").

66. *Royal Humane Society, Instituted 1774: The Annual Report. Published for the Anniversary Festival 1793 by W. Hawes, M.D. Register* ([London, 1793?]), 35 ("nothing left them," "small," "highly gratified").

67. RHS Committee minutes, December 9 ("Danger," "not consistent") and December 11, 1782, RHSA.

68. *Royal Humane Society, Instituted 1774. Published for the Anniversary Festival 1792* ([London, 1792?]), 69–70; William Hawes, *An Address to the King and Parliament of Great Britain, on the Important Subject of Preserving the Lives of its Inhabitants* (London, 1782); *Reports of the Royal Humane Society instituted in the Year 1774, for the Recovery of Persons Apparently Drowned for the Years MDCCLXXXVII, MDCCLXXXVIII, and MDCCLXXXIX*, 433–434.

69. Kariann Akemi Yokota, *Unbecoming British: How Revolutionary America Became a Postcolonial Nation* (New York: Oxford University Press, 2011).

70. John Warren, *An Eulogy on The Honourable Thomas Russell, Esq. Late President of the Society for Propagating the Gospel Among the Indians and Other, in North America; the Humane Society of the Commonwealth of Massachusetts; the Agriculture Society; the Society for the Advice of Immigrants; the Boston Chamber of Commerce; and the National Bank in Boston* (Boston, 1796), 13, 15, 29, 15 ("new channels").

71. Warren, *An Eulogy on The Honourable Thomas Russell*, 26 ("unbounded"), 20–22.

72. Warren, *An Eulogy on The Honourable Thomas Russell*, 22 ("godlike design"), 12 ("precarious nature"), 22 ("shipwreck'd mariner"); *A Continuation of the Proceedings of the Humane Society of . . . Massachusetts*, 2 ("lives and property").

73. *Royal Humane Society, Instituted 1774: The Annual Report. Published for the Anniversary Festival 1793*, 31.

74. John Clarke, *A Discourse, Delivered Before the Humane Society of the Commonwealth of Massachusetts; at the Semi-annual Meeting, Eleventh of June 1793* (Boston, 1793), 31; *Royal Humane Society, Instituted 1774: The Annual Report. Published for the Anniversary Festival 1793*, 29; John Bartlett, *A Discourse on the Subject of Animation* (Boston, 1792), 23. N.B. The MHS report gives August 1792 as date that the first three honorary members were named but the letter announcing the honorary membership from the MHS printed in the RHS report is dated July 25, 1792.

75. Thomas Barnard, *A Discourse, Delivered Before the Humane Society of the Commonwealth of Massachusetts. At the Semiannual Meeting, June 10, 1794* (Boston, 1794), 21. On Andrew Brown, see George Shepperson, "Andrew Brown," *Dictionary of Canadian Biography Online*, http://www.biographi.ca/009004-119.01-e.php?&id_nbr=2770, accessed February 6, 2013. Brown traveled to Boston with a letter of introduction to Jeremy Belknap. S. S. Blowers to Jeremy Belknap, September 24, 1791; Andrew Brown to Jeremy Belknap, June 14, 1793; Andrew Brown to Jeremy Belknap, December 31, 1793; Belknap Papers, 161.B (Reel 5), MHS; *A Statement of Premiums Awarded by the Trustees of the Humane Society of Massachusetts, from July 1817 to April 1829* (Boston, 1829), 49; [Halifax] *Royal Gazette and Nova Scotia Advertiser*, December 16, 1794.

76. Marq de Villiers and Sheila Hirtle, *Sable Island: The Strange Origins and Curious History of a Dune Adrift in the Atlantic* (New York: Walker, 2004), 146–231.

77. *Reports of the Humane Society instituted in the Year 1774, for the Recovery of Persons Apparently Drowned. For the Year MDCCLXXVIII* [London, 1779], 103; *Royal Humane Society, Instituted 1774: The Annual Report. Published for the Anniversary Festival 1793*, 28, 32.

78. See Chapter 5, this volume.

79. *Reports of the Royal Humane Society instituted in the Year 1774, for the Recovery of Persons Apparently Drowned for the Years MDCCLXXXVII, MDCCLXXXVIII, and MDCCLXXXIX*, 353 ("this common cause").

80. *Royal Humane Society, Instituted 1774: The Annual Report. Published for the Anniversary Festival 1793*, 29 ("your endeavours").

81. John Lathrop, *A Discourse Before the Humane Society, in Boston: Delivered on the Second Tuesday of June, 1787* (Boston, 1787), 7; *Pennsylvania Packet*, September 5, 1780; *Society for the Recovery of Persons Aparently Drowned. Instituted M.D.CC.L.XX.IV.* [London, 1774], 4, 5; Lathrop, *A Discourse Before the Humane Society, in Boston*, 19, 20, 21; Clarke, *A Discourse, Delivered Before the Humane Society of the Commonwealth of Massachusetts*, 31–32; Brooks, *A Discourse Delivered Before the Humane Society of the Commonwealth of Massachusetts*, 15.

82. The Pennsylvania Abolition Society was not a public subscription charity but required members to be elected. *The Constitution of the Pennsylvania Society, for Promoting Abolition, and the Relief of Free Negroes, Unlawfully Held in Bondage. Begun in the Year 1774, and Enlarged on the Twenty-third of April, 1787. To Which Are Added in the Acts of the General Assembly of Pennsylvania, for the Gradual Abolition of Slavery* (Philadelphia, 1787), 6 ("during their residence"); Delaware Abolition Society constitution, *New York Daily Advertiser*, August 26, 1788 ("during their residence" quotation in its constitution also); *The Constitution of the Humane Society of the State of New York* (New York, 1795), 7.

83. *An Account of the Scots Society in Norwich, in Great Britain. Founded in 1775* (Norwich, 1783), 10; C. A. Struve to the Royal Humane Society, *Royal Humane Society, 1774 … The Annual Report published for the Anniversary Festival by W. Hawes M.D.* [London, 1798], 17.

84. On debates over American foreign policy and attitudes toward foreign events in the 1790s, see Stanley Elkins and Eric McKitrick, *The Age of Federalism: The Early American Republic, 1788–1800* (New York: Oxford University Press, 1993); Rachel Cleves, *The Reign of Terror in America: Visions of Violence from Anti-Jacobins to Antislavery* (New York: Oxford University Press, 2009). For a perceptive arguing that with the Constitutional Convention, Americans shifted away from their global aspirations to a national focus, see J. M. Opal, *Beyond the Farm: National Ambitions in Rural New England* (Philadelphia: University of Pennsylvania Press, 2008), 13.

85. Bartlett, *A Discourse on the Subject of Animation* MHS—first letter 32, 33, 34 ("relieve the unfortunate," "behold with rapture," "intimate alliance").

86. On the Pennsylvania Abolition Society, see Newman, *The Transformation of American Abolition*, 15–17. On the Republican ties of the leaders of the Humane Society of the State of New York, see Alfred F. Young, *The Democratic Republicans of New York: The Origins 1763–1797* (Chapel Hill: Published for the Institute of Early American History and Culture, Williamsburg, Virginia, by the University of North Carolina Press, 1967), 400. On the *Royal Humane Society, Instituted 1774: The Annual Report. 1796 By William Hawes M.D.* [London, 1796], quotation 46.

87. Hawes, *An Address to the King and Parliament of Great Britain, on the Important Subject of Preserving the Lives of its Inhabitants.* Hawes gave lectures on resuscitation but the school he envisioned was not established. *Annual Report of the Humane Society. 1809* (London, 1809), 5.

88. On the RHS's national vision and hope for government support at its beginning, see *Reports of the Society for the Recovery of the Apparently Drowned. Part II* (1774) 34, 35. For its hope for a national establishment in the early 1780s, see *Reports of the Royal Humane Society instituted in the Year 1774, for the Recovery of Persons Apparently Drowned for the Years MDCCLXXXIII and MDCCLXXXIV* [London], 164.

89. For a genealogy of established and attempted humane societies, see Moniz, "Labours in the Cause of Humanity in Every Part of the Globe," 359–364.

90. *Reports of the Royal Humane Society instituted in the Year 1774, for the Recovery of Persons Apparently Drowned for the Years MDCCLXXXVII, MDCCLXXXVIII, and MDCCLXXXIX*, 398–399, 356–361, 456 ("every necessary assistance").

91. On Murray, see John Burke, *Burke's Landed Gentry*, vol. 2 (London, 1846), 903; Arthur H. Plaisted, *The Manor and Parish Records of Medmenham* (London, 1925), 140–141; Charles Murray to William Hawes, *Reports of the Royal Humane Society instituted in the Year 1774, for the Recovery of Persons Apparently Drowned for the Years MDCCLXXXVII, MDCCLXXXVIII, and MDCCLXXXIX*, 398, 399, 400 ("may be extended").

92. On the importance of common Protestantism for British American ties and then on the betrayals of that shared heritage, see Stephen Conway, "From Fellow-Nationals to Foreigners: British Perceptions of the Americans, circa 1739–1783," *William and Mary Quarterly* 59 (2002): 65–100; P. J. Marshall, *The Making and Unmaking of Empires: Britain, India, and America, c. 1750–1783* (Oxford: Oxford University Press, 2005), 205, 333–335. On the waning of transatlantic Protestant ties, see Katherine Carte Engel, "The SPCK and the American Revolution: The Limits of International Protestantism," *Church History* 81:1 (2012): 77–103.

93. *Reports of the Royal Humane Society instituted in the Year 1774, for the Recovery of Persons Apparently Drowned for the Years MDCCLXXXVII, MDCCLXXXVIII, and MDCCLXXXIX*, 246.

94. *Royal Humane Society. Instituted 1774* ([London, 1790]), 3; John Coakley Lettsom to William Hawes, *Royal Humane Society, Instituted 1774: The Annual Report. Published for the Anniversary Festival 1793*, September 26, 1792, 30.

95. William Hawes to the Massachusetts Humane Society Corresponding Secretary, June 23, 1796, *The Annual Report 1797 by W. Hawes M.D.* [London, 1798], 38. The letter was also published in Chandler Robbins, *A Discourse Delivered Before the Humane Society of the Commonwealth of Massachusetts, at their Semiannual Meeting, June 14th 1796* (Boston, 1796), 25. See also Hawes's comments about the ties connecting the United States and Britain prompted by news of the founding of the Humane Society of the State of New York. *Royal Humane Society. Instituted 1774. The Annual Report Published for the Anniversary Festival 1795 by William Hawes M.D.*, 37.

CHAPTER 7

1. James Currie to Benjamin Rush, April 11, 1793 ("fruitless war," "no man can predict"), Rush Manuscripts, vol. 3, Library Company of Philadelphia (LCP).

2. John Coakley Lettsom to Sir Mordaunt Martin, April 4, 1791, in Thomas Joseph Pettigrew, *Memoirs of the Life and Writings of the late John Coakley Lettsom: with a Selection from his Correspondence*, 3 vols. (London, 1817), vol. 2, 45 ("cry of the poor"). John Lathrop to John Coakley Lettsom, November 9, 1790, in Pettigrew, *Memoirs of . . . Lettsom*, vol. 2, 445 ("break the chains," "sufferings," "reconciled").

3. Wilfrid Prest, *Albion Ascendant: English History 1660–1815* (Oxford: Oxford University Press, 1998), 292–294; Thomas Dunn, *Discourse, Delivered in the New Dutch Church, Nassau-street, on Tuesday, the 21st October, 1794, Before the New York Society for the Information and Assistance of Persons emigrating from Foreign Countries* (New York, 1794), 18 ("proscribed"); on the Birmingham riots against supporters of the French Revolution, see Jenny Uglow, *The Lunar Men: Five Friends Whose Curiosity Changed the World* (New York: Farrar, Straus and Giroux, 2002), 437–445.

4. John Coakley Lettsom to Sir Mordaunt Martin, October 15, 1793, in Pettigrew, *Memoirs of . . . Lettsom*, vol. 2, 74 ("present useless crusades," "in favour," "unwise").

5. Paul A. Fideler, *Social Welfare in Pre-Industrial England: The Old Poor Law Tradition* (Basingstoke, Hampshire: Palgrave Macmillan, 2006), 178. Prest, *Albion Ascendant*, 294–299.

6. John Lathrop to John Coakley Lettsom, January 21, 1794, in Pettigrew, *Memoirs of . . . Lettsom*, vol. 2 448 ("break the yoke").

7. Rachel Hope Cleves, "A Scene of Confusion and Blood: The American Reaction against the French Revolution," in *The Reign of Terror in America: Visions of Violence from Anti-Jacobins to Antislavery* (Cambridge: Cambridge University Press, 2009), 58–103; John Lathrop to John Coakley Lettsom, January 21, 1794, in Pettigrew,

Memoirs of . . . Lettsom, vol. 2, 449 ("warmth," "knew some of the men"), 448 ("wild and extravagant").

8. Philipp Ziesche, *Cosmopolitan Patriots: Americans in Paris in the Age of Revolution* (Charlottesville: University of Virginia Press, 2010), esp. chap.4.

9. Gordon S. Wood, "The Crisis of 1798–1799" in *Empire of Liberty: A History of the Early Republic* (New York: Oxford University Press, 2009), 239–275.

10. Ashli White, "The Contagion of Rebellion," in *Encountering Revolution: Haiti and the Making of the Early American Republic* (Baltimore: Johns Hopkins University Press, 2010), 124–175.

11. On immigration in the 1790s in general, see Marilyn C. Baseler, "Immigrants and Politics in the 1790s," in *"Asylum for Mankind": America, 1607–1800*, 243–309 (Ithaca, NY: Cornell University Press, 1998); on Irish immigration in the 1790s, see David A. Wilson, *United Irishmen, United States: Immigrant Radicals in the Early Republic* (Ithaca, NY: Cornell University Press, 1998); on St. Dominguens, see White, *Encountering Revolution*, 5.

12. Edmund Burke, "Speech at Bristol Previous to the Election 6 September 1780," in W. M. Elofson, ed., with John A. Woods, *The Writings and Speeches of Edmund Burke*, vol. 3 (Oxford: Clarendon Press, 1996), 637–638 ("of all men"). Evan Radcliffe, "Revolutionary Writing, Moral Philosophy, and Universal Benevolence in the Eighteenth Century," *Journal of the History of Ideas* 54 (1993): 221–240; Evan Radcliffe, "Burke, Radical Cosmopolitanism, and the Debates on Patriotism in the 1790s," *Studies in Eighteenth-Century Culture* 28 (1999): 311–339. On the fate of universal benevolence and cosmopolitanism in the 1790s, see Thomas J. Schlereth, *The Cosmopolitan Ideal in Enlightenment Thought* (Notre Dame, IN: Notre Dame University Press, 1977), 132–134; W. Caleb McDaniel, "Philadelphia Abolitionists and Antislavery Cosmopolitanism," in Richard Newman and James Mueller, eds., *Antislavery and Abolition in Philadelphia: Emancipation and the Long Struggle for Racial Justice in the City of Brotherly Love*, 149–173 (Baton Rouge: Louisiana State University Press, 2011), 159–161. On the fortunes of popular democratic cosmopolitanism, see Seth Cotlar, *Tom Paine's America: The Rise and Fall of Transatlantic Radicalism in the Early Republic* (Charlottesville: University of Virginia Press, 2011).

13. John Haygarth, *A Sketch of a Plan to Exterminate the Casual Small-Pox from Great Britain; and to Introduce General Inoculation* (London, 1793), 25 ("not solely," "objects of disgust," "most guilty,"), 24 ("acts of beneficence"), 25 ("neighbours and fellow-citizens"). For the waning of cosmopolitanism in the abolitionist movement, see J. R. Oldfield, *Transatlantic Abolitionism in the Age of Revolution: An International History of Anti-slavery, c. 1787–1820* (Cambridge: Cambridge University Press, 2013), chap. 4.

14. John Sylvester John Gardiner, *A Sermon Delivered Before the Humane Society, of the Commonwealth of Massachusetts, at their Semiannual Meeting, June 14, 1803*

(Boston, 1803), 11 ("specious veil"), 11–12 ("conceal[ed] . . . indifference"), 11 ("if we did not love those best").

15. This shift coincided with greater British acceptance and waning critiques of its imperial role in India. See P. J. Marshall, "The Moral Swing to the East: British Humanitarianism, India and the West Indies" in *"A Free though Conquering People": Eighteenth-Century Britain and Its Empire* (Aldershot: Ashgate, 2003), 69–95.

16. Major Carroll to William Hawes, August 27, 1795, *Royal Humane Society, Instituted 1774: The Annual Report. 1796 By William Hawes M.D.* [London, 1796], 44.

17. John Lathrop to William Hawes, July 24, 1798, in *Royal Humane Society, 1774, Annual Report 1799 by W. Hawes M.D.* (London, [1799]), 28 ("fierce and cruel," "threaten desolation"); Patrick Colquhoun to Thomas Eddy, September 12, 1808, in Samuel L. Knapp, *The Life of Thomas Eddy* (1834; rpt. New York: Arno Press, 1976), 226 ("permanent union"); John Coakely Lettsom to Jedidiah Morse, February 22, 1804 ("advantageous"), Gratz Collection, Case 12, Box 21 (European Physicians and Scientists), Historical Society of Pennsylvania, Philadelphia.

18. Benjamin Rush to the president of the Massachusetts Humane Society, March 9, 1793, in John Clarke, *A Discourse, Delivered Before the Humane Society of the Commonwealth of Massachusetts; at the Semi-annual Meeting, Eleventh of June 1793* (Boston, 1793), 32 ("fellow citizen").

19. Morgan Rhees, *The Good Samaritan. An Oration Delivered on Sunday Evening, May 22nd, 1796, In Behalf of the Philadelphia Society for the Information and Assistance of persons Emigrating from Foreign Countries* (New York, 1796), 13 ("great number," "pittance".)

20. Dunn, *Discourse, Delivered in the New Dutch Church*, 13.

21. Thomas Eddy to Patrick Colquhoun, July 15, 1803, in Knapp, *The Life of Thomas Eddy*, 201 ("Many of the evils"); DeWitt Clinton, *An Address to the Benefactors and Friends of the Free School Society, Delivered at the Opening of that Institution, in their New and Spacious Building* (New York, 1810), 7, 10 ("poor and distressed"), 12; DeWitt Clinton, *An Oration on Benevolence, Delivered Before the Society of Black Friars, in the City of New-York, at Their Anniversary Festival, on the 10th November 1794* (New York, 1795), 18; Clinton, *An Address to the Benefactors and Friends of the Free School Society*, 5 ("no privilged orders," "equality of rights"), 16 ("fertile soil").

22. See *Reports of the Royal Humane Society instituted in the Year 1774, for the Recovery of Persons Apparently Drowned for the Years MDCCLXXXVII, MDCCLXXXVIII, and MDCCLXXXIX* [London, 1790], 456; *Royal Humane Society, 1774, Annual Report 1801 by W. Hawes M.D.* (London, 1801), 8; *Annual Report of the Humane Society 1809* (London, 1809), 13.

23. In 1799, the corresponding secretary was new to the job. Perhaps that situation explains the omission of the Royal Humane Society letter that year. In 1802, the Royal Humane Society letter was not reprinted in the Massachusetts Humane Society report, but the report referred to the letter and other materials sent by the Royal Humane Society; Clarke, *A Discourse, Delivered Before the Humane Society of the Commonwealth of Massachusetts, ... Eleventh of June, 1793*, 31; Brooks, *A Discourse Delivered Before the Humane Society of the Commonwealth of Massachusetts, June 9th, 1795*, 15; Chandler Robbins, *A Discourse Delivered Before the Humane Society of the Commonwealth of Massachusetts, at their Semiannual Meeting, June 14th 1796* (Boston, 1796), 25; John Fleet, *A Discourse Relative to Animation, Delivered Before the Humane Society of the Commonwealth of Massachusetts, at their Semiannual Meeting June 13th, 1797* (Boston, 1797), 17; William Walter, *A Discourse Delivered Before the Humane Society of the Commonwealth of Massachusetts, at the Semiannual Meeting Twelfth of June, 1798* (Boston, 1798), 33; Isaac Hurd, *A Discourse Delivered in the Church in Brattle Street, in Boston, Tuesday, June 11th, 1799, Before the Humane Society of the Commonwealth of Massachusetts* (Boston, 1799); Thomas Thacher, *A Discourse Delivered at Boston, Before the Humane Society of the Commonwealth of Massachusetts, June 10th, 1800* (Boston, 1800), 19–20; Jedidiah Morse, *A Sermon Preached Before the Humane Society of the Commonwealth of Massachusetts, at their Semi-annual Meeting, June 9th, 1801* (Boston, 1801), 31–32; Eliphalet Porter, *A Discourse Delivered Before the Humane Society of the Commonwealth of Massachusetts, at their Semiannual Meeting, June 8, 1802* (Boston, 1802), 23; Gardiner, *A Sermon Delivered Before the Humane Society, of the Commonwealth of Massachusetts, at their Semiannual Meeting, June 14, 1803*, 21; John Clark Howard, *A Discourse Delivered Before the Humane Society of the Commonwealth of Massachusetts, at their Semiannual Meeting, June 12, 1804* (Boston, 1804), 30–32; Thomas Gray, *The Value of Life and Charitable Institutions* (Boston, 1805), 25–26.

24. Compare, for instance, the letters of 1792 and 1805, *Royal Humane Society, Instituted 1774: The Annual Report. Published for the Anniversary Festival 1793 by W. Hawes, M.D. Register* (London, 1793), 29; *Royal Humane Society. Annual Report, 1806 by W. Hawes M.D.* (London, 1806), 60.

25. *Appendix* ([Boston?], [1810]), 23–32. N.B. The Massachusetts Humane Society did not print a full report in 1810, but only printed the materials that usually went in the appendix.

26. Gardiner, *A Sermon Delivered Before the Humane Society, of the Commonwealth of Massachusetts*, 12 ("begin at home"); Isaac Huntingford, *A Sermon Preached at the Anniversary of the Royal Humane Society, in St. James's Church, Westminster, on Sunday, April 24, 1803* (London, 1803), 25 ("every human Being").

27. *An Account of the First Festival of the Royal Jennerian Society for the Extermination of the Small-pox, on Thursday, May 17, 1803. Extracted from the Gentleman's Magazine* [London], 1 ("elegant dinner"), 2 ("plaudits," "ready to burst").

28. *An Account of the First Festival of the Royal Jennerian Society for the Extermination of the Small-pox, on Thursday, May 17, 1803. Extracted from the Gentleman's Magazine*, 2 ("overcome and opprest, "confessed he had not," "every friend of humanity," "describe ... the ravages," "that its terrors," "every medical gentleman," "every civilized part," "enlightened country").

29. *An Account of the First Festival of the Royal Jennerian Society for the Extermination of the Small-pox, on Thursday, May 17, 1803. Extracted from the Gentleman's Magazine*, 5 ("rescuing from the grave," "could possibly result").

30. Richard B. Fisher, *Edward Jenner 1749–1823* (London: Deutsch, 1991).

31. Edward Jenner to Jean de Carro, November 27, 1799, in Genevieve Miller, ed. *Letters of Edward Jenner and Other Documents Concerning the Early History of Vaccination* (Baltimore: Johns Hopkins University Press, 1983), 9–10; Levi Bartlett to Benjamin Waterhouse, November 5, 1800 ("inoculating freely"), Bartlett Family Papers, Series A 1,11 NH Medical Society 1800–45 and undated, New Hampshire Historical Society (NHHS), Concord, New Hampshire.

32. Agreement between B. Billings, Wm. Parsons, Thomas S. Ranney, L. Bartlett, Josiah Bartlett, and Benjamin Waterhouse, September 18, 1800, Bartlett Family Papers, Folder D 1, 11, NHHS. On Benjamin Waterhouse's attempt to maintain a monopoly on vaccine distribution in the United States, see John B. Blake, *Benjamin Waterhouse and the Introduction of Vaccination: A Reappraisal* (Philadelphia: University of Pennsylvania Press, 1957), 14–24.

33. On individuals (either medical men or laypeople) vaccinating the poor for free, see, for instance, John Baron, *The Life of Dr. Jenner, M.D.*, vol. 1 (London, 1838), 433, 592–593; Benjamin Waterhouse, *A Prospect for Exterminating the Smallpox* (Cambridge, 1802), 66–71; on women vaccinators, see Fisher, *Edward Jenner*, 89; Lady Brodhead to Edward Jenner, n.d., Jenner Papers, 5232/25, Wellcome Library; Miss Story's Vaccinations, 5244/74, Charles Murray, Royal Jennerian Society [Correspondence], Wellcome Library.

34. John Z. Bowers, "The Odyssey of Smallpox Vaccination," *Bulletin of the History of Medicine* 55 (1981): 17–33, see esp. 26–33.

35. Fisher, *Edward Jenner*, 87–91, 95–97

36. Fisher, *Edward Jenner*, 101.

37. James Smith to Edward Jenner, May 14, 1807 ("first successful"), Jenner Papers, 5232/12, the Wellcome Library of the History and Understanding of Medicine, London; *Longworth's New York City Directory for 1802* (New York, 1802), 117.

38. Fisher, *Edward Jenner*, 96 ("had been set on foot," "bear the odium"), 135, 136.

39. Minutes of the Board of Directors of the Royal Jennerian Society for the Extermination of Smallpox (RJS), December 3, 1802 ("promoting universal vaccination") (MS 4302), Wellcome Library, London.

40. On the men involved in the Royal Jennerian Society, see Fisher, *Edward Jenner*, 135–138. On their roles in the Royal Humane Society, see the reports of the Royal Humane Society. On Jenner's role as Severn Humane Society medical assistant, see *Reports of the Royal Humane Society instituted in the Year 1774, for the Recovery of Persons Apparently Drowned for the Years MDCCLXXXV and MDCCLXXXVI* (London, 1787), 160. The Royal Humane Society report identifies only "Mr. Jenner, Berkeley." Fisher says that Jenner was the first medical man in his family so presumably it is the same Jenner. Fisher, *Edward Jenner*, 20.

41. On the controversary over vaccination, see Fisher, *Edward Jenner*, 80–104, 112, 157–165, 194–195.

42. *Royal Humane Society, 1774, Annual Report 1803 by W. Hawes M.D.* (London, 1803), 47 ("the support of").

43. On the Royal Jennerian Society, especially Jenner's interactions with it, see Fisher, *Edward Jenner*, 132–204. The number of RJS stations varied over time in large part because of lack of patients, though "great irregularities . . . in the attendance of the Inoculators" cannot have helped. On the stations, see, for instance, Fisher, *Edward Jenner*, 146, 147; RJS General Court Minutes (MS 4303), March 7, 1804; March 26, 1806; quotation about irregularities, RJS Medical Council Minutes (MS 4304), October 3, 1805. On children as the main patient population for vaccination, see John Epps, *The Life of John Walker* (London, 1831), 92. On distribution and franking privileges, see RJS Board of Directors Minutes (MS 4302), March 31, 1803; April 7, 1803; Fisher, *Edward Jenner*, 145; RJS Medical Council Minutes (MS 4304), January 1, 1806; May 1, 1806; Minutes of the RJS Board of Directors 1805–1809 (MS 4305), April 3, 1806. For the RJS 1804 annual report, see RJS General Court Minutes (MS 4303), March 7, 1804 ("6134 charges of matter"). On the RJS request that recipients of cowpox matter vaccinate for no charge and send in reports, see RJS Medical Council Minutes (MS 4304), April 3, 1806. On the collapse of the charity, see Fisher, *Edward Jenner*. 172–204, esp. 172–178.

44. Minutes of the RJS General Court, March 6, 1805 ("gratuitous diffusion") (MS 4303), Wellcome Library.

45. "Extract of a Letter Written by Dr James S Stringham of New York to Dr Duncan, concerning Vaccine Inoculation," *Annals of Medicine for the Year 1801* (Edinburgh, 1802), 473 ("It must . . . be").

46. C. E. Wengel to Edward Jenner, July 15, 1807, Jenner Papers (MS 5232/13), Wellcome Library; Helenus Scott to Edward Jenner, n.d., in John Baron, *The Life of Edward Jenner, M.D.*, vol. 1 (London, 1838), 412; *Third Festival of the Royal Jennerian Society* (from the *Gentleman's Magazine*, June 1805), 524; James Smith

to Edward Jenner, May 14, 1807 ("the following record"), Jenner Papers (MS 5232/12), Wellcome Library.

47. James Smith to Edward Jenner, May 14, 1807, Jenner Papers (MS 5232/12), Wellcome Library; Lord Elgin to Jean De Carro, December 23, 1800, in Baron, *The Life of Edward Jenner*, 415; John Rule to John Walker, August 14, 1815 (4809), Royal College of Physicians, London; Benjamin Waterhouse to John Coakley Lettsom, April 14, 1801, Benjamin Waterhouse Papers (MS 7801), Wellcome Library. On various methods of non-human transmission, see also Bowers, "The Odyssey of Smallpox Vaccination," 21–22.

48. On James Smith, see Whitfield J. Bell, "Dr. James Smith and the Public Encouragement for Vaccination for Smallpox," *Annals of Medical History*, 3rd series 2 (1940): 500–517. On Crawford's role in smallpox vaccination, see Bell, "Dr. James Smith and the Public Encouragement for Vaccination for Smallpox," 502, and John Ring, *A Treatise on the Cow-pox; Containing a History of Vaccine Inoculation, and an Account of the Various Publications, which Have Appeared on that Subject, in Great Britain and other Parts of the World. Part I.* (London, 1801), 459.

49. James Smith to Edward Jenner, May 14, 1807 ("vaccine matter," "almost insuperable," "method of preseving," "active much longer"), Jenner Papers, 5232/12, Wellcome Library.

50. Bell, "Dr. James Smith and the Public Encouragement for Vaccination for Smallpox," 504; James Smith to Edward Jenner, May 14, 1807 ("many years of happiness"), Jenner Papers, 5232/12, Wellcome Library.

51. Bell, "Dr. James Smith and the Public Encouragement for Vaccination for Smallpox," 504–506.

52. *Address of the Royal Jennerian Society* ([London], 1803), 24 ("So completely"); Jefferson quotation, Hopkins, *The Greatest Killer*, 310.

53. RJS Board of Directors Minutes, May 9, 1805 (MS 4302), Wellcome Library, London; RJS General Court Minutes, September 4, 1805 (MS 4303), Wellcome Library. In 1807, the RJS Medical Council nominated three other foreign honorary members. RJS Medical Council Minutes, September 4, 1805 (MS 4304), Wellcome Library.

54. Besides the charities in New York and Baltimore, American charities providing vaccination included the Philadelphia and Charleston dispensaries. See *A Comparative View of the Natural Small-pox, Inoculated Small-pox, and Vaccination in their Effects on Individuals and Society* (Philadelphia, 1803) and *The Physicians of the Charleston Dispensary, to the Patients of that Institution* (Charleston, 1802.)

EPILOGUE

1. Benjamin Waterhouse to Dr. Tilton, December 30, 1813, Gratz Collection, American Literary Miscellaneous (Case 6, Box 24), Historical Society of Pennsylvania, Philadelphia.

2. On the early-modern concept of "charity," see Christine Leigh Heyrman, "A Model of Christian Charity: The Rich and the Poor in New England 1630–1730" (Ph.D. diss., Yale University, 1977); Conrad Edick Wright, *The Transformation of Charity in Postrevolutionary New England* (Boston: Northeastern University Press, 1992), 17–22; Paul S. Seaver, *Wallington's World: A Puritan Artisan in Seventeenth-Century London:* (Stanford, CA: Stanford University Press, 1985), 103. On the original meaning of the word "philanthropy," see Wright, *The Transformation of Charity*, 120–121.

3. *Account of the Society of Friends of Foreigners in Distress; With the Nature and View of the Institution: Also the Plan and the Regulations* (London, 1814), 4, 5, 66. The [London] *Times*, May 7, 1931, 9.

4. Katherine M. J. McKenna, *A Life of Propriety: Anne Murray Powell and Her Family, 1755–1849* (Montreal: McGills-Queen's University Press, 1993), 234.

5. For instance, on Rush's student, David Hosack, and his protégé, John Wakefield Francis, see Christine Chapman Robbins, *David Hosack: Citizen of New York* (Philadelphia: American Philosophical Society, 1964); on Hosack's and Francis's philanthropic activities, see John Wakefield Francis Papers, Manuscripts and Archives Division, New York Public Library.

6. John T. Cumbler, *From Abolition to Rights for All: The Making of a Reform Community in the Nineteenth Century* (Philadelphia: University of Pennsylvania Press, 2008); Anne M. Boylan, *The Origins of Women's Activism: New York and Boston, 1797–1840* (Chapel Hill: University of North Carolina Press, 2002), 67–68.

7. Ian Tyrrell points to the transformative effects of reformers' overseas activities as fostering a "historical experience" of humanitarianism in a later generation. I see both that transformation and a collective historical experience of expansive moral responsibility occurring earlier. Ian Tyrrell, *Reforming the World: The Creation of America's Moral Empire* (Princeton, NJ: Princeton University Press, 2010), 98.

8. Daniel T. Rodgers, *Atlantic Crossings: Social Politics in a Progressive Age* (Cambridge, MA: Belknap Press of Harvard University Press, 1998).

9. Rodgers, *Atlantic Crossings: Social Politics in a Progressive Age*, 60–75, esp. 62 on Americans in German universities. Thomas Adam, *Buying Respectability: Philanthropy and Urban Society in Transnational Perspective, 1840s to 1930s* (Bloomington: Indiana University Press, 2009), 15–17, 59–60.

10. Thomas Eddy to Patrick Colquhoun, May 19, 1815, in Samuel L. Knapp, *The Life of Thomas Eddy* (1834; rpt. New York: Arno Press, 1976), 230–231.

11. W. Caleb McDaniel, "Philadelphia Abolitionists and Antislavery Cosmopolitanism," in Richard Newman and James Mueller, eds., *Antislavery and Abolition in Philadelphia: Emancipation and the Long Struggle for Racial Justice in the City of Brotherly Love*, 149–173 (Baton Rouge: Louisiana State University Press, 2011), 165–166; on the Convention and the conflict it caused among abolitionists, see

W. Caleb McDaniel, "Conflict and Continuity in Transatlantic Abolitionism," in *The Problem of Democracy in the Age of Slavery: Garrisonian Abolitionists and Transatlantic Reform* (Baton Rouge: Louisiana State University Press, 2013), 66–86.

12. Betty Fladeland, *Men and Brothers: Anglo-American Antislavery Cooperation* (Urbana: University of Illinois Press, 1972), 300–301; McDaniel, *The Problem of Democracy in the Age of Slavery*; Bonnie S. Anderson, *Joyous Greetings: The First International Women's Movement, 1830–1860* (Oxford: Oxford University Press, 2000); Brian Harrison, *Drink and the Victorians: The Temperance Question in England, 1815–1872* (Pittsburgh: University of Pittsburgh Press, 1971), 196.

13. George Wilson Pierson, *Tocqueville in America* (Baltimore: Johns Hopkins University Press, 1938); Tyrrell, *Reforming the World*; Adam, *Buying Respectability*. The phrase "philanthropic tourism" is from J. H. Dekker, "Transforming the Nation and the Child: Philanthropy in the Netherlands, Belgium, France and England, c. 1780–c.1850," in Hugh Cunningham and Joanna Innes, eds., *Charity, Philanthropy and Reform from the 1690s to 1850*, 130–147 (New York: St. Martin's Press, 1998), 137–139.

14. For scholars who see Americans' donations for sufferers abroad as episodic before the late nineteenth century, see Merle Curti, *American Philanthropy Abroad* (New Brunswick, NJ: Rutgers University Press, 1963), 5; Tyrrell, *Reforming the World*, 99. See also Michael Barnett, *Empire of Humanity: A History of Humanitarianism* (Ithaca, NY: Cornell University Press, 2011), 82. Bruno Cabanes sees the central role of transnational networks in humanitarianism as a development of World War I. Bruno Cabanes, *The Great War and the Making of Modern Humanitarianism* (Cambridge: Cambridge University Press, 2014), 4.

15. Tyrrell, *Reforming the World*, 19–25. On Europeans preference for "international" bodies versus Americans' "world" approach, see 25. In Tyrrell's view, Americans' "world" approach was more revolutionary because "it promised to intervene in individual lives irrespective of nation."

16. Tyrrell, *Reforming the World*, 21.

17. Curti, *American Philanthropy Abroad*, 10–137; Tyrrell, "Blood, Souls, and Power" in *Reforming the World*, 98–119.

18. Olivier Zunz, "'For the Improvement of Mankind,'" in *Philanthropy in America: A History* (Princeton, NJ: Princeton University Press, 2012), 8–43, 22 ("well-being of mankind").

19. Barnett, *Empire of Humanity*, 76–82.

20. Kathleen D. McCarthy, *American Creed: Philanthropy and the Rise of Civil Society 1700–1865* (Chicago: University of Chicago Press, 2003), 193–197.

21. Barnett, *Empire of Humanity*, 82–87; on the emergence of mass philanthropy, see Zunz, "The Coming of Mass Philanthropy," in *Philanthropy in America*, 44–75; on ordinary Americans' donations to European sufferers during World War I, see Julia F. Irwin, *Making the World Safe: The American Red Cross and a Nation's*

Humanitarian Awakening (Oxford: Oxford University Press, 2013). Other scholars who consider World War I a turning point for humanitarianism include Cabanes, *The Great War and the Making of Modern Humanitarianism*, and Keith David Watenpaugh, *Bread from Stones: The Middle East and the Making of Modern Humanitarianism* (Oakland: University of California Press, 2015).

22. Barnett, *Empire of Humanity*, 101–103; see also 22 for Barnett's view that humanitarian feeling expands in response to crises of faith. For the view that the work of humanitarian organizations reflects not an international community but "an international order, dominated by the United States," see David Rieff, *Bed for the Night: Humanitarianism in Crisis* (New York: Simon and Schuster, 2002), 8.

23. Barnett, *Empire of Humanity*, 111–112; on the post–World War II construction of an international humanitarian order, see also Gerard Daniel Cohen, *In War's Wake: Europe's Displaced Persons in the Postwar Order* (New York: Oxford University Press, 2012); on the Peace Corps, see Elizabeth Cobbs Hoffman, *All You Need Is Love: The Peace Corps and the Spirit of the 1960s* (Cambridge, MA: Harvard University Press, 1998). Similarly, in the United States, the federal government's role in disaster relief developed in the latter half of the twentieth century. See Ted Steinberg, *Acts of God: The Unnatural History of Natural Disaster in America* (New York: Oxford University Press, 2000). On natural disaster relief as part of foreign assistance, see Julia F. Irwin, "Raging Rivers and Propaganda Weevils: Transnational Disaster Relief, Cold War Politics, and the 1954 Danube and Elbe Floods," *Diplomatic History* (Advance Access, published online October 8, 2015).

24. Barnett, "It's a Humanitarian's World," in *Empire of Humanity*, 161–170. Humanitarian intervention was not new in the late twentieth century. See Gary J. Bass, *Freedom's Battle: The Origins of Humanitarian Intervention* (New York: Alfred A. Knopf, 2008).

25. On the long-standing principles of humanitarianism, see Barnett, *Empire of Humanity*, 2. For one Cold War–era humanitarian organization balancing its principles of impartiality with partnership with the United States, see Irwin, "Raging Rivers and Propaganda Weevils."

26. On the recent crisis in humanitarianism, see Barnett, *Empire of Humanity*, 195–198; Rieff, *Bed for the Night*. Bruno Cabanes argues that the rights-based approach to humanitarianism burgeoned after World War I. Cabanes, *The Great War and the Making of Modern Humanitarianism*, 6–7.

27. Barnett, *Empire of Humanity*, 197.

Bibliography

PRIMARY SOURCES
Manuscript Collections

Bodleian Library, Oxford
Letters to John Howard, MS English Misc. c. 332
British Library, London
Hardwicke Papers
Papers Relative to a Monument to John Howard
Correspondence of Arthur Young
Francis A. Countway Library of Medicine, Boston
Benjamin Waterhouse Papers
Records of the Boston Dispensary
Historical Society of Pennsylvania, Philadelphia
Clifford Correspondence
Howard Edwards Collection
Etting Collection
Gratz Collection
Old Swedes Church Gloria Dei Burial Records
Library of Congress, Washington, DC
Manuscripts of Dr. Bray's Associates, Facsimiles from English Archives, Society
for the Propagation of the Gospel in Foreign Parts
Library Company of Philadelphia
Benjamin Rush Manuscripts
Maryland Historical Society, Baltimore
"A Letter Addressed to Lieutenant General Mathew on the means of preventing
the method of treating and origins of the Diseases most prevalent and which
prove most destr[uctive] to the Natives of Cold Climates visiting or residing in
Warm Countries by John Crawford, M.D," Box 130, Manuscript Collections of
the Medical and Chirurgical Faculty of Maryland
Correspondence of John Crawford

Massachusetts Historical Society, Boston
Jeremy Belknap Papers
Massachusetts Humane Society Papers
James Murray Papers
James Murray Robbins Papers

New York Academy of Medicine
Bard Collection
D[avid] Hosack: Copies of Letters and Documents

New-York Historical Society
Murray Family Papers

New York-Presbyterian Hospital-New York Weill Cornell Medical Center Archives
New York Hospital Board of Governors Minutes, Vols. 1–3

New York Public Library
John Griscom Correspondence
John Wakefield Francis Papers

Pennsylvania Hospital Archives, Philadelphia
Philadelphia Dispensary Minute Books, 1786–1806 and 1807–1839
Philadelphia Humane Society Annual Meeting Minutes 1793–1839
Philadelphia Humane Society Managers' Minutes, Vols. 1 and 2

Rhode Island Historical Society, Providence,
Gilbert Deblois Letterbooks

Royal College of Physicians, London
John Rule to John Walker, August 14, 1815

Royal Humane Society Archives, London
First Minute Book, 1774–1784

Wellcome Library for the History and Understanding of Medicine, London
Letter from John Crawford to unknown recipient, January 28, 1789, Naval Hospital Barbados 1789
"Memorial of Doctor [John] Crawford (the Chief Surgeon of the Colony of Demerary) to the Lord of the Treasury" (n.d.)
Jenner Papers
John Coakley Lettsom Papers
Royal Jennerian Society Correspondence
Minutes of the Board of Directors Minutes of the Royal Jennerian Society for the Extermination of Smallpox, [1802–1805]
Minutes of the Board of Directors of the Royal Jennerian Society for the Extermination of Smallpox, 1805–1809
Minutes of the General Court of the Royal Jennerian Society for the Extermination of Smallpox, [1803–1806]

Minutes of the General Court of the Royal Jennerian Society for the Extermination of Smallpox, 180–1808

Minutes of the Medical Council of the Royal Jennerian Society for the Extermination of Smallpox, [1803–1807]

Benjamin Waterhouse Papers

Published Collections of Primary Sources

Baron, John. *The Life of Dr. Jenner, M.D.* 2 vols. London, 1838.

Basker, James G., ed. *Amazing Grace: An Anthology of Poems about Slavery.* New Haven, CT: Yale University Press, 2002.

Boswell, James. *Life of Johnson.* Ed. R. W. Chapman. Intro. Pat Rogers. Oxford World's Classics edition. Oxford: Oxford University Press, 1998.

Bridenbaugh, Carl, ed. *Gentleman's Progress: The Itinerarium of Dr. Alexander Hamilton 1744.* Chapel Hill: Published for the Institute of Early American History and Culture, Williamsburg, Virginia, by the University of North Carolina Press, 1948.

Butterfield, Lyman H., ed. *Letters of Benjamin Rush.* 2 vols. Princeton, NJ: Published for the American Philosophical Society by Princeton University Press, 1951.

Corner, Betsy C. and Christopher C. Booth, eds. *Chain of Friendship: Selected Letters of Dr. John Fothergill of London, 1735–1780.* Cambridge, MA: Belknap Press of Harvard University Press, 1971.

Corner, George W., ed. *The Autobiography of Benjamin Rush: His "Travels Through Life" together with his Commonplace Book for 1789–1813.* Princeton, NJ: Published for the American Philosophical Society by Princeton University Press, 1948.

Currie, William Wallace. *Memoir of the Life, Writings, and Correspondence of James Currie, M.D. F.R.S. of Liverpool, Fellow of the Royal College of Physicians, Edinburgh, London Medical Society, &c. &c.* London, 1831.

Elofson, W. M. with John A. Woods, eds. *The Writings and Speeches of Edmund Burke.* Vol. 1. Oxford: Clarendon Press; New York: Oxford University Press, 1996.

Field, John. *Correspondence of John Howard, Not Before Published.* London, 1855.

The Journal of Dr. John Morgan of Philadelphia from the City of Rome to the City of London 1764 Together with a Fragment of a Journal Written at Rome, 1764 and a Biographical Sketch [by Julia Harding Morgan]. Philadelphia, 1907.

Klepp, Susan E. *"The Swift Progress of Population": A Documentary and Bibliographic Study of Philadelphia's Growth, 1642–1859.* Philadelphia: American Philosophical Society, 1991.

Lambert, Sheila. *House of Commons Sessional Papers.* Vol. 69. Wilmington, DE: Scholarly Resources, 1975.

Lawrence, Christopher and Fiona A. Macdonald, eds. *Sambrook Court: The Letters of J. C. Lettson at the Medical Society of London.* London: Wellcome Trust Centre for the History of Medicine at University College London, 2003.

"Letters of Thomas Coram." *Proceedings of the Massachusetts Historical Society* 56 (1923): 15–56.

Manuscripts of the Earl of Egmont. Diary of the First Earl of Egmont (Viscount Percival), Vol. 2: 1734–1738. London, 1920.

Paine, Thomas. *Common Sense and Related Writings.* Edited with an Introduction by Thomas P. Slaughter. Boston: Bedford/St. Martin's, 2001.

Parkinson, Charlotte, ed. *The Society for the Relief of Women and Children: 1797–1997: An Exploration of the Minutes and Records from 1797–1997 of the Society for the Relief of Women and Children.* [New York], 2000.

Percival, Edward, ed. *Memoir of the Life and Writings of Thomas Percival M.D.* London, 1807.

Pettigrew, Thomas Joseph. *Memoirs of the Life and Writings of the Late John Coakley Lettsom, M.D.; LL.D; F.R.S; F.A.S.; F.L.S.; &c. &c. &c. With a Selection from his Correspondence.* 3 vols. London, 1817.

Sokoll, Thomas, ed. *Essex Pauper Letters 1731–1837.* Oxford: Published for the British Academy by Oxford University Press, 2001.

Sprigge, Timothy. *The Correspondence of Jeremy Bentham.* Vol. 3. London: Athlone, 1968.

Woods, John A., ed. "The Correspondence of Benjamin Rush and Granville Sharp, 1773–1809." *Journal of American Studies* 1 (1967): 1–38.

Books and Pamphlets

Abstract of the Evidence Delivered Before a Select Committee of the House of Commons, in the Years 1790 and 1791; on the Part of the Petitioners for the Abolition of the Slave Trade. London, 1791.

An Abstract of the Proceedings of the Scots Society in Norwich, November 30, 1780. Norwich, n.d.

Account of the Dublin General Dispensary and Humane Society. Established at the Dispensary Court, No. 28, Temple-Bar, for the Purpose of Administering Medical and Surgical Assistance to the Sick Poor of the City, and of Recovering Persons Apparently Dead from Drowning, Suffocating, or Other Accidents. Dublin, 1793.

An Account of the Expenditure, and General Management of the Affairs, of the Society in Scotland for Propagating Christian Knowledge: Contained in a Report Drawn up by a Committee of their Number, Appointed for that Purpose. Edinburgh, 1796.

An Account of the First Anniversary Festival of the Royal Jennerian Society for the Extermination of the Small-pox, on Thursday, May 17, 1803, Extracted from the Gentleman's Magazine. London, n.d.

An Account of the General Dispensary for the Relief of the Poor. London, 1772.

Account of the New York Hospital. New York, 1811.

An Account of the Philadelphia Dispensary, Instituted for the Medical Relief of the Poor. Philadelphia, 1802.

An Account of the Proceedings of the Society of Universal Good-will, from the Beginning of 1784. To the End of the Year 1787. Norwich, 1787.

An Account of the Rise, Constitution and Management, of the Society in Scotland, for Propagating Christian Knowledge. London, 1714.

An Account of the Scots Society, in Norwich, from Its Rise in 1775, Until It Received the Additional Name of the Society of Universal Good-will, in 1784. To Which Are Added the Articles, President's Address, &c. &c. 2nd ed. Norwich, n.d.

An Account of the Scots Society in Norwich, in Great Britain. Founded in 1775. Norwich, 1783.

Account of the Society of Friends of Foreigners in Distress; With the Nature and View of the Institution: Also the Plan and Regulations. London, 1814.

An Account of the Society for Promoting Religious Knowledge Among the Poor. London, 1759.

An Account of the Society for Promoting Religious Knowledge Among the Poor. London, 1763.

An Account of the Society for Promoting Religious Knowledge Among the Poor. London, 1769.

The Act of Incorporation, Constitution and By-laws of the Philadelphia Society for the Information of Persons Emigrating from Foreign Countries. Philadelphia, 1797.

Address of the Royal Jennerian Society. [London], 1803.

Address of the Royal Jennerian Society, for the Extermination of Small-Pox, with the Plan, Regulations, and Instructions for Vaccine Inoculation. London, 1803.

An Address to the Citizens of Baltimore and its Vicinity, Containing a Concise Account of the Baltimore General Dispensary, Its By-laws, and Other Matters Worthy of Notice. Baltimore, 1812.

Address to the Public, Respecting the Establishment of a Lunatic Asylum at Edinburgh. Edinburgh, 1807.

Aikin, John. *A View of the Life, Travels, and Philanthropic Labors of the Late John Howard.* Philadelphia, 1794.

Aitken, John. *Medical Improvement: An Address Read to the Medical Society.* Edinburgh, 1777.

Appendix [to the Massachusetts Humane Society annual discourse; the discourse was not printed that year.] [Boston, 1810]

Articles and Regulations Proposed for the Society of Universal Good-will, in London, or Elsewhere, 1789. Norwich, 1789.

Baldwin, Richard. *Baldwin's New Complete Guide to All Persons who Have Any Trade or Concern with the City of London.* [London], [1768].

Barnard, Thomas. *A Discourse, Delivered Before the Humane Society of the Commonwealth of Massachusetts. At the Semiannual Meeting, June 10, 1794.* Boston, 1794.

Bard, John. *A Letter from John Bard . . . to the Author of Thoughts on the Dispensary.* New York, 1791.

Bard, Samuel. *A Discourse Upon the Duties of a Physician, with Some Sentiments, on the Usefulness and Necessity of a Public Hospital.* New York, 1769.

Bartlett, John. *A Discourse on the Subject of Animation. Delivered Before the Humane Society of the Commonwealth of Massachusetts. June 11, 1792.* Boston, 1792.

Bartlett, Josiah. *An Oration Occasioned by the Death of John Warren, M.D. Past Grand Master. Delivered in the Grand Lodge of Massachusetts, at a Quarterly Meeting, In Boston, June 12, 1815.* Boston, 1815.

Bath Humane Society, Instituted in the Year 1805; Supported by Voluntary Contributions. Bath [England], 1806.

Bayley, Richard. *A Letter from Doctor Richard Bayley, to Doctor John Bard . . . [A]n Answer to a Part of his Letter Addressed to the Author of Thoughts on the Dispensary.* New York, 1791.

Bell, Andrew. *An Analysis of the Experiment in Education, Made at Egmore, Near Madras.* 3rd ed. London, 1807.

Berkeley, George. *A Sermon Preached Before the Incorporated Society for the Propagation of the Gospel in Foreign Parts, at their Anniversary Meeting in the Parish-Church of St. Mary-le-Bow, on Friday, February 18, 1731.* London, 1732.

Biddle, Clement. *The Philadelphia Directory.* Philadelphia, 1791.

Bisse, Philip. *A Sermon Preach'd Before the Incorporated Society for the Propagation of the Gospel in Foreign Parts; at their Anniversary Meeting in the Parish of St. Mary-le-Bow, on Friday, the 21st of February, 1717.* London, 1718.

A Brief Account of the New York Hospital. New York, 1804.

Brocklesby, Richard. *Private Vertue and Public Spirit Display'd: in a Succinct Essay on the Character of Capt. Thomas Coram, who Deceased the 29th of March and Was Inter'd in the Chapel of the Foundling Hospital (a Charity Established By His Solicitation) April 3d 1751.* London; Boston, 1751.

Brooks, John. *A Discourse Delivered Before the Humane Society of the Commonwealth of Massachusetts, June 9th, 1795.* Boston, 1795.

Brown, James Baldwin. *Memoirs of the Public and Private Life of John Howard, the Philanthropist, Compiled from his own Diary . . . His Confidential Letters; the Communications of his Surviving Relatives and Friends; and other Authentic Sources of Information.* 2nd ed. London, 1823.

Browne, P. *The History of Norwich, from the Earliest Records to the Present Time.* Norwich, 1814.

Buchan, William. *Domestic Medicine: Or A Treatise on the Prevention and Cure of Diseases by Regimen and Simple Medicines.* London, 1784.

Butler, Joseph. *Butler's Fifteen Sermons Preached at the Rolls Chapel.* Ed. T. A. Roberts. London, 1970.

Clarke, John. *A Discourse, Delivered Before the Humane Society of the Commonwealth of Massachusetts, at their Semiannual Meeting, Eleventh of June 1793*. Boston, 1793.

Clarkson, Thomas. *An Essay on the Impolicy of the Slave Trade. In Two Parts. To Which is Added, an Oration on the Necessity of Establishing at Paris, a Society to Promote the Abolition of the Trade and Slavery of the Negroes. J. P. Brissot de Warville*. Philadelphia, 1788.

Clarkson, Thomas. *The History of the Rise, Progress and Accomplishments of the Abolition of the African Slave-Trade, By the British Parliament*. Philadelphia, 1808.

Clerke, Sir William. *Thoughts upon the Means of Preserving the Health of the Poor, by Prevention and Suppression of Epidemic Fevers. Addressed to the Inhabitants of Manchester, and the Several Populous Trading Towns, Surrounding and Connected with It*. London, 1790.

Clinton, DeWitt. *An Address to the Benefactors and Friends of the New York Free School Society, Delivered at the Opening of that Institution, in their New and Spacious Building*. New York, 1809.

Clinton, DeWitt. *An Oration on Benevolence, Delivered Before the Society of Black Friars, in the City of New-York, at Their Anniversary Festival, on the 10th November 1794*. New York, 1795.

Cogan, Thomas, trans. *Memoirs of the Society Instituted at Amsterdam in Favour of Drowned Persons, for the Years 1767, 1768, 1769, 1770, and 1771. Translated from the original by Thomas Cogan, M.D.* London, 1773.

[Collins, William]. *The Slave Trade; a Poem. Written in the Year 1788. Dedicated to the Gentlemen, who Compose that Truly Noble, Generous, and Philanthropic Society for the Abolition of the Slave Trade*. London, 1793.

Colman, Henry. *A Discourse Delivered in the Chapel Church, Boston, Before the Humane Society of Massachusetts*. Boston, 1812.

Colquhoun, Patrick. *A New and Appropriate Education for the Labouring People*. London, 1806.

A Comparative View of the Natural Small-pox, Inoculated Small-pox, and Vaccination in their Effects on Individuals and Society. Philadelphia, 1803.

The Constitution of the Humane Society of the State of New York. New York, 1795.

The Constitution of the Pennsylvania Society, for Promoting Abolition, and the Relief of Free Negroes, Unlawfully Held in Bondage. Begun in the Year 1774, and Enlarged on the Twenty-third of April, 1787. To Which Are Added in the Acts of the General Assembly of Pennsylvania, for the Gradual Abolition of Slavery. Philadelphia, 1787.

Continuation of the Account of the Pennsylvania Hospital: From the First of May 1754, to the Fifth of May 1761. Philadelphia, 1761.

A Continuation of the Proceedings of the Humane Society of the Commonwealth of Massachusetts, from the second Tuesday in June 1788, to the second Tuesday in June 1789. Boston, 1789.

Coombe, Thomas. *The Influence of Christianity on the Condition of the World: A Sermon, Preached in Trinity Chapel, Conduit Street, on Sunday, December 13, 1789.* London, 1790.

Cooper, Samuel. *A Sermon Preached in Boston, New-England, Before the Society for Encouraging Industry, and Employing the Poor; August 8, 1753.* Boston, 1753.

Cornwallis, Frederick. *A Sermon Preached before the Incorporated Society for the Propagation of the Gospel in Foreign Parts.* London, 1756.

Coxe, John Redman. *A Short View of the Importance and Respectability of Medicine. Read Before the Philadelphia Medical Society, on the 7th of February, 1800.* Philadelphia, 1800.

Cugoano, Ottobah. *Thoughts and Sentiments on the Evil and Wicked Traffic and Slavery of the Human Species, Humbly Submitted to the Inhabitants of Great-Britain.* London, 1787.

Danforth, Thomas. *A Discourse, Before the Humane Society, of the Commonwealth of Massachusetts. Boston, June 14, 1808.* [Boston], 1808.

Darwin, Erasmus. *The Botanic Garden.* 1791; rpt. Merton, Yorkshire.

Dingley, Amasa. *An Oration. On the Improvement of Medicine: Pronounced before a Respectable Auditory of Citizens, in the Federal Hall in the City of New York; . . . on the 16th January, 1794.* New York, 1795.

Duncan's New York City Directory for 1791. [New York, 1791].

Dunn, Thomas. *Discourse, Delivered in the New Dutch Church, Nassau-Street, on Tuesday, the 21st October, 1794, Before the New York Society for the Information and Assistance of Persons Emigrating from Foreign Countries.* New York, [1794].

Emerson, William. *A Discourse Delivered in the First Church, Boston, on the Anniversary of the Massachusetts Humane Society, June 9, 1807.* Boston, 1807.

Entick, John. *A New and Accurate Survey of London, Westminster, Southwark, and Places Adjacent.* 4 vols. London, 1766.

Equiano, Olaudah. *The Life of Olaudah Equiano, or Gustavus Vassa the African Written by Himself.* Edited with an introduction by Paul Edwards. Harlow, 1992.

Extracts from the Reports of the Royal Humane Society, Which Fully Evince the Utility of an Air Machine, Invented by Mr. White. [London?], 1790.

Extracts from the Reports of the Royal Humane Society, Which Fully Evince the Utility of an Air Machine, Invented by Mr. White. [London?], 1794.

Fleet, John. *A Discourse Relative to Animation, Delivered Before the Humane Society of the Commonwealth of Massachusetts, at their Semiannual Meeting June 13th, 1797.* Boston, 1797.

Fothergill, Anthony. *An Essay on the Preservation of Shipwrecked Mariners, in Answer to the Prize Questions Proposed by the Royal Humane Society.* London, 1799.

A Further Account of the Success attending the Attempts Made at Liverpool, for the Recovery of Drowned Persons: Extracted from the Reports of the London Humane Society. [London? 1785?].

Gardiner, John Sylvester John. *A Sermon Delivered Before the Humane Society, of the Commonwealth of Massachusetts, at their Semiannual Meeting, June 14, 1803.* Boston, 1803.

General Instructions for the Agents of the Scots Society at Norwich, and the Branches Thereof. Norwich, 1780.

A General Report of the Workington and Harrington Dispensary for the Year 1796. Workington, 1796.

George, Daniel. *An Almanack for the Year 1780.* Newbury, 1780.

Gibson, John. *The Unlimited Extent and Final Blessedness of God's Spiritual Kingdom: A Sermon, Preached Before the Society for Propagating Christian Knowledge, At their Anniversary Meeting, In the High Church of Edinburgh, on Friday, June 3, 1768.* Edinburgh, 1768.

Gray, Thomas. *The Value of Life and Charitable Institutions. A Discourse Delivered before the Humane Society of the Commonwealth of Massachusetts, at their Semi-Annual Meeting, June 11th, 1805.* Boston, 1805.

Greene, Edward Burnaby. *Ode to the Humane Society.* London, 1784.

Hanway, Jonas. *An Account of the Marine Society, Recommending the Piety and Policy of the Institution.* London, [1759].

Hardie, James. *The Philadelphia Directory and Register for 1794.* Philadelphia, 1794.

Harris, Thaddeus Mason. *A Discourse Delivered before the Humane Society of the Commonwealth of Massachusetts.* Boston, 1806.

Hawes, William. *An Address to the King and Parliament of Great Britain, on the Important Subject of Preserving the Lives of its Inhabitants ... With an Appendix, in which is Inserted a Letter from Dr. Lettsom to the Author.* London, 1782.

Hawes, William. *The Transactions of the Royal Humane Society.* Vol. 1 of 2 vols. [London, 1795].

Haygarth, John. *An Inquiry How to Prevent the Small-Pox. And Proceedings of a Society for Promoting General Inoculation at stated periods, and preventing the Natural Smallpox in Chester.* Chester, England, 1784.

Haygarth, J. *A Private Letter Addressed to the Right Reverend Dr. Porteus, the Late Lord Bishop of London; to Propose a Plan which Might Give a Good Education to All the Poor Children in England, at a Moderate Expense (Printed at His Lordship's Desire).* New edition. Bath and London, 1812.

Haygarth, J. *A Sketch of a Plan to Exterminate the Casual Small-Pox from Great Britain; and to Introduce General Inoculation.* London, 1793.

History of the Humane Society of Massachusetts. Boston, 1845.

History of the Humane Society of the Commonwealth of Massachusetts: with a Selected List of Premiums awarded by the Trustees, from its Commencement to the Present Time, and a List of the Members and Officers. Prepared by Direction of the Trustees. Boston, 1876; rpt. Michigan Historical Reprint Series.

Hogan, Edmund. *The Prospect of Philadelphia and Check on the Next Directory.* Philadelphia, 1795.

Hopkins, Samuel. *Historical Memoirs, Relating to the Housatunnuk Indians: Or, An Account of the Methods used, and Pains taken, for the Propagation of the Gospel among that Heathenish Tribe, and the Success Thereof, under the Ministry of the late Reverend Mr. John Sergeant.* Boston, 1753.

Hosack, David. *An Enquiry into the Causes of Suspended Animation from Drowning; with the Means of Restoring Life.* New York, 1792.

Howard, John. *The State of the Prisons in England and Wales, with Some Preliminary Observations, and an Account of Some Foreign Prisons.* London, 1777.

Howard, John. *An Account of the Present State of Prisons . . . in the Norfolk Circuit.* London, [1789].

Howard, John. *An Account of the Present State of Prisons . . . in the Oxford Circuit.* London, [1789].

Howard, John. *An Account of the Principal Lazarettos of Europe: With Some Papers Relative to Plague.* Warrington, 1789.

[Howard, John.] *Appendix; Containing Observations Concerning Foreign Prisons and Hospitals: Collected by Mr. Howard, in his Concluding Tour.* Ed. John Aikin. [London, 1791].

Howard, John Clark. *A Discourse Delivered Before the Humane Society of the Commonwealth of Massachusetts, at their Semiannual Meeting, June 12, 1804.* Boston, 1804.

Huntingford, George Isaac. *A Sermon Preached at the Anniversary of the Royal Humane Society, in St. James's Church, Westminster, on Sunday, April 24, 1803.* London, 1803.

Hurd, Isaac. *A Discourse Delivered in the Church in Brattle Street, in Boston, Tuesday, June 11th, 1799, Before the Humane Society of the Commonwealth of Massachusetts.* Boston, 1799.

Information for Emigrants to the New England States. Boston, 1795.

Information to Those Who Are Disposed to Migrate to South-Carolina. Charleston, 1795.

The Institution of the Humane Society of the Commonwealth of Massachusetts. Boston, 1786.

The Institution of the Humane Society of the Commonwealth of Massachusetts. Boston, 1788.

The Institution of the Humane Society of the Commonwealth of Massachusetts: with the Rules for regulating said Society, and the Methods of Treatment to be used with Persons apparently dead; with a Number of recent Cases proving the happy Effects thereof. Boston, 1788.

The Institution of the Merrimack Humane Society, With the Rules for Regulating Said Society, and the Methods of Treatment to Be Used with Persons Apparently Dead. Newburyport, 1803.

The Institution of the Merrimack Humane Society. Newburyport, 1809.

Jamieson, John. *The Sorrows of Slavery, a Poem. Containing a Faithful Statement of Facts Respecting the African Slave Trade.* London, 1789.

Johnson, Alexander. *A Short Account of a Society at Amsterdam Instituted in the Year 1767 for the Recovery of Drowned Person; With Observations Shewing the Utility and Advantage that Would Accrue to Great Britain from a Similar Institution Extended to Cases of Suffocation by Damps in Mines, Choaking, Strangling, Stifling, and other Accidents.* London, 1773.

Johnson, Samuel. *A Dictionary of the English Language.* 2 vols. London, 1755.

Kendall, James. *A Discourse Delivered in King's Chapel, Boston, Before the Humane Society of Massachusetts, at their Semiannual Meeting, June 8, 1813.* Boston, 1813.

Lathrop, John. *A Discourse Before the Humane Society, in Boston: Delivered On the Second Tuesday of June, 1787.* Boston, 1787.

Lathrop, John. *A Discourse Before the "Society for Propagating the Gospel Among Indians, and Others, in North-America." Delivered on the 19th of January, 1804.* Boston, 1804.

Lettsom, John Coakley. *Hints Designed to Promote Beneficence.* Vol. 1 (of 1 vol.) London, 1797.

Lettsom, John Coakley. *Hints Designed to Promote Beneficence, Temperance, and Medical Science.* 3 vols. London, 1801.

Lettsom, John Coakley. *Memoirs of John Fothergill.* 4th ed. London, 1786.

London Vaccine Institution, for Inoculating and Supplying Matter Free of Expense. London, 1813.

Longworth's New York City Directory for 1802. New York, 1802), p. 117. See also Martyn, Benjamin. *Reasons for Establishing the Colony of Georgia, with Regard to the Trade of Great Britain, the Increase of Our People, and the Employment and Support It Will Afford to Great Numbers of Our Own Poor, as Well as Foreign Persecuted Protestants.* London, 1733.

Mather, Cotton. *Bonifacius. An Essay Upon the Good, that Is to Be Devised and Designed, by Those who Desire the Great End of Life, and To Do Good While They Live.* Boston, 1710.

Medical Register. London, 1780.

Medical Register. London, 1783.

"Memoir of Thomas Cogan, M.D., One of the Founders of the Royal Humane Society." *The Annual Biography and Obituary, for the Year 1819.* London, 1819.

A Memorial of the Case of the German Emigrants Settled in the British Colonies of Pensilvania, and the Back Parts of Maryland, Virginia, &c. London, 1754.

Mills, Henry. *Schools Commended. The Invaluable Blessing of a Sound, Useful, and Pious Education especially that of School Learning; with a Particular View to Archbp Whitgift's Foundation, in Croydon Surry.* London, 1732.

Morgan, John. *A Discourse upon the Institution of Medical Schools in America; Delivered at a Public Anniversary Commencement, Held in the College of Philadelphia May 30 and 31.* Philadelphia, 1765.

Morse, Jedidiah. *A Sermon Preached Before the Humane Society of the Commonwealth of Massachusetts, at their Semiannual Meeting, June 9th, 1801.* Boston, 1801.

[Murray, John.] *An Enquiry into the Origin, Progress, & Present State of Slavery: With a Plan for the Gradual, Reasonable, & Secure Emancipation of Slaves. By a Member of the Society of UNIVERSAL GOODWILL in London and Norwich.* London, 1789.

Newton, John. *Thoughts Upon the African Slave Trade.* London, 1788.

The New York City Directory for 1789. New York, 1789.

The New York City Directory for 1790. New York, 1790.

The New York Directory and Register for the Year 1794. New York, 1794.

[New York Hospital]. *Charity Extended to All. State of the New York Hospital for the Year 1797.* [New York, 1798].

New-York Society for the Information and Assistance of Persons Emigrating from Foreign Countries. New York, 1794.

Parkman, Francis. *A Sermon Delivered at the Internment of the Rev. John Lathrop. Pastor of the Second Church in Boston, who Died Jan. 4, 1816, in the Sixty-Sixth Year of His Age, and Forty-Eighth of his Ministry.* Boston, 1816.

Paxton, John. *The Philadelphia Directory for 1813.* Philadelphia, 1813.

[Philadelphia Dispensary]. *A Comparative View of the Natural Small-Pox, Inoculated Small-Pox, and Vaccination in their Effects on Individuals and Society.* Philadelphia, 1803.

[Philadelphia Humane Society]. *Directions for Recovering Persons, Who Are Supposed to Be Dead, from Drowning, Also for Preventing & Curing the Disorders, Produced by Drinking Cold Liquors, and By the Actions of Noxious Vapours, Lightning, and Excessive Cold and Heat, Upon the Human Body.* Philadelphia, [1788].

The Physicians of the Charleston Dispensary, to the Patients of that Institution. Charleston, 1802.

Pietas Hallensis: Or a Publick Demonstration of the Foot-steps of a Divine Being Yet in the World: In a Historical Narration of the Orphan-House, and Other Charitable Institutions, at Glaucha near Hall in Saxony. Trans. Josiah Woodward. London, 1705.

Pietas Romana et Parisiensis, or a Faithful Relation of the Several Sorts of Charitable and Pious Works Eminent in the Cities of Rome and Paris. Oxford, 1687.

Plan of the Finsbury Dispensary, St. John's Square, Clerkenwell, for Administering Advices and Medicines to the Poor. [London, 1794?].

Plan of the Philadelphia Dispensary for the Medical Relief of the Poor. Philadelphia, 1787.

Plan of the Philadelphia Dispensary for the Medical Relief of the Poor. Philadelphia, 1808.

Plan of the Westminster General Dispensary. Instituted 1774. London, 1776.

Porter, Eliphalet. *A Discourse Delivered Before the Humane Society of the Commonwealth of Massachusetts, at their Semiannual Meeting, June 8, 1802.* Boston, 1802.

The Power of Faith: Exemplified in the Life and Writings of Mrs. Isabella Graham of New-York. New York, 1816.

Pratt, Samuel Jackson. *Emma Corbett.* 2 vols. 5th ed. London, 1783.

Pratt, Samuel Jackson. *Gleanings through Wales, Holland, and Westphalia; With the Views of War and Peace at Home and Abroad.* Vol. 1. 2nd ed. London, 1796.

[Pratt, Samuel Jackson]. *Humanity, or The Rights of Nature, A Poem; In Two Books. By the Author of Sympathy.* London, 1788.

Proceedings at the Annual and Other Meetings of the Scots Society in Norwich, in 1778, 1779, and 1780. Norwich, 1780.

Proceedings of the Committee Appointed to Manage the Contributions Begun at London Dec. XVIII MDCCLVIII for Cloathing French Prisoners of War. London, 1760.

Public Characters, or Cotemporary [sic] Biography. Baltimore, 1803.

[Proclamation, September 4, 1738]. By His Excellency Jonathan Belcher [of Massachusetts.]

Report of the Central Committee at Paris, on the Subject of Vaccine or Cowpox; Made on the 24th November, 1802. London, n.d.

A Report of the Infirmary, Dispensary, Lunatic Hospital, and Asylum in Manchester. From the 25th of June, 1793, to the 24th of June, 1794. [Manchester, 1794].

The Reports of the Society for Bettering the Condition and Improving the Comforts of the Poor. Vol. 2. 4th ed. London, 1805.

The Report of the Society for Bettering the Condition and Increasing the Comforts of the Poor. Vol. 3. London, 1802.

Reports of the Society for the Recovery of the Apparently Drowned. Part II. [London], 1774.

Reports of the Sunderland Humane Society, From It's [sic] Institution in September 1791, to the Commencement of the Year 1793. Sunderland, 1793.

Rhees, Morgan. *The Good Samaritan. An Oration Delivered on Sunday Evening, May 22nd, 1796, In Behalf of the Philadelphia Society for the Information and Assistance of Persons Emigrating from Foreign Countries.* New York, 1796.

Ring, John. *A Treatise on the Cow-pox; Containing a History of Vaccine Inoculation, and an Account of the Various Publications, which Have Appeared on that Subject, in Great Britain and other Parts of the World. Part I.* London, 1801.

Robbins, Chandler. *A Discourse Delivered Before the Humane Society of the Commonwealth of Massachusetts, at their Semiannual Meeting, June 14, 1796.* Boston, 1796.

Robinson, James. *The Philadelphia Directory for 1809.* Philadelphia, 1809.

Robinson, James. *The Philadelphia Directory for 1810.* Philadelphia, 1810.

[Royal Humane Society]. *A Brief Account of the Humane Society.* [London], 1789.

[Royal Humane Society]. *Brief Account of the Royal Humane Society.* [London], 1792.

[Royal Humane Society]. *Society for the Recovery of Persons Apparently Drowned. Instituted M.D.CC.L.XX.IV.* [London, 1774]. (1)

[Royal Humane Society]. *Society for the Recovery of Persons Apparently Drowned. Instituted M.D.CC.L.XX.IV.* [London, 1774]. (2)

[Royal Humane Society]. *The Plan of an Institution for Affording Immediate Relief to Persons Apparently Dead, from Drowning. And also for Diffusing a General Knowledge of the Manner of Treating Persons in a Similar Critical State, from Various Other Causes; Such as Strangulation by the Cord, Suffocation by Noxious Vapours, &c. &c. Published by Order of the Society.* London, 1774.

[Royal Humane Society]. *Plan and Report of the Society for the Recovery and Persons Apparently Drowned.* [London, 1774].

[Royal Humane Society]. *Plan and Reports of the Society Instituted at London . . . for the Recovery of Persons Apparently Drowned.* [London, 1775].

[Royal Humane Society]. *Report of the Society Instituted in the Year 1774, for the Recovery of Persons Apparently Drowned.* [London, 1775].

[Royal Humane Society]. *Reports of the Humane Society instituted in the Year 1774, for the Recovery of Persons Apparently Drowned. For the Year MDCCLXXVI.* [London, 1776].

[Royal Humane Society]. *Reports of the Humane Society instituted in the Year 1774, for the Recovery of Persons Apparently Drowned. For the Year MDCCLXXVII.* [London, 1778].

[Royal Humane Society]. *Reports of the Humane Society instituted in the Year 1774, for the Recovery of Persons Apparently Drowned. For the Year MDCCLXXVIII.* [London, 1778].

[Royal Humane Society]. *Reports of the Humane Society instituted in the Year 1774, for the Recovery of Persons Apparently Drowned for the Years MDCCLXXIX and MDCCLXXX.* [London, 1781].

[Royal Humane Society]. *Reports of the Humane Society instituted in the Year 1774, for the Recovery of Persons Apparently Drowned for the Years MDCCLXXXI and MDCCLXXXII.* [London, 1782/3?].

[Royal Humane Society]. *Reports of the Humane Society instituted in the Year 1774, for the Recovery of Persons Apparently Drowned for the Years MDCCLXXXIII and MDCCLXXXIV.* [London, 1784/5?].

[Royal Humane Society]. *Reports of the Humane Society instituted in the Year 1774, for the Recovery of Persons Apparently Drowned for the Years MDCCLXXXIV and MDCCLXXXVI.* [London, 1787].

[Royal Humane Society]. *Reports of the Royal Humane Society instituted in the Year 1774; with an Appendix of Miscellaneous Observations on the Subject of Suspended Animation. For the Years MDCCLXXXVII, MDCCLLXXXVIII and MDCCLXXIX.* [London, 1790].

[Royal Humane Society]. *Royal Humane Society. Instituted 1774.* [For 1790]. [London, 1790].

[Royal Humane Society]. *Royal Humane Society, Instituted 1774. Published for the Anniversary Festival 1791.* [London, 1791?].

[Royal Humane Society]. *Royal Humane Society, Instituted 1774. Published for the Anniversary Festival 1792.* [London, 1792?].

[Royal Humane Society]. *Royal Humane Society, Instituted 1774: The Annual Report. Published for the Anniversary Festival 1793 by W. Hawes, M.D. Register.* [London, 1793?].

[Royal Humane Society]. *Royal Humane Society, Instituted 1774: The Annual Report. Published for the Anniversary Festival 1794 by W. Hawes M.D. Register.* [London, 1794?].

[Royal Humane Society]. *Royal Humane Society, Instituted 1774: The Annual Report. Published for the Anniversary Festival 1795 by William Hawes M.D.* [London, 1795?].

[Royal Humane Society]. *Royal Humane Society, Instituted 1774: The Annual Report. 1796 By William Hawes M.D.* [London, 1796?].

[Royal Humane Society]. *The Annual Report 1797 by W. Hawes M.D.* [London, 1797?].

[Royal Humane Society]. *Royal Humane Society, 1774 ... The Annual Report, published for the Anniversary Festival 1798 by W. Hawes M.D.* [London, 1798].

[Royal Humane Society]. *Royal Humane Society, 1774, Annual Report 1799 by W. Hawes M.D.* London, [1799].

[Royal Humane Society]. *Royal Humane Society, 1774, Annual Report 1800 by W. Hawes M.D.* London, [1800].

[Royal Humane Society]. *Royal Humane Society, 1774, Annual Report 1801 by W. Hawes M.D.* London, [1801].

[Royal Humane Society]. *Royal Humane Society. Established 1774, for the Restoration of Human Life ... Annual Report, 1802 by W. Hawes M.D.* London, [1802].

[Royal Humane Society]. *Royal Humane Society. 1774, Annual Report 1803 by W. Hawes M.D.* London, [1803].

[Royal Humane Society]. *Royal Humane Society. For the Restoration of Human Life ... Annual Report, 1804 by W. Hawes M.D.* London, [1804].

[Royal Humane Society]. *Royal Humane Society. Annual Report, 1805 by W. Hawes M.D.* London, [1805].

[Royal Humane Society]. *Royal Humane Society. Annual Report, 1806 by W. Hawes M.D.* London, [1806].

[Royal Humane Society]. *Royal Humane Society. Annual Report, 1807 by W. Hawes M.D.* London, [1807].

[Royal Humane Society]. *Royal Humane Society. Annual Report, 1808 by W. Hawes M.D.* London, [1808].

[Royal Humane Society]. *Annual Report of the Royal Humane Society 1809.* London, [1809].

[Royal Humane Society]. *Annual Report of the Royal Humane Society 1810.* London, [1810].

[Royal Humane Society]. *Annual Report of the Royal Humane Society 1811.* London, [1811].

[Royal Humane Society]. *Annual Report of the Royal Humane Society for the Recovery of the Apparently Drowned 1812.* London, 1812.

[Royal Humane Society]. *Annual Report of the Royal Humane Society. 1813.* London, 1813.

[Royal Humane Society]. *Annual Report of the Royal Humane Society. 1814.* London, 1814.

[Royal Humane Society]. *Annual Report of the Royal Humane Society. 1815.* London, 1815.

[Royal Humane Society]. *Annual Report of the Royal Humane Society. 1820.* London, 1820.

Rules and By-Laws of the Baltimore General Dispensary. Baltimore, 1803.

Rules of the City Dispensary for the Medical Relief of the Poor. Instituted at New York. February 1, 1791. New York, 1791.

Rules of the (New York) City Dispensary, for the Medical Relief of the Poor. [n.d., c. 1792].

Reports of the Sunderland Humane Society, From It's [sic] Institution in September 1791, to the Commencement of the Year 1793. Sunderland, 1793.

Say, Benjamin. *An Annual Oration Pronounced Before the Humane Society of Philadelphia, on the Objects & Benefits of Said Institution; the 28th day of February, 1799.* Philadelphia, 1799.

Secker, Thomas. *A Sermon Preached Before the Incorporated Society for the Propagation of the Gospel in Foreign Parts, at their Anniversary Meeting in the Parish-Church of St. Mary-le-Bow, on Friday, February 20, 1740–1.* London, 1741.

Shaw, Lemuel. *A Discourse, Delivered Before the Officers and Members of the Humane Society of Massachusetts, 11 June, 1811.* Boston, 1811.

Short Account of the Rise, Progress, and Present State of the Lunatic Asylum at Edinburgh. Edinburgh, 1812.

Sketch of the Origin and Progress of the Humane Society of the City of New York. New York, 1814.

Smith, Adam. *The Theory of Moral Sentiments.* 1759; Prometheus books edition, New York, 2000.

Smith, James. *The Additional Letters of Humanitas.* [Baltimore], 1801.

Smith, William. *A Brief History of the Rise and Progress of the Charitable Scheme, Carrying on by a Society of Noblemen and Gentlemen, for the Relief and Instruction of Poor Germans.* Philadelphia, 1755.

Some Account of the Pennsylvania Hospital, from Its First Rise to the Beginning of the Fifth Month, Called May 1754. Philadelphia, 1754.

Stafford, Cornelius William. *The Philadelphia Directory for 1798.* Philadelphia, 1798.

Stanfield, James Field. *The Guinea Voyage. A Poem. In Three Books.* London, 1789.

A Statement of Premiums Awarded by the Trustees of the Humane Society of Massachusetts, from July 1817 to April 1829. Boston, 1829.

Stephen's Philadelphia Directory, for 1796. Philadelphia, 1796.

Stoddard, Solomon. *Question Whether GOD Is Not Angry with the Country for Doing So Little Towards the Conversion of the Indians?* Boston, 1723.

Summary Account of the Rise and Progress of the Society in Scotland for Propagating Christian Knowledge. Edinburgh, 1783.

Swain, John Hadley. *A Sermon Preached at St. Martin's in the Fields, London, on Sunday, March 30, and at Hampstead Church, Middlesex, on Sunday, May 25, 1783, for the Benefit of the Humane Society.* London, 1783.

Thacher, Thomas. *A Discourse Delivered at Boston, Before the Humane Society of the Commonwealth of Massachusetts, June 10th, 1800.* Boston, 1800.

Third Festival of the Royal Jennerian Society. (From the *Gentleman's Magazine,* June 1805.)

Thompson, Benjamin, Count Rumford. *Essays, Political, Economical, and Philosophical.* 3 vols. London, 1796.

Tudor, William. *A Discourse Delivered Before the Humane Society, at their Anniversary, May, 1817.* Boston, 1817.

Turell, Ebenezer. *The Life and Character of the Reverend Benjamin Colman, D.D. late Pastor of a Church in Boston New-England. Who Deceased August 29th 1747.* Boston, 1749.

Walter, William. *A Discourse Delivered Before the Humane Society of the Commonwealth of Massachusetts, at the Semiannual Meeting Twelfth of June, 1798.* Boston, 1798.

Warren, John. *An Eulogy on The Honourable Thomas Russell, Esq, Late President of The Society for Propagating the Gospel Among the Indians and Others, in North America; the Humane Society of the Commonwealth of Massachusetts; the Agriculture Society;the Society for the Advice of Immigrants; the Boston Chamber of Commerce; and the National Bank in Boston.* Boston, 1796.

Waterhouse, Benjamin. *On the Principle of Vitality. A Discourse Delivered in the First Church in Boston, Tuesday, June 8th, 1790. Before the Humane Society of the Commonwealth of Massachusetts.* Boston, 1790.

Waterhouse, Benjamin. *A Prospect for Exterminating the Smallpox.* Cambridge, 1802.

Watkins, Tobias. *An Eulogium on the Character of Brother John Crawford.* Baltimore, 1813.

Wheelock, Eleazar. *A Plain and Faithful Narrative of the Original Design, Rise, Progress and Present State of the Indian Charity-School at Lebanon, in Connecticut.* Boston, [1763].

White, Daniel Appleton. *An Address to the Members of the Merrimack Humane Society, at their Anniversary Meeting, in Newburyport, Sept. 3, 1805.* Newburyport, 1805.

Whitefield, George. "Continuation of the Account and Progress &c. of the Orphan House" (1746). In *The Works of the Reverend George Whitefield,* Vol. 3. London, 1771.

Williams, Helen Maria. *A Poem on the Bill Lately Passed for Regulating the Slave Trade.* London, 1788.

Wood, William. *The Christian Duty of Cultivating a Spirit of Universal Benevolence Amidst the Present Unhappy National Hostilities. A Sermon Preached at Bradford in Yorkshire, Before an Assembly of Dissenting Ministers, and Published at Their Request.* Leeds, 1781.

Newspapers and Periodicals

American Museum
[Edinburgh] *Annals of Medicine for the Year 1801*
The [London] *Annual Biography and Obituary, for the Year 1819*
Barbados Gazette
Barbados Mercury
Boston Magazine
[Baltimore] *Companion and Weekly Miscellany*
[London] *Gazetteer and New Daily Advertiser,* January 12, 1778.
Gentleman's Magazine
Hibernian Magazine
Memoirs of the Medical Society of London, Instituted 1773
[London] *Monthly Magazine*
New York Daily Advertiser
The [Baltimore] *Observer*
Royal American Magazine
[Halifax] *Royal Gazette and Nova Scotia Advertiser*

Electronic Sources

Readex America's Historical Newspapers, University of Michigan, Ann Arbor, Michigan, http://infoweb.newsbank.com.proxy.lib.umich.edu/.
The Papers of Benjamin Franklin, www.franklinpapers.org.

SECONDARY SOURCES

Abraham, James Johnston. *Lettsom: His Life, Times, Friends and Descendants.* London, William Heinemann Medical Books, 1933.

Abruzzo, Margaret. *Polemical Pain: Slavery, Cruelty, and the Rise of Humanitarianism.* Baltimore: Johns Hopkins University Press, 2011.

Adam, Thomas. *Buying Respectability: Philanthropy and Urban Society in Transnational Perspective, 1840s to 1930s.* Bloomington: Indiana University Press, 2009.

Alexander, John K. *Render Them Submissive: Responses to Poverty in Philadelphia, 1760–1800.* Amherst: University of Massachusetts Press, 1980.

Alleyne, Warren. "It So Happened." [Barbados] *Sunday Sun of the Nation.* May 31, 1998.

Anderson, Benedict R. O'G. *Imagined Communities: Reflections on the Origin and Spread of Nationalism.* London: Verso, 1983.

Anderson, Fred. *Crucible of War: The Seven Years' War and the Fate of Empire in North America.* New York: Vintage Books, 2001.

Andrew, Donna T. Comp. *London Debating Societies, 1776–1799.* London: London Record Society, 1994.

Andrew, Donna T. and Randall McGowen. *The Perreaus and Mrs. Rudd: Forgery and Betrayal in Eighteenth-Century London.* Berkeley: University of California Press, 2001.

Andrew, Donna T. *Philanthropy and Police: London Charity in the Eighteenth-Century* Princeton, NJ: Princeton University Press, 1989.

Armstrong, Eva V. and Claude K. Deischer. "Dr. Henry Moyes, Scotch Chemist." *Journal of Chemical Education* 24 (1947): 169–174.

Axtell, James. "The White Indians." In *The Invasion Within: The Contest of Cultures in Colonial North America,* 302–327. Oxford: Oxford University Press, 1985.

Bailyn, Bernard. *The Ideological Origins of the American Revolution.* Enlarged edition. Cambridge, MA: Belknap Press of Harvard University Press, 1992.

Baker, James. *The Life of Sir Thomas Bernard, Baronet.* London, 1819

Bannet, Eve Tavor. *Empire of Letters: Letter Manuals and Transatlantic Correspondence, 1688–1820.* Cambridge: Cambridge University Press, 2005.

Barker, Hannah. *Newspapers, Politics, and Public Opinion in Late Eighteenth- Century England.* Oxford: Clarendon Press, 1998.

Barnett, Michael. *Empire of Humanity: A History of Humanitarianism.* Ithaca, NY: Cornell University Press, 2011.

Barry, Jonathan. "Publicity and the Public Good: Presenting Medicine in Eighteenth-century Bristol." In *Medical Fringe and Medical Orthodoxy, 1750–1850,* 29–39. Ed. W. F. Bynum and Roy Porter. London: Croom Helm, 1987.

Barry, Jonathan. "Urban Associations and the Middling Sort." In *The Middling Sort of People: Culture, Society and Politics in England, 1550–1800,* 84–112. Ed. Jonathan Barry and Christopher Brooks. New York: St. Martin's Press, 1994.

Baseler, Marilyn C. "Immigrants and Politics in the 1790s." In *"Asylum for Mankind": America, 1607–1800,* 243–309. Ithaca, NY: Cornell University Press, 1998.

Bass, Gary J. *Freedom's Battle: The Origins of Humanitarian Intervention.* New York: Alfred A. Knopf, 2008.

Baumgartner, Leona. "John Howard (1726–1790) Hospital and Prison Reformer." *Bulletin of the History of Medicine* 7 (1939): 486–625.

Bell, Richard. *We Shall Be No More: Suicide and Self-Government in the Newly United States.* Cambridge, MA: Harvard University Press, 2012.

Bell, Whitfield J. "Benjamin Franklin and the German Charity Schools." *Proceedings of the American Philosophical Society* 99: 6 (1955): 381–387.

Bell, Whitfield J. "Dr. James Smith and the Public Encouragement for Vaccination for Smallpox." *Annals of Medical History,* 3rd series 2 (1940): 500–517.

Bell, Whitfield J. "Philadelphia Medical Students in Europe, 1750–1800." *Pennsylvania Magazine of History and Biography* 67 (1943): 1–29.

Bell, Whitfield J. *John Morgan Continental Doctor.* Philadelphia: University of Pennsylvania Press, 1965.

Bellows, Barbara L. *Benevolence among Slaveholders: Assisting the Poor in Charleston 1670–1860.* Baton Rouge: Louisiana State University Press, 1993.

Bender, Thomas, ed. *The Antislavery Debate: Capitalism and Abolitionism as a Problem in Historical Interpretation.* Berkeley: University of California Press, 1992.

Berg, Maxine. *Luxury and Pleasure in Eighteenth-Century Britain.* Oxford: Oxford University Press, 2005.

Berlin, Ira. *Many Thousands Gone: The First Two Centuries of Slavery in North America.* Cambridge, MA: Belknap Press of Harvard University Press, 1998.

Bickham, Troy O. *Making Headlines: The American Revolution as Seen through the British Press.* Dekalb: Northern Illinois University Press, 2009.

Bickham, Troy O. *Savages within the Empire: Representations of American Indians in Eighteenth- Century Britain.* Oxford: Oxford University Press, 2005.

"Biography of Dr. Amos Windship (1745–1813)." *Publications of the Colonial Society of Massachusetts* 25 (1924): 141–171.

Bittle, William G. and R. Todd Lane. "Inflation and Philanthropy in England: A Re-Assessment of W. K. Jordan's Data." *Economic History Review* 29 (1976): 203–210.

Black, Jeremy. *The English Press 1621–1861.* Thrupp, Stroud, Gloucestershire: Sutton, 2001.

Blake, John B. *Benjamin Waterhouse and the Introduction of Vaccination: A Reappraisal.* Philadelphia: University of Pennsylvania Press, 1957.

Black, Jeremy. *British Abroad: The Grand Tour in the Eighteenth Century.* New York: St. Martin's Press, 1992.

Booth, Christopher. *John Haygarth, FRS: A Physician of the Enlightenment.* Philadelphia: American Philosophical Society, 2005.

Bossy, John. *Christianity in the West 1400–1700.* Oxford: Oxford University Press, 1985.

Bowden, Henry Warner. *American Indians and Christian Missions: Studies in Cultural Conflict.* Chicago: University of Chicago Press, 1981.

Bowers, John Z. "The Odyssey of Smallpox Vaccination." *Bulletin of the History of Medicine* 55 (1981): 17–33.

Boylan, Anne M. *The Origins of Women's Activism: New York and Boston, 1797–1840* Chapel Hill: University of North Carolina Press, 2002.

Breen, T. H. *American Insurgents, American Patriots: The Revolution of the People.* New York: Hill and Wang, 2010.

Breen, T. H. "'Baubles of Britain': The American and Consumer Revolutions of the Eighteenth Century." *Past and Present* 119 (1988): 73–104.

Breen, T. H. "An Empire of Goods: The Anglicization of Colonial America, 1690–1776." *Journal of British Studies* 25:4 (1986): 467–499.

Breen, T. H. *The Marketplace of Revolution: How Consumer Politics Shaped the American Revolution.* Oxford: Oxford University Press, 2004.

Brewer, John. "Commercialization and Politics." In Neil McKendrick, John Brewer, and J. H. Plumb. *Birth of a Consumer Society,* 253–260. Bloomington: Indiana University Press, 1982.

Brewer, John. *The Pleasures of the Imagination: English Culture in the Eighteenth Century.* New York: Farrar, Straus and Giroux, 1997.

Bridenbaugh, Carl. *Cities in Revolt: Urban Life in America, 1743–1776.* New York: Alfred A. Knopf, 1955.

Bridenbaugh, Carl. *Cities in the Wilderness: The First Century of Urban Life in America, 1625–1742.* 2nd ed. New York: Alfred A. Knopf, 1955.

Bridenbaugh, Carl and Jessica Bridenbaugh. *Rebels and Gentlemen: Philadelphia in the Age of Franklin.* New York: Reynal and Hitchcock, 1942.

Brock, Helen. "North America: A Western Outpost of European Medicine." In *The Medical Enlightenment of the Eighteenth Century,* 194–216. Ed. Andrew Cunningham and Roger French. Cambridge: Cambridge University Press, 1990.

Brown, Christopher Leslie. *Moral Capital: Foundations of British Abolitionism.* Chapel Hill: Published for the Omohundro Institute of Early American History and Culture, Williamsburg, Virginia, by the University of North Carolina Press, 2006.

Brown, Richard D. "The Emergence of Urban Society in Rural Massachusetts, 1760–1820." *Journal of American History* 61 (1974): 29–51.

Brown, Richard D. *Knowledge Is Power: The Diffusion of Information in Early America, 1700–1865.* New York: Oxford University Press, 1989.

Brown, Vincent. *The Reaper's Garden: Death and Power in the World of Atlantic Slavery.* Cambridge, MA: Harvard University Press, 2008.

Brownlow, John. *Memoranda; or Chronicles of the Foundling Hospital, Including Memoirs of Captain Coram, &c. &c.* London, 1847.

Brunton, Deborah C. "The Transfer of Medical Education: Teaching at the Edinburgh and Philadelphia Medical Schools." In *Scotland and America in the Age of Enlightenment,* 242–258. Ed. Richard B. Sher and Jeffrey R. Smitten. Princeton, NJ: Princeton University Press, 1990.

Bullock, Steven C. *Revolutionary Brotherhood: Freemasonry and the Transformation of the American Social Order, 1730–1840*. Chapel Hill: Published for the Omohundro Institute of Early American History and Culture, Williamsburg, Virginia, by the University of North Carolina Press , 1996.

Burgoyne, Cindy. "'Imprisonment the Best Punishment': The Transatlantic Exchange and Communication of Ideas in the Field of Penology, 1750–1820." Ph.D. diss., University of Sunderland, 1997.

Burke, John. *Burke's Landed Gentry*. Vol. 2. London, 1846.

Burstein, Andrew. "The Political Character of Sympathy." *Journal of the Early Republic* 21 (2001): 601–632.

Butler, Jon. *Awash in a Sea of Faith: Christianizing the American People*. Cambridge, MA: Belknap Press of the Harvard University Press, 1990.

Butler, Jon. *The Huguenots in America: A Refugee People in New World Society*. Cambridge, MA: Harvard University Press, 1983.

Butler, Jon. *Power, Authority, and the Origins of the American Denominational Order: The English Churches in the Delaware Valley 1680–1730*. Philadelphia: American Philosophical Society, 1978.

Bynum, W. F. "Hospital, Disease and Community: The London Fever Hospital, 1801–1850." In *Healing and History: Essays for George Rosen*, 97–115. Ed. Charles E. Rosenberg. New York: Dawson Science History Publications, 1979.

Bynum, W. F. "Physicians, Hospitals and Career Structures in Eighteenth-Century London." In *William Hunter and the Eighteenth-Century Medical World*, 106–123. Ed. W. F. Bynum and Roy Porter. Cambridge: Cambridge University Press, 1985.

Cabanes, Bruno. *The Great War and the Making of Modern Humanitarianism*. Cambridge: Cambridge University Press, 2014.

Cage, R. A. *The Scottish Poor Law 1745–1845*. Edinburgh: Scottish Academic Press, 1981.

Calam, John. *Parsons and Pedagogues: The S.P.G. Adventure in American Education* New York: Columbia University Press, 1971.

Campbell, Lyall. *Sable Island, Fatal and Fertile Crescent*. Windsor, Nova Scotia: Lancelot Press, 1974.

Camic, Charles. "Experience and Ideas: Education for Universalism in Eighteenth-Century Scotland." *Comparative Studies in Society and History* 25 (1983): 50–82.

Carretta, Vincent. *Equiano the African: Biography of a Self-Made Man*. Athens: University of Georgia Press, 2005.

Cash, Arthur. *John Wilkes: The Scandalous Father of Civil Liberty*. New Haven, CT: Yale University Press, 2006.

Cash, Philip. "Setting the Stage: Dr. Benjamin Waterhouse's Reception in Boston, 1782– 1788." *Journal of the History of Medicine and Allied Science* 1992 (47): 5–28.

Cashin, Edward J. *Beloved Bethesda: A History of George Whitefield's Home for Boys, 1740–2000*. Macon, GA: Mercer University Press, 2001.

Cassell, Ronald. *Medical Charities, Medical Politics: The Irish Dispensary System and the Poor Law, 1836–1872.* Rochester, NY: Boydell Press, 1997.

Chaplin, Joyce E. *An Anxious Pursuit: Agricultural Innovation and Modernity in the Lower South, 1730–1815.* Chapel Hill: Published for the Omohundro Institute of Early American History and Culture, Williamsburg, Virginia, by the University of North Carolina Press, 1993.

Charters, Erica. *Disease, War and the Imperial State.* Chicago: University of Chicago Press, 2014.

Chernow, Ron. *Washington: A Life.* New York: Penguin Press, 2010.

Clark, Charles E. "Early American Journalism: News and Opinion in the Popular Press." In *A History of the Book in America,* Vol. I: *The Colonial Book in the Atlantic World,* 347–366. Ed. Hugh Amory and David Hall. Cambridge: Cambridge University Press, 2000.

Clark, Peter. *British Clubs and Societies 1580–1800: The Origins of an Associational World.* Oxford: Oxford University Press, 2000.

Cleary, Patricia. *Elizabeth Murray: A Woman's Pursuit of Independence in Eighteenth-Century America.* Amherst: University of Massachusetts Press, 2000.

Cleves, Rachel Hope. *The Reign of Terror in America: Visions of Violence from Anti-Jacobinism to Antislavery.* Cambridge: Cambridge University Press, 2009.

Cody, Lisa Forman. "Living and Dying in Georgian London's Lying-in Hospitals." *Bulletin of the History of Medicine* 78 (2004): 309–348.

Cohen, Gerard Daniel. *In War's Wake: Europe's Displaced Persons in the Postwar Order.* Oxford: Oxford University Press, 2012.

Colley, Linda. *Britons: Forging the Nation 1707–1837.* New Haven, CT: Yale University Press, 1992.

Colley, Linda. *Captives: Britain, Empire, and the World, 1600–1850.* New York: Anchor Books, 2002.

Compston, H. F. B. *Thomas Coram Churchman, Empire Builder and Philanthropist.* London: SPCK, 1918.

Conway, Stephen. "From Fellow-Nationals to Foreigners: British Perceptions of the Americans, circa 1739–1783." *William and Mary Quarterly* 59 (2002): 65–100.

Copeland, David. "America 1750–1820." In *Press, Politics and the Public Sphere in Europe and North America, 1760–1820,* 140–158. Ed. Hannah Barker and Simon Burrows. Cambridge: Cambridge University Press, 2002.

Corfield, P. J. *The Impact of English Towns 1700–1800.* Oxford: Oxford University Press, 1982.

Cotlar, Seth. *Tom Paine's America: The Rise and Fall of Transatlantic Radicalism in the Early Republic.* Charlottesville: University of Virginia Press, 2011.

Cowell, Benjamin. *Spirit of '76 in Rhode Island: Or, Sketches of the Efforts of the Government and People in the War of the Revolution.* Boston, 1850.

Crane, Verner W. "Dr. Thomas Bray and the Charitable Colony Project, 1730." *William and Mary Quarterly*, 3rd series, 19:1 (1962): 49–63.

Crane, Verner W. "Philanthropists and the Genesis of Georgia." *American Historical Review* 27:1 (1921): 63–69.

Crowe, Charles. "Bishop James Madison and the Republic of Virtue." *Journal of Southern History* 30 (1964): 58–70.

Crowley, John E. *The Invention of Comfort: Sensibilities and Design in Early Modern Britain and Early America*. Baltimore: Johns Hopkins University Press, 2001.

Croxson, Bronwyn. "The Public and Private Faces of Eighteenth-Century London Dispensary Charity." *Medical History* 41 (1997): 127–149.

Cumbler, John T. *From Abolition to Rights for All: The Making of a Reform Community in the Nineteenth Century*. Philadelphia: University of Pennsylvania Press, 2008.

Cunningham, Hugh and Joanna Innes, eds. *Charity, Philanthropy and Reform: From the 1690s to 1850*. New York: St. Martin's Press, 1998.

Curti, Merle. *American Philanthropy Abroad*. New Brunswick, NJ: Rutgers University Press, 1963.

Dain, Angela. "An Enlightened and Polite Society." In *Norwich since 1550*, 193–218. Ed. Carole Radcliffe and Richard Wilson, with Christine Clark. London: Hambledon and London, 2004.

Dalrymple, William. *White Mughals: Love and Betrayal in Eighteenth-Century India*. New York: Viking, 2003.

Davidoff, Leonore and Catherine Hall. *Family Fortunes: Men and Women of the English Middle Class, 1780–1850*. Chicago: University of Chicago Press, 1987.

Davidson, Luke. "Raising Up Humanity: A Cultural History of Resuscitation and the Royal Humane Society of London, 1774–1808." Ph.D. diss., University of York, 2001.

Davis, David Brion. *Inhuman Bondage: The Rise and Fall of New World Slavery*. Oxford: Oxford University Press, 2006.

Davis, David Brion. *The Problem of Slavery in the Age of Revolution, 1770–1823*. Ithaca, NY: Cornell University Press, 1975.

Davis, Natalie Zemon. *The Gift in Sixteenth-Century France*. Madison: University of Wisconsin Press, 2000.

Dawson, Kevin. "Enslaved Swimmers and Divers in the Atlantic World." *Journal of American History* 92 (2006): 1327–1355.

Dayton, Cornelia H. and Sharon V. Salinger. *Robert Love's Warnings: Searching for Strangers in Colonial Boston*. Philadelphia: University of Pennsylvania Press, 2014.

Dekker, Jeroen J. H. "Transforming the Nation and the Child: Philanthropy in the Netherlands, Belgium, France and England, c. 1780–c. 1850." In *Charity, Philanthropy and Reform from the 1690s to 1850*, 130–147. Ed. Hugh Cunningham and Joanna Innes. New York: St. Martin's Press, 1998.

Demos, John. *The Unredeemed Captive: A Family Story from Early America.* New York: Alfred A. Knopf, 1994.

Devine, T. M. *Scotland's Empire 1660–1815.* London: Penguin Books, 2003.

Dierks, Konstantin. "The Familial Letter and Social Refinement in America, 1750–1800." In *Letter Writing as a Social Practice,* 31–41. Ed. David Barton and Nigel Hall. Amsterdam: John Benjamins, 1999.

Doerflinger, Thomas M. *A Vigorous Spirit of Enterprise: Merchants and Economic Development in Revolutionary Philadelphia.* Chapel Hill: Published for the Institute of Early American History and Culture, Williamsburg, Virginia, by the University of North Carolina Press, 1986.

Dorsey, Bruce. *Reforming Men and Women: Gender in the Antebellum City.* Ithaca, NY: Cornell University Press, 2002.

Drayton, Richard. *Nature's Government: Science, Imperial Government, and the "Improvement" of the World.* New Haven, CT: Yale University Press, 2000.

Duffy, Eamon. "*Correspondence Fraternelle*: The SPCK, the SPG, and the Churches of Switzerland in the War the Spanish Succession." In *Reform and the Reformation: England and the Continent c1500–c1750,* 251–280. Ed. Derek Baker. Oxford: Published for the Ecclesiastical History Society by Basil Blackwell, 1979.

Duffy, Eamon. "The Society of [*sic*] Promoting Christian Knowledge and Europe: The Background to the Founding of the Christenumsgesellschaft." In *Pietismus und Neuzeit,* 28–42. Ed. Martin Brecht, et al. Gottingen: Vandenhoeck and Ruprecht, 1982.

Duffy, John. *Epidemics in Colonial America.* Baton Rouge: Louisiana State University Press, 1953.

Duffy, John. "History of Public Health and Sanitation in the West since 1700." In *The Cambridge World History of Human Disease,* 200–206. Ed. Kenneth Kiple. Cambridge: Cambridge University Press, 1993.

Elkins, Stanley and Eric McKitrick. *The Age of Federalism: The Early American Republic, 1788–1800.* New York: Oxford University Press, 1993.

Elliott, J. H. *Empires of the Atlantic World: Britain and Spain in America 1492–1830.* New Haven, CT: Yale University Press, 2006.

Ellis, Frank H. "The Background of the London Dispensary." *Journal of the History of Medicine and Allied Sciences* 20 (1965): 197–212.

Engel, Katherine Carté. "The SPCK and the American Revolution: The Limits of International Protestantism." *Church History* 81:1 (2012): 77–103.

Epps, John. *The Life of John Walker.* London, 1831.

Eustace, Nicole. "The Sentimental Paradox: Humanity and Violence on the Pennsylvania Frontier." *William and Mary Quarterly* 65 (2008): 29–64.

Fideler, Paul A. *Social Welfare in Pre-Industrial England.* Houndsmill, Basingstoke, Hampshire: Palgrave Macmillan, 2006.

Fiering, Norman. "Irresistible Compassion: An Aspect of Eighteenth-Century Sympathy and Humanitarianism." *Journal of the History of Ideas* 37 (1976): 195–218.

Finger, Simon. *The Contagious City: The Politics of Public Health in Early Philadelphia.* Ithaca, NY: Cornell University Press, 2012.

Fisher, Richard B. *Edward Jenner 1749–1823.* London: Andre Deutsch, 1991.

Fissell, Mary E. *Patients, Power, and the Poor in the Eighteenth-Century Bristol.* Cambridge: Cambridge University Press, 1991.

Fladeland, Betty. *Men and Brothers: Anglo-American Antislavery Cooperation.* Urbana: University of Illinois Press, 1972.

Flavell, Julie. *When London Was Capital of America.* New Haven, CT: Yale University Press, 2010.

Forsythe, David. *The Humanitarians: The International Committee of the Red Cross.* Cambridge: Cambridge University Press, 2005.

Foster, Charles I. *An Errand of Mercy: The Evangelical United Front, 1790–1837.* Chapel Hill: University of North Carolina Press, 1960.

Fowler, Jonathan Allen. "Adventures of an 'Itinerant Institutor': The Life and Philanthropy of Thomas Bernard." Ph.D. diss., University of Tennessee, 2003.

Friedman, Lawrence J. and Mark D. McGarvie. *Charity, Philanthropy and Civility in American History.* Cambridge: Cambridge University Press, 2003.

Furstenberg, Francois. "Atlantic Slavery, Atlantic Freedom: George Washington, Slavery, and Transatlantic Abolitionist Networks." *William and Mary Quarterly* 68:2 (April 2011): 247–286.

Games, Alison. "Beyond the Atlantic: English Globetrotters and Transoceanic Connections." *William and Mary Quarterly,* 3rd series, 63 (2006): 675–692.

Games, Alison. *Web of Empire: English Cosmopolitans in an Age of Expansion, 1560–1660.* Oxford: Oxford University Press, 2008.

Gascoigne, John. *Science in the Service of Empire.* Cambridge: Cambridge University Press, 1998.

Gaustad, Edwin Scott. *The Great Awakening in New England.* 1957; reprint Chicago: Quadrangle Books, 1968.

Gevitz, Norman. "'But All Those Authors Are Foreign': American Literary Nationalism and Domestic Medical Guides." In *The Popularization of Medicine 1650–1850,* 232–251. Ed. Roy Porter. London: Routledge, 1992.

Glasson, Travis. *Mastering Christianity: Missionary Anglicanism and Slavery in the Atlantic World.* New York: Oxford University Press, 2012.

Glover, Richard. *Britain at Bay: Defence against Bonaparte, 1803–14.* London: Allen and Unwin, 1973.

Godfrey, Amy Margaret. "Divine Benevolence to the Poor: Charity, Religion and Nationalism in Early National New York, 1784–1820." Ph.D. diss, Northern Illinois University, 2007.

Golinski, Jan. *Science as Public Culture: Chemistry and Enlightenment in Britain, 1760–1820.* Cambridge: Cambridge University Press, 1992.

Goodman, Nathan. *Benjamin Rush Physician and Citizen 1746–1813.* Philadelphia: University of Pennsylvania Press, 1934.

Gould, Eliga. "American Independence and Britain's Counter-Revolution." *Past and Present* 154 (1997): 107–141.

Gould, Eliga. *Among the Powers of the Earth: The American Revolution and the Making of a New World Empire.* Cambridge, MA: Harvard University Press, 2012.

Gould, Eliga. *The Persistence of Empire: British Political Culture in the Age of the American Revolution.* Chapel Hill: Published for the Omohundro Institute of Early American History and Culture, Williamsbug, Virginia, by the University of North Carolina Press, 2000.

Granshaw, Lindsay. "The Rise of the Modern Hospital in Britain." In *Medicine in Society: Historical Essays*, 197–218. Ed. Andrew Wear. Cambridge: Cambridge University Press, 1992.

Green, Abigail. "Humanitarianism in Nineteenth-Century Context: Religious, Gendered, National." *Historical Journal* 57 (2014): 1157–1175.

Greene, Jack P. *Imperatives, Behaviors, and Identities: Essays in Early American Cultural History.* Charlottesville: University Press of Virginia, 1992.

Greene, Jack P. *Pursuits of Happiness: The Social Development of Early Modern British Colonies and the Formation of American Culture.* Chapel Hill: University of North Carolina Press, 1988.

Grell, Ole Peter and Andrew Cunningham, eds. *Health Care and Poor Relief in Protestant Europe.* London: Routledge, 1997.

Grell, Ole Peter, Andrew Cunningham, and Robert Jutte. *Health Care and Poor Relief in 18th and 19th Century Northern Europe.* Aldershot: Ashgate, 2002.

Grell, Ole Peter, Andrew Cunningham, and Bernd Roeck, eds. *Health Care and Poor Relief in 18th and 19th Century Southern Europe.* Aldershot: Ashgate, 2005.

Griffin, Clifford S. *Their Brothers' Keepers: Moral Stewardship in the United States, 1800–1865.* New Brunswick, NJ: Rutgers University Press, 1960.

Grigg, John A. "'How This Shall Be Brought About': The Development of the SSPCK's American Policy." *Itinerario* 3 (2008): 43–60.

Gross, Robert A. "Giving in America: From Charity to Philanthropy." In *Charity, Philanthropy, and Civility in American History*, ed. Lawrence J. Friedman and Mark D. McGarvie. Cambridge: Cambridge University Press, 2003.

Hackett, Paul. "Averting Disaster: The Hudson's Bay Company and Smallpox in Western Canada during the Late Eighteenth and Early Nineteenth Centuries." *Bulletin of the History of Medicine* 78 (2004): 575–609.

Halttunen, Karen. "Humanitarianism and the Pornography of Pain in Anglo-American Culture." *American Historical Review* 100 (1995): 303–334.

Hancock, David J. *Citizens of the World: London Merchants and the Integration of the British Atlantic Community, 1735–1785*. Cambridge: Cambridge University Press, 1995.

Hancock, David J. "Commerce and Conversation in the Eighteenth-Century Atlantic: The Invention of Madeira Wine." *Journal of Interdisciplinary History* 29 (1998): 197–219.

Hancock, David J. *Oceans of Wine: The Emergence of American Taste and Trade*. New Haven, CT: Yale University Press, 2009.

Hancock, David J. "The Trouble with Networks: Managing the Scots' Early-Modern Madeira Trade." *Business History Review* 79 (2005): 467–491.

Harris, Marc. "Civil Society in Post-Revolutionary America." In *Empire and Nation: The American Revolution in the Atlantic World*, 197–355. Ed. Eliga H. Gould and Peter S. Onuf. Baltimore: Johns Hopkins University Press, 2005.

Harrison, Brian. *Drink and the Victorians: The Temperance Question in England, 1815–1872*. Pittsburgh: University of Pittsburgh Press, 1971.

Harrison, John Anthony. "Blind Henry Moyes, 'An Excellent Lecturer in Philosophy.'" *Annals of Science* 13 (1957): 109–125.

Harrison, Richard. *Princetonians 1769–1775: A Biographical Dictionary*. Princeton, NJ: Princeton University Press, 1980.

Haskell, Thomas L. "Capitalism and the Origins of the Humanitarian Sensibility, Parts 1 and 2," *American Historical Review* 90 (1985): 339–361, 547–566.

Hawke, David Freeman. *Benjamin Rush: Revolutionary Gadfly*. Indianapolis: Bobbs-Merrill, 1971.

Haynes, Sam W. *Unfinished Revolution: The Early American Republic in a British World*. Charlottesville: University of Virginia Press, 2010.

Heal, Felicity. *Hospitality in Early Modern England*. Oxford: Clarendon Press, 1990.

Heitman, Francis B. *Historical Register of Officers of the Continental Army during the War of the Revolution, April 1775, to December 1783*. Revised ed. 1914; rpt. Baltimore: Clearfield, 1982.

Hendrickson, David C. *Peace Pact: The Lost World of the American Founding*. Lawrence: University Press of Kansas, 2003.

Heyrman, Christine Leigh. "The Fashion among More Superior People: Charity and Social Change in Provincial New England, 1700–1740." *American Quarterly* 34 (1982): 107–124.

Hilton, Boyd. *The Age of Atonement: The Influence of Evangelicalism on Social and Economic Thought, 1795–1865*. Oxford: Clarendon Press, 1988.

Hirschman, Albert. *The Passions and the Interests: Political Arguments for Capitalism before its Triumph*. Princeton, NJ: Princeton University Press, 1977.

Hitchcock, Tim. *Down and Out in Eighteenth-Century London*. London: Hambledon and London, 2004.

Hitchcock, Tim. "Pauper and Preachers: The SPCK and the Parochial Workhouse Movement." In *Stilling the Grumbling Hive: The Response to Social and Economic Problems in England, 1689–1750*, 145–166. Ed. Lee Davison, et al. New York: St. Martin's Press, 1992.

Hochschild, Adam. *Bury the Chains: Prophets and Rebels in the Fight to Free an Empire's Slaves.* Boston: Houghton Mifflin, 2005.

Hodson, Christopher. *Acadian Diaspora: An Eighteenth-Century History.* Oxford: Oxford University Press, 2012.

Hoffman, Elizabeth Cobbs. *All You Need Is Love: The Peace Corps and the Spirit of the 1960s.* Cambridge, MA: Harvard University Press, 1998.

Honour, Hugh. *The Image of the Black in Western Art.* Vol. 4:1. Cambridge, MA: Belknap Press of Harvard University Press, 1989.

Hont, Istvan and Michael Ignatieff. *Wealth and Virtue: The Shaping of Political Economy in the Scottish Enlightenment.* Cambridge: Cambridge University Press, 1983.

Hopkins, Donald R. *The Greatest Killer: Smallpox in History with a New Introduction.* Chicago: University of Chicago Press, 2002.

Horton, James Oliver and Lois E. Horton. *In Hope of Liberty: Culture, Community, and Protest among Northern Free Blacks, 1700–1860.* New York: Oxford University Press, 1997.

Houston, Alan. *Benjamin Franklin and Politics of Improvement.* New Haven, CT: Yale University Press, 2008.

Howard, D. L. *John Howard: Prison Reformer.* London: C. Johnson, 1958.

Howe, Mark A. DeWolfe. *The Humane Society of the Commonwealth of Massachusetts: An Historical Review, 1785–1916.* Boston, 1918.

Hunt, Lynn. *Inventing Human Rights: A History.* New York: W.W. Norton, 2007.

Iannini, Christopher. "'The Itinerant Man': Crevecouer's Caribbean, Raynal's Revolution, and the Fate of Atlantic Cosmopolitanism," *William and Mary Quarterly* 61 (2004): 201–234.

Ignatieff, Michael. *Just Measure of Pain: The Penitentiary in the Industrial Revolution, 1750–1850.* New York: Pantheon, 1978.

Innes, Joanna. "The 'Mixed Economy of Welfare' in Early Modern England: Assessments of the Options from Hale to Malthus (c. 1683–1803)." In *Charity, Self-Interest and Welfare in the English Past*, 139–180. Ed. Martin Daunton. New York: St. Martin's Press, 1996.

Innes, Joanna. "State, Church and Voluntarism." In *Charity, Philanthropy and Reform from the 1690s to 1850*, 15–66. Ed. Hugh Cunningham and Joanna Innes. New York: St. Martin's Press, 1998.

Innes, Joanna. "The State and the Poor: Eighteenth-Century England in European Perspectives." In *Rethinking Leviathan: The Eighteenth-Century State in Britain and Germany*, 113–132. Ed. John Brewer and Eckhart Hellmuth. London: German Historical Institute, Oxford University Press, 1999.

Irvin, Benjamin. *Clothed in Robes of Sovereignty: The Continental Congress and the People Out of Doors*. New York: Oxford University Press, 2011.

Irwin, Julia F. *Making the World Safe: The American Red Cross and a Nation's Humanitarian Awakening*. Oxford: Oxford University Press, 2013.

Irwin, Julia F. "Raging Rivers and Propaganda Weevils: Transnational Disaster Relief, Cold War Politics, and the 1954 Danube and Elbe Floods." *Diplomatic History* (Advance Access, published online October 8, 2015).

Isaac, Rhys. *The Transformation of Virginia 1740–1790*. Chapel Hill: Published for the Institute of Early American History and Culture, Williamsburg, Virginia, by the University of North Carolina Press, 1982.

Jackson, Maurice. *Let This Voice Be Heard: Anthony Benezet, Apostle of Atlantic Abolition*. Philadelphia: University of Pennsylvania Press, 2009.

Jacob, Margaret C. *Living the Enlightenment: Freemasonry and Politics in Eighteenth-Century Europe*. Oxford: Oxford University Press, 1991.

Jacob, Margaret C. *Strangers Nowhere in the World: The Rise of Cosmopolitanism in Early Modern Europe*. Philadelphia: University of Pennsylvania Press, 2006.

Jaffee, David. "The Village Enlightenment in New England, 1760–1820." *William and Mary Quarterly*, 3rd series, 47 (1990): 327–346.

James, Sydney V. *A People Among Peoples: Quaker Benevolence in Eighteenth- Century America*. Cambridge, MA: Harvard University Press, 1963.

Jasanoff, Maya. *Edge of Empire: Lives, Culture, and Conquest in the East, 1750-1850*. New York: Alfred A. Knopf, 2005.

Jasanoff, Maya. *Liberty's Exiles: American Loyalists in the Revolutionary World*. New York: Alfred A. Knopf, 2011.

John, Richard R. *Spreading the News: The American Postal System from Franklin to Morse*. Cambridge, MA: Harvard University Press, 1995.

Johnson, Paul E. *A Shopkeeper's Millennium: Society and Revivals in Rochester, New York, 1815-1837*. New York: Hill and Wang, 1978.

Jones, M. G. *The Charity School Movement*. Cambridge: Cambridge University Press, 1938.

Jordan, Winthrop D. *White over Black: American Attitudes Towards the Negro, 1550-1812*. 1968; New York: W. W. Norton & Co., 1977.

Jordan, W. K. *The Charities of London, 1480-1660*. London: George Allen & Unwin Ltd., 1960.

Jordan, W. K. *The Charities of Rural England, 1480-1660*. London: George Allen & Unwin Ltd, 1961.

Jordan, W. K. *Philanthropy in England, 1480-1660*. New York: Russell Sage Foundation, 1959.

Juster, Susan. *Disorderly Women: Sexual Politics & Evangelicalism in Revolutionary New England.* Ithaca: Cornell University Press, 1994.

Kaplan, Catherine O'Donnell. *Men of Letters in the Early Republic.* Chapel Hill: Published for the Omohundro Institute of Early American History and Culture, Williamsburg, Virginia, by the University of North Carolina Press, 2008.

Karras, Alan L. *Sojourners in the Sun: Scottish Migrants in Jamaica and the Chesapeake, 1740–1800.* Ithaca: Cornell University Press, 1992.

Kellaway, William. *The New England Company 1649-1776: Missionary Society to the American Indians.* New York: Barnes and Noble, 1962.

Kendrick, T. D. *The Lisbon Earthquake.* London: Methuen, 1956.

Keys, Barbara. *Reclaiming American Virtue: The Human Rights Revolution of the 1970s* Cambridge: Harvard University Press, 2014.

Kidd, Thomas S. *The Protestant Interest: New England after Puritanism.* New Haven: Yale University Press, 2004.

Kilpatrick, Robert. "'Living in the Light': Dispensaries, Philanthropy and Medical Reform in Late Eighteenth-Century London." In *The Medical Enlightenment of the Eighteenth Century*, 254–280. Eds. Andrew Cunningham and Roger French. Cambridge: Cambridge University Press, 1990.

King, Steven. *Poverty and Welfare in England 1700-1850: A Regional Perspective* Manchester: Manchester University Press, 2000.

Kingdon, Robert M. "Social Welfare in Calvin's Geneva." *American Historical Review* 76 (1971): 50–69.

Kirsch, George B. *Jeremy Belknap.* New York: Arno Press, 1982.

Kleingeld, Pauline. "Six Varieties of Cosmopolitanism in Late Eighteenth-Century Germany." *Journal of the History of Ideas* 60 (1999): 505–524.

Klingberg, Frank J. *Anglican Humanitarianism in Colonial New York.* Philadelphia: The Church Historical Society, 1940; rpt. 1971.

Klingberg, Frank J. *Codrington Chronicle: An Experiment in Anglican Altruism on a Barbados Plantation, 1710-1834.* Berkeley: University of California Press, 1949.

Klingberg, Frank J. *Contributions of the S.P.G. to the American Way of Life.* Philadelphia: Church Historical Society, 1943.

Knapp, Samuel L. *The Life of Thomas Eddy.* 1834; reprint edition, New York, 1976.

Knott, Sarah. *Sensibility and the American Revolution.* Chapel Hill: Published for the Omohundro Institute of Early American History and Culture, Williamsburg, Va., by the University of North Carolina Press, 2009.

Knott, Sarah. "Sensibility and the American War for Independence," *American Historical Review* 109 (2004): 19–40.

Kolchin, Peter. *American Slavery 1619-1877.* New York: Hill and Wang, 1993. 1st rev. ed. 2003.

Kraus, Michael. *The Atlantic Civilization: Eighteenth-Century Origins.* Ithaca: Published for the American Historical Association, Cornell University Press, 1949.

Krebs, Daniel. *A Generous and Merciful Enemy: Life for German Prisoners of War during the American Revolution.* Norman: University of Oklahoma Press, 2013.

Lambert, David and Alan Lester. "Geographies of Colonial Philanthropy." *Progress in Human Geography* 28 (2004): 320–341.

Lambert, Frank. *'Pedlar in Divinity': George Whitefield and the Transatlantic Revivals, 1737-1770.* Princeton: Princeton University Press, 1994.

Langford, Paul. *A Polite and Commercial People: England, 1727-1783.* Oxford: Clarendon Press, 1989.

Landau, Norma. "The Laws of Settlement and the Surveillance of Immigration in Eighteenth-Century Kent." *Continuity and Change* 3 (1998): 391–420.

Landau, Norma. "The Regulation of Immigration, Economic Structure and Definitions of the Poor in Eighteenth-Century England." *The Historical Journal* 33 (1990): 541–571.

Langstaff, J. Brett. *Dr. Bard of Hyde Park.* New York: E.P. Dutton & Co., 1942.

Laqueur, Thomas W. "Bodies, Details, and the Humanitarian Narrative." In *The New Cultural History.* Ed. Lynn Hunt, 176–204. Berkeley: University of California Press, 1989.

Laqueur, Thomas W. "Mourning, Pity, and the Work of Narrative in the Making of 'Humanity.'" In *Humanitarianism and Suffering: The Mobilization of Empathy,* 31–57. Eds. Richard Ashby Wilson and Richard D. Brown. Cambridge and New York: Cambridge University Press, 2009.

Larabee, Eric. *The Benevolent and Necessary Institution: The New York Hospital 1771-1971.* Garden City: Doubleday & Co., Inc., 1971.

Lawrence, Susan C. *Charitable Knowledge: Hospital Pupils and Practitioners in Eighteenth-Century London.* Cambridge: Cambridge University Press, 1996.

Lees, Lynn Hollen. *The Solidarities of Strangers: The English Poor Laws and the People, 1740-1948.* Cambridge and New York: Cambridge University Press, 1998.

Lloyd, Katherine and Cindy Burgoyne. "The Evolution of a Transatlantic Debate on Penal Reform, 1780-1830." In *Charity, Philanthropy and Reform From the 1690s to 1850,* 208–227. Eds. Hugh Cunningham and Joanna Innes. Houndmills, Basingstoke, Hampshire, 1998.

Lloyd, Katherine M. R. "Peace, Politics & Philanthropy: Henry Brougham, William Roscoe and America 1808-1868." Ph.D. diss., University of Oxford, 1996.

Lloyd, Sarah. "Pleasing Spectacles and Elegant Dinners: Conviviality, Benevolence, and Charity Anniversaries in Eighteenth-Century London." *Journal of British Studies* 41 (2002): 23–57.

Lobo, Francis M. "John Haygarth, Smallpox and Religious Dissent in Eighteenth-Century England." In *The Medical Enlightenment of the Eighteenth Century.*

Eds. Andrew Cunningham and Roger French, 217–253. Cambridge: Cambridge University Press, 1990.

Longmore, Paul. *The Invention of George Washington*. Charlottesville: University of Virginia Press, 1999.

Loudon, I. S. L. "The Origins and Growth of the Dispensary Movement in England." *Bulletin of the History of Medicine* 55 (1981): 322–342

Mann, Bruce. *Republic of Debtors: Bankruptcy in the Age of American Independence.* Cambridge, Mass.: Harvard University Press, 2002.

Marble, Allan Everett. *Surgeons, Smallpox, and the Poor: A History of Medicine in Nova Scotia, 1749-1799*. Montreal & Kingston: McGills-Queen's University Press, 1993.

Marshall, P. J. *The Making and Unmaking of Empires: Britain, India, and America c. 1750-1783*. Oxford: Oxford University Press, 2005.

Marshall, P. J. "The Moral Swing to the East: British Humanitarianism, India and the West Indies." In P. J. Marshall. *A Free though Conquering People,'* 69–95. 986; reprint Aldershot, Hampshire, 2003.

Marshall, P. J. *Remaking the British Atlantic: The United States and the British Empire after American Independence.* Oxford: Oxford University Press, 2012.

Marshall, P. J. "Who Cared about the Thirteen Colonies? Some Evidence from Philanthropy." In *'A Free though Conquering People': Eighteenth-Century Britain and Its Empire*, 53–67. Ed. P. J. Marshall. 1999; reprint Aldershot, Hampshire: Ashgate, 2003.

McCarthy, Kathleen D. *American Creed: Philanthropy and the Rise of Civil Society, 1700-1865*. Chicago: The University of Chicago Press, 2003.

McClellan, James E.III. *Science Reorganized: Scientific Societies in the Eighteenth Century*. New York: Columbia University Press, 1985.

McClure, Ruth. *Coram's Children: The London Foundling Hospital in the Eighteenth Century*. New Haven: Yale University Press, 1981.

McCusker, John J. and Russell R. Menard. *The Economy of British America, 1607-1789.* Chapel Hill: Published for the Institute of Early American History and Culture, Williamsburgh, Va., by the University of North Carolina Press, 1985.

McDaniel, W. Caleb. "Philadelphia Abolitionists and Antislavery Cosmopolitanism." In *Antislavery and Abolition in Philadelphia: Emancipation and the Long Struggle for Racial Justice in the City of Brotherly Love*, 149–173. Eds. Richard Newman and James Mueller. Baton Rouge: Louisiana State University Press, 2011.

McDaniel, W. Caleb. *The Problem of Democracy in the Age of Slavery: Garrisoanian Abolitionists and Transatlantic Reform*. Baton Rouge: LSU Press, 2013.

McKendrick, Neil, John Brewer, and J. H. Plumb. *Birth of a Consumer Society*. Bloomington: Indiana University Press, 1982.

McKenna, Katherine M. J. *A Life of Propriety: Anne Murray Powell and Her Family, 1755–1849*. Montreal & Kingston: McGill-Queen's University Press, 1994.

Meranze, Michael. *Laboratories of Virtue: Punishment, Revolution, and Authority in Philadelphia, 1760-1835.* Chapel Hill: University of North Carolina Press, 1996.

Middlekauff, Robert. *The Glorious Cause: The American Revolution, 1763-1789.* Oxford and New York: Oxford University Press, 1982, 2005.

Midgley, Clare. *Women Against Slavery: The British Campaigns, 1780-1870.* London: Routledge, 1992.

Miller, Genevieve. *The Adoption of Smallpox Inoculation in England and France.* Philadelphia: University of Pennsylvania Press, 1957.

Miller, Samuel. *Memoirs of the Rev. John Rodgers, D.D. Late Pastor of the Wall-Street and Brick Churches, in the City of New-York.* New York, 1813.

Mitchison, Rosalind. *The Old Poor Law in Scotland: The Experience of Poverty, 1574–1845.* Edinburgh: Edinburgh University Press, 2000.

Mohl, Raymond. "The Humane Society and Urban Reform in Early New York, 1787–1831." *New-York Historical Society Quarterly* 54 (1970): 30–52.

Mohl, Raymond. "Humanitarianism in the Preindustrial City: The New York Society for the Prevention of Pauperism." *Journal of American History* 57 (1970): 576–599.

Mohl, Raymond. *Poverty in New York, 1783-1825.* New York: Oxford University Press, 1971.

Moniz, Amanda Bowie. "'Labours in the Cause of Humanity in Every Part of the Globe': Transatlantic Philanthropic Collaboration and the Cosmopolitan Ideal, 1760-1815." Ph.D diss., The University of Michigan, 2008.

Moniz, Amanda Bowie. "Saving the Lives of Strangers: Humane Societies and the Cosmopolitan Provision of Charitable Aid." *Journal of the Early Republic* 29 (Winter 2009): 607–640

Morgan, Rod. "Divine Philanthropy: John Howard Reconsidered." *History* 62 (1977): 388–410.

Morris, R. J. "Voluntary Societies and British Urban Elites, 1780-1850." In *The Eighteenth-Century Town 1688-1820*, 338–366. Ed. Peter Borsay. London, 1990.

Mulcahy, Matthew. *Hurricanes and Society in the British Greater Caribbean, 1624–1783.* Baltimore: The Johns Hopkins University Press, 2006.

Mullan, John. *Sentiment and Sociability: The Language of Feeling in Eighteenth-Century.* Oxford: Clarendon Press, 1998.

Namier, Sir Lewis and John Brooke. *The House of Commons.* Vol. 2. New York: Published for the History of Parliament Press by Oxford University Press, 1964.

Nash, Gary. *Forging Freedom: The Formation of Philadelphia's Black Community 1720–1840.* Cambridge, Mass. and London: Harvard University Press, 1988.

Nash, Gary. "Poverty and Politics in Early American History." In *Down and Out in Early America*, 2–9. Ed. Billy G. Smith. University Park: Pennsylvania University Press, 2004.

Nash, Gary. "Poverty and Poor Relief in Pre-Revolutionary Poor Relief." *William and Mary Quarterly*, 3rd series, 33:1 (1976): 3–30.

Nash, Gary. *The Urban Crucible: The Northern Seaports and the Origins of the American Revolution*. Cambridge, MA: Harvard University Press, 1986.

Neem, Johann N. *Creating a Nation of Joiners: Democracy and Civil Society in Early National Massachusetts*. Cambridge, MA: Harvard University Press, 2008.

Newman, Richard S. *Freedom's Prophet: Bishop Richard Allen, the AME Church, and the Black Founding Fathers*. New York: New York University Press, 2008.

Newman, Richard S. *The Transformation of American Abolitionism: Fighting Slavery in the Early Republic*. Chapel Hill: University of North Carolina Press, 2002.

Newman, Simon P. "American Political Culture and the French and Haitian Revolutions: Nathaniel Cutting and the Jeffersonian Republicans." In *The Impact of the Haitian Revolution in the Atlantic World*, 72–89. Ed. David P. Geggus. Columbia: University of South Carolina Press, 2001.

Newman, Simon P. *Embodied History: The Lives of the Poor in Early Philadelphia*. Philadelphia: University of Pennsylvania Press, 2003.

North, Eric McCoy. *Early Methodist Philanthropy*. New York: [The Methodist Book Concern], 1914.

O'Brien, Susan. "Eighteenth-Century Publishing Network in the First Years of Transatlantic Evangelicalism." In *Evangelicalism: Comparative Studies of Popular Protestantism in North America, the British Isles, and Beyond, 1700–1990*, 38–57. Ed. Mark A. Noll, David W. Bebbington, and George A. Rawlyk. New York: Oxford University Press, 1994.

O'Connell, Neil J. "George Whitefield and Bethesda Orphan-House." *Georgia Historical Quarterly* 54 (1970): 41–62.

O'Donnell, John M. "Cullen's Influence on American Medicine." In *William Cullen and the Eighteenth Century Medical World*. Ed. A. Doig, J. P. S. Ferguson, I. A. Milne, and R. Passmore. Edinburgh: Edinburgh University Press, 1993.

One Hundred Years of History of the Baltimore General Dispensary. Baltimore, 1901.

O'Shaughnessy, Andrew. *An Empire Divided: The American Revolution and the British Caribbean*. Philadelphia: University of Pennsylvania Press, 2000.

Oldfield, J. R. *Popular Politics and British Anti-slavery: The Mobilisation of Public Opinion against the Slave Trade 1787–1807*. Manchester: Manchester University Press, 1995.

Oldfield, J. R. *Transatlantic Abolitionism in the Age of Revolution: An International History of Anti-slavery, c. 1787–1820*. Cambridge: Cambridge University Press, 2013.

Oliver, John Rathbone. "An Unpublished Autograph Letter from Dr. John Crawford (1746–1813) to General William Henry Winder (1755–1824)." *Bulletin of the Institute of the History of Medicine* 4 (1936): 145–151.

Opal, J. M. *Beyond, the Farm: National Ambitions in Rural New England*. Philadelphia: University of Pennsylvania Press, 2008.

Owen, David. *English Philanthropy 1660–1960*. Cambridge, MA: Belknap Press of Harvard University Press, 1964.

Parrish, Susan Scott. *American Curiosity: Cultures of Natural History in the Colonial British Atlantic World*. Chapel Hill: Published for the Omohundro Institute of Early American History and Culture, Williamsburg, Virginia, by the University of North Carolina Press, 2006.

Pencak, William. *Jews and Gentiles in Early America*. Ann Arbor: University of Michigan Press, 2005.

Pennington, Edgar Legare. "The Work of the Bray Associates in Pennsylvania." *Pennsylvania Magazine of History and Biography* 58:1 (1934): 1–25.

Pernick, Martin. "Back from the Grave: Recurring Controversies over Defining and Diagnosing Death in History." In *Death: Beyond Whole-Brain Criteria*, 17–74. Ed. Richard M. Zaner. Dordrecht: Kluwer Academic, 1988.

Peterson, Mark A. *The Price of Redemption: The Spiritual Economy of Puritan New England*. Stanford, CA: Stanford University Press, 1997.

Phillips, Joseph W. *Jedidiah Morse and New England Congregationalism*. New Brunswick, NJ: Rutgers University Press, 1983.

Pierson, George Wilson. *Tocqueville in America*. Baltimore: Johns Hopkins University Press, 1938.

Plaisted, Arthur H. *The Manor and Parish Records of Medmenham*. London, 1925.

Plumb, J. H. "The Acceptance of Modernity." In *Birth of a Consumer Society*, 316–334. Ed. Neil McKendrick, John Brewer, and J. H. Plumb. Bloomington: Indiana University Press, 1982.

Pocock, J. G. A. *Virtue, Commerce, and History: Essays of Political Thought and History, Chiefly in the Eighteenth Century*. Princeton, NJ: Princeton University Press, 1985.

Porter, Dorothy and Roy Porter. *Patients' Progress: Doctors and Doctoring in Eighteenth-Century England*. Stanford, CA: Stanford University Press, 1989.

Porter, Roy. "Cleaning up the Great Wen: Public Health in Eighteenth-Century London." In *Living and Dying in London*. Ed. W. F. Bynum and Roy Porter. *Medical History Supplement* No. 11, 1991.

Porter, Roy. *The Creation of the Modern World: The Untold Story of the British Enlightenment*. New York: W. W. Norton, 2000.

Porter, Roy. "The Gift Relation: Philanthropy and Provincial Hospitals in Eighteenth-Century England." In *The Hospital in History*, 149–178. Ed. Lindsay Granshaw and Roy Porter. London: Routledge, 1989.

Porter, Roy. "Lay Medical Knowledge in the Eighteenth Century: Evidence from the *Gentleman's Magazine*." *Medical History* 29 (1985): 138–168.

Porter, Roy. "The Rise of Medical Journalism in Britain to 1800." In *Medical Journals and Medical Knowledge: Historical Essays*, 6–28. London: Routledge, 1992.

Porter, Roy and Mikalus Teich, eds. *The Enlightenment in National Context*. Cambridge: Cambridge University Press, 1981.

Powell, John Harvey. *Bring Out Your Dead: The Great Plague of Yellow Fever in Philadelphia in 1793*. 1949; reprint, New York: Arno Press, 1970.

Poynter, J. R. *Society and Pauperism: English Ideas on Poor Relief, 1795–1834*. London: Routledge and Kegan Paul, 1969.

Prest, Wilifrid. *Albion Ascendant: English History 1660–1815*. Oxford: Oxford University Press, 1998.

Price, Jacob M. "The Imperial Economy, 1700–1776." In *The Oxford History of the British Empire: The Eighteenth Century*, 78–104. Ed. P. J. Marshall. Oxford: Oxford University Press, 1998.

Prochaska, F. K. *Women and Philanthropy in Nineteenth-Century England*. Oxford: Oxford University Press, 1980.

Pybus, Cassandra. "Billy Blue: An African American Journey through Empire in the Long Eighteenth Century." *Early American Studies* 5 (2007): 252–288

Pybus, Cassandra. "'A Less Favourable Specimen': The Abolitionist Response to Self-Emancipated Slaves in Sierra Leone, 1793–1808." *Parliamentary History* 26, Issue Supplement S1 (2007): 97–112.

Radcliffe, Evan. "Burke, Radical Cosmopolitanism, and the Debates on Patriotism in the 1790s." *Studies in Eighteenth-Century Culture* 28 (1999): 311–339.

Radcliffe, Evan. "Revolutionary Writing, Moral Philosophy, and Universal Benevolence in the Eighteenth Century." *Journal of the History of Ideas* 54 (1993): 221–240.

Reid-Maroney, Nina. "Scottish Medicine and Christian Enlightenment at the Pennsylvania Hospital, 1775–1800." In *Nation and Province in the First British Empire: Scotland and the Americas, 1600–1800*, 245–264. Ed. Ned C. Landsman. Lewisburg: Bucknell University Press, 2001.

Richards, Eric. "Scotland and the Uses of Atlantic Empire." In *Strangers within the Realm: Cultural Margins of the First British Empire*, 67–114. Ed. Bernard Bailyn and Philip D. Morgan. Chapel Hill: Published for the Institute for Early American History and Culture, Williamsburg, Virginia, 1991.

Richards, Jeffrey H. "Samuel Davies and the Transatlantic Campaign for Slave Literacy in Virginia." *Virginia Magazine of History and Biography* 111:4 (2003): 333–378.

Richardson, David. "Shipboard Revolts, African Authority, and the Atlantic Slave Trade." *William and Mary Quarterly*, 3rd series, 58:1 (2001): 69–92.

Rieff, David. *A Bed for the Night: Humanitarianism in Crisis*. New York: Simon and Schuster, 2002.

Riley, James C. *The Eighteenth-Century Campaign to Avoid Disease*. New York: St. Martin's Press, 1987.

Rippy, J. Fred. *Joel R. Poinsett: Versatile American*. Durham, NC: Duke University Press, 1935.

Risch, Erna. "Immigrant Aid Societies before 1820." *Pennsylvania Magazine of History and Biography* 60 (1936): 15–34.

Risse, Guenter B. "Medicine in the Age of Enlightenment." In *Medicine in Society: Historical Essays*, 149–196. Ed. Andrew Wear. Cambridge: Cambridge University Press, 1992.

Rivers, Isabel. "The First Evangelical Tract Society." *Historical Journal* 50:1 (2007): 1–22.

Roberts, M. J. D. *Making English Morals: Voluntary Associations and Moral Reform in England, 1787–1886.* Cambridge: Cambridge University Press, 2004.

Robinson, William H. *Phillis Wheatley and Her Writings.* New York: Garland, 1984.

Robbins, Christine Chapman. *David Hosack: Citizen of New York.* Philadelphia: American Philosophical Society, 1964.

Rodgers, Daniel T. *Atlantic Crossings: Social Politics in a Progressive Age.* Cambridge, MA.: Belknap Press of Harvard University Press, 1998.

Roney, Jessica Choppin. *Governed by a Spirit of Opposition: The Origins of American Political Practice in Colonial Philadelphia.* Baltimore: Johns Hopkins University Press, 2014.

Rose, Craig. "The Origins and Ideals of the SPCK 1699–1716." In *The Church of England c. 1689–c.1833: From Toleration to Tractarianism*, 172–190. Ed. John Walsh, Colin Haydon, and Stephen Taylor. Cambridge: Cambridge University Press, 1993.

Rose, Craig. "Politics and the London Royal Hospitals, 1683–92." In *The Hospital in History*, 123–148. Ed. Lindsay Granshaw and Roy Porter. London: Routledge, 1989.

Rosenberg, Charles E. *The Care of Strangers: The Rise of America's Hospital System.* New York: Basic Books, 1987.

Rosenberg, Charles E. *Caring for the Working Man: The Rise and Fall of the Dispensary Movement.* New York: Garland, 1989.

Rosenberg, Charles E. "Health in the Home: A Tradition of Print and Practice." In *Right Living: An Anglo-American Tradition of Self-Help Medicine and Hygiene*, 1–20. Ed. Charles E. Rosenberg. Baltimore: Johns Hopkins University Press, 2003.

Rosenberg, Charles E. "Medical Text and Social Context: Explain William Buchan's *Domestic Medicine*." In *Explaining Epidemics and Other Studies in the History of Medicine*, 32–56. Cambridge: Cambridge University Press, 1992.

Rosenthal, Joel. *The Purchase of Paradise: Gift Giving and the Aristocracy, 1307–1485.* London: Routledge and Kegan Paul, 1972.

Rozario, Kevin. "'Delicious Horrors': Mass Culture, the Red Cross, and the Appeal of Modern American Humanitarianism." *American Quarterly* 55:3 (2003): 417–455.

Rubin, Miri. *Charity and Community in Medieval Cambridge.* Cambridge: Cambridge University Press, 1987.

Schlenther, Boyd Stanley. "'To Convert the Poor People in America': The Bethesda Orphanage and the Thwarted Zeal of the Countess of Huntingdon." *Georgia Historical Quarterly* 78 (1994): 225–256.

Schlenther, Boyd Stanley. "Religious Faith and Commercial Empire." In *The Oxford History of the British Empire: The Eighteenth Century*. Ed. P. J. Marshall. Oxford: Oxford University Press, 1998–1999.

Schlereth, Thomas J. *The Cosmopolitan Ideal in Enlightenment Thought.* Notre Dame, IN: University of Notre Dame Press, 1977.

Schultz, Edward T. *History of Freemasonry in Maryland.* Vol. 2. Baltimore: J. H. Medairy, 1885.

Seaver, Paul S. *Wallington's World: A Puritan Artisan in Seventeenth-Century London.* Stanford, CA: Stanford University Press, 1985.

Sensbach, Jon. *Rebecca's Revival: Creating Black Christianity in the Atlantic World.* Cambridge, MA: Harvard University Press, 2005.

Shaw, Caroline. *Britannia's Embrace: Modern Humanitarianism and the Imperial Origins of Refugee Relief.* New York: Oxford University Press, 2015.

Sheridan, Richard B. "The Guinea Surgeons on the Middle Passage: The Provision of Medical Services in the British Slave Trade." *The Interdisciplinary Journal of African Historical Studies* 14:4 (1981): 601–625.

Shields, David S. *Civil Tongues and Polite Letters in British America.* Chapel Hill: Published for the Institute of Early American History and Culture, Williamsburg, Virginia, by the University of North Carolina Press, 1997.

Shipton, Clifford K., ed. *Sibley's Harvard Graduates.* Vol. 15 of 18 vols. Boston: Massachusetts Historical Society, 1970.

Shipton, Clifford K., ed. *Sibley's Harvard Graduates.* Vol. 17 of 18 vols. Boston: Massachusetts Historical Society, 1970.

Shyrock, Richard Harrison. *Medicine and Society in America 1660–1860.* Ithaca, NY: Cornell University Press, 1972.

Siena, Kevin. *Venereal Disease, Hospitals and the Urban Poor: London's 'Foul Wards,' 1600–1800.* Rochester, NY: Rochester University Press, 2004.

Silver, Peter. *Our Savage Neighbors: How Indian War Transformed Early America.* New York: W.W. Norton, 2008.

Simey, Margaret B. *Charitable Effort in Liverpool in the Nineteenth Century.* Liverpool: Liverpool University Press, 1951.

Sirota, Brent S. *Christian Monitors: The Church of England and the Age of Benevolence, 1680–1730.* New Haven, CT: Yale University Press, 2014.

Slack, Paul. *The English Poor Law, 1531–1782.* Cambridge: Cambridge University Press, 1995.

Slack, Paul. "Hospitals, Workhouses, and the Relief of the Poor in Early Modern England." In *Health Care and Poor Relief in Protestant Europe, 1500–1700,* 234–251. Ed. Ole Peter Grell and Andrew Cunningham. London: Routledge, 1997.

Slack, Paul. *Poverty and Policy in Tudor and Stuart England.* London: Longman, 1998.

Slack, Paul. *From Reformation to Improvement: Public Welfare in Early Modern England.* New York: Oxford University Press, 1999.

Smith, Billy G., ed. *Down and Out in Early America.* University Park: Pennsylvania State University Press, 2004.

Smith, Billy G., ed. "Inequality in Late Colonial Philadelphia: A Note on Its Nature and Growth." *William and Mary Quarterly*, 3rd series, 41 (1984): 629–645.

Smith, Billy G., ed. "Introduction: The Best Poor Man's Country." In *Down and Out in Early America*, xiv–xviii. Ed. Billy G. Smith. University Park: Pennsylvania State University Press, 2004.

Smith, Billy G., ed. *The "Lower Sort": Philadelphia's Laboring People, 1750–1800*. Ithaca, NY: Cornell University Press, 1990.

Smith, Billy G., ed. "The Material Lives of Laboring Philadelphians, 1750–1800." *William and Mary Quarterly*, 3rd series, 38:2 (1981): 164–202.

Smith, Joseph Jencks. *Civil and Military List of Rhode Island, 1647–1800*. Providence, 1900.

Snell, K. D. M. *Annals of the Labouring Poor: Social Change and Agrarian England, 1660–1900*. Cambridge: Cambridge University Press, 1985.

Snell, K. D. M. *Parish and Belonging: Community, Identity and Welfare in England and Wales, 1700–1950*. Cambridge: Cambridge University Press, 2006.

Snell, K. D. M. "Pauper Settlement and the Right to Poor Relief in England and Wales." *Continuity and Change* 6 (1991): 375–416.

Snyder, Sarah B. *Human Rights Activism and the End of the Cold War: A Transnational History of the Helsinki Network*. New York: Cambridge University Press, 2011.

Solkin, David H. *Painting for Money: The Visual Arts and the Public Sphere in Eighteenth-Century England*. New Haven, CT: Published for the Paul Mellon Centre for Studies in British Art by Yale University Press, 1992.

Spadafora, David. *The Idea of Progress in Eighteenth-Century Britain*. New Haven, CT: Yale University Press, 1990.

Sparrow, W. J. *Knight of the White Eagle: A Biography of Sir Benjamin Thompson, Count Rumford*. London: Hutchinson, 1964.

Steele, Ian K. *The English Atlantic 1675–1740: An Exploration of Communication and Community*. New York: Oxford University Press, 1986.

Steinberg, Ted. *Acts of God: The Unnatural History of Natural Disaster in America*. Oxford: Oxford University Press, 2000.

Stevens, Laura M. *The Poor Indians: British Missionaries, Native Americans, and Colonial Sensibility*. Philadelphia: University of Pennsylvania Press, 2004.

Stewart, Larry. "The Edge of Utility: Slaves and Smallpox in the Early Eighteenth Century." *Medical History* 29 (1985): 54–70.

Stott, Anne. *Hannah More: The First Victorian*. Oxford: Oxford University Press, 2003.

Stout, Harry S. *The Divine Dramatist: George Whitefield and the Rise of Modern Evangelicalism*. Grand Rapids, MI: William R. Eerdmans, 1991.

Szasz, Margaret Connell. *Scottish Highlanders and Native Americans*. Norman: University of Oklahoma Press, 2007.

Taylor, Alan. *American Colonies*. New York: Viking, 2001.

Taylor, James Stephen. "The Impact of Pauper Settlement 1691–1834," *Past and Present* 73 (1976): 42–74.

Taylor, James Stephen. *Jonas Hanway Founder of the Marine Society: Charity and Policy in Eighteenth-Century Britain.* London: Scolar Press, 1985.

Tercier, John Anthony. *Contemporary Deathbed: The Ultimate Rush.* Houndsmill, Basingstoke, Hampshire: Palgrave Macmillan, 2005.

Tiffany, Nina Moore. *Letters of James Murray Loyalist.* Boston, 1901.

Todd, Janet. *Sensibility: An Introduction.* London: Methuen, 1986.

Thomas, E. G. "The Old Poor Law and Medicine," *Medical History* 24 (1980): 1–19.

Thomas, Keith. *Man and the Natural World: Changing Attitudes in England 1500–1800.* Oxford: Oxford University Press, 1983.

Thompson, H. L. *Thomas Bray.* London: SCPK, 1954.

Thomson, Elizabeth. "The Role of Physicians in the Humane Societies of the Eighteenth Century." *Bulletin of the History of Medicine* 37 (1963): 43–51.

Thorne, Susan. "'The Conversion of Englishmen and the Conversion of the World Inseparable': Missionary Imperialism and the Language of Class in Early Industrial Britain." In *Tensions of Empire: Colonial Cultures in a Bourgeois World,* 238–262. Ed. Frederick Cooper and Ann Stoler. Berkeley: University of California Press, 1997.

Tolles, Frederick. *Quakers and the Atlantic Culture.* New York: Macmillan 1960.

Transactions of the College of Physicians of Philadelphia. 3rd series, Vol. 9, 1887.

Tully, Alan. *Forming American Politics: Ideals, Interests, and Institutions in Colonial New York and Pennsylvania.* Baltimore: Johns Hopkins University Press, 1994.

Turley, David. "British Antislavery Reassessed." In *Rethinking the Age of Reform: Britain 1750–1850,* 182–199. Ed. Arthur Burns and Joanna Innes. Cambridge: Cambridge University Press, 2003.

Turley, David. *The Culture of English Antislavery, 1780–1860.* London: Routledge, 1999.

Tyrrell, Ian. *Reforming the World: The Creation of America's Moral Empire.* Princeton, NJ: Princeton University Press, 2010.

Uglow, Jenny. *The Lunar Men: Five Friends Whose Curiosity Changed the World.* New York: Farrar, Straus and Giroux, 2002.

Underdown, David. *Fire from Heaven: The Life of an English Town in the Seventeenth Century.* New Haven, CT: Yale University Press, 1992.

Van Horne, John C. "Joseph Solomon Ottolenghe (ca. 1711–1775): Catechist to the Negroes, Superintendent of the Silk Culture, and Public Servant in Colonial Georgia." *Proceedings of the American Philosophical Society* 125:5 (1981): 398–409.

Van Horne, John C. *Religious Philanthropy and Colonial Slavery: The American Correspondence of the Associates of Dr. Bray.* Urbana: University of Illinois Press, 1985.

Vertovec, Steven and Robin Cohen, eds. *Conceiving Cosmopolitanism: Theory, Context, and Practice.* Oxford: Oxford University Press, 2002.

Vibert, Faith. "The Society for the Propagation of the Gospel in Foreign Parts: Its Work for the Negroes in North America before 1783." *Journal of Negro History* 18:2 (April 1933): 171–212.

Villiers, Marq de and Sheila Hirtle. *Sable Island: The Strange Origins and Curious History of a Dune Adrift in the Atlantic.* New York: Walker, 2004.

Waldstreicher, David. *In the Midst of Perpetual Fetes: The Making of American Nationalism, 1776–1820.* Chapel Hill: Published for the Omohundro Institute of Early American History and Culture, Williamsburg, Virginia, by the University of North Carolina Press, 1997.

Wagner, Gillian. *Thomas Coram, Gent. 1688–1751.* Woodbridge, UK: Boydell Press, 2004.

Walters, Ronald. *American Reformers 1815–1860.* New York: Hill and Wang, 1978.

Ward, W. R. *The Protestant Evangelical Awakening.* Cambridge: Cambridge University Press, 1992.

Waring, Joseph Ioor. *A History of Medicine in South Carolina.* (Charleston: South Carolina Medical Society, 1967).

Watenpaugh, Keith David. "Between Communal Survival and National Aspiration: Armenian Genocide Refugees, the League of Nations, and the Practice of Interwar Humanitarianism." *Humanity* 5:2 (2014).

Watenpaugh, Keith David. *Bread from Stones: The Middle East and the Making of Modern Humanitarianism.* Oakland: University of California Press, 2015.

Weber, Samuel E. "The Charity School Movement in Pennsylvania." Ph.D. diss., University of Pennsylvania, 1905.

Welch, Pedro L. V. *Slave Society in the City: Bridgetown, Barbados 1680–1834* Kingston, Jamaica: J. Currey, 2003.

Wheeler, Rachel S. *To Live upon Hope: Mohicans and Missionaries in the Eighteenth-Century Northeast.* Ithaca, NY: Cornell University Press, 2008.

Whelan, Kevin. "The Green Atlantic: Radical Reciprocities between Ireland and America in the Long Eighteenth Century." In *A New Imperial History: Culture, Identity and Modernity in Britain and the Empire 1660–1840,* 21623-8. Ed. Kathleen Wilson. Cambridge: Cambridge University Press, 2004.

White, Ashli. "The Dangers of Philanthropy." In *Encountering Revolution: Haiti and the Making of the Early American Republic,* 51–86. Baltimore: Johns Hopkins University Press, 2010.

Wiberly, Stephen Edward Jr. "Four Cities: Public Poor Relief in Urban America 1700–1775." Ph.D. diss., Yale University, 1975.

Williams, Carolyn. "'The Luxury of Doing Good'": Benevolence, Sensibility, and the Royal Humane Society." In *Pleasure in the Eighteenth Century,* 77–107. Ed. Roy Porter and Marie Mulvey Roberts. New York: New York University Press, 1996.

Williams, William H. "The 'Industrious Poor' and the Founding of the Pennsylvania Hospital." *Pennsylvania Magazine of History and Biography* 97 (1973): 431–443.

Wilson, Adrian. "Conflict, Consensus and Charity: Politics and the Provincial Voluntary Hospitals in the Eighteenth Century." *English Historical Review* 111 (1996): 599–619.

Wilson, Adrian. "The Politics of Medical Improvement in Early Hanoverian England." In *The Medical Enlightenment of the Eighteenth Century*, 4–39. Ed. Andrew Cunningham and Roger French. Cambridge: Cambridge University Press, 1990.

Wilson, Bird. *Memoir of the Life of Bishop White*. Philadelphia, 1839.

Wilson, David A. *United Irishmen, United States: Immigrant Radicals in the Early Republic*. Ithaca, NY: Cornell University Press, 1998.

Wilson, Julia. "An Early Baltimore Physician and His Medical Library." *Annals of Medical History* 4 (1942): 63–80.

Wilson, Julia. "Dr. John Crawford, 1746–1813," *Bulletin of the School of Medicine University of Maryland* 25 (1940): 116–132.

Wilson, Kathleen. "Urban Culture and Political Activism in Hanoverian England: The Example of Voluntary Hospitals." In *The Transformation of Political Culture: England and Germany in the Late Eighteenth Century*, 165–184. Ed. Eckhart Hellmuth. London: German Historical Institute, Oxford University Press, 1990.

Wilson, Renate. "Halle Pietism in Colonial Georgia." *Lutheran Quarterly* 12 (1998): 271–301.

Wilson, Renate. "Pietist Universal Reform and the Care of the Sick and the Poor: The Medical Institutions of the Francke Foundation and the Social Context." In *Institutions of Confinement: Hospitals, Asylums, and Prisons in Western Europe and North America, 1500–1950*, 133–152. Ed. Norbert Finzsch and Robert Jutte. New York: Cambridge University Press, 1996.

Wilson, Renate. *Pious Traders in Medicine: A German Pharmaceutical Network in Eighteenth-Century North America*. University Park: Pennsylvania State University Press, 2000.

Wilson, Richard Ashby and Richard D. Brown, eds., *Humanitarianism and Suffering: The Mobilization of Empathy*. Cambridge: Cambridge University Press, 2009.

Winch, Julie. *James Forten, Gentleman of Color*. Oxford: Oxford University Press, 2002.

Wolf, Eva Sheppard. *Race and Liberty in the New Nation: Emancipation in Virginia from the Revolution to Nat Turner's Rebellion*. Baton Rouge: Louisiana State University Press, 2006.

Wood, Gordon S. *The Americanization of Benjamin Franklin*. New York: Penguin Press, 2004.

Wood, Gordon. *Empire of Liberty: A History of the Early Republic*. Oxford: Oxford University Press, 2009.

Wood, Gordon. *The Radicalism of the American Revolution*. New York: Vintage Books, 1991.

Woodward, John. *To Do the Sick No Harm: The British Voluntary Hospital Movement to 1875*. London: Routledge and Kegan Paul, 1974.

Wright, Conrad Edick. *The Transformation of Charity in Postrevolutionary New England*. Boston: Northeastern University Press, 1992

Yokota, Kariann Akemi. *Unbecoming British: How Revolutionary America Became a Postcolonial Nation*. Oxford: Oxford University Press, 2011.

Young, Alfred F. *The Democratic Republicans of New York: The Origins 1763–1797*. Chapel Hill: Published for the Institute of Early American History and Culture, Williamsburg, Virginia, by the University of North Carolina Press, 1967.

Ziesche, Philipp. *Cosmopolitan Patriots: Americans in Paris in the Age of Revolution*. Charlottesville: University of Virginia Press, 2010.

Zuckerman, Arnold. "Plague and Contagionism in Eighteenth-Century England: The Role of Richard Mead. *Bulletin of the History of Medicine* 78 (2004): 273–308.

Zunz, Olivier. *Philanthropy in America: A History*. Princeton, NJ: Princeton University Press, 2012.

Electronic Sources

American National Biography Online. www.anb.org.

Dictionary of Canadian Biography Online. http://www.biographi.ca/.

Oxford Dictionary of National Biography. http://www.oxforddnb.com/.

Index

Printed in the USA/Agawam, MA
July 6, 2017

654581.007